THE LIFE OF
MARY
QUEEN OF SCOTS

THE LIFE OF
MARY
QUEEN OF SCOTS
AN ACCIDENTAL TRAGEDY

RODERICK GRAHAM

PEGASUS BOOKS
NEW YORK

THE LIFE OF MARY QUEEN OF SCOTS

Pegasus Books LLC
80 Broad Street
5th Floor
New York, NY 10004

First Pegasus Books edition 2009

Library of Congress Cataloging-in-Publication Data is available.

ISBN: 978-1-60598-049-2

10 9 8 7 6 5 4 3 2 1

Printed in the United States of America
Distributed by W. W. Norton & Company, Inc.
www.pegasusbooks.us

TO

Jane and Peter, Marian and Hugh
(originally Anna Throndsen and Erik Rosencrantz),
Michael and Melissa, and Robert and Valerie

Thank you for your friendship

Contents

❦

PART IV : *England, 1568–87*

List of Illustrations

❧

Preface

❧

Mary Stewart was the victim of a golden childhood snatched away by widowhood, and her tragedy was an accidental one. This book seeks neither to blacken her character, by portraying her as a murderess of husbands, nor to sanctify her as the lonely champion of her faith, but to recount the circumstances which formed her character and to explain the events which determined her fate.

Mary was undoubtedly one of the great beauties of her era. Since the golden age of Hollywood, many technical tricks have been used to enhance the beauty of the subject when photographing the stars: the focus of the camera might not be entirely sharp, the lens might be smeared with oil or grease, sometimes a gauze might be stretched across the front of the lens – often with holes strategically placed to allow the sitter's eyes to sparkle – and smoke might even be diffused across the studio; all that before the negatives passed into the hands of the retouchers. The result has been a totally unreal icon of beauty. This is how we now see not only a Garbo or Dietrich, but also many of today's celebrities. The same gauze, smoke and retouching have been liberally applied to the memory of Mary Stewart.

She was born in Scotland to a French mother, crowned at the age of nine months and, to avoid a forced marriage with an English prince, was sent at once for safekeeping to her relatives in France. Here she was educated to be a fairy princess, betrothed to the Dauphin – sadly, he was retarded both mentally and physically – and she was destined to become a glittering queen of France. When she gained the throne, her uncles and their allies ruthlessly used her position to wield power for themselves until she was rendered useless by the death of the feeble boy-king. Therefore, still a virgin and now a widow at the age of eighteen years and seven months, her career in France was over, and, with her carefully protective education abandoned, she returned to Scotland.

She had been educated in a time of aggressively masculine rulers and had been taught the skills of female empowerment by two eminently powerful women of contrasting personalities: Diane de Poitiers and Catherine de Medici. She had seen direct female rule in its full effect under her cousin Elizabeth I of England, but such was the gilded cage that had been constructed around her that she never put any of her lessons into practice. She had been thoroughly taught the skills of, and excelled at, life in a Renaissance court, accepting extravagant praise, riding, dancing, singing, organising masques and pageants, flirting and presiding over a bejewelled court of lavish splendour. She knew nothing of politics or international diplomacy – except where it involved the marriage of her friends. Now, deprived of the advice of her uncles, she had to rule Scotland alone.

Mary, during her short time in Scotland, lived on a self-created fantasy island of delights modelled on the Valois court of France. At her arrival, in 1561, the nobility had looked for leadership, hopefully one working to their advantage, and had found instead a disinterested docility. Having assured the people that she would not interfere with their religion, Mary had taken no further interest in their affairs, provided that they adored her as she rode past on her progresses away from her court at Holyrood. Her council ran the country, she signed what she was advised to sign and made suitable noises towards her southern neighbour. Mary had no interest at all in politics, and on the rare occasions when she attended Privy Council meetings she took her embroidery.

As a marriage prospect she carried with her everywhere the twin infections of religion and dynasty. Mary did not govern personally and gave no firm instruction to her council to rule on her behalf. This left the sometimes divided nobility trying, occasionally, to interpret her whims, thus causing a near fatal separation of monarchy and legislature.

The skills required to decorate the court of France as a beautiful and graceful queen were very different to those needed to control a naturally quarrelsome nation just emerging from the Reformation. Having, metaphorically, been coached in the skills of a talented amateur to play selected exercises on the harpsichord with grace and charm to a sycophantic audience, she was suddenly thrust onto a very public platform to play entire Beethoven sonatas on a concert grand piano. Mary simply ignored this daunting task and was finally deposed by her exasperated aristocracy, escaping to leave a civil war raging while she threw herself on the mercy of her cousin Elizabeth Tudor.

In England, Mary endured a form of house arrest of varying severity until, stupidly, she made an identifiable endorsement of a plot to assassinate Elizabeth. The latter was finally forced to act and Mary Stewart was executed aged forty-four.

Mary was an enthusiastic dancer, gracefully slim and tall – her first dancing partner of her own height was her husband-to-be Henry Darnley – with fair, probably red-gold hair and a clear complexion. She was an enthusiastic horsewoman, often riding astride, and seldom happier than when at full gallop with the sun on her back.

Men fell in love with her at an amazing rate, often with disastrous consequences. A French court poet hid in her bedroom and was executed for his pains, a Scottish earl tried to abduct her and was declared insane, and some fell on their knees with declarations of undying love.

Mary lived, over two periods, for eleven years and six months in Scotland, thirteen years in France, and seventeen years and nine months in England, but she remained at heart a princess of France, more at home speaking French amid the châteaux of the Loire than anywhere else. She never took charge of her life, but was controlled by events, and the few decisions she did make all ended tragically.

I have kept the modernisation of spelling and grammar to the minimum required for clarity and have dated the turning of the year at 1 January. There were three principal currencies in use during Mary's lifetime – Scottish merks, crowns and pounds; English pounds, shillings and pence (£, s, d) and French livres tournois and crowns – and, unfortunately, there is no convenient factor by which we can multiply sums to convert to modern values. However, by the end of the sixteenth century an English professional – teacher, shopkeeper, or parson – could live comfortably on £20 annually (£90 Scots, 160 livres, 100 French crowns).

Since weaponry was an integral part of male life, some explanations may be necessary. All males carried a dagger, which in Scots was called a 'whinger', and occasionally a long sword or rapier. In battle, swords were either of the rapier variety or the basket-hilted broadsword. The claymore was a two-handed sword used best on horseback. The 12-foot-long Scottish pike was used in a phalanx or 'schiltron' formation to repel cavalry. Firearms were, apart from cannon, relative newcomers and were mainly an early form of musket called variously 'arquebus', harquebus', 'hagbut' or 'hackbut'. To avoid unnecessary confusion I have called them arquebus throughout.

Acknowledgements

Above all I must thank my publisher, Hugh Andrew, who suggested to me that he felt the time to be ripe for a balanced biography of Mary Stewart. Without his initial support, this book would never have been written. A place beside Hugh Andrew must be given to my wife, Fiona, for listening, with every sign of cheerful interest, to two years' worth of often repetitious conversation about Mary. Fiona then took on the task of initial copy-editing, brushing aside my irritation when she pointed out, for example, that Mary was unlikely to have been crowned on two different dates. It was a labour of Hercules, carried out smilingly, and I thank her for it.

Andrew Simmons, as managing editor at Birlinn, gave help and encouragement in huge quantities, along with the most tactful of suggestions, while providing eagle-eyed editors to clarify my sometimes presumptuous narrative. Laura Esslemont and Peter Burns ransacked picture libraries to make a pleasure out of a chore.

Dr Jenny Wormald of St Hilda's College, Oxford and the University of Edinburgh, read the manuscript and made extremely helpful suggestions. Michael Lynch, Professor Emeritus of Scottish History at the University of Edinburgh, read the manuscript for historical veracity and gracefully suggested corrections. Owen Dudley Edwards, formerly Reader in History at the University of Edinburgh, gave invaluable information on the various canonisation campaigns with breathless enthusiasm.

Technical help from the Royal Armouries at Leeds on Henri II's fatal joust and a weather report for the night of Darnley's murder from the Nautical Almanac Office filled in two vital blanks.

Medical advice from Professor I.M.L. Donaldson, Dr Morrice McCrae and Dr Peter Bloomfield helped with diagnoses made at a distance of 500 years. Kenneth Dunn, Senior Curator of Manuscripts at the National Library of Scotland, corrected my attempts at Latin translations, and the issue staff, both there and at the library of the University of Edinburgh, found books and manuscripts with their customary skill and helpfulness.

However, none of these people can be held responsible for the way in which their advice and information have been presented and any errors are mine.

Family Trees

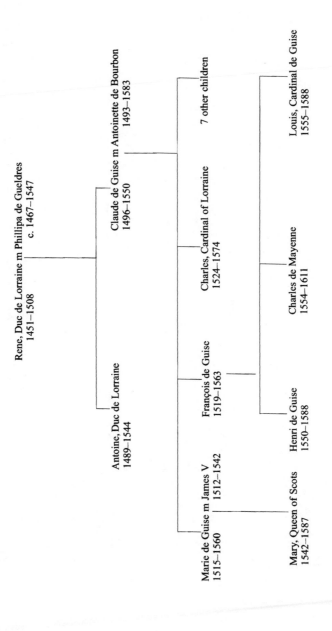

Guise

Rene, Duc de Lorraine m Phillipa de Gueldres
1451–1508   c. 1467–1547

Antoine, Duc de Lorraine
1489–1544

Claude de Guise m Antoinette de Bourbon
1496–1550   1493–1583

Marie de Guise m James V
1515–1560   1512–1542

François de Guise
1519–1563

Charles, Cardinal of Lorraine
1524–1574

7 other children

Mary, Queen of Scots
1542–1587

Henri de Guise
1550–1588

Charles de Mayenne
1554–1611

Louis, Cardinal de Guise
1555–1588

Valois

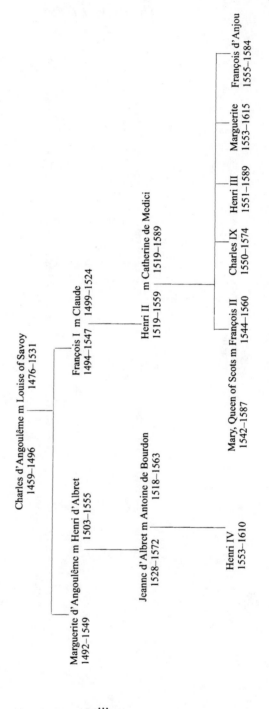

Charles d'Angoulême m Louise of Savoy
1459–1496   1476–1531

François I m Claude
1494–1547   1499–1524

Henri II   m Catherine de Medici
1519–1559   1519–1589

François II   Charles IX   Henri III   Marguerite   François d'Anjou
1544–1560   1550–1574   1551–1589   1553–1615   1555–1584

Mary, Queen of Scots m
1542–1587

Marguerite d'Angoulême m Henri d'Albret
1492–1549   1503–1555

Jeanne d'Albret m Antoine de Bourdon
1528–1572   1518–1563

Henri IV
1553–1610

Tudors/Stewarts

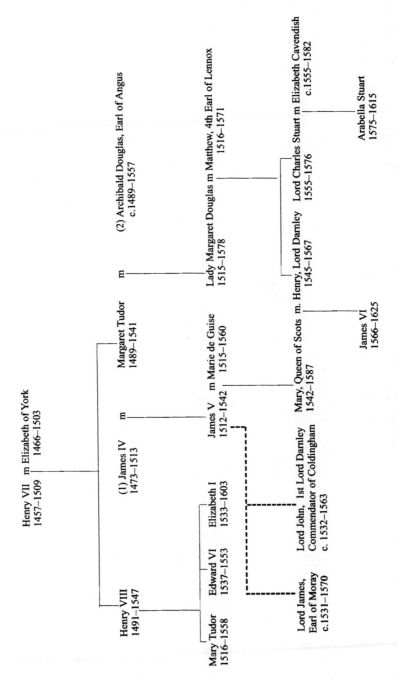

Henry VII m Elizabeth of York
1457–1509   1466–1503

Henry VIII
1491–1547

Margaret Tudor   m   (2) Archibald Douglas, Earl of Angus
1489–1541   c.1489–1557

(1) James IV
1473–1513

Mary Tudor   Edward VI   Elizabeth I
1516–1558   1537–1553   1533–1603

James V m Marie de Guise
1512–1542   1515–1560

Lady Margaret Douglas m Matthew, 4th Earl of Lennox
1515–1578   1516–1571

Lord James,   Lord John, 1st Lord Darnley
Earl of Moray   Commendator of Coldingham
c.1531–1570   c. 1532–1563

Mary, Queen of Scots m. Henry, Lord Darnley
1542–1587   1545–1567

Lord Charles Stuart m Elizabeth Cavendish
1555–1576   c.1555–1582

James VI
1566–1625

Arabella Stuart
1575–1615

xix

Lennox/Arran

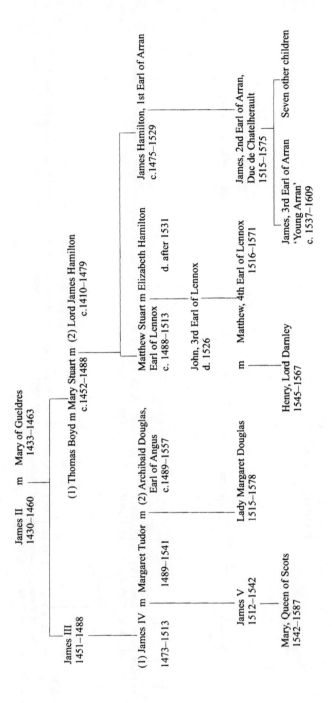

James II
1430–1460

m

Mary of Gueldres
1433–1463

James III
1451–1488

(1) Thomas Boyd m Mary Stuart m (2) Lord James Hamilton
               c.1452–1488   c.1410–1479

Matthew Stuart m Elizabeth Hamilton
Earl of Lennox   d. after 1531
c. 1488–1513

James Hamilton, 1st Earl of Arran
c.1475–1529

(1) James IV m Margaret Tudor m (2) Archibald Douglas,
1473–1513   1489–1541   Earl of Angus
                          c.1489–1557

John, 3rd Earl of Lennox
d. 1526

James V
1512–1542

Lady Margaret Douglas
1515–1578

m

Matthew, 4th Earl of Lennox
1516–1571

James, 2nd Earl of Arran,
Duc de Chatelherault
1515–1575

Mary, Queen of Scots
1542–1587

Henry, Lord Darnley
1545–1567

James, 3rd Earl of Arran
'Young Arran'
c. 1537–1609

Seven other children

xx

PART I

Scotland 1542–48

CHAPTER ONE

As goodly a child as I have seen

※

Early in the morning of 8 December 1542 armed messengers left the warmth of the Linlithgow Palace guardrooms at the gallop, their breath steaming in the sudden chill and their horses' hooves striking sparks from the frozen cobbles outside the forecourt. Behind them the new white walls of the south façade gleamed in a reflection of the snow-covered ground. After only a few yards they passed the church of St Michael before plunging down the steep hill into the town, where they took their separate icy roads. Heavy snowfalls had blanketed the country in one of the worst winters of the century. The horsemen were all carrying the urgent news that Marie de Guise, Queen of Scotland, was safely delivered of a child. As her previous two children had died, more than usual care had been taken over the birth of this child in a first-floor room in the palace, and the messengers had been on standby since her labour had begun.

Of these messengers, by far the most important was the man heading for the royal hunting lodge of Falkland Palace, where James V was lying, gravely ill. With little daylight and only one prearranged horse stage, the messenger would lodge for the night twenty miles distant at Stirling before turning east across Fife. His package was heavily sealed, secured in a saddlebag, and he did not know its precise contents, although the rumours in the guardrooms had all been of the queen's successful confinement. Since he had been given two loaded pistols as well as his broadsword and dagger, he knew it was a vital despatch and that, given the rumoured condition of the king's health, speed was of the utmost importance.

In Stirling, he slept in his clothes with his sword by his side and a pistol on top of his package under his pillow. Early next day he left Stirling while it was still dark to cover the thirty-five miles to Falkland Palace, where he finally delivered his despatch. It was immediately unsealed by a courtier, who read the document, frowned, and took the news to King James, now lying in his bed in his sickroom. At first the news was good in that the queen had survived childbirth and was safely delivered of a healthy child. The bad news which followed was that the child was a girl, to be called Mary. It was her mother's name, and 8 December was also the feast of the Immaculate Conception of the Virgin. It is possible that Mary was actually born the day before and the record was subsequently changed to allow what would be seen as a happy coincidence of dates.

James V had not been with his queen, but since royal fathers were seldom present at their wives' confinements, this was not unusual. What was unusual was that, a few days earlier, James had been personally leading a raiding force of 18,000 Scotsmen in a crossing of the English border at the Solway Firth. To invade Henry VIII's England at this time was like poking a stick at a very angry bear, and James knew it.

On the expedition, James had set up his headquarters twenty miles north of the border at Lochmaben, and the raiding party set out under the command of Oliver Sinclair, James's loathed favourite, to cross the River Esk. Raiding parties were not unusual in the Border area, where a precise delineation of the frontier was impossible to achieve, and widespread cattle and sheep stealing, combined with kidnap and extortion, were carried out under patriotic banners. The area was generally known as the 'Debatable Lands' and even today, for imaginative tourists, its undoubted beauty is tinged with the feeling that hostile horsemen may be lying in wait just over the next hill.

The raiders entered England and burnt property belonging to the Grahams, but achieved nothing except to warn the English that a Scots army was nearby. The English deputy warden of the West March caught up with the Scots who were re-crossing the

River Esk on their way home. With 'spears of the borders to prick at them [he] set upon their hinder ends and struck down many'. The Scots were then trapped by the rapidly rising tide in the Solway Estuary and the retreat turned into a total shambles. The incoming tide drowned many, while others were trapped in the marshes of Solway Moss or simply surrendered to whoever they could find to prevent their certain slaughter. One sorry remnant was overtaken in Liddesdale and sent home barefoot, clad only in their shirts. In the bitter November weather few survived. The English pursuit continued until 12 December, being now justified as retribution for a cattle raid. Their haul, apart from prisoners, amounted to 1,018 cattle, 4,240 sheep and 400 horses.

It was when James realised the extent of the losses that he fell into a deep depression and turned north, accompanied by only his personal retinue. There are reports that he first travelled to Tantallon Castle on the south-eastern coast of the River Forth to say farewell to his mistress, who was being cared for by the wife of Oliver Sinclair, but he certainly rode to Edinburgh and put some of his personal affairs in order before visiting his wife, Marie, awaiting the birth in Linlithgow.

The Palace of Linlithgow, technically the private property of the queen, was lavishly furnished in the latest French style; warm fires, rich tapestries and all the comforts that a Renaissance prince might expect welcomed James as he rode through his new southern gatehouse, itself modelled on that at Vincennes, outside Paris. Frozen, but still impressive, there was an elaborate fountain in the courtyard, covered in splendid carvings of mermaids, minstrels and heraldic beasts in the contemporary French style and built by James to please his queen. But James's depression was severe, and none of the luxuries held any further interest for him. He spent two days with his pregnant wife, during which her ladies tried to prevent his gloom from distressing her, before saying goodbye and riding to his hunting lodge at Falkland in Fife.

In happier times Linlithgow Palace had been a particular project for James and Marie, and together they had closely supervised its building and decoration. As the king rode into the new palace on this occasion, these were only distant memories since, back in Edinburgh following the calamity at Solway Moss, he had prophesied that he would be dead in fifteen days. His domestic servants, anxious to make arrangements, asked him where he would hold his Christmas court and were told, 'I cannot tell, choose ye the place. But this I can tell you, on Yule day you will be masterless and the realm without a king.' He retired to his chamber at Falkland, inconsolable as the detail of his losses at Solway Moss bore in on him.

Although few men had been killed, a large number of the nobility had been taken prisoner and their ransom would cost James large amounts of money that he did not have. He was crying out, 'Is Oliver taken? Oh! Fled Oliver!' to the distress of his servants. At the age of thirty, James Stewart was undergoing a total collapse under the stresses of kingship. Mourning the loss of the men he had led into a foolish encounter was the final torment and he was dying of grief for his shortcomings as a ruler. The chronicler Lindsay of Pitscottie says that he was 'near strangled to death' by the extreme melancholy.

This latest news of his daughter's birth was not received with any happiness by James who, according to legend, said, 'It cam wi' a lass and it'll gang wi' a lass,' before turning his face away from his attendants to await his death.

This prophecy, if that is what it was, is difficult to interpret. The Stewart dynasty was certainly founded 'by a lass' when Marjory Bruce, the daughter of the victor of Bannockburn, married Walter the Steward, and David II's crown descended to their son, Robert the Steward. Stewart rule did finally end in 1714 with the death of the childless Queen Anne, but it is unlikely that James was so farseeing. It is far more probable that he meant that the king felt that it would be impossible for the factious and troublesome kingdom of Scotland to be ruled by a queen alone.

The queen-to-be who would undertake this task was, as yet, only two days old, and a close watch was being kept on her during her first dangerous days of life; it was a time when infant

6

mortality was high and, as her mother knew all too well, certainly no respecter of royalty. The practice, at least in France, was to have a priest attend the delivery so that, as soon as the cord was cut, the child could be baptised, but there is no evidence that this was done in Mary's case. Under the supervision of one Janet Sinclair, a team of nurses kept constant watch over the royal baby, who, at this moment, only knew that she was hungry and was yelling loudly in the first of many celebrated royal tantrums. She was immediately taken from her cradle and given to a wet nurse to be fed. This lady had been chosen with care, having nursed several babies, some even her own, to a healthy infancy. Royal or noble ladies did not nurse their own children since the sooner their lactation ceased, the sooner they would be fertile again and ready to fulfil their *raison d'être* – like the prized mares and pedigree bitches in the stables and kennels – to continue the bloodline.

Marie knew that her marriage to James V had been entirely political and expedient. Henry VIII's Reformation and Dissolution of the Monasteries had been about to engulf Scotland, and to stem this heretical tide James sought an alliance with France. Thus, on 1 January 1537 François I of France gave his twenty-year-old daughter Madeleine to be James's queen in the cathedral of Notre Dame in Paris. James returned to Scotland, happy that he had forged a bond of Catholicism with Henry's greatest enemy. He received a dowry of 100,000 livres and an annual payment of 125,000 livres, always a welcome increase to the treasury of a comparatively poor Scottish king. The marriage was also, extraordinarily, a love match. James had been in negotiation for the hand of Marie de Vendôme, but, on seeing the beauty of Madeleine, switched his suit. Unfortunately, the fragile Madeleine died of influenza within two months of arriving in Scotland, but, nothing daunted, James returned to France. This time he was engaged to Marie de Guise et Lorraine, daughter of two of the most dominant people in France. Her father was Claude, Duc de Guise, and her mother was Antoinette de Bourbon, a terrifying virago, a glance from whom was said to frighten even the king. Marie had previously been married to the Duc de Longueville, but was widowed at the age of twenty-two, with one surviving son, François, now the young duke in his father's place.

Marie had none of the fragility of Madeleine but was tall, high-busted and striking. Any sixteenth-century suitor could see that she would breed healthy children. Henry VIII had proposed marriage to her after Jane Seymour died giving birth to Prince Edward, but Marie replied that while her figure was big, her neck was small and she would rather not. François I – always keen to provoke Henry VIII – agreed a suitable second dowry for her wedding to James and the marriage was performed with Lord Maxwell standing proxy for James. On 18 May 1538, in the presence of the French royal court, Lord Maxwell placed his leg beside Marie in her bed and the marriage was deemed to have been consummated. In June she came to Scotland where James and she remarried in the cathedral of St Andrews before setting out on a triumphal tour. She duly praised the elegance and civilisation of Scotland, and, although she knew that James was still visiting a mistress at Tantallon Castle, she behaved as a dutiful daughter of the House of Guise and smiled graciously at everyone she met. She started to learn Scots, at which she became proficient, but sent homesick letters to her mother and to François. He wanted to see his mother again but did not want to visit Scotland so, touchingly, he sent her a piece of string knotted to show how tall he was growing. Like all grand-mothers-to-be, Antoinette, Marie's mother, sent copious amounts of gossip and advice to her daughter, especially in her time of pregnancy. She was to consult only French doctors. 'The Queen will only be well if she washes her hair at least once a month or cuts her hair short, for her greasy hair makes her catch cold. She must not let herself be bled.'

Then, when she had delivered two princes and was at last crowned queen and felt that she could relax her diplomatic adoration of all things Scottish, she had craftsmen, luxuries and even seedling trees sent from France. There was always a highly practical side to Marie's nature and she put her own comforts high on her list, resulting in strong French Renaissance influences in the royal court. But now, only four years after her marriage, with both her princes tragically dead, she was about to become a widow.

James V finally departed this life at midnight on 14 December 1542, and immediately the rumour mill started to turn. The king had been poisoned; he had been smothered with his pillow by fanatical churchmen or equally fanatical heretics – all the usual hysteria flowed in abundance, since the truth was too banal. The king had suffered vomiting and diarrhoea, had previously contracted venereal disease, was prone to the unspecified fevers that abounded at the time and was in a state of deep depression, having lost his favourite, Oliver Sinclair, and invoked the wrath of his belligerent neighbour, Henry Tudor. In legend he is thought to have died of grief, but today we would give his probable cause of death as dysentery. John Knox said, 'All men lamented that the realm was left without a male to succeed.' The ruler of Scotland was now a six-day-old girl.

The news that reached England was, firstly, that the child was very weak and then, on the same day, that the child was dead. English courtiers were wise always to give Henry good news while they worked out how to give him any unwelcome tidings and it was not until after James's death that Henry was told that Mary was alive and healthy. The ripples of bad news were enthusiastically spreading, and by Christmas the reports reaching far-off Hungary were that both mother and child were at death's door.

In fact they were far from it, and as soon as Janet Sinclair thought the weather was dry enough and Queen Marie fit enough, the baby was wrapped in warm blankets and carried the few hundred yards to St Michael's Church, where she was baptised at the font wrapped in a chrisom, or christening robe, of white taffeta, as a symbol of her innocence. If Mary died within a month of her birth then the chrisom would be used as a shroud. She was then carried to the high altar, at which she was confirmed as a member of the Roman Catholic faith. The christening party then returned to the palace for celebrations, albeit muted ones as the court was in official mourning.

Henry Tudor, as Mary's great-uncle, was also respectfully observing this period of mourning. The temptation for the ageing king must have been great. After the debacle of Solway Moss, Scotland was leaderless, many of its nobility were in English prisons and the country was in disarray. But John Lisle, who was gathering an army for Henry in the north-east of England, wrote, 'seeing that God hath thus disposed his will of the said King of Scots, [we] thought it should not be to your Majesty's honour that we your soldiers should make war or invade on a dead body or upon a widow, or on a young suckling his daughter.' Scotland was ripe for Henry to pluck, but his agile brain saw that with tact and diplomacy he might bring Scotland under Tudor rule peaceably and, what was always a consideration for the Tudors, cheaply.

Gaining the subservience of his northern neighbour had been a lifetime ambition of Henry's, and he had attempted to negotiate with James V earlier in the year. It was when James simply failed to appear at a conference at York to discuss this that Henry, infuriated, sent a punitive raiding party north. The Scots' successful repulse of this raid at Haddonrigg had encouraged James to make the disastrous foray in response at Solway Moss, leaving Scotland open to swift retribution.

Now a girl had succeeded to the crown, and girls, once married, were subservient to their husbands. Henry had a five-year-old son, Edward, who could grow into a usefully dynastic husband, so he decided, for the moment, to wait.

The Scots now faced another long period of regency with an infant monarch. This was not new, and the tale of kingship and regency under the James Stewarts is a sorry one, but briefly told. James I became king at the age of twelve, but was a prisoner of the English until he was thirty and later stabbed to death in a palace privy by his nobles when he was forty-three. His son James II was aged six when his father was murdered, but he reigned until his thirtieth year (1460) when a cannon he was inspecting blew up, leaving a nine-year-old James III to rule. At the age of thirty-seven he was running from the Battle of Sauchieburn when his nobles caught up with him and killed him on the spot. Their feeble comment upon this murder was that 'the king happened to be slain'. His son, James IV, was then fifteen and had been involved in the revolt against his father, for which act he did penance by wearing an iron belt next to his skin for the rest of his life. He did preside successfully over an energetic Scottish Renaissance court until his death at the folly-driven slaughter at Flodden put his son, James V, on the throne at the age of eighteen months. Mary was the youngest monarch to wear the crown, but she was far from the first child to succeed to the throne.

The effects of these recurrent crises were twofold. Firstly, the nobility had become accustomed to existing without an effective sovereign. The system of feudal government with all power and land tenure descending from a king had been established with great care by the Normans but now had become fragile. Swearing fealty to a sovereign lord for the land you had personally taken by the sword became farcical when that sovereign lord was still in a cradle or, at best, a fresh-faced boy of fifteen. In the cases of two of the royal successions, the very lords who were swearing fealty had been party to the death of the new king's father. Knees were dutifully bent and heads were bowed but the reality was very different. Scotland was a loose and occasionally uneasy federation of lordships held together in a governing council only by family ties and the overwhelming need for peace. The crown had the ultimate control of the law, but in his own lands the lord had total personal power of 'pit and gallows'. These lords were not the ignorant thugs they are often thought to be: for the most part they had been given a classical education, spoke Latin and French with ease and had travelled widely. Many had seen the European Renaissance and had brought aspects of it back to their own castles. Though still ready with a sword, they were sophisticated and cultured men in a comparatively prosperous country. Their tenants were no worse off than the inhabitants of Gascony, Piedmont or Ex-tremadura, and they shared the hardships of life common to all peasants in the sixteenth century. King James V himself 'plen-ished the country with all kinds of craftsmen out of other countries' and even maintained a 'Keeper of the Royal Parrots' among his numerous courtiers.

The second result of the loss of power at the centre was that the only unity of purpose evident among the nobility was represented by their occasional combining under the king to thwart any invasion by England, and any royal campaign to cross the border and invade England was undertaken reluctantly. The motive to defend the realm was often superseded by the thought of booty, and when that became difficult the wish to return north became paramount. The last Stewart to learn this bitter lesson was Charles Edward Stewart in 1746.

Obviously, to prevent a state of near anarchy it was imperative that a regent, or governor, was appointed as soon as possible. He would take over the palaces and treasure of the king and receive the income from his estates until the new sovereign took power for herself; the governor would also be the most influential man in the kingdom. Immediately, David Beaton, Cardinal-Archbishop of St Andrews, stepped into the gap. He was fifty years old, an experienced diplomat and a dedicated Catholic – in spite of numerous mistresses and illegitimate offspring. He was a supporter of a Franco-Scottish alliance and a bitter opponent of Henry VIII's reformation of the English Church. He now presented Scotland with what he claimed to be the late king's will, passing power to a committee of four governors – the earls of Huntly, Moray, Argyll and Arran – with himself as chief of the council and 'tutor testamentary' to the princess whom he memorably described as a 'skittering [inconsequential] lass'. Since the will was detailed in its instructions for the education of a princess, James must have written it in the four days between 10 and 14 December, while he was dying. But he was unconscious for most of the time and lucid for none of it; he called for no secretaries, gave no instructions and apparently died intestate.

The king had died in Beaton's arms and the cardinal was rumoured to have gained the royal signature to a blank document which he afterwards completed as the king's will. It was all very neat. Beaton's 'will' was clearly an opportunistic forgery made with the help of one Henry Balfour, and it was immediately challenged by the Earl of Arran.

James Hamilton, 2nd Earl of Arran, had, in fact, an extremely close hereditary claim to the throne himself. His grandfather had married Mary Stewart, the sister of James III, and so James had royal Stewart blood in his veins. However, his grandfather may not have been free to marry Mary since his dubious divorce from his previous wife was tacitly accepted without any solid proof. Arran could, therefore, have been the son of a bastard. An undoubtedly legitimate descendant was the Earl of Lennox, but his claim came entirely from the female line and thus was weaker. It was from this line that Henry Darnley sprang. But if the child Mary should die – always a strong possibility – then Arran could claim the crown for himself.

Arran was, however, one of the most incompetent and vacillating men ever to draw hesitant breath in Scotland. Every move he made was for his own personal gain and advancement, but he lacked the wit or constancy to determine where that gain might lie or how to pursue it. He allied himself at first with Marie de Guise and Catholic France, then changed sides to join John Knox and the Reformation. He made very sure, however, that by January 1542 he was confirmed in the office of governor, where his first act was to appoint Cardinal Beaton as chancellor. Then, with a volte-face which would come to typify the man, he threw the cardinal into prison. He was highly relieved when Henry released the noblemen captured at Solway Moss without asking for any ransom, but it never occurred to him to look this particular gift horse in the mouth.

Henry VIII had the same ambition for personal power, but, unlike Arran, he knew precisely how to achieve it. His cheapest, and most effective, way to bring Scotland into his orbit was for the young Mary to marry Prince Edward, and so the nobles were released on condition that they supported this plan. Oaths of fealty and agreements of loyalty were struck, rewards were promised and Arran unwittingly welcomed back a faction totally committed to English domination. Better to be a rich earl under an English king than a poor one under an indecisive governor and a French dowager.

James V was buried with full royal pomp on 10 January 1543 in Holyrood Abbey beside Madeleine and his two dead sons. He had not had a happy reign. His ruthless expertise at raising money from his nobility struck fear into the clergy, who were well aware of the king's Tudor uncle's enthusiasm for looting churches and monasteries, and felt that they could easily be next to be fleeced. James had, however, put in place the basis for contemporary Scots law, founding the High Court of Justiciary in 1532 – albeit based on the Northern Italian courts of Pavia – and he left a treasury of £26,000 Scots. He was also said to be 'well-plated'; in other words he had a considerable hoard of gold and silver plate. This was a popular form of investment as it could be quickly melted down in time of need. The same was true of the gold chains worn by the nobility. The sixteenth-century historian John Leslie called James the 'poor man's king – a maintainer of justice, an executor of the laws and a defender of the innocent and pure'.

The dowager queen was still at Linlithgow Palace with her daughter, but was well aware of the incompetent machinations of Arran. History has accused Marie de Guise of many things but incompetence has never been one of them. Wisely, since she had her own plans for her daughter, Marie now made sure that the infant Mary stayed at Linlithgow in her personal care rather than that of Arran. She was well aware of the importance of her new daughter as a dynastic prize, knowing that Henry would be keen to gain control over both her and her daughter. Henry's warden of the Marches, Viscount Lisle, had said of Mary, 'I would she and her nurse were in my lord prince's house.'

The first official approach came when Mary was less than four months old. Sir Ralph Sadler rode into Holyrood Palace as

Henry's ambassador to negotiate a marriage treaty. Sadler was 'of low stature . . . well skilled in all exercises and remarkable for both strength and activity'. He was a professional diplomat, trained under Thomas Cromwell and no stranger to Scotland. He had attempted to separate James V from his French alliances, but James had 'weighed the profuse liberality of François I against the niggard present of a set of horses'. A propitiative gift of a mere six geldings had been sent by the parsimonious Henry.

Now, in late March, Sadler was met by Arran, who told him that he would have no objection to the marriage and that the assent of the Scottish estates, could be guaranteed provided Henry dealt with Arran alone. This made it clear that bribes and guarantees of Arran's continuation as governor would be needed. Sadler hinted that a marriage between Arran's son, James Hamilton, and Henry's daughter, Princess Elizabeth, might be considered, but Arran was unimpressed by this and made it clear that his current price was a single payment of £1,000. He promised Sadler support for Henry's religious reformation but, in private, he continued to practise as a Catholic. Arran would cheerfully have sold Sadler the furniture in the palace, all of which, as governor, he had the power to dispose of. The Englishman realised very quickly that Arran represented a problem that could simply be bought off or threatened into submission. Therefore Sadler's next move was to Linlithgow where, he was certain, a Guise queen mother would be made of sterner stuff.

Sadler, as a properly cautious ambassador, insisted on seeing the infant himself – a not uncommon practice – and Marie instructed the nurses to unwrap the five-month-old baby for him. Sadler was even allowed to hold Mary on his knee while the royal nurses watched anxiously, but Mary gurgled winsomely and Sadler became the first of many men who fell under the spell of Mary Stewart, describing her as 'as goodly a child as I have seen and as like to live, with the grace of God'.

The child was wrapped up again and removed for her feed

while Sadler and Marie discussed the possibility of a marriage to Edward. Knowing her devotion to the Catholic faith and her strong ties with France, he expected that she would object violently and he would have to return to the venal Arran. But Sadler did not know that on 20 February Marie had received a letter from Charles Brandon, Duke of Suffolk and Henry's lord lieutenant of the Borders, telling her that the marriage was 'not only to the high advancement of [her] daughter but also thereby shall cease much trouble and effusion of blood'. It was an offer she was not supposed to be able to refuse, but such threats only brought grim smiles of determination to the face of Marie de Guise. Marie knew what Sadler's expectations would be and now completely outflanked him by agreeing to every demand. She was 'most willing and comfortable to [his] majesty's purpose', and even to having the child removed to safekeeping in London. She had, of course, no intention of doing any of this.

Arran had dismissed her French ambassadors and was attempting, ineffectually, to isolate Marie by trying to have her correspondence intercepted. However, she had already smuggled out one letter to her mother, who was gathering allies in François I's court against the possibility of trouble in Scotland. By agreeing completely, if insincerely, with Sadler, Marie sidelined Arran. Sadler could now deal directly with the queen mother and forget Arran. He could reassure Henry that he had influence over the real power, while Marie quietly continued with her own agenda.

Marie knew that, however idyllic Linlithgow Palace was, it could never withstand a siege, and she knew that a weakling like Arran would quickly turn to violence when thwarted. She called Arran 'the most inconstant man in the world, for whatsoever he determineth today, he changeth tomorrow'. To ensure her continuing custody of Mary, her mother had already started sending covert loads of treasure, plate and furnishings to her own castle of Stirling, which was much more easily defended.

Stirling Castle, which Marie held in her own right as part of her marriage settlement, stands, like Edinburgh's, high on a rock with an eagle's viewpoint over the surrounding countryside. It is all but impregnable. Once there, the infant would be secure, but Arran, who had got wind of her plans, forbad Marie to leave Linlithgow. The dowager queen continued to subvert Sadler, telling him that Arran would break his word, wait until Henry was dead and then marry Mary to his own son and seize the throne himself. Marie had no evidence for this except that most people were willing to believe the worst of Arran, and Sadler was inclined to believe her. In fact, as it turned out, there was no need to implement the move to Stirling, since Marie's Guise connections in France were beginning to bear fruit.

The intelligence from France was that François was financing Mary's uncle the Duc de Guise to raise an army, if it should be needed. In the event, François sent Matthew Stuart, Earl of Lennox, Arran's rival in the line of inheritance, to Scotland. (While living in exile, Lennox had become a French citizen and changed the spelling of Stewart to Stuart, the French version of his name.) Lennox came prepared for conflict and occupied his castle at Dumbarton on the north coast of the Clyde – another impregnable rock-perched stronghold. Cardinal Beaton – called by Henry 'the best Frenchman in Scotland' – had been moved from prison to his own stronghold at St Andrews, and the Catholic lords were gathering around him. Henry, impatient and sickened by the lack of results in Scotland, now ordered Arran to move the child to Edinburgh Castle. The impotent Arran, since he had no power to do this without a confrontation with Marie, Lennox and Beaton, prevaricated. His feeble excuse was that the baby was teething and could not be moved. The two sides were now clearly defined. Marie, Beaton and Lennox had the growing backing of François and were in possession of the infant Mary. Arran had a few of the lords, who were fulfilling their promises given to Henry during their imprisonment after Solway Moss, and Henry himself was breathing down Arran's neck, demanding action.

Tudor patience was very limited and Henry's had run out. 'The king's majesty causeth such preparations of force and power to be made on the borders, as in case these promises, gentle handling and reasonable communication take not effect, the king's majesty may use his own princely power and strength.' He let Arran know that he would send a treaty to be agreed with the implied threat that if it was not immediately agreed to Scotland could expect an English invasion. This was the Treaty of Greenwich, and on 1 July 1543 it was duly agreed with no great enthusiasm. Henry, above all, wanted Scotland to be tied to him by treaty and to be unlikely to call for French help, while he himself had the freedom to look across the Channel for an opportunity to invade France. The terms of the treaty were therefore surprisingly favourable to Scotland. Mary would stay in Scotland until she was aged ten, and Henry would send a nobleman and his wife to supervise her education when she was of a suitable age. In other words he wanted Edward's bride to speak English, not French or Scots. On her tenth birthday Mary would marry Prince Edward in England, the implication being that she would not return to Scotland. The terms of the dowry were agreed, although both sides knew they could be renegotiated. Astonishingly, Henry agreed that the kingdom of Scotland should 'retain its ancient laws and liberties'. He was guaranteeing Scotland's independence for ten years, with the promised marriage postponed for the same period. In the manner of these treaties, both sides knew that everything could change in this space of time, and all the parties involved set about making what profit they could from it.

In the meantime, Sadler was receiving the inevitable requests for money to secure the loyalty of the Scottish lords. These ranged from £100 from the Earl Marischal and the Earl of Angus, through £300 for Lord Maxwell, up to the £1,000 for Arran himself. Arran assured Sadler that he could control the Scottish lords: 'If they would not do their duties to him he would notify the world of their disloyalty and would seek help of England and all parts of the world to be revenged on them.' If his adversaries opposed him he would 'surely stick' to Henry, and all the strongholds south of the Forth 'should be ready at [Henry's] commandment'. He now wanted to have a contract of marriage between Elizabeth and his son, and hinted that his purchasing loyalty for Henry had meant that he had had to melt some of his own plate into coin, but the immediate payment of £1,000 would put matters right. Sadler, wisely, had withheld this money since he felt that Arran's use of it would be 'unfruitful', but in July he released the funds. The effect of this was that by August, Arran was asking for another £5,000.

To Sadler's disquiet, Arran still wanted to have close supervision over Mary, in case she was whisked away to France. This was beginning to look more likely as Marie had formed a formal alliance with Beaton and Lennox and their troops were gathering at Linlithgow. There was a rumour that French ships were lying off the coast, although no one had actually seen them directly. Sadler wanted Mary to be taken to Stirling, out of the way of possible armed conflict, and, since this was precisely what Marie wanted, she was delighted to oblige.

On 27 July, Mary, accompanied by Lennox with 2,500 cavalry and 1,000 infantry, travelled to Stirling in state along the path taken by the messenger who had delivered the news of her birth to James V. She was only some eight months old, still being suckled by her wet nurse, but no one who saw the procession could have been in any doubt that it was the progress of a queen. Mary was firmly in the care of Marie de Guise, and Arran had no further negotiating power.

The castle was, if anything, more impregnable than Edinburgh. It had also received the attentions of James V and had magnificent carved roundels in the French style and a great hall that, it was rumoured, could seat 400. Thanks to Marie's clandestine removals from Linlithgow it was furnished to the standards expected of a royal palace. The castle was the first royal building in Scotland to have a Chapel Royal. There were gardens within the walls and here Mary could be brought to womanhood in perfect safety. Even Sadler, used as he was to his king's extravagances at Hampton Court, was impressed and reported of the mother and child, 'she is very glad to be at Stirling. Her daughter did grow apace and soon she would be a woman if she took of her mother who is indeed the largest stature of women.' Although in later life her weight would become a major problem for her, Marie was still an attractively tall woman.

Henry, trying desperately to keep control of a deteriorating situation at 500 miles distant, now asked that only Mary be lodged in the castle and that her mother be lodged in the town with only limited visiting rights. He was quite right in diagnosing what everybody on the ground could see: Marie was totally in charge of the situation. His request was simply ignored.

Sadler, however, cautious as usual, asked to see the child Mary again and she was obediently displayed, in good health after recovering from a bout of chickenpox. Arran, realising that he had now lost any chance of deceiving anybody, decided, as he usually did, to join the winning side and met Beaton, who arranged for him to make a public confession of his apostasy and to receive absolution. Arran also gave his son, James Hamilton, into the cardinal's care in the castle of St Andrews. Now, all the power of Scotland was united around Mary, and her mother could proceed immediately to the next vital stage.

Mary's coronation took place on 9 September 1543. She was exactly ten months old and can have remembered nothing of it in later life. The ceremony was held in the Chapel Royal in Stirling with, according to Sadler, 'such solemnity as they do use in this country, which is not very costly'. Arran carried the crown – as his descendant, the Duke of Hamilton does to this day – Lennox carried the sceptre and Argyll the sword of state. Mary was carried by her mother, and Beaton, in the scarlet vestments of a cardinal, conducted the ceremony. The crown had last been worn by James V at the coronation of Marie; now it was being held by the cardinal above the tiny queen's head. She was duly anointed with the holy oil mixed with balm – chrism – and immediately became God's anointed. She was now possessed of certain holy powers – such as curing scrofula, or the King's Evil, with a touch – and her wearing of the crown, with the secular power represented by it, had been given to her by divine right. She was, in effect, two people in one: Mary Stewart, a ten-month-old baby, and Queen Mary, verging on being half human and half divine in one body. In later life, when speaking as queen, to show the presence of both elements she would refer to herself as 'we'. Adherence to these quasi-medieval beliefs would contribute to the end of the reign of the house of Stewart 200 years later.

The new queen behaved extremely badly throughout the ceremony, screaming constantly so that no one could hear the nobility pledging their often hypocritical allegiance. The heralds, whose duty it was to announce Mary's lengthy new titles in full, simply gave up the task, and while Janet Sinclair put her new queen in her night cradle the court attended a ball in the great hall. The pro-English lords were absent, and there now seemed no possibility of them being able to carry out their promises to Henry. Marie de Guise had demonstrated that she was not simply the queen mother, to be respected and quietly bypassed, but a woman of skill and determination, representing a Franco-Scottish power base that could not be ignored. Henry was left with his Treaty of Greenwich, now worthless, and never again would he trust the Scots.

Although it was autumn, the court could still for the moment enjoy itself with hawking, hunting and dancing. Musicians and painters flocked to Stirling, and Marie, for once free of her dynastic cares, started to enjoy the pleasures of young widow-hood. She was twenty-eight years old and sexually attractive, so her simplest way to ensure the loyalty of her squabbling nobility was to play the marriage game. Arran could be bought by power and money but Lennox's favour could be bought with the flicker of an eyelash. He was cosmopolitan, having been a lieutenant in the Garde Écossaise, a group of aristocratic mercenaries who acted as the French king's personal bodyguard. He was sophis-ticated and could easily beguile the ladies of the court with his elegant manner.

Such a flirtation with one person could be dangerous unless balanced by another, and Marie had a perfect foil in Patrick Hepburn, Earl of Bothwell. He had already been exiled for arrogant unruliness and was reputed, wrongly, to be a royal bastard – a slander he did nothing to correct. Hereditary lord admiral, he was entitled to the profits from the sales of all ships wrecked on the coasts of Scotland, giving him a steady and dependable income. His castles were Crichton, near Edinburgh, and the grim tower of Hermitage in the Middle March, held on the royal behalf, but from where he could challenge or welcome any force from England as the fancy took him. His behaviour would have been recognisable to the knights of the twelfth century, with violence as the immediate answer to any problem; today he would enthusiastically embrace the code of honour of the Mafia. He was married, but as soon as he realised that he could soon be the stepfather of the queen he gained a rapid annulment.

Lennox and Bothwell vied as to who should be the 'most gallzeart in their clothing' and 'behaved themselves in the queen's presence sometimes in dancing, sometimes in shooting, sometimes in singing and jousting and running of the great horse at the lists, with all other knightly games that might satisfy the queen'. They were carrying out the sort of courtship which had delighted Eleanor of Aquitaine 400 years previously in her Courts of Love. The chronicler Lindsay of Pitscottie said Marie's court 'was like Venus and Cupid in the time of fresh May'.

The commanding presence of the court was undoubtedly Marie, the queen dowager, but the jewel at its heart was the infant Queen Mary. Marie made sure that the child was treated with the dignity due to her, and when she was allowed to watch the court dancing its galliards and pavanes, the ladies and gentlemen would bow gravely to the child before taking their first steps. When the ever-watchful Janet Sinclair decided it was time for Mary to be taken to bed, the chamberlain would call out, 'The Queen retires!' The dancing would stop and the entire company would drop onto one knee. Mary would never have seen the armed guards who surrounded her at a discreet distance, but would have been aware of the attention she was paid by courtiers privileged enough to come near to her. Hardened warriors like Bothwell would boast that the infant queen had smiled at them and they lifted their caps to her as she watched concourses of men on horseback ride out with birds of prey on their forearms, although she was too precious to be allowed to join them beyond the castle walls. Her young world was full of music, either at frequent balls or, more regularly, in the Chapel Royal, where sacred music by Robert Carver and Robert Johnson accompanied the Mass. She could not have remembered any precise details of this time, but the first adult influences on her infant mind were of music, dancing and courtly obeisance. She would not have known of the desperate scheming taking place just below the surface of the glittering court.

Marie was an expert at playing the game of courtship, but Bothwell could only think one step ahead and spoiled the game by publicly announcing Marie's non-existent promise of marriage. Lennox now felt he was an abandoned lover and slouched away to sulk in his fortress at Dumbarton. At a stroke, Marie's carefully constructed unity looked as if it might fall apart.

There was, of course, the strong possibility of help from France, and the Duchesse Antoinette wrote to her daughter, 'I do not doubt that the King for his part will give you all the help he can. Your brother the Duc d'Aumale and I will petition him.' Realising that Marie was now in trouble, François I acted by sending a fleet, money, arms and matériel and two ambassadors, de Brosse and Mesange. Lennox promptly seized the treasure, but was reminded that, as a French citizen, by doing so he was committing treason. He knew that the French had a short way with traitors, involving a long and painful death, and was immediately reconciled to Marie's cause. Lennox now extracted a promise of marriage from Marie, and she agreed with Arran that Lennox and he had the authority to administer the kingdom jointly. In return Lennox allowed the ambassadors to distribute 59,000 crowns among the nobility, and the unity of the First Estate which Marie had achieved, having wobbled dangerously, was restored.

Arran, like Marie, had naturally not meant any of his praises of

23

Lennox, and he took the extreme action often rashly favoured by the slighted coward; he immediately marched against him at Glasgow Muir and was badly trounced. But Lennox now knew that his chance of sole power in Scotland was illusory, and he fled south to London where, on 29 June 1544, he married Henry VIII's niece, Lady Margaret Douglas. Their son was Henry Darnley.

Marie's court now had French ambassadors and their retinues restored, and she was enjoying her motherhood free from political conflicts. Arran and Beaton were her allies and she could regard the defection of Lennox as one less complication. The infant queen was where a daughter should be – in the direct care of her mother – and adored by everyone. Marie had gained a total victory without a shot being fired or a drop of blood being spilt, and it did not escape her notice that Henri, the French Dauphin, and his Italian bride, Catherine de Medici, had, at last, become parents of a son, François, so a Catholic dynastic marriage across the Channel could now be regarded as a strong possibility.

Henry, whose fury was increasing daily, now rashly seized and burnt some innocent Scots merchantmen and so gave the Scottish parliament the excuse to make an official repudiation of the Treaty of Greenwich. The Act of the Scottish Parliament stated, 'The King of England has violate [sic] and broken the said peace . . . the said contracts to be expired in themselves and not be kept in time coming.' By 11 November letters in the name of eleven-month-old Mary were sent to Charles V, the Holy Roman Emperor, asking for protection for Scottish ships trading to Lower Germany, i.e. Hamburg and Lübeck. Her seals were in the hands of Arran, and the council and the letters acknowledged the presumed fact that Scotland was now at war with England. Henry had written a furious letter to Arran in October accusing him of having gone back on his word – a word which had cost Henry £1,000 to acquire. Henry's herald warned Arran and the council that death and destruction were at hand, causing Beaton to assure Henry that he was as desirous as any subject of either realm to 'entertain the concord' that had existed between Henry and his late king. Beaton did not mean it, and Henry believed not a word of it. He said that Beaton 'worketh only to please France'.

Sadler was isolated and under surveillance. 'I am not able to do his majesty the service where my poor heart would . . . the whole body of the realm is inclined to France,' he wrote. In England, Henry had started on the long decline of his later years, his ulcerated leg swelling to such a degree that he was intermittently confined to bed and, in spite of the careful nursing of his last wife, Catherine Parr, was in continual pain. His temper had always been short and now he was in a constant rage against Marie and the Scots for their repudiation of the Treaty of Greenwich. He had never made empty threats and had no intention of starting now.

On 20 December 1543, Henry's herald, Henry Ray, Berwick Pursuivant, told the Scots that the raid at Solway Moss a year before was regarded in London as an act of war, and therefore Scotland should now make ready to do everything to please Henry or defend itself.

In May of 1544, the Earl of Hertford disembarked 15,000 men at Granton, three miles north of Edinburgh. His instructions were precise and savage.

CHAPTER TWO

One of the most perfect creatures

꙰

Mary was now eighteen months old, sturdy and starting to grow tall, even as a toddler, playing in the spring sunshine with her attentive nurses inside the safety of Stirling Castle. She was naturally unaware that to possess her had become the urgent aim of the rulers of Western Europe.

Three powerful men ruled most of the continent. In England it was the 53-year-old Henry VIII, unchallenged domestically but aware that his northern border could be threatened by Scotland. He knew that, alone, Scotland was too poor to mount more than annoying border-raids, but Henry was the only Protestant king in Europe, and Scotland could count on support – moral from Rome and practical from France. In contrast, Henry's English reformation had made him no friends.

France was ruled by the equally flamboyant fifty-year-old François I. Since coming to the throne the two men had been rival Renaissance princes, either at war with each other or outdoing each other in extravagant splendour. Their meeting on the Field of the Cloth of Gold in 1520 was meant to celebrate amity but was, in reality, a spectacle of two peacocks displaying in front of each other. The only thing of consequence was that Henry met an English lady-in-waiting at the French court called Anne Bullen or Boleyn.

François was under constant threat from the Spanish Nether-lands in the north and from Spain itself across the Pyrenees in the south. Spain and the Netherlands were under the rule of the 44-year-old Charles V, the Holy Roman Emperor. Charles also ruled Austria and had a power base in northern Italy from which he could, of course, attack France from the south-east through Savoy. François had fought a tragically unsuccessful war here with Charles, ending with his capture at the Battle of Pavia in 1525. Most of the French aristocracy were either killed or captured and François himself became Charles's prisoner in Spain for a year. He was finally released in exchange for his sons; thus the future Henri II became, in his turn, a prisoner in Spain for two years. Charles was a fanatical Catholic and the Spanish Netherlands represented the northern end of his pincer-like grasp on France. The Netherlands were only separated from England by the English Channel at its narrowest.

These pieces of the jigsaw interlocked all too neatly, and throughout the century the three rivals bickered, drew up treaties, formed alliances and carried out constant military incursions. But now there was a marriageable princess, albeit a toddler, and marriage alliances were the strongest alliances of all. Henry had Prince Edward as his heir, although the seven-year-old boy, whose birth had cost his mother, Jane Seymour, her life, was weak and unlikely to live long, a fact that no one at court was foolhardy enough to mention to the king. Edward would be firmly educated in the Protestant faith by Archbishop Thomas Cranmer. But if Henry could neutralise the threat from a Scottish–French alliance then he could, with a free hand, turn his attentions south to France itself.

François now had a grandson of equal age to Mary, whose mother was a Guise, and who could, therefore, be relied on to favour a French marriage. Also, the child would almost certainly be raised as a good Catholic. In 1546 François had suggested that Mary might marry the son of Christian, King of Denmark, since he could rely on Marie in Scotland to favour France. With England's eastern shores put under threat by Denmark, the French king could totally encircle Henry, remove the menace of English aggression and be free to deal with Charles V. The far-sighted plan came to nothing.

Charles, in his turn, had a son Philip, married to Mary of Portugal, who might yet produce a suitable son. For the moment Charles could wait.

Henry, however, could not and the result of his impatience had been the hasty Treaty of Greenwich, now cancelled by the infuriating Scots. At the end of January 1544, Henry had written to the Earl of Suffolk at Newcastle ordering him to assemble an army of 20,000 to invade Scotland in May, and in March Suffolk was instructed to flood the Borders with a network of spies. He was given six weeks to bring the kingdom to its knees with what the English government called the Enterprise of Scotland, although it is now more commonly called the Rough Wooing. The wardens of the Border Marches would start a softening-up process by increasing raids and incursions. The preparations were all quite blatant as Henry had hoped that, thanks to intensive spying on both sides, the knowledge of his intentions would strike fear into the Scots and bring them to the negotiating table. It did nothing of the sort, producing only a stony silence from the Scottish parliament, but neither did it provoke them into strengthening the defences around the Firth of Forth.

The business of the court at Stirling continued as normal with Marie begging Pope Paul III to allow Isabel, Prioress of North Berwick Abbey, to be replaced by Margaret Home. The reason for her enforced retirement was exhaustion caused by the stress of continual English raiding, thus making evident that the increasing campaign of military incursions was now reaching to within twenty miles of Edinburgh. Four days later, on 24 January, Marie wrote to Rome again, asking that Arran's half-brother, John Hamilton, be given the bishopric of Dunkeld, with its income. 'In this age religion is to be supported not only with dignity but with substance in riches.' On 1 February, Henry wrote to Charles V assuring him that his realms would not be troubled; in other words, he was asking for a guarantee of non-intervention. It was granted, provided the emperor could rely on equal support for a local problem of his own in Austria. Henry agreed.

At the end of April, Hertford was so well advanced in putting his forces together that he held a procession through the streets of Newcastle with '3,000 northern horsemen, in jacks [leather jerkins] with spears, 28 nobles and gentlemen in black velvet with gold chains, 3 trumpets and 3 clarions, 3 officers of arms in tabards, a gentleman bearing a naked sword, the Earl in rich apparel, 4 pages richly clothed, 28 servants in livery and, finally, 5,000 foot soldiers'. No one could be in any doubt that a full-scale invasion was now under way, and, on 1 May, Sadler was instructed to offer final terms. Henry wanted the marriage and delivery of Queen Mary before her tenth birthday, an agreement of perpetual peace, renunciation of all amity with France, no foreign agreements without Henry's agreement, an unconditional promise that Scotland would be England's active ally in war, and an assurance that Arran might continue as governor, provided he continued to be well disposed towards Henry.

When there was no response to this offer, Hertford set sail with precise instructions from the Privy Council. He had received them a month previously, and despite him pointing out some practical difficulties they were, in the main, unchanged. As an example of state-authorised savagery they remain unequalled, even by Hitler's SS or the depredations visited on Croatia by the Serbians during the 1990s.

'Put all to fire and sword; burn Edinburgh town, so razed and defaced when you have sacked and gotten what you can of it, as there may remain forever a perpetual memory of the vengeance God lightened on them for their falsehood and disloyalty. Do not tarry at the castle; sack Holyrood House and as many towns and villages about Edinburgh as you may conveniently. Sack Leith and burn and subvert it and all the rest, putting man, woman and child to fire and sword without exception where any resistance may be made against you, and this done, pass over to Fifeland and extend like extremities and destructions in all towns and villages whereunto ye may reach conveniently, not forgetting among the rest to spoil and turn upside down the cardinal's town of St Andrews, as the upper stone may be nether, and not one stick standing by another sparing no creature alive. Spend one month there spoiling and burning.'

29

It was an over-ambitious task but Hertford set about carrying it out with grim efficiency. He landed in Fife on 3 May, burned St Monans and seized the shipping lying in the harbour before resting overnight on the island of Inchkeith. He landed unopposed at Granton on the next day and unshipped his artillery in four hours, seizing more boats, including a galley, the *Salamander*, François I's personal gift to Marie. He was able to disembark his entire force and camp overnight before advancing on Edinburgh the next day, where he met the Scottish army of 6,000. He put Henry's terms to Adam Otterburn, Provost of Edinburgh, and had them rejected. According to the *Diurnal of Occurrents* the Provost 'ordered the Edinburgh men home. They [the English] besieged the castle, but they were little or nothing better, for the castle slew many of their men, and thereafter, on the next day, they burnt Edinburgh and despoiled the same, then passed to Leith again without any impediment.' In fact, Hertford spent three days burning and pillaging in Edinburgh. He then burned the castle of Craigmillar and ravaged the countryside surrounding Edinburgh as far as Dunbar in the east and Queensferry in the west. He destroyed the Chapel of Our Lady of Loretto in Musselburgh as well as the orchards at Seton, 'The fairest and the best that we saw in all that country.' Crossing the Forth again he advanced as far as Kinghorn but realised that he could never reach St Andrews in the time Henry had allowed him.

In Stirling, plans were made to transport Mary, first to the Highlands, where it was 'not possible to come by her', then to the cathedral at Dunkeld, where Arran's brother was now bishop. Hertford was within six miles of Stirling when he was forced by lack of time to turn for home. He and his men 'sent home spoil and gunshots, returned home on foot through the main country of Scotland, burning both pile, fortress and town which was in their way and lost scant 40 persons'. Hertford recorded the destruction of the abbeys of Kelso, Jedburgh, Dryburgh and Melrose, 7 monasteries, 16 castles, 5 market towns, 253 villages, 13 mills and 3 hospitals. He had slain 192 Scots in battle, taken 816 prisoners and was driving 10,386 cattle,

12,242 sheep and 200 goats south as booty, as well as 850 bolls* of corn. In all the towns the civilian populations had been slaughtered. Hertford had been given his strict timescale because Henry had been planning to invade France with a view to seizing Boulogne, and Hertford now rode south to join these invasion forces.

Hertford's invasion had been a disaster for Scotland. One effect of it was, however, to strengthen the view held in Scotland that Mary should now marry in France. Help was promised from François and Marie's stock had risen hugely as Arran's had fallen, with Marie now sitting on the council, and it was clear that from now on she would have personal control of the choice of a husband for Mary.

Having helped Henry to win back Boulogne from François, Hertford returned to Scotland in February 1545 and once again slaughtered and burned in the border country, but when he met a Scottish army at Ancrum Moor on 27 February, it was no longer under the sole command of the inept Arran. The Scots forces were now in the more capable hands of the Earl of Angus and, for the first time in his career, Hertford was routed.

Both sides drew breath and for a year concentrated on making alliances and restocking treasuries for the inevitable restart of hostilities. Mary continued her gilded childhood in the safety of Stirling Castle, where she was starting to speak the Scots tongue of her nurses. The behaviour of the court, however, followed Marie's tastes and French fashions prevailed. Mary accepted that regular attendance at Mass was a normal part of life, as was the formality of aristocratic attendance on her. Had it been possible for her to be taken on journeys around Stirling she might have gleaned some knowledge of life beyond the court, but security made this impossible, and her nurses' enthusiasm in their adoration of the queen in their care went some way to compensating for her claustrophobic existence. She had no knowledge of the events unfolding in East Lothian.

*A boll equalled 6 English bushels, or 24 pecks, or 48 gallons.

On the night of 16 January 1546 the Earl of Bothwell's soldiers, acting on orders from Cardinal Beaton, arrested a group of men in Ormiston, a village near Haddington. Bothwell's various amorous pursuits had caused him to fall out of favour with Marie – he was 'in glondours', or disgrace – and his efforts in the Catholic cause restored his position. The cardinal's target had been George Wishart, a Protestant reformer who had been gaining support wherever he preached. Wishart was under the personal protection of his 'sword-bearer', John Knox. Knox, a St Andrews University graduate and ordained priest, had been converted to the reformed cause by Wishart and was now one of a growing number of Protestant apostates.

Wishart was taken under arrest to St Andrews – the other men were allowed to 'escape' – and tried under circumstances that would have shamed Stalin's show trials. Inevitably he was found guilty, and on 18 February 1546 the cardinal, in a colossal misjudgment, had him burned to death at a stake conveniently placed outside the castle. In fact, it was so conveniently placed that the cardinal could watch Wishart's torments from cushioned ease while enjoying his dinner and wine.

His misjudgment became evident three months later, early on the morning of 29 May, when five men, whose quarrel with Beaton was, in fact, political rather than religious, entered the castle. Repairs were taking place and workmen were going to and fro unchallenged, so the assassins entered easily, threw the porter into the moat and narrowly missed seeing Marion Ogilvie, Beaton's mistress, leaving the castle after the cardinal and she had spent the night 'busy at their accounts'. Beaton was now 'resting . . . after the rules of physic'. Having gained entry, the men admitted sixteen more conspirators, broke down the door of the cardinal's room and, in spite of his pleas – 'Fie, fie! I am a priest!' – stabbed him to death. To make sure that this act came to the attention of the public, they hung his body at the foot of the castle walls, where it was thoroughly abused by the townsfolk – 'Ane called Guthrie pisched in his mouth.' Awaiting the inevitable reprisals, the assassins withdrew into the castle and prepared for a siege.

Henry VIII was jubilant, and, for a time, it was wrongly believed that the assassins – now called the Castilians – were acting under his orders. Arran, needless to say, hesitated. Since his son had been in the castle and was now held as a prisoner, this was not surprising, but it allowed the Castilians time to beg for help from Henry. Henry had only recently made peace with France after his seizure of Boulogne and he knew that his interference in Scotland could jeopardise this fragile agreement. But in this case Henry was being invited to invade Scotland as a liberator, and St Andrews would provide an excellent port of entry. It was very tempting. However, on 28 January 1547, before he could do anything, he died, leaving the kingdom to his ailing nine-year-old son, who became Edward VI, under the protectorship of the Earl of Hertford, recently created the Duke of Somerset.

Hardly had news of this change of power been digested than word came from France that François I had died and his son Henri II was now king. Henri had never enjoyed good relations with his father and it is said that when Anne de Pisseleu, Duchesse d'Étampes, François's mistress, heard the news of his death, she fainted on the spot. However, Henri did enjoy good relationships with the Guise faction, and he was keen that Mary should marry his son, now the Dauphin. He proved his good intentions towards Scotland by sending a fleet to St Andrews under the command of Leon Strozzi. Where Arran had procrastinated, Strozzi acted, bombarding the castle into submission and taking the Castilians prisoner on 29 July 1547. He released Arran's son, held the nobility for ransom and sent the rest of the Castilians, including Knox, to what were presumed to be slow deaths as galley slaves. Once again the tide of danger receded from Scotland and Marie could congratulate herself on keeping the marriage prospects with France alive.

On 27 August 1547 Somerset arrived at Berwick with a fresh army to finish what he had failed to do over two years previously – 'to bring to good effect the most godly purpose of the marriage . . . to make her, being now but Queen of thy realm, as Queen of both realms'. What was not stated, but which was implicit, was that while Mary might very well become Queen of England, Edward would certainly become King of Scotland.

Somerset had learned that his previous slash-and-burn methods had achieved nothing, so on this invasion he used different tactics. He advanced steadily up the east coast, building temporary forts as he went and supplying his army from the sea, where a fleet followed his advances. For almost a fortnight the campaign was largely bloodless. Then, on 10 September 1547, he reached the village of Pinkie, some seven miles from Edinburgh and within range of the guns on his ships. There, a surprise awaited him.

The Scots were well aware of his advance and had, for once, drawn themselves up in an organised position on a hill overlooking the River Esk. There were three divisions under Angus and Huntly, but Arran was in the centre, in overall charge. His uncertainty in what should have been an invulnerable defensive position is indicated by the fact that on the night before the battle, presuming defeat, he dictated his will and begged the French to protect his children. All he had to do was wait, since if Somerset tried to cross the river he could easily be cut down. Instead Arran stupidly ordered Angus to cross the river and attack. Strongly protesting that it was a disastrous move, Angus did so and managed to make a foothold on the eastern bank of the Esk. He weathered a vigorous cavalry counter-attack from Somerset but was eventually forced to fall back towards the Highland levies under Argyll. 'At this instant the Highlanders, who, unable to resist their plundering propensities, were dispersed over the field stripping the slain, mistook this retrograde movement for a flight and, seized with a sudden panic, began to run off in all directions.' Now the ships in the Forth began to bombard the fleeing Highlanders, who had no idea where the fire was coming from – they did not expect to be attacked by ships – and promptly left the field altogether. The English pressed home their counterattack and Angus's line broke, now fleeing into Huntly's troops, who took them for advancing Englishmen and opened fire on them at point-blank range. Arran galloped for Edinburgh as fast as his horse would carry him. Over 10,000 Scots lay dead, and from Pinkie to Edinburgh 'for the space of five miles the ground was strowed [sic] with dead bodies'. Thus in Scottish memory 10 September 1547 lives on as 'Black Saturday'. The road to Edinburgh was open and, turning for the capital, Huntly remarked, 'I hold well with the marriage but I like not the wooing.'

The Norroy King of Arms, Edward VI's herald, was instructed to tell the Scottish council, 'God has shown his power in giving his grace the late victory. Enjoin the queen and council to deliver the young queen to the Protector to be suitably nourished and brought up with her husband as Queen of England as he promises to do on his honour, failing which he will use all means to bring it about by force.'

Marie's first instinct on hearing the news was for the safety of Mary, who now might very easily be carried as a captive to England. Lord Erskine, who, with Lord Livingstone, was one of the queen's guardians, was put in charge and the royal nursery was hastily packed up. No doubt the child Mary thought the sudden commotion was all a great game, but it was deadly serious. Erskine's family had, for fifty years, been commendators of the abbey of Inchmahome – laymen governing ecclesiastical benefices and receiving their incomes from the foundation. The abbey lay fourteen miles north-west of Stirling, and Mary was removed there while the guns of Stirling Castle guarded the road. Even if an approach could have been made, the abbey was on a tiny island in the middle of the Lake of Menteith so that only light defences were necessary. Although Mary was now being drawn further into the edges of the Highlands and separated from her mother, it was an idyllic place, with the small abbey buildings surrounded by trees giving onto grassland that stretched down to the water. It was Mary's first experience of an enforced exile on a Scottish lake-island and, accompanied by her personal court with four girl companions her own age, there were games among the autumn trees at the lakeside, making her exile far from unpleasant. Her second isle-bound exile would not be so agreeable.

35

Somerset did not set about a siege of Edinburgh Castle but, leaving a token force at Broughty Castle outside Dundee, returned to England in October at the end of the campaigning season. Marie had her daughter restored to her side at Stirling and the little queen's three-week-long exile was over.

Marie realised that Scotland's only chance of survival lay now in a formal alliance with France, and the French ambassador, Henri Cleutin, Sieur d'Oysel, sailed for France in late November with 'certain points which neither the Queen Dowager nor the Governor would commit to any but him', which were firm terms for a marriage between Mary and the Dauphin. Somerset realised that if he delayed any longer there would be French reinforcements in Scotland; at the end of February, he pre-empted this by launching a first incursion under Lord Grey of Wilton, who reached Haddington. Here he left a holding garrison which was joined in April by a greater force in order to occupy Haddington fully and establish it as a base for the future occupation of the Lowlands. Arran moved to besiege the town while rumours flew that he was intending to seek terms from Grey and join the English. True to form, Arran certainly intended to be on the winning side, but it was proving difficult for him to make a choice, after which he would switch his allegiance with no conflict of conscience.

The worsening situation made it clear that Mary had to be moved again and this time the intention was plain: she went to the castle of Dumbarton, situated above the best available harbour for a flight to France. The effect of these hasty removals from her mother on the four-year-old Mary is unknown, but in March of 1548 she fell ill. Inevitably the rumours flew that she was about to die, thus leaving Somerset with no reason to continue the campaign, and Henri II with no future Dauphine. In the event, Mary was simply running through the normal illnesses of childhood: she had already suffered chickenpox and was now in the grip of measles, though in the sixteenth century either one could have been fatal. However, she survived, and the savage courting dance of the two combatants continued.

With news of the French commitment came a touching letter to Mary from her eleven-year-old half-brother François, Duc de Longueville, in which he told her how he was every day practising to be at ease in armour and was learning how to tilt on horseback. As soon as he became proficient in fighting, he wrote, he intended to come and defend his half-sister against those who wanted to harm her. Less charmingly, but more practically, Henri II had now made up Arran's vacillating mind by offering his son, James Hamilton, a marriage to the daughter of the Duc de Montpensier, and promising to create a French duchy for Arran himself when the marriage treaty was agreed.

Then on 21 June 1548 a message was sent to the Earl of Shrewsbury: 'There be French galleys and other ships of France at Leith and have landed 5 or 6 thousand men which be Italians or Gascons . . . and they make very great brags and their saying is that they will come to Haddington. But I think it is too hot for them, they will be busy.' In command was the Sieur d'Essé and his companion Jean de Beaugué, who had a very low regard for the Scots forces. In company with Marie, who had arrived in person, the French now set about a vigorous siege of Haddington. While this was more than occupying the English, Marie presided at a tented parliament held outside the town on 7 July. Their business was simple. In exchange for driving the English out of Scotland, Mary would be betrothed to François, the Dauphin, while Henri promised that the independence of Scotland would be guaranteed as it had been in the past. Marie could no longer take the risk of defending Scotland with the incompetent Arran in charge and gladly signed the treaty. Once the seals were attached, Arran became the Duc de Châtelherault with a pension of 12,000 livres annually. This was roughly seventy-five times the annual earnings of a typical English doctor or schoolmaster, and did not take account of rents from the duchy which might well double that amount.

French ships were sent to Dumbarton by a roundabout route, and the French commander, de Beaugué, met Mary and her court for the first time:

There are a large number of virtuous and brave French gentlemen who are established as the guard for the Queen, who only allow access to her when guaranteed in writing by the Queen Dowager, one of the wisest Princesses on earth. Having the agreement of the Princes and great lords of the kingdom that the Queen be conveyed to France, to be educated beside the Queen, [Henri II] has given orders that Villegaignon leaves harbour, with four galleys, which will sail from France between the German sea and the Pethea-lantique sea [Pentland Firth] past the Orkneys, a journey never before undertaken by galleys. At Dumbarton the Queen will embark on the galley *Reale* with Monseigneur Brézé, who has hastened from the king, to accompany this Princess, aged between five and six years, one of the most perfect creatures one could hope for on all the earth.

Mary was actually four years and seven months old, so the old soldier de Beaugué was deceived by her already impressive stature. Since she was travelling not as a fugitive or into enforced exile but as a sovereign queen visiting her husband-to-be, there was nothing furtive about Mary's departure. She now had her own court, which would accompany her to France. The lords Livingstone and Erskine were her guardians and accompanied Lord James Stewart, her eldest half-brother, as well as Robert and John Stewart, two younger half-brothers. All three were the illegitimate sons of James V. Lord James's mother was Margaret Erskine, who may well have been the model for Dame Sensualitie in David Lindsay's *Ane Satyre of the Thrie Estaitis*. Acting as the female chamberlain of this miniature court, and also illegitimate, being a daughter of James IV and the Countess of Bothwell, was Lady Fleming, a vigorous widow whose husband, Malcolm, had been killed at Pinkie ten months previously. She was not mourning him conspicuously. Janet Sinclair, Mary's former nurse, was now her governess. Including various ladies' maids and menservants, the royal suite numbered some thirty people.

It also included four personal companions of Mary's own age, the 'Four Maries'. These girls had been Mary's companions at Inchmahome and were all of noble birth – Mary Fleming could even claim royal blood as a granddaughter of James IV. Mary Seton, accompanied by her brother, the young Lord Seton, was the daughter of Marie Pieris, a maid-of-honour to Marie de Guise, and became Mary's personal hairdresser for most of her life. Mary Beaton, whose love of romantic literature would equal Mary's own, was related to the assassinated Cardinal Beaton, while Mary Livingston, an enthusiast for dancing and riding, was the daughter of one of Mary's guardians. The queen's personal maids-of-honour were always known as 'Marie' in Scotland, the word deriving from the Icelandic 'Maer' or virgin, although how the word came into the Scots tongue is obscure. In any case, these four girls were also actually called Mary.

All five girls, one distinctly taller than the others, were dressed with the full formality of their rank as miniature adults – a portrait of Mary as a child shows her capped and corseted with no concession to her youth. On 29 July 1548 the five-strong infant entourage, in long formal dresses and with their little heads held high, walked down a gangplank and onto the *Reale*, Henri II's personal galley. Mary had bidden a tearful farewell to her mother, but she probably did not realise the full import of what was happening. Like all royal children she was more accustomed to the company of her nurses and governesses than her mother, so often preoccupied with state business.

Artus de Maillé, Sieur de Brézé, a member of the Guise faction and a relative of Diane de Poitiers, Henri's mistress, had been sent by the king as the royal representative and escort. He kept Marie well informed with letters sent whenever the ship made landfall, and on 31 July he wrote, 'the queen your daughter fares as well and is, thank God, as cheerful as you have seen her for a long time'. In his next letter he assured Marie, 'the queen fares exceedingly well and has not yet been ill on the sea'; then, on 3 August, he informed her that that 'in spite of very strong winds which tossed the galley most severely, the queen has never been ill. This makes me think she will suffer little on the open sea.' De

Brézé's ease of communication and anticipation of 'the open sea' is made clear on 6 August when their ship had only travelled as far as Lamlash on the Isle of Arran, eighty miles from Dumbarton. Lady Fleming, in particular, was impatient at the lack of progress and demanded to be put ashore until the weather improved. Villegaignon, who was a professional sailor and observed no niceties towards imperious ladies, told her that she had two options. She could either stay on board or drown. Better weather did arrive and now gave them a quicker journey, although off the coast of Cornwall de Brézé reported, '[the] weather was wondrous wild with the biggest waves I ever saw in my life'. Heavy seas smashed the ship's rudder but the crew, being the most expert in France, replaced it, and on 15 August, after a voyage of seventeen days, the royal party landed at Roscoff in Brittany. Mary, de Brézé wrote, 'prospers as well as ever you saw her. She has been less ill upon the sea than any one of her company so that she made fun those that were.' We must presume that her green, vomiting ladies forgave her, although her two guardians, the lords Erskine and Livingstone, took some days to recover. The royal party then travelled down the headland to St Pol-de-Léon, where an official welcoming party was waiting for them. Mary Stewart had arrived in the country of which she would, one day, be queen.

PART II

France, 1548–61

CHAPTER THREE

We may be very well pleased with her

҉

The voyage had been no more eventful than any other of the time, dependent on wind and tides. The galley slaves would not have been used if there had been a favourable wind, since they could make little headway against strong contrary winds, and they only represented an additional force in calm weather, though were crucial while manoeuvring in harbour. Mary may have seen the lash used on them, as it was a practice she later forbad, whatever the circumstances. The ships would have been only lightly armed since they offered no promise of profit for pirates, and an attack by English forces was extremely unlikely. Seizing the child on land could always be disguised as a 'rescue', but to take her from the King of France's personal galley while she was under his protection would have provoked an international incident from which even the hot-headed Somerset would draw back.

From Roscoff on 15 August 1548 Villegaignon had sent notice of Mary's arrival, and when they reached St Pol a first welcoming party was waiting for them, including a maître d'hôtel, who acted much as a local tour guide, and, bizarrely enough, the Duchesse d'Étampes, the mistress of François I. There was no official court position for the mistresses of dead kings; she, presumably, had got news of Mary's arrival through her gossip network, paid her own expenses and came out of curiosity. The entire nobility of France were agog to see the youngest monarch in Europe, who had already gained the status of a fairy queen. Villegaignon bade a relieved farewell to the royal party and was sent back to Scotland with men and ammunition for Marie's continuing siege of

Haddington. He was also rewarded by being made Admiral of Brittany.

Mary now travelled twelve miles inland to Morlaix, where she made a state entry on 20 August. This was her first experience of the French countryside, and, since in France she did not need the armed guards that surrounded her everywhere in Scotland, she was able to satisfy her youthful curiosity. She had been taught four or five useful words of greeting and thanks in French, but in any case French was a foreign tongue there. Brittany had only been absorbed into France fourteen years earlier and most people spoke only Breton.

The boundaries of the kingdom were much less extensive than those of today, especially on the east, where Savoy stretched westwards to include Nice. From there, the border ran northwards along the valley of the Meuse, putting Metz and Verdun into the Holy Roman Empire, before turning west to include Picardy, but not Artois, which was in the Netherlands and therefore also under the rule of Charles V. There was a population of about 18 million compared to Scotland's 800,000, and, with its mild climate and fertile soil, its agriculture was the most prosperous in Europe – there had not been a crop failure for almost a century. The French chroniclers were romantic to a man, and in their reports it seemed that sunshine arrived with Mary and that bad weather only returned on her departure. Joachim du Bellay, a poet and aristocrat who had travelled from Scotland with her, constantly sang her praises in verse as, later, Pierre de Bourdeille, Seigneur de Brantôme, would do in prose. Du Bellay said that 'when in her highland garb she resembled a goddess in masquerade'. It is hard to imagine what fantasy passed for Highland dress in a court totally unacquainted with the reality.

Mary's journey was now across country to Nantes, where the royal party transferred to a barge to take them along the Loire. This should have been an idyllic journey, but at Ancenis, only a third of the way along the river, the young Lord Seton died of a 'stomach flux', probably as a result of food poisoning. Mary now had to comfort Seton's sister, Mary, and attend her first funeral

Mass. The first link with her Scottish past was broken. She also had to say farewell to de Brézé, who left on royal orders, passing his duties over to Antoinette de Bourbon, Mary's formidable grandmother.

Apart from her mother, Antoinette de Bourbon was the first scion of this ancient and powerful family that Mary had met. Antoinette was the wife of Claude, Duc de Guise, the son of René II de Lorraine and Philippa de Gueldres. Claude, whose two brothers were Jean, Cardinal of Lorraine, and Antoine, Duc de Lorraine, had, with Antoinette, nine children, all of whom were still alive. They were Mary's uncles and aunts, and numbered amongst themselves two dukes, one marquis, two cardinals, one grand prior and two abbesses, as well as Mary's mother, a queen regent. It was obviously vitally important that Mary make a good impression, and on 1 October 1548 Antoinette reported, 'She is very pretty indeed, and as intelligent a child as you could see. She is brunette, with a clear complexion and I think that when she develops she will be a beautiful girl, for her complexion is fine and clear and her skin white. The lower part of her face is very well formed, the eyes are small and rather deep-set, the face is rather long. She is graceful and self-assured. To sum up, we may be very well pleased with her.'

Despite her good impression of her granddaughter, Antoinette de Bourbon did not find the Maries handsome or even clean, but she thought Lady Fleming was impressive. Excluding Marie de Guise, Antoinette, who lived to the age of eighty-nine, was the first of a long series of women Mary would meet who were powerful in their own right and who neither depended on their husband's influence nor abandoned their femininity in the pursuit of personal power. At that moment, Antoinette wanted to establish her personal influence as Mary's substitute mother and to ensure that the infant queen became a member of the Guise faction before she was surrounded by Henri's court.

The royal courtiers were waiting for her at Carrières-sur-Seine, where she would lodge temporarily in the medieval fortress until the royal apartments in the château of St Germain-en-Laye were made ready. Through Henri's mistress, Diane de Poitiers, orders were sent that the current occupants of Carrières be lodged in the village. The château of St Germain-en-Laye was only a few miles from Paris, but readily defensible on a cliff overlooking the River Seine. Its foundations dated from the twelfth century, and although François I had rebuilt it entirely as a palatial country estate, it still housed a garrison of 3,000 soldiers. His son was continuing with the refurbishments. Henri's apartments were on the first floor, overlooking gardens laid out as elaborate parterres and pergolas, while the royal children were on the second floor with its sunny south-facing rooms. Henri was taking a personal interest in Mary's quarters, sending precise instructions for the furnishings. He also asked for assurances that none of the workmen employed for the renovations had any infectious diseases, and established that all the neighbouring villages were infection free, thus establishing a *cordon sanitaire* around Mary, whom he now referred to as 'my daughter'. She arrived in her temporary home at Carrières-sur-Seine on 16 October and was glad that her stay in the grim medieval castle was short. Henri had sent further instructions to Jean d'Humières, who was to be her chamberlain and, with his wife Françoise, in charge of the royal nursery, that 'she takes precedence over my daughters. She is a crowned queen and, as such I would have her honoured and served.' This meant, among other things, that she would have a cloth of state with her heraldic bearings hung over her chair and that her servants would kneel in her presence and walk backwards when withdrawing from it. Janet Sinclair would have found these formalities unnecessary but would have encouraged her little charge to behave with proper decorum and not give the French any opportunity to find the Scots' manners barbaric, as the poet Brantôme had found their language. The other royal children, meanwhile, were enthusiastically beginning the education of their exotic, high-ranking nursery companion in the complex structure of the royal household.

This household was headed by the king. Henri de Valois had been born on 31 March 1519, the second son of François I, and had had no thought of succeeding to the throne since his eldest brother, François, was in good health. When François I was released from his Spanish imprisonment in 1526 he ignored his sons and rode past them to liberty as they took his place as hostages, though the seven-year-old Henri was kissed goodbye by the tender-hearted Diane de Poitiers, eighteen years his senior. The princes' imprisonment was harsh. By the time of their release in 1530, the eleven-year-old Henri had become morose and withdrawn but he was greeted on his return to France by Diane, who started to take an interest in the young man. When he rode in his first joust, held to celebrate his release, he carried her colours of black and white on his lance. Three years later, she accompanied him to his wedding to Catherine de Medici, an Italian heiress only two months older than him. Catherine was the only daughter of Lorenzo de Medici and a niece of Pope Clement VII, so the marriage provided François with a useful power base in Italy. Diane, with the Constable of France – Anne, Duc de Montmorency – led the aristocratic faction opposing Catherine as a foreign upstart, with Montmorency unfairly calling her 'an Italian shopkeeper's daughter'. These nobles, equally unfairly, accused Catherine of poisoning Henri's elder brother when he died in 1536 after playing tennis in very hot weather and then drinking iced water, the water having been brought to him by his Italian secretary, Sebastian de Montecuculli. Since all Italians were thought to be expert with poisons, it seemed obvious to those that opposed her that Catherine was clearing a path to the throne of France for herself and her husband. Montecuculli, who was probably quite innocent, was tortured and, on the orders of François I, torn apart by horses.

Henri was now the married Dauphin in need of heirs, but Catherine had produced no children, and since Henri himself had fathered a bastard girl in 1537, the fault was laid entirely at the Dauphine's door, with calls being made for a papal annulment of the marriage. Diane, now Henri's mistress, adopted his illegitimate daughter as Diane de France. Then, to everyone's relief, in 1545, Catherine became pregnant with François, Mary's future husband. The Diane and Montmorency faction was still antagonistic towards Catherine, but she was supported by François I and was at the king's side during the illness which killed him in 1547. Catherine was now Queen of France and Henri was king with Diane as his *maîtresse en titre*, newly created Duchesse de Valentinois.

When Henri made an official entry – an *entrée joyeuse* – into Lyon in 1548, he was accompanied by Diane at his side. These splendid entries, according to the historian Sir Roy Strong, were 'an essential part of the liturgy of secular apotheosis'. The pageant included twelve 'Roman gladiators' fighting with two-handed swords, garlanded oxen ridden by naked girls – Henri was especially fond of this display – and a young woman dressed as the goddess Diana, leading a lion on a silver chain. Catherine made her entry the next day; Henri asked that it be late in the day so that 'her ugliness might pass unnoticed'. Diane was now associated with the goddess Diana, and her importance to Henri was marked symbolically in subtle ways – the royal monogram, for example which consisted of the letters 'H' and 'C' interlaced, but with the ends of the 'C' drawn to a point to represent the crescent moon, which was the symbol of Diana. Henri also adopted a monogram of two letter 'Ds' interlaced with his 'H'.

Diane has attracted legends as magnets attract iron filings. The poet Brantôme said of her, 'everyone around her breathed the air of eternal spring'. He also said that when he visited her in her seventieth year she looked no more than thirty; since she died at sixty-four, Brantôme's statements should be garnished with plentiful salt. Queen Catherine was unfairly eclipsed by Diane, but in spite of this she loved her flagrantly unfaithful husband, and carried out her queenly duties knowing that the bulk of the population thought of her as an Italian witch. It was into this uneasy *ménage à trois* that the six-year-old Scots queen was thrust.

Henri was determined that Mary should become a French woman as quickly as possible, and he began by sending her Maries away to a convent some four miles distant at Poissy where they would be taught French by the Prior François de Vieuxpont.

From then on, Mary and her Maries spoke French in public, though in private they would occasionally speak in Scots to each other through fits of girlish giggles. Scots became a private nursery language. Meanwhile, Mary had the company of the royal children and, on Henri's precise instruction, relayed to d'Humières by Diane, she shared a bedroom with Elisabeth, nicknamed Isabel, the king's three-year-old daughter, who would become Mary's closest companion in France.

Henri himself arrived at St Germain-en-Laye on 9 November 1548, when he 'found her [Mary] the prettiest and most graceful princess he ever saw, as have the queen and all the court', and Catherine said, 'the little Scottish queen has but to smile to turn all French heads'. De Brézé wrote to Marie, her now-anxious mother, on 11 November, 'I assure you, Madame, he [Henri] gave her the best welcome possible and continues to do so from day to day . . . he considers her no less than his own daughter. He will bring her up with the Dauphin in one court to accustom them to one another.' Henri also wrote to Marie, on 11 December, continuing his praises for Mary but also giving a hint of troubled waters ahead: 'I assure you, Madame, that you have sent a lady hither with the Queen your daughter who has pleased this company as much as the six most virtuous women in this country could have done . . . I mean Lady Fleming.'

Henri made sure of Mary's thorough education in French manners by placing her under the watchful eye of Diane, who continued to act as an intermediary between the king and d'Humières, even training the nurses for the royal nursery personally at her own château of Anet, north-west of Paris. Diane and Mary became close friends, and from the start Diane saw that Mary would grow into a considerable beauty, according to the strictures accepted for female beauty at the time. They were classified in eight groups of three:

3 things white, the skin, the teeth, and the hands.
3 things black, the eyes, the eyebrows, and the eye lashes.
3 things red, the lips, the cheeks, and the nails.

3 things long, the body, the hair, and the hands.
3 things short, the teeth, the ears, and the feet.
3 things narrow, the mouth, the waist, and the ankles.
3 things big, the arms, the thighs, and the calves.
3 things small, the breasts, the nose, and the head.

Of these, Mary already possessed what could be expected of a child for six and Diane could see that, with care, the other attributes would follow in time. She, herself, could tick all the boxes and was widely thought to possess a magic elixir which preserved her beauty. In fact her daily routine had no such magic; she rose at three, bathed in cold water, summer or winter, and then rode for three hours before returning to bed for reading and meditation. She administered her considerable estates herself with great efficiency and ate only sparingly. Amid a court ablaze with all the colours of the rainbow she dressed only in black and white, which were technically the colours of a widow in semi-mourning, but were also her heraldic colours. With her tall figure and upright bearing she stood out from everyone else and could not be ignored. Previously, it had been the custom of a royal mistress to appear with her left breast exposed as a sign that her heart was available to her lover, and Diane may well have done so on occasions. She is never shown thus in portraits, although in the many idealised representations of Diane as her alter ego Diana she often appears totally naked. Interestingly, Diane produced no royal bastards from her liaison with Henri in spite of both of them having children with other partners.

A crucial issue which concerned the court was how the child Mary would relate to her future husband, the Dauphin, even though the marriage was one of dynastic convenience and the principles of royal duty would have been thoroughly explained to Mary by Diane. This was all too necessary since the Dauphin was a complete contrast to the healthy and extrovert Mary, and his conception had been a major trial for Catherine. She knew that her position at court was still highly insecure while she had seemed incapable of producing an heir, and the poor woman had gone to extraordinary lengths to achieve her goal. Knowing of her husband's fecundity it is said that the desperate queen had holes bored in the floor above his bedchamber so that she could watch him in bed with Diane. Diane, in her turn, had coerced Henri to do his marital duty as often as possible. Menstrual cycles had been watched, astrological tables had been consulted, foul-smelling poultices had been applied and grisly potions had been drunk by the desperate 25-year-old Catherine. Her personal physician, Dr Fernel, had given her more practical advice, the details of which are unfortunately unknown to us today. Eventually, the welcome result had been Dauphin François. Inevitably, Catherine had been accused of having used witchcraft in order to conceive, though there is no evidence whatsoever to support this claim. In contrast to Mary's scantily attended christening in the cold of St Michael's Church in Linlithgow, François had been christened in the Chapel of St Saturnin at Fontainebleau, a month after his birth in January 1543. The ceremony, lit by 300 torches carried by the Royal Guard, had been attended by the nobility of France, the hierarchy of the Church and all foreign ambassadors, arrayed in their finest. François, however, was not the Dauphin that France that Henri had prayed for.

According to contemporaries he had an 'obstruction of the brain' which meant that he spoke through his nose – this was probably the result of adenoids – and red livid marks occasionally appeared on his face, which 'were sure signs of ill health and a short life'. Others said that the Dauphin was timid, bilious, with an underdeveloped intelligence and was incapable of sustained effort; 'Very good teachers have been provided for him . . . yet their success is very small.' He was undersized and thin, and seemed to the courtiers to be a prince destined to stay a child. But he tried to overcome his physical failings and astonished the court with his vivacity, loving hunting and weapons. In 1551, when he was only seven years old, he had archery butts built in the galleries at the Palace of Blois.

Though Mary and François had met in the nursery, they had yet to appear in public. This would happen on 4 December 1548 at St Germain, when Mary's uncle François, Duc de Guise, married Anne d'Este, daughter of the Duke of Ferrara. Protocol demanded that, as a crowned queen, Mary would dance with her limping fiancé immediately after Henri and Catherine had danced together, Lady Fleming having taught her enough simple steps to acquit herself with honour. She was a ready pupil and thoroughly enjoyed not only showing off her aptitude but also the physical pleasure of dancing, a joy that would stay with her for the rest of her life. At the ball, the tiny couple were led onto the floor by Diane and Lady Fleming, the musicians started a prearranged and reasonably slow melody and the display started. With her heavy brocade dress, embroidered with jewellery, and elaborately dressed hair, Mary was at first hesitant, but the music caught her and she started to enjoy herself, even though she found she was supporting the Dauphin. The entire court watched closely. Her limbs seemed straight, her feet were dainty in their satin slippers, and her smile was enchanting. To an audience expert in judging horses and cattle it seemed that she would probably breed healthy dauphins in her turn and the courtiers breathed a sigh of relief – all, that is, except the English ambassador, who saw the union of England's two greatest enemies made flesh in the two children. The dance ended, and Mary, stooping a little, kissed the Dauphin on the lips as formality required, while members of the court applauded and smiled reassuringly at each other. Lady Fleming led Mary to the king, who bent and kissed his little 'daughter' before complimenting Lady Fleming on the skills of her charge for rather longer than either Diane or Queen Catherine would have thought strictly necessary.

From the regular reports from d'Humières that Henri received he was able to reassure himself that Mary and his son 'got on as well together as if they had known each other all their lives'. Montmorency wrote to Marie in Scotland on 30 March 1549, 'I will assure you that the Dauphin pays her little attentions, and is enamoured of her, from which it is easy to judge that God gave them birth the one for the other.' This was due to the careful instruction of Diane, who taught Mary that her best way of ensuring the affection of the Dauphin was to cosset him and never to allow him to be over-ambitious, ensuring that whatever he attempted was well within his somewhat limited powers. It was through Mary's encouragement that François became so enthusiastic for outdoor pursuits, and their relationship was that of brother and sister with an overlay of courtly love. Mary never attempted to dominate her little fiancé, and Antoinette, as well as the king, was well pleased with the state of affairs in the nursery.

Henri was not so happy with the Scots in general. Many of the Garde Écossaise wanted to join Mary's personal service, but this was heavily discouraged. Although formed as a royal bodyguard from noble families in Scotland, they were mercenaries and had a reputation for arrogance, violence and vandalism, even leaving their graffiti on the walls of the chapel at Fontainebleau. They were also expensive to maintain, as were the forces supporting Marie de Guise in Scotland.

In December 1549 Henri had asked for the astronomical sum of 400,000 livres in taxation for his military expenses in Scotland, and he begged d'Humières not to increase Mary's court. Most of Mary's male servants had been sent home and replaced with Frenchmen, whilst the Maries had been sent away the previous year to Poissy. Mary's French was improving due to the facility young children have for learning new languages and, although she continued to understand Scots, French was now her everyday language. Attempts were made to replace Janet Sinclair. She was retained, although now, as only one amongst many servants, she had less personal contact with Mary and was the butt of constant jokes by the French servants for her continued Scottishness. Mary's Frenchification was proceeding successfully. Her governess, Lady Fleming, remained in charge of all Mary's female staff for reasons other than her domestic efficiency: she was now a regular occupant of the king's bed.

This ill-judged affair had the surprising result of uniting Diane and Catherine against Lady Fleming and Henri. Diane also felt that Henri was harming Mary's standing by encouraging infidelity among her household, but Montmorency saw a chance of destabilising Diane's position at court and made public the rumours that she had been supplanted. Although reluctantly tolerated by Catherine, Diane had many enemies and her considerable wealth made her loathed. Apart from her château at Anet, she had vineyards and estates throughout France, and on the death of François I she had seized the jewellery he had given to his mistress the Duchesse d'Étampes. Henri had also given her the château of Chenonceau and the rights to collect various taxes, and even placed a tax on church bells for her. Of this, Rabelais said, 'the king had hung the chimes of this kingdom on the neck of his mare'. Henri managed to ride out the scandal until one evening when Lady Fleming, who must have been drunk, loudly announced to the court, 'I have done all that I can and I am pregnant by the king, for which I count myself both honoured and happy. I now carry the royal blood and whatever flowers that may bring.' The child, a boy, was known as the Bastard of Angôuleme and Lady Fleming was swiftly returned to Scotland, to be replaced by the more strait-laced Mme de Parois as head of Mary's household.

Some care was taken to explain the change in governesses, and the truth was undoubtedly kept from Mary as she became more and more a princess of France. Being a queen of Scotland – a country of which she now had only hazy memories – had become of secondary importance. Mary's life in France was so vivid with new experiences that it took over from her past, except, of course, from her memories of her mother who was now planning to visit France. The first letter Mary wrote, in 1549, was to Marie. It was a very formal correspondence, in which she told her mother that de Brézé was to visit her with some news. Typical of any young girl writing in her 'best handwriting', Mary shortened the letter, saying that de Brézé would give her mother all the news, which was that Mary's grandfather Claude, Duc de Guise, had died at the age of fifty-four. Marie had been writing constantly, mainly to Antoinette, concerning the care of her daughter, especially in religious matters. She was to attend Mass daily and had two personal chaplains, Guillaume de Laon, provided by Henri, and the Prior of Inchmahome, who had accompanied her on the voyage from Dumbarton and remained with her at his own expense, no doubt to the relief of Henri.

In April 1550, Mary was delighted to receive the news that her mother was planning a visit to France, although not solely for the funeral of Claude, which Mary was thought too young to attend. Mary's uncle, François de Guise, inherited the dukedom. Her letter to her mother about the impending visit is much less formal and shows that she had become fluent in written French by this stage. Meanwhile, Marie wrote to Diane as to the correct mourning in current fashion. It would have been more appropriate to consult Catherine, but Marie, French to her roots, regarded Catherine's dress sense as Italian – they had never met – and, therefore, barbaric.

Marie did not come to France entirely for family reasons. The English forces had finally retreated from Scotland, leaving Henri's French garrisons free to return home, as were his forces from Boulogne, which was back in French hands, and he was planning a gala celebration in Rouen. Marie brought with her the entire Scottish court, hoping, as did happen, that their support for her as queen regent would be strengthened after receiving suitable pensions from Henri for their loyalty. In other words, they were getting a free foreign holiday, plus handsome bribes which she, herself, could not afford. Marie knew how to appease her Scottish aristocracy.

Mary and her mother met on 25 September 1550 and, in October, came to Rouen as part of an *entrée joyeuse* Henri had arranged to celebrate the return of Boulogne to France and the final pacification of Scotland. This meant the withdrawal of French troops and the saving of much French money, although even without this welcome bonus Marie and her daughter were guests of honour. However, now the daughter far outshone the mother. Mary was seven years and ten months old and still tall for her age, so Nicolas de Moncel, her tailor, had supplied the precocious child with violet, scarlet and yellow velvets, plain

Holland linen, white and blue Venetian satin, violet and black taffeta with pink and white caps, as well as embroidered aprons worn over skirts of cloth of silver. She glittered as she sat on Henri's right in the royal stand while the procession passed before them led by the dignitaries of Rouen, who uncovered their heads and bowed as they passed. They were followed by 2,000 soldiers escorting ragged English captives in chains – these 'prisoners' were probably citizens of Rouen clad in brand-new rags. Four canvas and wood elephants carried flaming pots on their backs, surrounded by Roman gladiators, bowing to a huge cart drawn by plumed horses and carrying 'Henri' and his 'family' – more volunteer citizens in borrowed plumes. Next, winged horses drew a carriage with figures of fame and victory. Classical warriors carried poles with models of the forts at Boulogne and Calais and giant banners on which were painted artists' impressions of Haddington, Dundee and Broughty Castle. Finally, there was a floating island on which naked 'Brazilian' natives – Rouennais citizens painted pink – were duly overcome by French soldiers. (Henri was keen to establish a colony in Brazil, and in 1555 Admiral Villegaignon would lead an unsuccessful expedition to what is now Rio de Janiero.) There was a mock sea battle fought on the Seine and a solemn Te Deum sung in the cathedral. Henri and Mary adored every minute of it. The following day the display was repeated for the benefit of Queen Catherine, although this time the spectacle was marred when one of the ships in the sea battle actually did sink and the actors playing the crew were drowned in the fast-flowing Seine.

It was during her mother's visit that Mary, while staying at Amboise, had her first whiff of danger. Robert Stewart, one of the archers of the Garde Écossaise, was an escaped prisoner from those taken at St Andrews after the siege of the castle. He had changed his name and now had access to the royal apartments at Amboise. He attempted to poison Mary's food but was discovered. He fled to England and was captured and returned to France, where, under torture, he confessed and was executed. The actual facts were kept from Mary, but the increased security and heightened palace gossip would have intrigued and excited the young queen.

A more sombre note was struck when Mary's half-brother, the fifteen-year-old François, Duc de Longueville, who had sent his mother Marie the knotted string showing his increase in height, died in Amiens. Marie had nursed him at his end and was heartbroken when he died. Mary was now her only surviving child, and she knew that she would have to leave France and her daughter very soon. Heavy hints were being dropped about the expense of keeping her and her Scottish attendants in the royal household, and she left in the late autumn of 1551 after a tearful parting with her daughter. She could have remained in the family home at Joinville and she even considered joining a convent, but she knew that her duty lay in governing Scotland as regent for her daughter. Mary and her mother would never meet again.

CHAPTER FOUR

The most amiable Princess in Christendom

૨૬

Mary's life as the Dauphine was peripatetic in the extreme, constantly moving around the royal palaces. But principally now for Mary the Palace of St Germain formed all her memories of childhood as Scotland faded into the distance. St Germain was near enough to Paris for Henri to attend to business, but far enough away from the capital to allow rural relaxation, much as, in Scotland, Linlithgow Palace sat at a convenient distance from Edinburgh. Mary appeared enthusiastically in masquerades at St Germain, where she, as the Delphic Sybil, prophesied love and happiness for the Dauphin when she became Queen of Britain, to the polite applause of the indulgent court. Her education in dynastic ambition was beginning at a young age.

The Louvre in Paris, very much a working palace used by Henri II for business, was being thoroughly rebuilt and so was seldom visited by the royal children. Outside Paris, the country palaces nearly all owed their existence to the royal passion for hunting and the nearest to Paris was Fontainebleau, thirty-five miles to the south. It had been a hunting lodge since the eleventh century, but François I transformed it into a Renaissance jewel. Francesco Primaticcio, the Mantuan painter and architect, decorated the great rooms, installed exact replicas of classical statues and looked after the royal collection of pictures, although François I had himself acquired the Mona Lisa directly from Leonardo da Vinci. It was as lavishly Renaissance as François's liberal purse would allow. The beautiful Linlithgow Palace of Mary's birth would have fitted neatly into one of its courtyards.

To the south-west of Paris the River Loire swings westwards to the sea, and it was along its banks that a string of palaces hung like jewels on a necklace. Nearest to Paris was Chambord, the grandest of them all and a favourite of Henri's. This vast palace, covered by innumerable turrets and spires, sits beside the River Cossen; François had wanted to divert the Loire but was dissuaded, although, even then, building the palace nearly bankrupted him. It was elaborately decorated without and within, containing over 400 rooms, all fashionably plastered and painted. In the central great hall was a double helix staircase said to have been designed by Leonardo himself. Even the roof was a fairyland fantasy with crocketted towers, lanterns and intricately carved dormer windows. The thousands of nooks and crannies invited the confidences, intrigues and assignations which played a great part in the life of glittering society. Mary and the Dauphin were watched affectionately as they played games where she was the damsel in distress and he her gallant knight. There was a special terrace from which the ladies could watch the gentlemen returning from hunting or look down on the pageants and jousts on the forecourt below.

As soon as she was able to read it, Mary was introduced to the best-selling book of the time, *Amadis de Gaul*. This was a French translation of a Spanish romance by Garci Rodríguez de Montalvo, telling of the adventures of Amadis, the flower of chivalry, who rescues his love, Oriana, from her captivity while defeating all the enemies of her father. This book had an enormously wide readership among the romantically minded courtiers of the day and had a powerful influence on its female readers. Diane d'Antouins, who was to become the first mistress of Henri IV, even changed her name to Corysande, one of the heroines of the book. It was a highly romantic flashback to the days of Arthur and his knights, though here the quest was not for the Grail but for pure love. Standing on the terrace of Chambord, the impressionable Mary saw this fantasy made reality as armoured knights rode in the lists with their mistresses' colours on their lances. Since careful nurses removed their charges in time, she would not have seen how, as the heat of the afternoon grew and

59

exhaustion inflamed tempers, the gallantry of the joust was often replaced by vindictive violence: lances were cast aside to be replaced with axes and maces, and the exhausted knights-errant of the morning were carried off on blood-stained stretchers.

At Chambord Mary and the Dauphin would ride through the vast parkland – armed guards and ladies-in-waiting keeping a discreet distance – and hunt enthusiastically for the game obligingly driven towards them. One of the innovations Catherine de Medici had imported from Italy was the practice of wearing a pair of serge drawers under her skirts that allowed her to ride astride without affording a view of the royal limbs, and Mary soon adopted the fashion. She had two horses as gifts from Henri, Bravane and Mme la Réale, and, with the Dauphin mounted on either Enghien or Fontaine, she had some of the most carefree times of her childhood.

Mary also received the formal education suitable for a royal princess. On orders from Henri, Catherine saw to it that Mary was taught with her own children under their schoolmasters, Claude Millot and Antoine Fouquelin, while her spiritual education was undertaken by Pierre Lavane and Jacques Amyot. Mary's own chaplain, Guillaume de Laon, had charge of her communion vessels, which travelled with her wherever she celebrated Mass, in case she should contract any infection from vessels shared with others. The close-knit court of Catherine displayed a strict morality, at least in contrast to the licentiousness of François I's day, and casual amorous intrigues were officially frowned upon. After marriage, the maintenance of a mistress was deemed acceptable, as in Henri's case, but unofficial and temporary liaisons came under the heading of vulgar immorality.

In the cosmopolitan court Mary now spoke French fluently and, with the facility of children, easily learned some Italian and Spanish, as well as Latin and Greek, although with more difficulty. She is credited with having written Latin 'themes' when she was twelve years old in the form of letters of a hundred or so words each, to her 'sister' and best friend Elisabeth, the eldest of Henri's daughters. These letters are packed with classical allusions and read as if they come from a scholar of the time who had read all of Cicero, Plato and Plutarch, and Erasmus's colloquy *Diluculum*, as well as the more obscure Politian. They even included a letter to Calvin recommending that he study Socrates's view of immortality. Overall, their underlying theme is to praise classical education for women. But the Latin, in Mary's clear handwriting, appears on the recto, with the French text written in another hand on the verso. It has been suggested that the French text was written by a tutor and that Mary had simply translated it into Latin as an exercise; it seems very unlikely that any child, except a precocious genius, could have achieved that breadth of reading by the age of twelve to enable her to compose them unaided.

Mary delivered a Latin oration 'of her own composition' to the court, for which she was certainly heavily coached. Here her chosen subject, or, more likely, the subject chosen for her, was a defence of the access of women to the liberal arts. The arch-flatterer Brantôme found it wonderful to 'see that learned and beautiful queen declaiming thus in Latin, which she understood and spoke admirably'; though it is very unlikely that he was actually present. In later life, when forced into conversations in Latin, she had to use an interpreter, and she had no enthusiasm for scholarship as such. Mary's cousin, Elizabeth Tudor, enjoyed a facility with Latin, and she spoke both it and Greek freely. By contrast, scholastically, Mary Stewart was a dutiful plodder.

Mary was, however, a patron of poetry and supported the young poets who inhabited the court in the hope of commissions. They rejected the classical styles of the Latin and Greek poets and championed the use of French as a language flexible enough for secular as well as spiritual subjects, and one capable of carrying a powerful emotional message to the common people. This circle of seven poets, calling themselves the Pléiade (the astronomical group of seven stars) was led by Pierre de Ronsard and Joachim du Bellay. Given their rejection of the classical modes, it is curious that they took the same name as a group of

Greek poets flourishing in Alexandria in the third century BC. Ronsard had been a page at the court of Madeleine, the tragic queen to James V, and du Bellay had accompanied Mary on her voyage from Scotland. Now both men dedicated poetry to the young queen. Having poets worshipping her was simply something she grew to expect.

Mary was learning to embroider – a pastime that she often turned to throughout her life. She could now sew and knit, and in 1551 there was an order for 32 sols' worth of wool. She learned music, played the guitar and sang the songs of Marot with her sister princesses. Clément Marot was a poet and the translator of the Psalms into French, set to music by Claude Goudimel and Loys Bourgeois. Mary also learned 'genteel' cooking – the making of preserves and sweetmeats, above all a pâté of sugar, cinnamon and powdered violets – and she was joined by the other princesses in pretending to be simple bourgeois housewives busying themselves in their kitchens.

The seventeenth-century French historian Mezeray summed up what the French court and people thought of Mary: 'Nature had bestowed upon her everything that is necessary to form a complete beauty. And beside this she had a most agreeable turn of mind, a ready memory and a lively imagination. All these good natural qualities she took care likewise to embellish, by the study of the liberal arts and sciences especially painting, music and poetry insomuch that she appeared to be the most amiable Princess in Christendom.' By 1551 this amiable princess had sixteen dresses, ranging from cloth of silver to mere satin, six cotton aprons, three skirts of differing materials, three caps, two farthingales, two overskirts, a cloak and a fur muff. Jehan du Chauvrais, her furrier, looked after her sable and wolf skins, while Pierre Daujon, the embroiderer, sewed on the goldsmith Mathurin Lussault's 22-carat gold buttons enamelled in black and white – the heraldic colours of Diane de Poitiers – and assorted chains and collars, as well as looking after her gold belts enamelled in white and red. She had so many jewels and costumes that three brass chests were especially made to hold them while she was travelling. The other princesses were less splendidly provided for, but since they were of lower rank they did not seem to be jealous. When indoors she occasionally played cards with the Dauphin and on one occasion won the trifling amount of 79 sols 6 deniers, while on another, remembering Diane de Poitiers's advice, she wisely lost 45 sols 4 deniers.

Mary's household, now administered by Claude d'Urfé, had expanded since Jean d'Humières's death on 18 July 1550. For her personal use were eight grooms and eight stable boys, thirty-six maids of honour, eleven honorary receptionists, eight secretaries, nine ushers, twenty-eight valets, four porters, four lodging directors, four wardrobe masters, the treasurer Jacques Bochetel, two comptrollers-general, five doctors, three apothecaries, four surgeons and four barbers. There were fifty-seven kitchen staff and forty-two to look after the cellars, but only one porter to carry water to be used for toilet purposes as well as drinking, which was much 'to the detriment of the general sobriety and toilet care'. There was also a floating population of court musicians, poets, jesters and dancers, as well as jugglers and acrobats.

On one day, 8 June 1553, the court ate twenty-three dozen loaves, eighteen sides of beef, eight sheep, four calves, twenty capons, one hundred and twenty pigeons, three kids, six geese and four hares – at the cost of 152 livres, 4 sols 12 deniers, or £2,736 in today's currency. Unsurprisingly, Mary occasionally suffered from faintness due to over-eating. Henri II's accounts show an annual expenditure of 74,982 livres for his personal domestic costs in one year, although this represents only a fraction of the royal expenditure. When the court, or even a single member of it, moved – which it did frequently – then the entire household moved as well, in a vast train of closely guarded carts, with the king's entourage carrying all the apparatus of justice and administration.

Less formally, Henri, accompanied by only a few body servants, would visit the spectacular château of Chenonceau, the personal gift he had made to Diane de Poitiers. Bought by François I in 1535, Chenonceau stood beside a mill at the foot of a bridge on the banks of the River Cher, a tributary of the Loire. Diane de Poitiers stamped her personality everywhere, Primaticcio's portrait of Diane as Diana the Huntress having pride of place in the royal bedchamber. Diane commissioned a garden to be laid out in the French style, although later Catherine added a garden in the Italian style and built a long gallery supported by a bridge across the river. This is the palace we see now, but, even with those changes of Catherine's, Chenonceau is still emphatically Diane's.

Henri had the reputation of being uneasy in conversation with ladies, but Diane spoke to him as a man, and it was to Chenonceau he would come to visit his mistress and listen to her advice. He was also a frequent visitor to the Château d'Anet, Diane's own property, some fifty miles north-west of Paris. It was designed to her personal specifications by Philibert de l'Orme and was, at the same time, both a temple to Diana and a Renaissance country mansion. The surrounding estate was laid out with equal care, and according to Brantôme it was 'for the king a terrestrial paradise – mysterious wooded nooks for the secrets of love, a vast carpet of verdure for the hunt or for riding and a barrier of hills against indiscretions and importunates – a veritable fairy castle'.

Mary and her Dauphin frequently visited the Château d'Anet to be free from the rigid formality of the court and act out the trysts and assignations they had read about in *Amadis*. Here also Diane would supervise Mary's formal studies while gently introducing her to the art of maintaining her own personality as a woman in the aggressively male world of Henri's court. It was essential that men were seen to be in complete control and that all initiatives were theirs alone. Thus, all major topics had to be approached from a tangent, avoiding direct confrontation by praising a man for an idea which he had not yet dreamt of, or for his firmness when he was clearly vacillating. Promises of sex to be given or withheld were the weakest of weapons in the royal court, as the exiled Lady Fleming had discovered. Diane's power lay not in her bed but in her brain, and she stressed to the young princess that it was more with her intellect than anything else that Mary could take power when she came to rule as a queen consort. Mary could maintain her own court and exercise a measure of control over her husband, avoiding an existence as a mere breeder of princes and princesses. As a queen regnant she would no longer need to rely on manipulating men to do her bidding but could command them directly. Since the idea of being a queen regnant would have meant contemplating a return to Scotland which was very far from her teenage mind, Mary, sadly, received this excellent advice with an eager smile and deaf ears.

Catherine, not unnaturally, wanted more and more to bring the care of the royal children under her sole control and Henri, quite naturally, resented the cost of maintaining Mary's court at his own expense. The Scots had similar reservations over paying for the upkeep of an absent queen whose annual expenses were in the region of £12,000 Scots, almost half the entire royal revenue. Even these sums did not include Mary's expenditure on horses, ponies and stabling.

The Scots were eventually persuaded to continue these payments by Marie de Guise, and on 1 January 1554 the twelve-year-old Mary wrote to tell her mother that she now had her own household and had invited her uncle Charles, the Cardinal of Lorraine, to dinner. He became a crucial influence in her education and was also her spiritual mentor. She would hear him celebrate Mass in his private chapel accompanied by the exquisite sacred music of Jacques Arcadelt. However, Mary received no practical advice on politics from her uncles. They regarded her simply as a key which would one day open the sluice gates of influence for the Guise family, a carte d'entrée to royal power.

The Guise faction, especially François, Duc de Guise, was already united with Catherine in their dislike of the constable, Montmorency, Diane's ally and a favourite of Henri's. Now that Mary had her own court they could start to use her to bring their feuding into the open. The Cardinal of Lorraine was always at her elbow with advice and, through her, the Guise family set about strengthening their already powerful position. Mary blithely hoped to ride both horses and assured her mother that all her uncles were as solicitous for her comfort, as was Diane de Poitiers. Having managed to have his niece declared to be of age, 'at eleven years and a day', the cardinal put into motion his scheme to extend Guise power in Scotland. It was very simple: since Mary was a sovereign queen, there was now no need for Châtelherault to share the regency with Marie de Guise, who could become the sole regent on her daughter's behalf. As Henri, wisely, did not trust Châtelherault at all, he encouraged the scheme, and in April 1554 Marie became sole regent. On the cardinal's advice Mary sent her mother several sheets of paper, blank except for her signature, 'MARIE'. This was the signature she used for the rest of her life, always in block capitals and always in French.

In France, Mary was now able to choose her own guardians, and, to no one's surprise, she opted for her Guise uncles along with the king, thus putting the Guise family next in importance to the ruling Valois dynasty. She told her mother, 'I can assure you, Madame, that nothing which comes from you shall be known through me.'

Mary's spending continued to increase, however, and as she grew she needed new dresses, some of cloth of gold. Then, to the horror of her housekeeper, Mme de Parois, she intended to give some old dresses to her aunts, the abbesses of St Pierre and Farmoutiers, to be cut up and used as richly-embroidered altar frontals. This crisis came at the end of 1555 and Mary told her mother of it in a letter on 28 December. De Parois had exploded in fury, since the disposition for sale of cast-offs was one of the fringe benefits of royal service, and she accused Mary of trying to impoverish her. Mary might have been persuaded by the cardinal or her mother that she was, as a thirteen-year-old, exceeding her authority, but Mary knew that as a sovereign queen she could not be overruled, so she maintained her position that she had been maligned by a servant and de Parois, under a

66

certain amount of duress, resigned. Mary's first display of power was an act of petty malevolence against a defenceless servant.

In his picture of Hollywood, *Adventures in the Screen Trade*, William Goldman tells us that one of the distinguishing marks of a star is that they know that from the moment they awaken until they go to sleep, no one will ever disagree with them about anything they say, no matter how outlandish. Four hundred and fifty years previously, Mary Stewart had just discovered this extremely dangerous power.

Mary had reacted to de Parois's complaint by insisting on exerting her power as a queen, but, had she been overruled, she would have left herself no room in which to manoeuvre. Diane de Poitiers's tactics would have been to persuade the cardinal that her wishes were also his and he would then have removed de Parois on her behalf. Catherine de Medici would simply have had an already well-prepared alternative in case of opposition. Mary's direct approach verged on a childish tantrum and the effect on her was a physical collapse. This happened frequently when she was challenged and her collapses consisted of vomiting, dizziness, acute depression and bouts of crying, lasting anything from a few days to several weeks. Her normally robust physical health nearly always gave way when reality intruded upon her fantasy existence as a fairy princess, although, on this occasion in 1556, it seems that she had contracted the 'quartan ague', actually a recurrent summer fever similar to malaria. Later, she certainly did contract smallpox and thus was at a serious risk of death. Even if she survived, there was a grave possibility of extreme disfigurement, but Catherine put her daughter-in-law-to-be in the hands of her own Dr Fernel, who masterminded Mary's recovery with her looks unimpaired.

Mary would have taken little interest in the shifting of the tectonic plates of diplomacy when, on 6 July 1553, the sickly boy-king of England Edward VI died, probably of tuberculosis. The threat to France by England lessened as Mary Tudor succeeded him, and the new queen, devotedly Catholic, set about putting a severe brake on the progress of the Protestant Reformation.

However, when Mary Tudor married Philip II of Spain, son of Charles V, France was again surrounded by hostile powers. The threat of invasion became a reality when, in 1557, Philip II mobilised his forces in the Netherlands. His ally, the Duke of Savoy, invaded and was met by Montmorency with the French forces at St Quentin, later the site of one of the bloodiest battles of the First World War. This earlier battle was equally bloody, resulting in a total defeat for the French, with Montmorency and his sons among the 400 French noblemen taken prisoner and marched off to Brussels. Henri immediately sent for the Duc de Guise and gave him sweeping powers of retaliation. Freeing his enemy Montmorency was not seen as a priority by the duke. However, acquiring glory for the name of Guise was, and he made a raid on the fort of Calais, poorly defended by the English. On 1 January 1558, the town fell to France. Mary Tudor felt the loss of England's last foothold in France keenly, declaring that if her heart were to be opened after her death, people would find the word 'Calais' engraved on it. Henri held an *entrée joyeuse* into Calais and the Duc de Guise was made Lieutenant-General of France. The final link binding the king and the house of Guise was now ready to be forged.

A marriage between Mary, as a daughter of the house of Guise, and François de Valois would form the strongest bond possible, as well as answering Henri's need to encircle England. In Scotland, Marie de Guise, who was trying to stem the tide of the Scottish Reformation, was enthusiastic about having the next king of France as her son-in-law. A significant number of the Scottish nobility had rejected her government and signed the First Band (or Bond). They were later known as the Protestant Lords of the Congregation, and, although Marie de Guise had effectively stalemated these men, there were growing signs of an alternative, Protestant, government beginning to come into existence. It was still nascent, and indeed its spiritual leader, John Knox, had travelled to Dieppe, only to be sent back into exile at Geneva, with John Calvin, having been told that the time for his return was not yet ripe.

Prior to the capture of Calais, and easily foreseeing what was to come, Marie de Guise sent nine commissioners to France to negotiate the terms of the marriage. With the diplomatic skill instinctive to the Guises she was careful to include Lord James Stewart, Mary's half-brother; Gilbert Kennedy, Earl of Cassilis; and John Erskine of Dun, all three men Protestants, but totally reliable in their defence of Scotland's liberties. They were all enthusiastic about the marriage since it might very well mean that Mary would live out her life in France, leaving Scotland open for their own exercise of power in a council of regency. At this time Mary certainly had no plans to return.

The terms of the marriage agreement were largely what had been agreed at Haddington and came as no surprise to the commissioners, but what did come as a shock was that the French negotiations were supervised by Diane de Poitiers. These men had dealt, reluctantly and unsatisfactorily, with the queen regent, Marie, and here was another Frenchwoman, neither a queen nor a regent, but in their Protestant eyes, simply the king's whore. There were no ministers of state or chancellors attending and the negotiations were to be very straightforward. In fact, Henri could afford to be as generous as the Scots requested since he had put into action plans for an alternative, secret, treaty.

Once the Scots lords had recovered their composure after meeting the haughty beauty Diane, negotiations began. The agreement on the table reiterated Mary's pledge to preserve the freedom, liberties and privileges of Scotland; on marriage the young couple would be the King-Dauphin and Queen-Dauphine, but François would be King of Scotland until he succeeded to the French throne, when he would become king of both nations. All Frenchmen would be naturalised Scotsmen and eventually all Scotsmen would, similarly, be naturalised Frenchmen,* but in the meantime Scotland would be governed on

*This was not repealed until 1906.

behalf of the absent royal children by Marie, Queen Regent. If Mary died without heirs, then the crown would revert to the next heir by blood. Since this was the Duc de Châtelherault, both sides prayed fervently that this would never happen. If François died first, which seemed likely, Mary would receive a payment of 600,000 livres, and her male issue would inherit both crowns, while, under the Salic laws of France, her female issue would inherit only the Scottish crown.

The only disputed point was that François would not receive the Scottish crown for his coronation as had been requested, but instead would be given all the powers of the crown matrimonial, that is to say, he would rule as monarch of Scotland and would sign state papers with Mary, his signature taking precedence. The French did not ask that Mary, although a queen, bring a dowry to France and the Scots were not asked to distribute lands to French nobles. Throughout all these negotiations the French behaved with surprising docility. Mary was awarded the duchies of Touraine and Poitou as a wedding portion.

Mary was at Fontainebleau and took no part in any of the negotiations. Under the benign eye of her mother-in-law to be, Catherine de Medici, she was, like all young brides, beset with tailors and dressmakers. The situation in Scotland was too fragile for Marie de Guise to attend her daughter's wedding, but Antoinette de Bourbon was appointed to attend as her proxy. This was disappointing, as Mary had seen so little of her real mother, but aside from this, all the wedding arrangements proceeded calmly.

At Fontainebleau, on 4 April 1558, Mary signed three documents unknown to the Scots negotiators. The first document was a 'Gift made by Mary Stewart to King Henri II'. It declared that the gift was being made in consideration of 'the singular and perfect affection which the kings of France have shown in protecting Scotland against England', and thanked Henri for keeping Mary in France and for paying her considerable expenses. As recompense, if Mary should die without heirs then Scotland and any other titles which were hers would fall to the king of France. This 'donation' was witnessed by the cardinal – to make sure Mary's nerve held – flanked by the secretary of state, Côme Claussé and by Monsieur Bourdin, a notary. The second document, also a 'donation', was made after counsel from 'the most reverend and most illustrious Cardinal de Lorraine and the Duc de Guise'. This stipulated that, should Mary die childless, the king of France would continue to enjoy the income of Scotland until a payment of 1 million livres d'or, or, more outrageously, such a sum as would repay France for the cost of its garrisons in Scotland and of Mary's upkeep and education in France, was made. It would be all but impossible for Scotland to raise such a vast sum for many years and simply meant that Scotland would become a debtor département of France. Mary also gave total possession of the kingdom of Scotland to the King of France and his successors. In the third document she abrogated any other agreement made in her name that might have prejudiced the two new agreements. This last document was signed by François as well. Mary had blithely given Scotland to France and renounced the agreement made by the Lords of the Congregation. The reason for a low-key negotiation, lightly supervised by Diane de Poitiers, was now quite clear. Henri knew that the real agreement would be engineered satisfactorily by the Guise family, so he could safely ignore the Scotsmen. It was totally scandalous for a Scottish monarch to sign away the future of her kingdom – even a kingdom that she never intended to rule.

Mary was fifteen and a half years old and has been excused for what can be seen as an act of total betrayal of her country on account of her age and the inevitable reassurances from her uncles that signing the donations was the correct course of action. They had been the supervisors of her education as a princess of France. However, she knew that the representatives of the Lords of the Congregation were in France; she had met her half-brother, Lord James Stewart, and spoken to the commissioners 'as a woman of age and knowledge'. If she did not understand what she was signing then all the accounts of her precocity are no more than courtly eulogies, though it is certainly clear that she was all too willing to blindly accept the advice of her uncles. Understandably, in the days immediately before their wedding most brides are often incapable of much rational thought, but Mary was not most brides; she already knew the Dauphin well and had treated him as a younger, rather backward brother to be protected from harm. She had no sexual anticipation. It was a purely dynastic marriage. What is possible is that Mary had become totally French and held little regard for a Scotland she now thought of as an alien country. The historian Allan White says, 'Scotland for Mary was only a sideshow in the far more exciting arena of European dynastic politics.' Her future life would be in France as its queen and, since all teenagers appear to believe in their own immortality, making provisions for her affairs after her death was of no consequence to her.

Fifteen days later the 'handfasting' or betrothal took place in the great hall of the Louvre as the Cardinal of Lorraine joined the couple's hands together in public and they formally agreed to marry each other. François obviously adored Mary, but it was the adoration of a schoolboy for his elder sister, and he was clearly no match, physically or mentally, for her. He stuttered and had a tendency to dribble, he was physically clumsy with a twisted spine, giving him a peculiarly lop-sided appearance, and his lack of application to his studies meant that he appeared slow-witted. His stunted growth and vocal abnormality might be explained by primary hypopituitarism, a defect in the growth of the pituitary gland. Another unfortunate effect of this condition is that the Dauphin's testicles never grew normally; in other words, he was sterile and would breed no future kings.

The couple, who had been closely observed by the court, were affectionate in each other's company and had their own private jokes and signals, but Mary was looking after her Dauphin in the same way she had cared for her dolls and talked to her ponies when not so very much younger. But on every side she had been told, 'One day you will marry the Dauphin and one day you will be Queen of France.' The time for the first step was four days away and Mary Stewart was ready to do her duty.

Henri now wanted to demonstrate as clearly as possible to the world at large that Mary was a bride of France. In an England still reeling from the loss of its last Continental foothold it was presumed that Mary Tudor would die childless; the next in line for the throne was the Protestant Princess Elizabeth. In French eyes she was a bastard and the proper order of succession would be that Mary Stewart should succeed to the English throne. In the meantime, her marriage would give Henri direct control of the Scots armies to use against England. It would also be the first marriage of a Dauphin in Paris for 200 years, and therefore it would be the most spectacular ceremony the king could devise.

Ambassadors came from across Europe. The papal legate, Cardinal Trivulzio, brought messages of goodwill from Rome. All eyes focused on Paris, where the inhabitants had been aware of the forthcoming wedding for some weeks as 'there was not an artisan who did not have some hard cash for his labour' and nearly everyone had a friend, neighbour or relative who was a pastry-cook, embroiderer, confectioner or carpenter; the preparations were evident for all to see. Paris had grown greatly from medieval times with Henri's rebuilding of the old Palace of the Louvre on the eastern fringes and the city itself now spread over both banks of the Seine. The heart of the city was still the ancient Cathedral of Notre Dame on its island and the citizens would have followed with great interest the construction of the temporary buildings in the square facing it.

There was a twelve-foot-high covered walkway or bridge which lead from the Bishop of Paris's palace to a large platform in front of the west door and then continued into the interior of the cathedral itself. This walkway was decorated with the insignia of Mary and Henri, carpeted with Turkey carpets and covered with blue silk emblazoned with gold fleurs-de-lis. The canopy of the walkway fluttered gently in the breeze on the morning of Sunday, 24 April 1558. The crowd had been assembling from first light, thronging to the foot of the platform, and every available window and roof on the square was packed with locals and their friends, all equipped with plentiful food and wine.

73

While they waited patiently in the sunshine, watching the colourful Swiss Guard take their positions around the platform and listening to their band, Mary was only a few hundred yards away in the palace of Eustache du Bellay, Bishop of Paris, finishing her dressing and managing to write a hasty letter to her mother. The letter is made doubly charming by being full of mistakes in spelling and grammar – even crowned queens are nervous on their wedding day. She tells Marie that she is one of the happiest ladies on earth to have the king and queen treat her as their own daughter-in-law, and to give her jewels and plate. She hopes that Marie will understand that everything she has done she has done for her sake – although how this justifies her signing the secret 'donations' of Fontainebleau is impossible to understand – and she says that the cardinal will write at length with details. She ends by apologising for such a short and badly written letter, explaining that the royal princesses are giving her no peace. At this point she would have been able to hear music coming from the square where the Swiss mercenaries' flute and drum band was playing as the nobles and ambassadors gathered on the tiered seating arranged for them. It was time for her to join the royal procession.

The aldermen of Paris, in new robes of crimson and yellow satin trimmed with scarlet fur, had met at seven o'clock, and at nine, fortified by wine and accompanied by archers, crossbow-men and musketeers, mounted their mules, also clad in silks, and processed from the Parlement – in today's Paris, the Courts of Justice – to their seats on the platform. Then, at half past ten, François, Duc de Guise, took charge. He was in his most splendid clothes, a 'panache' of white feathers springing from his cap, and was delightedly aware that he was acting as master of ceremonies in place of his still-imprisoned rival, Constable Montmorency.

Consorts of musicians took over from the band of the Swiss Guard and played more elaborately, with trumpets, flutes, oboes, viols and violins. Judges in their robes and members of the Parlement, in scarlet robes with furred hoods, were already on the platform. As the royal procession neared the cathedral, de Guise signalled for the dignitaries on the platform to go into the church. This cleared the view of the actual wedding for the crowd, which was, after all, the principal purpose of this expensive exercise. The royal procession consisted of a hundred of the gentlemen of the king's court, followed by the princes of the blood, wearing their coronets and carrying their insignia. The lesser churchmen followed them with jewelled copes and mitres sparkling in the spring sunshine, before elaborate fanfares and choirboys carrying silver candelabra welcomed the archbishops with Mary's uncle Charles, Cardinal of Lorraine and Cardinal Trivulzio, who had his own large gold crucifix carried in front of him. The Duc de Guise took centre stage and waited for the royal party, led by the Dauphin, who was accompanied by his younger brothers, Charles and Henri. Dauphin François, who hated public pomp, limped and looked as if he would rather be anywhere than standing before the people of Paris. In any case he, like many bridegrooms since, was of no interest to the crowd, who had come especially to the see the Scots queen.

Mary had decided to flout convention and to appear in white – traditionally the French colour of mourning – and she drew gasps and cheers from the crowd. In contrast to the limping Dauphin she walked with great dignity and drew herself up to her full height, smiling to left and right. Her dress had a traditional train held by two maids of honour, and it was encrusted with diamonds; her initial 'M' was embroidered with rubies and emeralds and she glittered like a human jewel. Around her neck she wore the 'Great Harry', a massive jewelled pendant given to her by Henri. It consisted of the letter 'H' encrusted with diamonds and surmounted by three other large diamonds. It was all set in gold and a pigeon's-egg-sized ruby hung from a gold chain. Unlike the other ladies of the court, Mary wore her hair down, knowing how beautiful it looked and how its girlish simplicity would be seen in contrast to her gold crown, studded with pearls, diamonds, sapphires, rubies and emeralds, and surmounted by a huge carbuncle which was rumoured to have cost over half a million gold crowns. King Henri supported her right arm and the Duc de Guise held her left. Then, almost as an afterthought, Queen Catherine walked with a crowd of duchesses and ladies in waiting. Most of Catherine's jewels were in the hands of Diane de Poitiers, who was, of course, nowhere to be seen.

Henri took a ring from his own finger and gave it to the Cardinal Archbishop of Rouen who, in the plain sight of every-one – the princes of the blood, the foreign ambassadors, and the people of Paris – performed the marriage ceremony. France now had a Dauphine. The royal couple then left with the platform party to celebrate Mass in the cathedral, which was also carpeted throughout. High leather chairs had been installed in the choir for the judiciary and legislature while the royal couple knelt on cloth-of-gold cushions.

Outside, the reason for the crowd's eagerness to be near the platform became clear. At a signal from the Duc de Guise the heralds shouted 'Largesse' three times and showers of gold and silver coins were thrown into the crowd. A Scots student gave an account of the mêlée which followed: 'The gentlemen took their cloaks, gentlewomen their farthingales, merchantmen their gowns, masters in art their hoods, students their peaked caps, and religious men had their scapulars violently riven from their shoulders to gather the showers of money.' A giant Franciscan friar got more of the money than his neighbours: 'he kept it as alms to the praise of God and honour of this most godly and triumphant marriage. I was somewhat busy among the rest and got three sous.' This near riot severely crushed the people at the front of the crowd and they now begged the heralds to stop.

Unaware of all this, Mary and François heard the Bishop of Paris say Mass in the royal chapel and another shower of largesse was thrown across the nave while the nobility tried – unsuccess-fully – not to look like avaricious beggars. When the newly-weds emerged from the cathedral they made another circuit of the platform but, unlike their modern equivalents, they did not kiss, although it is said that the roars of the crowd were heard a mile distant in St Denis.

Finally the royal party made the short walk back to the bishop's palace for a private banquet at which Mary's crown was held above her head by the chevalier of the chamber, Monsieur de St Sevet. Solid gold crowns are heavy, especially for a sixteen-year-old queen, and Mary knew that her next duty was to dance with her father-in-law. With her hair flowing free, she could dance with enough vigour to show herself at her best, and the court duly cheered their new Dauphine. Her next duty was to dance with her husband, but Henri tactfully led her to his daughter Elisabeth, so the Dauphin's clumsiness and the disparity in size of the couple would not be made obvious.

All this was exhausting enough but was merely the prologue to the main event of the day. At four o'clock the royal party left the bishop's palace for a horseback procession to the Palace of the Parlement. Mary and Catherine were carried in a litter with the Cardinals of Lorraine and Bourbon riding beside them, but instead of following the most direct route they turned off the Ile de la Cité onto the right bank of the Seine before returning by the Pont du Change, thereby letting the greatest number of people see their new Dauphine. Back at the palace the king helped Mary dismount, while the Duc de Navarre helped the Dauphin as they processed into the great hall preceded by 200 gentlemen-in-waiting as well as the heralds of France and Scotland. The company sat at a marble table covered by a cloth of gold studded with gems. 'One had to say that the Elysian Fields would not have been more beautiful or more delightful.' The king commanded that all Scots be given the password for entrance, but a mob 'using the guard ungently' crowded in and, for a moment, there was a near riot. The Scots student reported, 'After the second service the heralds called "largesse" and were given a gold cup worth 400 crowns. The cup came from the royal cupboard, some twelve degrees or steps in height furnished with all manner of plate of massy gold and silver but the most part gold. But there was [sic.] so many kinds of most excellent music with such dancing, sundry plays and triumphing and so many displays of bravery and princely pastime that I should be over prolix to describe them.'

After supper the tables were cleared and Mary danced again with the Princess Elisabeth. After this dance everyone walked through to the Chamber of Advocates, a heavily gilded room decorated with tapestries depicting the victories of Caesar, where a pageant awaited them. First there was a parade of the seven planets, then twenty-five canvas horses led in a young prince clad in cloth of gold. Two white warhorses drew a triumphal chariot with lutes, harps and citterns, twelve unicorns were ridden by young princes, and a chariot carried in the nine muses. All of this took two hours but it was said that the audience found it too short. More dancing followed, then six ships came in on a sea of silver silk, fanned from beneath to make waves and from above to billow out the silken sails. Each ship had a member of the royal family masked in cloth of gold and as the ships stopped by the tables, the ladies were escorted on board and left the party. Henri escorted Mary; Catherine chose François, and the formal events of the day were over, although the ambassadors and other guests continued revelling until dawn. Next day there were lesser weddings in the cathedral and then Henri held a three-day-long tournament outside the Palais de Tournelles – now the Place des Vosges – half a mile distant on the right bank. The Scot Richard Maitland of Lethington, a minor poet, a civil servant whose son would be Mary's principal secretary, wrote without any sense of irony:

> Scots and French now live in unity
> As they were brothers born in one country.
> Clear now of all suspicion,
> One to the other to keep true fraternity,
> Defend each other both by land and sea.

Henri had wanted the world to note the new marriage and alliance and, although the expense had been crippling, he had been triumphantly successful. By the end of all this Mary was, unsurprisingly, 'ill-disposed'.

CHAPTER FIVE

She cannot long continue

꿎

In Edinburgh the celebrations for Mary's marriage were, since the common people had not the slightest interest in it, much more muted, costing a mere £183 9s 9d and consisting mainly of the monstrous cannon Mons Meg firing a single shot. It carried for two miles and fell harmlessly in the fields to the north-west of the city. Of greater interest in Scotland was the mysterious death at Calais of four of the marriage treaty commissioners during their return to Scotland. Poison was immediately suspected, but a plot hatched by the French is extremely unlikely since it was greatly to the advantage of France that the marriage agreement, apparently so advantageous to the Scots government, be ratified by them without further delay. It was, after all, considering the secret Treaty of Fontainebleau, quite worthless.

Mary wrote as a married woman to her mother in a letter on 16 September 1558. Writing like any young bride worried for the health of a new husband who has gone abroad on active service, she tells Marie that the king – 'the king my husband' – was encamped in Picardy where various maladies were current. In all probability, the treaty commissioners had died from one of these. Mary knew that one purpose of the campaign was to negotiate the release of Anne de Montmorency. Since Philip had returned to Spain on account of Mary Tudor's childlessness, he was keen to seek some kind of peace with France. Having the Constable of France and other nobles in his prisons, and knowing that Henri could not afford another major campaign, Philip felt the time was right to bring Henri to the negotiating table.

Henri, having already made all Scotsmen French citizens,

could now claim that he was, in fact, king of both countries. The Scots felt that they were gaining parity, but the French knew that Scotland was simply becoming a *département* of France. With this assurance and the hostility of Philip towards his wife, Mary Tudor, cutting off any alliance from across the Channel, Henri was equally happy to negotiate with Spain.

However, before this could happen, the political chessboard was once more upset when on 17 November 1558 Mary Tudor died. She had already suffered two hysterical pregnancies and had been unfeelingly rejected by Philip as ugly, sexually repellent and infertile. She was heartily loathed by the bulk of the population for her extreme Catholicism – the many martyrdoms of her reign had earned her the nickname of 'Bloody Mary'. She may have died from the seemingly inconsequential cause of influenza, which was the commonest cause of death in 1557. This tragically unhappy woman was now succeeded by her 25-year-old half-sister Elizabeth.

Elizabeth Tudor was a complete contrast to Mary Stewart. She had been tutored by the scholar Roger Ascham, who said of her, 'Her study of true religion and learning is most eager. Her mind has no womanly weakness, her perseverance is equal to that of a man, and her memory long keeps what it quickly picks up. She talks French and Italian as well as she does English, and has often talked to me readily and well in Latin, moderately in Greek.' She had practical experience of the politics of self-preservation, having spent time in the Tower of London in 1554 while her cousin Mary Stewart was establishing her own court in France. Her childhood had been one of hardship and constant threat of death, while Mary had basked in the uncritical adoration of her uncles. Elizabeth's lifelong companion was to be the devoted and brilliantly devious William Cecil. Together they were already the most formidable political team in Europe.

For Henri, Elizabeth's accession was devastating news, and his first move was to have long-standing consequences for Mary. He declared Elizabeth illegitimate: since her father's divorce from Catherine of Aragon had been declared invalid by the Pope his marriage to Elizabeth's mother, Anne Boleyn, was therefore bigamous. Thus, the throne was vacant and the nearest claimant by blood was Henri's new daughter-in-law, Mary. The heralds proclaimed her Queen of Scotland, England and Ireland and from henceforth her arms carried the quarterings of all these states. The poets got to work praising Mary as a new prodigy, uniting France and Scotland with England, but in practical terms this achieved little except to infuriate Elizabeth. The English ambassador reported that 'the young queen bore not the arms of England of her own notion, but by command of her father the late king and so seemed to excuse it. Her majesty [Elizabeth] thinks this excuse either very strange or very imperfect.' Neither Cecil nor Elizabeth believed a word of this.

What was more practical were the diplomatic arrangements made by France with England and Spain as part of the Treaty of Cateau-Cambrésis. All three participants were on the edge of bankruptcy and exhausted by war. Henri was under extreme pressure from Diane to negotiate the return of Montmorency from prison in Brussels; appeasing Philip was therefore important to him. In return for the peace, Henri gave up all his conquests in Italy, abandoned his claim to Savoy and allowed England the chance to repossess Calais in eight years. Marriage alliances would cement these agreements. Marguerite, Henri's sister, was to marry Emmanuel-Philibert, Duke of Savoy, while Mary's childhood friend Princess Elisabeth was to be the bride of the recently widowed Philip of Spain. Both these engagements were entirely dynastic, since neither woman was consulted, and Mary now had her first personal taste of the realpolitik which dominated affairs of state: with the marriage of Elisabeth, she was peremptorily to lose a close friend.

As Queen and King of Scotland, on 21 April 1558, Mary and François sent a letter to Elizabeth with their endorsement of the treaty, vowing their love, hoping for peace and friendship and assuring her she would get nothing but good news from the bearer of the letter, who was in transit to Scotland as a counsellor of the queen regent. He was William Maitland of Lethington, whom Knox found to be 'a man of sharp wit and reasoning' and who was the most astute political mind in Scotland. His nickname was 'Michael Wylie', a corruption of Machiavelli, and he would become Mary's chief minister in Edinburgh. He was able to offer Mary good advice but always put the interests of Scotland and himself at the forefront of his counsel, unlike Diane, who advised Henri to his own personal advantage first. Mary had no such disinterested counsellor.

On reviewing the situation of her northern neighbour, Elizabeth had been advised that in Scotland 'the fortresses are all in the hands of the French, and of the Queen Dowager, who, being a Frenchwoman, it may be said that everything is in the power of his most Christian Majesty who keeps some twenty thousand infantry there as garrison. That force being sufficient as in two days they can send over as many troops as they please.' This was hugely threatening and Elizabeth was delighted that the young couple signed a treaty that had been made at Upsettlington in Berwickshire, declaring peace between England and Scotland, without any claims on the English throne. This seemed to draw a very satisfactory line under Câteau-Cambrésis and she instructed her ambassador, Nicholas Throckmorton, to 'have good countenance towards them'. On 28 May 1559, Mary and François signed this treaty and, since François stuttered too badly on such occasions, Mary declared on his behalf that Elizabeth was 'her good cousin and sister'. The witnesses were Henri and Catherine, for once without what had now become the normal presence of her Guise uncles.

Neither were the uncles present at the reception afterwards where Mary's escort was the newly freed Constable Montmorency, who was keen to show Throckmorton the loyalty of France. Throckmorton warned the constable that his mistress the queen would 'find the public display of Mary's arms strange', especially when the couple had signed a treaty disclaiming any right of inheritance. The constable dodged the question by saying that he was in a Brussels prison when the arms were painted, and since Elizabeth carried the fleur-de-lis of France on her arms it was lawful for the Queen of Scotland, being of the house of England and so near to the crown, to carry the arms of England. The first diplomatic sabre-rattling over this issue passed off peaceably.

With the return of Montmorency, Diane's influence was increasing again and her granddaughter married the constable's son. None of this pleased the Guises, especially when Montmorency's nephew, Admiral Coligny ('admiral' was a rank that applied equally to soldiers and sailors, and Gaspard de Coligny was, in modern terms, a general) embraced the Protestant cause, which was close to the heart of Elizabeth. Henri's view was that since the crown was Catholic, any deviation toward the Reformation was not simply heresy, but far worse. It was, quite simply, treason and could be dealt with by civil means without involving the clerical power of Mary's uncles, whose influence was, for the moment, slipping away.

Throckmorton also noticed that Mary was unwell and she soon had to retire from court in a state of nervous collapse. He found Mary and Henri's daughter, Marguerite, 'somewhat sickly' and on 24 May, visitors said she was 'very ill, pale and green and withal short-breathed and it is whispered among them [the French court] that she cannot live long'. By 18 June, one of Mary's attendants felt that she 'was very evil at ease and to keep her from fainting were fain to bring her wine from the altar . . . I never saw her look ill . . . she cannot long continue'. In fact, Mary was suffering from chlorosis, or the 'green-sickness', an adolescent anaemia brought about by irregularities in her menstrual cycle.

The news of Mary's imminent death was, of course, exactly what Elizabeth wanted to hear. Since she, like the Scots, had no knowledge of the secret Treaty of Fontainebleau, safely in Henri's hands, she believed that Mary's death would put the crown of Scotland into the easily bought hands of Châtelherault and her path to servile pacification north of the Tweed would be clear. It would also remove a troublesome claimant to her own throne – thought by many, who proclaimed Elizabeth's illegitimacy, to be the true heir to Henry VIII – a claim displayed in Mary's heraldry itself. These arms were found 'prejudicial to the

Queen her state and dignity' by Elizabeth's loyal College of Arms.

These disputes over who carried what as their arms may seem petty to us today, but in a time without newspapers or television they represented the public signature of the sovereign. Most people would recognise that anyone displaying arms was a person of importance and the royal arms would be universally known, as would the arms of a local nobleman.

Mary had, in the year since her wedding in April 1558, gone from being the fairy princess gleaming with jewels to a political pawn. Largely unaware of the danger of the heraldic claims made on her behalf, she was now overtaken in importance by Montmorency, and was losing status thanks to her uncles' temporary eclipse. Diane had taken no part in all of this, since, wisely, she was at Anet with the king, but Montmorency had fulfilled her wishes to gain supremacy over the Guises completely. The effect on Mary was typical. Whenever reality forced her to go against her wishes, or if she felt that she was being ignored, she collapsed physically. The manipulative lessons of Diane and Catherine may have been learnt, but she still lacked the political skill to put them into practice.

Much more to Mary's taste were the preparations for the two weddings arising from the Treaty of Câteau-Cambrésis, although the first of them would deprive her of her childhood friend, Princess Elisabeth. These weddings were an essential move for Henri since they would cement a Catholic alliance with Spain and prevent any possibility of a similar alliance between Elizabeth of England and Philip. So keen was Henri on such a Franco-Spanish bond that he suggested his youngest daughter, Marguerite, as a bride for Philip's son, Don Carlos. Philip, however, had decided on a single marriage and the Duke of Alba left the Netherlands with over a thousand in his retinue to act as proxy. Henri was disappointed in Philip's non-appearance, only to be brusquely told that kings of Spain do not fetch their brides.

On 22 June 1559 the Duke of Alba placed his naked foot in a bed already occupied by Elisabeth and their toes touched. He smiled and, while his valet replaced his hose, the courtiers applauded. Elisabeth was now Isabel de la Paz, Queen of Spain, although she would not travel to Spain until 30 January 1560.

The Duke of Savoy had arrived in Paris with a similar entourage on the previous day (21 June) and on the 27th he vowed his betrothal to Henri's sister, another Marguerite, who, still unmarried at thirty-six, was eager for her wedding to be held on 4 July as well. This would strengthen the clause of the treaty returning Savoy to its duke, who had been ousted by François I. The betrothal took place, not as Mary's had at the Louvre, but at the Palais de Tournelles, where Henri planned a grand tournament to last five days in the Rue Sainte-Antoine in front of the palace. It was all supervised with great enthusiasm by Henri himself, who was in his element recreating the legendary past. The paving stones and street-side stalls had been taken away and replaced with an amphitheatre, raised boxes for the ladies, stabling for horses, an armoury and a tiltyard. There were triumphal arches with rooms for dressing, and, on each side, twenty-foot-high pillars surmounted by figures of victory. The royal box, with cloth-of-gold hangings studded with fleurs-de-lis, held Catherine and Henri, for once tactfully separated from Diane de Poitiers by Mary and her dauphin. The Dukes of Alba and Savoy, with their brides and fiancées, were in private boxes on either side.

On 28 June 1559, a company of lancers from the Dauphin's company jousted successfully and the next day the *gens d'armes* from the noble houses of France followed them. The climax came on 30 June when François de Guise, Alfonso d'Este, Prince of Ferrara, and the Duc de Nemours challenged all comers. Henri, clothed in the black and white of Diane, with black-and-white feather plumes on his helmet and a black-and-white scarf on his lance, also entered the lists. The two heralds which came before the king were Scots, 'fair set out with the King Dolphin and Queen Dolphin's arms as all the world might easily perceive'.

Jousting is punishing physically, requiring strength as well as

85

horsemanship since the object of the exercise is to break your lance, usually made of ash, on your opponent's shield or armour. Deflecting the blow does not count for so much since withstanding the impact while unseating your opponent is the principal purpose. In the same year, at jousts held for the accession of Elizabeth in London, the Earl of Essex had met fifteen challengers and had broken fifty-seven lances. Essex, however, was a lusty teenager; Henri had turned forty, with a greying beard, although, with his usual male bravado, he made no concessions to his age and was still astonishing the court by playing enthusiastic tennis. The ever gloomy Throckmorton, having noted the continuing display of Mary's quartered arms, reported that the king 'overmuch exercised himself at tennis and other pastimes [and] was driven into a disease called vertigo'. Henri made his first two courses of jousting successfully enough, but on the third, against Gabriel de Lorges, Comte de Montgomery, the captain of the Garde Écossais, the king was nearly unhorsed. De Lorges, tactfully, acknowledged the king as the victor but Henri was having none of it and challenged de Lorges to run again. Catherine and the Dauphin begged him to let the matter rest and de Lorges at first refused to ride, but Henri, as his sovereign lord, commanded him and they hastily remounted, Henri on a Turkish stallion given to him by the Duke of Savoy.

The two horsemen met, and their lances shattered, but with disastrous results, as Antoine de Caraccioli, Bishop of Troyes wrote to Corneille Musse, Bishop of Bonito: 'The king was struck on the gorget [the piece of armour protecting the throat] the lance broke, but the visor was not strapped down and several splinters wounded the king above the right eye. He swayed from the force of the blow and the pain, dropping his horse's bridle, and the horse galloped off to be caught and held by the grooms. Helped from his horse, his armour taken off and a splinter of a good bigness, was removed.' The jousting attendants immediately surrounded the prostrate king and administered rosewater and vinegar but failed to revive him. Throckmorton thought that 'the hurt seemed not to be great' and judged him to be 'but in

86

little danger'. The king fainted twice more and 'lay like one amazed'. The Dauphin also fainted.

The king was taken to his chamber in the palace, the gates were locked and no one was allowed entrance. The unfortunate de Lorges begged the king to cut off his hand or his head but Henri said that de Lorges had done nothing requiring pardon, since he had been ordered to run the course and had 'carried himself like a brave knight and a valiant man-at-arms'. Surgeons with forceps extracted some further smaller splinters from his face, purged him with rhubarb and chamomile, took twelve ounces of blood, purged him again, applied 'refrigeratives' and gave him barley-gruel. Overnight he 'had a very evil rest, whereof there was great lamentations'. By next morning the entire royal family and the influential nobility were in urgent attendance. Montmorency told Elisabeth that the worst that could happen would be the loss of an eye and optimistic statements were issued, although they deceived no one. 'There was good hope that he might recover as all his surgeons declared.' However, Throckmorton now had little hope: 'The king was very weak and to have the sense of all his limbs almost benumbed . . . he moved neither hand nor foot.'

The surgeons feared that the major splinter might have pierced the pia mater, the innermost membrane enveloping the brain, and even penetrated the brain itself. To find out more, they acquired the severed heads of recently executed criminals and drove similar splinters through their foreheads, but these experiments revealed nothing conclusive. André Vesalius, the most eminent anatomist in Europe and surgeon to Philip II, came hotfoot from Brussels but even he could do nothing. The king was dying. Several ambassadors and courtiers have recorded various versions of the king's last words, but it seems likely that Henri simply swam in and out of consciousness in his sickroom, crowded as it was with doctors and family members. On the fourth day after the accident, it became clear that the wound was now seriously infected and the king fell into a violent fever.

Even if kings are dying, the dynastic business of the state must continue, and the marriage of the Duke of Savoy and Henri's sister, Marguerite, took place. Since it was clear to everyone that Henri was nearing the end and that the wedding could not take place while the court was in mourning, it became now a matter of urgency. It could not be the splendid triumph that Henri had planned for his sister's wedding, and perhaps not one to rival Mary's, but at least it could be another demonstration of Valois splendour in the July sunshine. Perhaps those watching would forget that the nuptuals cemented a treaty returning French-held territories to their rightful, mainly Italian, owners.

In the present woeful circumstances no member of the royal family dared travel more than a few hundred yards from the king's bedside and the ceremony was held in the nearby church of St Paul. Since Henri had fallen into a fitful sleep from which he was unlikely to awaken, the marriage took place at midnight in the sombre interior of the church already half-prepared for mourning. In the darkened chapel sat Catherine, in floods of tears, knowing that she was about to become a widow in a foreign country. Mary and the Dauphin sat holding on to each other in the hastily fetched royal thrones, fearful of what almost inevitably lay in store for them. Somehow Marguerite and the Duke of Savoy got through the ceremony and Marguerite rushed back to her brother's side.

Next day the king received the final sacrament, and on 10 July 1559 at one o'clock in the afternoon he went into 'a gigantic spasm and monstrous flailing of his limbs', then fell back on his bed. A doctor put his ear to the king's chest then straightened, shaking his head, as a priest laid a crucifix on Henri's chest. The Dauphin fainted again and was carried from the room. With a rustle of silks, everyone else, including Catherine de Medici, turned from looking at the now-dead king and dropped to their knees in front of Mary Stewart. At that moment the teenage Queen of Scots had also become the Queen of France.

CHAPTER SIX

She universally inspires great pity

꿎

In the streets workmen hastily tore down the festive hangings put up to celebrate Marguerite's wedding and replaced them with funeral wreaths as cannon fired solemn salutes. 'Hardly had Henri closed his mouth when François, Duc de Guise and his brother Charles, Cardinal of Lorraine had seized the person of the king [François] and his brothers, [and] taken them to the Louvre along with the two queens, leaving the king's body to the royal guard and the princes of the blood.' Mary went first to St Germain – she was told it was for her own safety – and Catherine went to Medan, a few miles upriver, while the Guise *coup d'état* reached its completion in Paris.

In Paris, by 13 July 1559, three days after Henri's death, it was reported that 'the house of Guise ruleth and doth all about the French king. What will succeed further is unknown until the King of Navarre's coming, which is uncertain.' The King of Navarre, Antoine de Bourbon, was a vociferous antagonist of the Guise faction. He claimed that, since he was only fifteen, François could not appoint his own council and therefore Antoine, as the closest in blood, should be appointed regent; his arrival in Paris had been expected daily since the death of Henri. But on 18 July 'the French king hath given him [the King of Navarre] to understand that the Cardinal of Lorraine and the Duc de Guise shall manage his whole affairs'. Antoine was a Bourbon who could trace his descent directly from Louis IX (St Louis) and had married Jeanne d'Albret, the niece of François I. However, fortunately for the Guise brothers, he was rarely other than weak, vacillating and indecisive.

'The Cardinal of Sens, keeper of the seals is displaced, and M. Olivier who was chancellor heretofore is likely to enter that office again.' Olivier de Lenville, an ally of the Guises, was appointed Chancellor of France and obtained the keys of the royal treasures along with 'some precious rings', while the cardinal and the Duc de Guise took over the Louvre itself and, with it, the instruments of power. The king was smothered in flattery and guided by them while the keys to cabinets were sought and, if they could not be found, the locks were shattered. Then François was told that the brothers had made everything safe and he would soon be united with his beloved wife. Within three or four days the king gave everything in the management of the royal affairs that had been Constable Montmorency's into the hands of the Cardinal and the Duc de Guise. They seized the confiscations that had been made by the king and distributed them among their friends. 'It was not hard to believe that the house of Guise wished to seize the crown; they might claim that the kingdom belonged to the house of Lorraine, as the direct issue of Charlemagne, and had been usurped by Hugh Capet.' (Hugh Capet had seized the crown in 987 and the Valois rulers claimed descent from him.)

Mary and Catherine were reunited with the Guise brothers at the Louvre where 'they set about bending the king to their will, never allowing him to meet anyone without the presence of one of them'. Catherine, frozen in grief and, following the Italian fashion for mourning, dressed now in black, which she wore until her death, sat in her rooms, which were draped with black silk and lit only by two candles, to receive the condolences of the foreign ambassadors. Mary stood behind her and replied on her behalf, dressed now in the white mourning clothes of the French court. The Queen Mother – Catherine refused the title of 'Queen Dowager' – set about wreaking vengeance on Diane de Poitiers, who had been forbidden to visit the dying king and, prepared for the inevitable, had fled to Anet, where the news of Henri's death was brought to her with an official request by Mary for the return of the jewels given to her by the king. These jewels had originally been given to Anne d'Étampes, François I's mistress, but were now returned to Catherine, whose next request was for the château of Chenonceau. If any château in France symbolised the relationship of Henri and Diane, it was this, and Catherine set about marking her own personality on it. She planted new gardens, this time in the Italian style, and built a huge gallery on the bridge over the Cher. Oddly enough she did not efface the monograms of 'H' and the crescent 'C'. Catherine offered Diane the château of Chaumont in its place – a château neither of them had liked – but Diane remained at Anet where she took no further part in the affairs of France. She was visited by her personal friends, including Mary, and she died there in 1567. She was buried in an exquisite tomb of her own design in her private chapel. She had been the companion of Henri since he was a boy and had stood beside him throughout his life, protecting, as she believed, France from the influence of Italy. While she was often domineering in public, in private she had been a friend to Mary.

Her château passed through many hands until, in 1795, the revolutionary Committee of Surveillance broke open the tomb and hung her remains, stripped of their funeral clothes, in public view, having first cut off her hair to sell as souvenirs. Shocked by this revolutionary fanaticism, the women of the village covered her corpse with strips of paper torn from a ruined house and she was reburied in a grave near to the chapel.

The unfortunate de Lorges, who had been the cause of Henri's injury, was officially displaced from the captainship of the Garde Écossaise and 'in his place is entered one Monsieur d'Ou . . . a mere Frenchman, who liketh not the Scotsmen all the best'. De Lorges converted to the Protestant cause and fled to England from the wholesale persecution of St Bartholomew's Eve in 1572. He returned to France in 1574 and took part in a rising of Norman Protestants during which he was captured, tried and found guilty of treason. Catherine personally watched him being beheaded and quartered.

The two Guise brothers could not have made this *coup d'état* effective alone; they needed royal authority and to gain this, they needed influential access to François. In other circumstances

Catherine would simply have taken her sickly son and through him would have controlled the nation, but with their kinswoman Mary as queen, the Guise ambitions were readily achieved.

Mary was, as usual, protective of François, and the teenage couple relapsed into the affectionate intimacy of their childhood. Nevertheless, Mary was encouraged to flex her muscles and to use her now undoubted power. Using the king as a mouthpiece and Mary as the ventriloquist, the Guises were able to control France. Catherine was sidelined and, while not an actual prisoner, the idea of giving her some freedom of political movement was, for the moment, postponed.

Mary had been used to controlling her court in domestic matters, but now ministers of state, generals and chancellors were eager to please her. This was heady stuff and she never allowed herself to realise that she was merely a shadow for her uncles. The chapel royal was filled with the music of the royal composers Clément Jannequin and Claudin de Sermisy, both of whom provided risqué chansons for Mary's after-dinner entertainment. De Sermisy provided at least one drinking song:

> Hey, hey, hey, the woods!
> We are praying to God the king of kings
> To preserve this good French wine
> Thus we will drink six draughts for three.
> Hey, hey, hey, the woods!
> In order to clear our voices
> Let us drink as much again, I am going for it
> Hey, hey, hey, the woods!

Whether Mary joined in the drinking – possibly an explanation for the frequent royal indispositions – is pure speculation. Another song filled with the melancholy of unrequited love gave an unwittingly unhappy prediction of Mary's future.

> I have walked a hundred thousand steps for you
> And done much folly,

Lived without rules or limits.
So now I am lost in melancholy.
Alas! What will be my life?
Nothing remains but unhappiness.
A thousand sorrows for one solitary pleasure!

At this time, however, Mary was the happiest young woman in Europe. All the natural wishes of a sixteen-year-old girl were heard and granted. She was indulged and she was denied nothing, while all the time she was being cynically manipulated. This was another dangerous reinforcement of her belief, like that of a Hollywood film star, that no one would ever disagree with her.

Throckmorton reported that 'the Queen of Scotland . . . is a great doer here, and takes all upon her'. René de Bouillé, a French historian, said, 'The feeble organisation of the king could only have one outcome, the single passion of which his beautiful and gracious consort was the object.' And Mary Stewart, out of respect, out of admiration, and out of past experience, was prepared to use all her influence to increase and affirm the status, salutary if sometimes dangerous, of her uncles. François, on their instructions, dismissed Montmorency from the court, and his rooms were occupied by the Cardinal of Lorraine, while the Duc de Guise had taken the former apartments of Diane de Poitiers.

Henri's body was embalmed, and after a funeral Mass in Notre Dame he was buried in the Cathedral of St Denis. The last official act of Montmorency as Constable of France was to throw his baton of office into the tomb and cry out, 'Le roi est mort', then, after three paternosters had been said, he retrieved the baton and called, 'Vive le roi!'

So began what wits of the time called the reign of the three kings: François de Valois, François de Guise, and Charles, Cardinal of Lorraine. The Guise family at last held the power which for years had been their dreams, and Mary Stewart had made it possible. She had been educated to be Queen of France and carefully tutored to accept the advice of her uncles.

93

However, Mary had learned from Diane that the Guise power had to be expressed through François, and she was only too willing to guide him.

The king now became the focus for anti-Guise sentiments led by Louis de Condé, brother of the still-vacillating King of Navarre. He was the reverse of his brother, being vigorous and outspoken, and had recently converted to Protestantism. It was when this Louis de Condé fomented a plot to overthrow the brothers and seize the king in 1560 that a new word entered the vocabulary of French Protestantism: the plotters met at the port of Hugues on the west coast of France and from then on French Protestants became known as Huguenots.

The conflict between Huguenot, or Protestant, and Catholic was to dominate the remainder of Mary's life. The roots of the conflict had started to thrive many years previously in a growing popular disaffection with the Church of Rome. In many ways the Church had grown top-heavy, controlling every aspect of daily life, from baptism through marriage, to death and burial. It administered all schools and universities, where learning, like all church services, was conducted in Latin, a language which the common people did not understand. Equally, the Bible was closed to the populace and remained untranslated from St Jerome's Latin. The Mass was a mystery experienced only by the priesthood and merely witnessed at a discreet distance by the laity. Access to heaven – after a suitable period in purgatory – was obtained only through the good offices of the priesthood. Saints, however, were presumably multilingual and could be prayed to in the vernacular and anywhere.

In the fourteenth century the devastating spread of the Black Death had carried off nearly a third of Europe's population, in spite of the ardent, though wholly impotent, prayers of the Church. Conflict over papal elections had resulted in the Great Schism which produced rival popes in Rome and in Avignon, each solemnly declaring that they alone spoke the absolute indisputable truth, but who only held power so long as their secular masters had use for them. Then, in England at the end of

94

the century, John Wycliffe, a distinguished scholar, set about a refutation of much of the dogma of the Church. He led a band of poor priests into the countryside, preaching to the people and, what was even more shocking, using an English translation of the Bible. Thomas Carlyle, the nineteenth-century historian, called Wycliffe 'The deep-lying tap-root of the whole tree'. Although Wycliffe was allowed to die in peace, his Bohemian follower, Jan Hus, was not so lucky, and he became the first martyr of the reformers. More than a hundred years later, the Dutch scholar, Desiderius Erasmus, like Wycliffe, managed to survive in spite of preaching a form of humanist Christianity across Europe, even being a welcome guest of the rigidly conservative Catholic, Thomas More.

Then, on 31 October 1517, the Augustinian monk Martin Luther lost his admittedly short temper in Wittenberg. The popular appeal of his reforms and condemnations of papal corruption spread to the princes within the Holy Roman Empire who themselves rose against the Catholic Emperor Charles V. At first Charles tolerated their demands, but in 1529 he withdrew his decree of toleration. The princes protested and the followers of their movement got their name – Protestants. Inevitably there were splits inside the movement, with Anabaptists calling for all property to be held in common. Attacking the ownership of property was going far too far and they were put down with sadistic savagery.

Switzerland, still a loose confederation of city-states, became an established refuge for Protestants, and by August 1535 Geneva was a Protestant republic. In the following year the preacher appointed to the Cathedral of St Pierre was a Frenchman from Picardy, Jean Cauvin, now known as John Calvin. His co-religionist George Wishart had been preaching the doctrines of the Helvetic Confession in Scotland when he was martyred by Beaton in 1546. In his turn, John Knox had spent part of his exile in Geneva during the reign of Mary Tudor. The movement had taken root among most of the nobility in Scotland, many joining it to make a political protest against what they saw as the

Frenchification of their country. The movement had had no charismatic leader until, on 2 May 1559, Knox finally returned to Scotland and what had previously been protest turned into a civil war in all but name.

In France, the secular discontent with the arrogant power of the House of Guise was now given a religious element as Catholics and Huguenots formed battlelines. For Mary herself, the Catholic faith was an integral part of life. She had attended Mass daily, and occasionally more often. Her own chaplain had performed the ceremony and heard her childish confessions in her own chapel, often with her childhood companions. It was as normal and as comforting to her as breathing fresh air or washing her face. Mary had none of the fervour of the Huguenots, whom her late father-in-law had regarded simply as traitors from the lower classes. Mary's experiences of the lower classes were either as cheering crowds or as servants whom she treated with kindness and who adored her with more than sycophantic servility. Her half-brother Lord James Stewart's conversion to the Protestant cause in Scotland shocked her more because it put him in opposition to her mother than because she thought his eternal soul was in danger. However, she did persuade François to write to him rapping his knuckles; Stewart wrote back unrepentantly, hoping that François might convert. It was puzzling to Mary that French noblemen could object to her uncles or her husband on religious grounds, and both Catherine and her uncles saw to it that she knew as little as possible about it. Heresy was, after all, part of the mysterious world inhabited by men and part of the politics of the court, in which she took no great part. Mary had been told what was expected of her – a nursery full of heirs to the throne – and Diane would have told her that, given the physical condition of her husband, she should not be over-eager to achieve this. On her wedding night she and her Dauphin would have been put to bed together, but the court had no great expectation of triumphantly blood-stained sheets on the next morning and, for the moment, Mary was happy to continue in a marriage of friendship, rather than physical love.

Mary was now content in her role as Queen of France, Scotland and England, having her plate engraved with 'Franciscus et Maria, Dei Gratia Franciae, Scotiae, Angliae et Hibernae, Rex et Regina'. It was less than tactful to serve Throckmorton from it. He had been advised by Elizabeth and Cecil to start courting Catherine since 'she hath in deed and in effect the authority (though not in name) of Queen Regent'. The grip of the Guise brothers extended as far as Scotland, for on 3 August 1559 the royal couple sent signed sheets of blank paper to Marie de Guise for distributing gifts in their names. François appeased Elizabeth by using only the traditional styles and seals, but Mary thoughtlessly continued to use 'Maria, Dei Gratia, Regina Franciae, Scotiae, Angliae et Hiberniae'.

By 27 August, Guise control was complete; when Throckmorton delivered a letter to François, he merely scanned it and replied that he thanked Elizabeth for her letter and told Throckmorton that he would do whatever his uncles advised. The letter was then passed to Mary, who read it more carefully, thanked Elizabeth and said she would do whatever her uncles advised. The protests by the King of Navarre came to nothing: 'the house of Guise doth all and the King of Navarre meddleth not'. Neither Mary nor François now had any real power.

Mary was, in fact, preparing to take part in her next great pageant, the coronation of François in the cathedral of Rheims. As an already crowned queen, Mary would be merely a spectator and, in any case, the queens of France were traditionally crowned in St Denis. Since the court was in mourning, the coronation could have been postponed, but worries over the king's health meant that this was not desirable. Mourning was still being observed and a command was issued that 'no noblemen or ladies shall be apparelled with any goldsmith's work, or embroidery but shall only wear velvet or other like, without any great show and that the next day they enter into the *deuil* [mourning] again and so continue for this twelvemonth'.

On 16 September 1559, the king arrived at Rheims in a great storm of wind and rain but nothing could diminish the spectacle of his entry. There was a 'machine of great invention', a sun burst which opened, allowing the king to approach a giant red heart which, in its turn, parted to reveal a nine-year-old girl in silver and cloth of gold who placed the keys to the city into his hands.

On Sunday, 17 September, Mary and François attended vespers, during which François presented a gold statue of his namesake St Francis of Assisi to the cathedral. This was now carpeted, and tapestries taken from the adjacent bishop's palace and from the Louvre, showing the coronation of Clovis and the victories of Scipio, were hung around the interior. Next morning, with sunlight pouring through the thirteenth-century stained glass, the royal procession moved the short distance from the palace where it had spent the night. Archbishop Charles, Cardinal of Lorraine in his full finery escorted François, who was dressed in plain white to signify his purity, as he was prepared for anointing. This was the most sacred part of the ceremony and was done with chrism kept in the abbey of St Rémi, two miles distant. So sacred was the chrism that when it was at the cathedral for the ceremony the three nobles who carried it were regarded as hostages of the abbey until its safe return.

Duly rendered sacred, François withdrew and changed into his coronation robes of blue velvet, lined with crimson taffeta and trimmed with ermine and gold fleurs-de-lis. He was then invested with the sceptre, as well as a baton of justice, and was given a ring in token of his marriage to France. Understandably, the fragile fifteen-year-old was staggering noticeably after what had been a five-hour ceremony, and so the gold crown was simply held above his head when he was led to his throne. The archbishop then shouted 'Vivat Rex!' which was echoed back by the congregation in the packed cathedral. Songbirds were released, a Te Deum was sung and the congregation relaxed.

The royal ladies were seated in a specially constructed box so that they could not only see but also be seen. Catherine once again wore the black of her native Italy and her daughters followed suit, but Mary wore the *deuil blanc* familiar from her portraits. It was the correct dress for a French queen in mourning and it sent the clear signal that she had no intention of allying herself with the Italian Medicis. Mary was a Guise. Throckmorton also noted that the arms of England, France and Scotland quartered were very 'brimly' set out above the city gates.

After the ceremony the congregation attended a state dinner where François, as a token of his new status, dined alone with the company seated around him. He was, however, tired and withdrew early, proceeded by pages carrying his regalia. This was far from the pomp enjoyed so much by his father. He now suffered from regular fainting fits and his inability to concentrate meant that he could have no part in the cabinets or meetings convened by the Guises. His fondness for hunting, provided he was never in any danger, proved an asset and he was encouraged to spend more time on horseback, albeit with armed guards in constant attendance. Mary was more fearless on horseback and rode with enthusiasm, on one occasion being swept from her horse by an overhanging branch. The hunt was in full cry and galloped past her without noticing her fall, to the extent that her headdress was ridden over; however, she redressed her hair, remounted and rejoined the chase, although 'she hath determined to change that kind of exercise' – a determination she did not, in fact, keep.

Royalty had probably the least privacy of any people in the kingdom, and since the lives of the royals were of constant interest to the court, rumours of their ill-health abounded. Mary was well past puberty and the frequency of her menstrual cycle would have been known to the whole court, all of whom were, against all probability, eager for signs of pregnancy. By December, Ralph Sadler in Scotland was writing 'we understand the Scottish Queen is not like to have any children'.

Mary was an enthusiastic gourmand, and at this time Catherine was introducing Italian recipes to the French kitchen, thus providing the basis for what we today think of as French cuisine, but Mary's weight at this time was never a matter for concern.

It was controlled by exercise and by occasional severe diets. Add all this to her savage depressions when attempts were made to thwart her and the litany of fainting fits and periods of bed rest become more understandable. Some of the wilder speculations about the royal couple's health were pure fabrication, such as a rumour on 15 November that François had contracted leprosy, although this probably arose from his occasional, but violent, bouts of eczema.

There were, however, very real fears over the health of Mary's mother, Marie de Guise, who was seriously ill in Edinburgh, where she had been fighting what was, to all intents and purposes, a civil war with the Lords of the Congregation. Marie de Guise had imported French troops – since Mary's wedding agreement had given the French Scots nationality, she could claim, somewhat speciously, that these troops did not represent a foreign intrusion – but was losing the struggle. In February 1560 the Lords had gained the assistance of Elizabeth through the Treaty of Berwick. Elizabeth was all too keen to help men who might not wholly support Mary's seeming usurpation of her titles and quartering of her arms. In England, Elizabeth's involvement with the Lords of the Congregation became known as 'The War of the Insignia'. Elizabeth would 'never assent that the realm of Scotland shall be knit to the crown of France otherwise than as it is already, only by marriage of the Queen to the French King'. Earlier in the month the Duc de Guise had written, hypocritically, to Marie, urging her to pull her French troops out of Scotland, and when Mary met Throckmorton on 27 February she asked him to assure Elizabeth that she, Mary, her cousin, would be a better neighbour than the rebels. The statement sounds like a piece of Guise sleight of hand. The Guises knew that Marie would ignore the letter, thus allowing Mary to make her assurance of friendship to Elizabeth. Neither Elizabeth nor Cecil would have given any credence to so obvious a ploy, but they would have been flattered that the Guises felt it necessary to make it.

In the event, Elizabeth had no time for such subtleties and in March she demanded that Mary 'utterly cease' quartering her arms, and order the withdrawal of French forces by 2 April. Elizabeth also called for a total recognition by all Scots that Mary was their sovereign; all principal offices were to remain in 'the natural manner of Scotland' and all bishoprics and estates of the Church to be conferred on native Scotsmen. In other words, Elizabeth demanded the removal of all French placemen.

Then, on 23 March, Cecil, via the Privy Council, sent a memorandum to Elizabeth. 'The Queen of Scots, her husband, and the house of Guise are mortal enemies of her person . . . their malice is bent against her person and they will never cease as long as she and the Scottish Queen lives'. Cecil, who understood his queen's fears, was moving from political advice to warning his queen of a personal threat to her life.

At the same time, François and Mary had come under direct threat themselves from the plot that had been formed at Hugues. The court was in residence at Blois on the Loire, where François could hunt in safety while Mary and Catherine heard sermons and attended Mass together. It was a peaceful interlude, but under the direction of the Seigneur de la Renaudie the plotters aimed to capture the Guise brothers, persuade the king to grant toleration to the Huguenots and then to set up a regency under Louis de Condé and the Bourbons. It was a hopelessly badly organised *coup d'état*: with 500 agents sent to recruit help from as far afield as England there was no possibility of the plot remaining secret. Once knowledge of the plot reached the court, the Duc de Guise ordered that they move immediately to the château of Amboise, fifteen miles downstream. This was on a cliff overlooking the river and practically impregnable to what was now in danger of becoming a rebel force. The rebels, many of whom were simply disgruntled countrymen, had no unified command but roamed the countryside while approaching Amboise, occasionally meeting and joining together, although never forming a coherent force. The rebel forces did include more than a few disaffected nobles from the growing number of anti-Guise elements in the country and, concerned that the rebels might find a significant leader in France's senior Huguenot, Louis de Condé, who was in attendance in the château, Catherine simply appointed him as chief of the king's bodyguard. In this new role, his presence inside the château was required to be constant.

In early March the first group of rebels had been captured and put to the rack. The main force was thenceforth taken piecemeal as it arrived to encircle the castle, while de la Renaudie himself was fortunately shot by an arquebusier – fortunately, because when the remainder were captured they were sadistically tortured before being executed in batches. To the surprise of the royal faction, many of the insurgents were German, Swiss, Savoyard, English and even Scots, acting not as mercenaries but as 'soldiers of the word of God'. There were so many prisoners that, for considerations of speed and economy, the Duc de Guise ordered many of them to be either sewn into sacks or tied together in groups of ten and thrown into the river to drown. Fifty-two more eminent rebels of noble blood were beheaded on a hastily built scaffold. The Duc and Catherine watched every execution in person and the corpses were then hung on the battlements for the citizens to see, while their heads were impaled on the balustrade outside the royal dining room: 'The streets of Amboise ran with blood, the river was covered with corpses, and all public places had gibbets.' Mary now had her first view of the bloody deaths caused by religious divisions, and she could not avoid having full knowledge of what was taking place. François wrote to the Bishop of Limoges that 'the death of a small number of unfortunates will be salutary for the good and peaceful order throughout all the kingdom'. Mary's friend Anne d'Este wept at the slaughter and it equally horrified Louise de Montmorency, the sister of the former constable. Eleanore de Condé and Mme de Crussol – described as a mainspring of the Huguenots – were also close to Mary, and Mary might well have been influenced by the political involvement of these powerful ladies. However, Mary herself took no part in the religious factionism affecting France. Since it involved less intellectual effort, Mary simply believed what her Guise uncles told her to believe.

The Duc de Condé attempted to draw the two sides together and made a personal appeal to François for greater toleration and for meeting of the Estates General (the nearest thing to a national parliament existing at the time), but on advice from the Guise brothers, François had Condé arrested and sentenced to death. The power of the brothers was now becoming intolerable to all outside the very tight circle surrounding the king, and even inside that circle Catherine felt that she had stood aside for long enough. She had realised from the moment Henri had died that she had no chance of asserting her personal power in the face of the Guise brothers and their total control of the king through Mary. Catherine had also realised that it was fruitless to fight a war she would inevitably lose and, therefore, stood aside while they gathered more power to themselves and made more enemies. She had never directly assisted those enemies – many were Huguenots and Catherine was a devout Catholic – but negotiations with Elizabeth and with Philip of Spain were taking place. Philip, married to Catherine's daughter, was now very worried at the growing pride of his northern neighbour and of its open encirclement of England, therefore he was more than willing to clip the Guise wings. If Elizabeth could be persuaded to act on behalf of the Protestant lords in Scotland, then Marie's rule as queen regent would be over and the first crack in Guise hegemony would appear. Thus, a Catholic monarch could support a Protestant one, if state interests demanded it.

By 25 April, having been queen for less than a year, even the politically naïve Mary realised that the intransigence of her uncles might lose her the kingdom of Scotland and 'wept bitterly and said that her uncles had undone her'. More bad news was coming from within Scotland itself. In Edinburgh, on 26 April, Marie herself was thought to be in danger of being captured by the Lords of the Congregation, and on receipt of the news, Giovanni Surian, the Venetian ambassador, reported that Mary 'shed most bitter tears incessantly and at length from anguish and sorrow and has taken to her bed'. Marie, exhausted by her constant battles with the Scots nobles, with English forces threatening her capital, and severely swollen with dropsy, died on 11 June 1560. In April she had told the French ambassador Henri Cleutin, Seigneur d'Oysel, who had become her chief adviser in Scotland, 'I am still lame and have a leg that assuageth not from swelling. If any lay his finger upon it it goeth in as into butter.' Dropsy is a morbid accumulation of fluid, often a symptom of vascular disorder, and the queen regent most probably died of cardiac failure. Her corpse was 'lapped in lead' and sailed for France on 19 October, to be buried in the Convent of St Pierre in Rheims where the abbess was her sister, Renée de Guise.

The news was kept from Mary for over two weeks, until 28 June, at which point, understandably, she fell into a severe depression. The news was broken to her by her uncle Charles, Cardinal of Lorraine, who had also been the brother of the dead queen regent, and 'she [Mary] passed from one agony to another'. The Venetian ambassador wrote to the doge, 'Your serenity may imagine the regret of these Guise lords, her majesty's brothers, as also of the most Christian Queen who loved her mother incredibly, and much more than daughters usually love their mothers.' After Mary's own death one of her most prized possessions was found to be a miniature of her mother.

Marie de Guise had had an unhappy life. The Protestant George Buchanan in his *History* said that 'she possessed an uncommon genius, and a mind strongly inclined to justice [but] was much under the influence of the Guise clan who marked out Scotland as the private property of their family'. Like all of her family she never learned to bend with the wind. With her death the Scottish civil war was all but over and Elizabeth could now dictate terms for withdrawal of her forces in what was to become the Treaty of Edinburgh.

After a month of bargaining, the Treaty of Edinburgh was signed on 6 July 1560, and Mary found that her uncles had indeed undone her, although Charles, Sieur de Randan, the French ambassador in Scotland, had begged Catherine to make peace before the cost of the French garrisons brought about 'the ruin and desolation of France'. Under the terms of the treaty, the

French forces would leave Scotland, the fortifications at Leith would all be dismantled, debts incurred by the French troops would be paid, a general amnesty would be given for all warlike deeds, Elizabeth would be implicitly recognised as the rightful queen of England, François and Mary would renounce all claims to the English throne, and a council of nobles would rule Scotland in Mary's absence, sending 'some persons of quality to remonstrate to them' concerning religion. Then, finally, 'The French King and Queen are by a special clause bound to the Queen of England to keep and perform the said covenants with the Scots'. The treaty was to be ratified by Mary and François within sixty days. In other words, Mary and François were free to do whatever Elizabeth wanted, otherwise she was authorised to invade. It was a total reversal of Guise policies, a denial of all the claims put forward by Henri and maintained by Catherine.

Throckmorton met Mary on 9 August and, for the first time, she asked to speak to him in Scots. It was not something she had done in public for many years and, apart from discomfiting an ambassador – always a favourite sport of royalty – Mary may have been rehearsing her tongue for a possible return to Scotland. On 22 August she met Throckmorton again, this time alone. Mary sat under her cloth of state and Throckmorton was placed on a low stool while she assured him that she would conform to whatever her husband resolved, 'for his will is mine.' These two meetings show Mary exercising her role as a sovereign queen in full charge of her own policies. The effect of the humbling terms imposed by the treaty had been to stiffen her pride and treat Throckmorton as an unimportant envoy from a minor supplicant. Much to his credit he was amused by this, but Mary's childish attitude was not lost on Cecil, who was most certainly not amused by it.

A rumour that Mary was pregnant arose again, but Throckmorton presumed the reason to be 'menstruum retentio'. With his normal sceptical view of court gossip he commented, 'It is a sport to see how this farce is handled.' The date for ratification of the treaty came and went with further bland assurances that until the wishes of the Scottish Estates were known and emissaries were sent from them no formal agreement could be expected from Mary and François.

The young couple had more pressing matters to deal with when, on 16 November, the king returned early from a hunt near Orléans with dizziness and ringing in his right ear. On Sunday he collapsed in church, and the pain in his head became chronic as he suffered discharges of fluid from his ear. François had always suffered from eczema, with florid patches appearing on his face, and respiratory infections, giving rise to foul-smelling breath, weakened his resistance to such complaints. The new inflammation caused a swelling 'the size of a large nut', and when doctors examined his left ear they discovered an open fistula from which pus was seeping. It seemed clear that the king was dying. In a letter of 4 December, Catherine acknowledged this unhappy fact while pointing out that France had a good supply of legitimate successors – 'all of whom are mine'. However, since François's brother Charles was only ten years old, the question of the inevitable regency had to be solved. Catherine did this brilliantly by summoning the feeble Antoine de Bourbon, King of Navarre, now himself a Huguenot but the nearest adult by blood to the throne. She immediately accused him of plotting treason. With his brother Condé already under sentence of death, and being 'naturally pliant and tractable', he offered Catherine the regency if she spared his life, and she agreed instantly. She made the Guise brothers embrace Antoine as a sign of forgiveness and ordered the release of Condé, thus neutralising her enemies at no cost to herself.

This masterstroke marked the end of Guise influence. Catherine had wisely stood aside in the face of what she, rightly, took to be the irresistible force of the Guise brothers allied with Mary's influence over François, but now she saw her chance and took it. As a girl she had studied not *Amadis de Gaul*, but Machiavelli's *The Prince* and Castiglione's *The Courtier*, where she would have read 'It is the office of a good courtier to know the nature and the inclination of his Prince, and so according to the business, and as occasion serveth, with slightness to enter into favour with him.' She would fill this office with enthusiasm. A later English ambassador said of Catherine, 'the truth is that she loveth and hateth as maketh most for her profit . . . as this woman can make her profit of times and occasions, and perchance seeketh to serve her turn without respect to right and wrong'. In other words she was the supreme pragmatist, in contrast to the romantic Mary.

The Cardinal ordered Masses of expiation, and prayers were said throughout France. The doctors lanced François's ear, which caused a temporary release of putrid matter through his mouth and nostrils. Mary nursed him constantly. On 3 December an abscess formed in the king's inner ear which spread to his brain and on 5 December he lost consciousness. Later that day he 'rendered his soul to God', and the ten-year-old Charles IX was King of France. The Cardinal of Lorraine broke the seals of François II in the presence of Charles and his mother. Mary Stewart, four days before her eighteenth birthday, was a royal widow.

The late king's skull was cut open and the doctors claimed that his brain was totally rotten and beyond any medicine, thus ensuring that they could not be blamed for any lack of skill. Mary's state was one of total collapse, reminiscent of Catherine's behaviour at the death of Henri. She remained in heavy mourning in a black draped room lit only by candles, weeping inconsolably. 'As heavy and dolorous a wife, as of right she had good cause to be, who, by long watching with him during his sickness and painful diligence about him . . . is not in best tune of her body, but without danger'. On 8 December Giovanni Surian summed up her state for his master, the Doge of Venice:

By degrees everyone will forget the death of the late king except the young queen, his widow, who, being no less noble minded than beautiful and graceful in appearance, the thoughts of widowhood at so early an age, and of the loss of a consort who was so great a king and who so dearly loved her, and also that she is dispossessed of the crown of France with little hope of recovering that of Scotland, which is her sole patrimony and dower, so afflict her that she will not receive any consolation, but, brooding over her disasters with constant tears and passionate and doleful lamentations, she universally inspires great pity.

Mary knew that, as had happened with Diane de Poitiers, on the day after François's death she would be required to hand over the jewels given to her by François, and so two inventories were drawn up on 6 December. The jewellery consisted mainly of large numbers of diamonds and rubies, in necklaces and crucifixes, some enamelled with the letter 'F', and the list runs for three pages. It is signed 'Charles' and was probably the first document he signed as king. Catherine added a receipt for the jewellery and an audit of Mary's personal staff was drawn up, showing that the four Maries were still in attendance, but listing 286 other courtiers and servants. Few of these were needed as Mary kept close mourning for fifteen days, and only persons in the nearest relationship to her were admitted, but ambassadors and courtiers buzzed with furious speculation.

Mary was now an eighteen-year-old woman of presumed, although as yet unproven, fertility and a widowed queen. The secret Treaty of Fontainebleau was now worthless, but Mary had huge personal land holdings in France as well as being able to claim the royal income of Scotland. On 20 December the boy-king Charles IX signed an order paying Mary an annual dowry of 60,000 livres to be derived from her holdings as Duchesse de Touraine and Poitou. Thus 'impoverishment followed her loss'. This is somewhat misleading, since she was still one of the richest women in France, even without her Scottish holdings, and still a very great prize for anyone who married her.

The court had buzzed with speculation from the moment it became clear that François was dying. Mary had sat by François's bedside, but Catherine and the brothers were far too occupied with the joint problems of the succession and the choice of Mary's next husband to do so. It was typical of Catherine to accept the inevitable with stoicism and to move forward at once. An early suggestion was that, given a papal dispensation, Mary might marry her brother-in-law Charles IX, but this idea was firmly rejected by Catherine. Catherine had, at first, treated Mary as one of her own daughters, but as Mary's power increased her hostility grew, until Mary's accession to the crown, when it became open. Mary, was, of course, protected by the Guises, but with the death of the king and Catherine's assumption of the regency everything changed. Now Catherine wished to have as little to do with Mary as possible and certainly would not contemplate her continuing as a daughter-in-law. The list of possible candidates for Mary's hand remained long and was entirely concerned with dynastic alliances.

While Mary wept for her loss, the various ambassadors reported the rumours. In Toledo the English ambassador Chamberlain had noticed talk of a union with Don Carlos of Spain, Philip II's heir. He was fifteen years old, a deformed hunchback, and was already starting to display the homicidal tendencies that would eventually lead to his perpetual imprisonment. In February 1561 de Quadra, Philip's ambassador to Elizabeth, reported, 'Lady Margaret Lennox is trying to marry her son Lord Darnley to the Queen of Scotland and I understand she is not without hope of succeeding. The parliament in Scotland has decided to recommend the queen to marry the Earl of Arran and, if she will not do so to withhold from her the government of the kingdom . . . things are in great confusion'. Darnley did appear in person in Orléans at the behest of his ever-ambitious mother, but he was well down the list of possible candidates. Young Arran was the Duc de Châtelherault's son, but an alliance there would put the possible inheritance into the hands of the house of Hamilton, a prospect that raised grave suspicions in the Scottish parliament. Furthermore, the mere suggestion of it would have driven Elizabeth to lose her already celebratedly short temper as she contemplated the most ambitious and unreliable dynasty in Scotland battering down her northern frontiers.

The list continued. François de Guise, Prior of St John, represented too close an alliance with the Guise clan. Eric XIV was the new King of Sweden, but also a Protestant, although this problem might be overlooked if Mary moved to Sweden. The other of the two Scotsmen proposed as husband also had barriers of faith. Lord James Stewart was Mary's half-brother, but, even if that problem could have been overcome, he had been the leader of the Protestant Lords of the Congregation and a bitter opponent of Mary's mother.

Mary, taking a leaf from her Tudor cousin's book, prevaricated, but, had necessity driven her, everyone would have assumed that she would marry according to political expediency and even the loathsome Don Carlos would not have been ruled out. This was far from the expectations of the enchanted princess waiting for her handsome champion. Mary had learned from Diane de Poitiers that such romantic notions were a dangerous luxury, but an apparent promise, followed by procrastination, would allow her to choose the time most opportune to satisfy her own ends.

Throckmorton noted that the Spanish ambassador was spending more time with Mary than his embassy required and he also found the court 'very much altered . . . [containing] not one of the house of Guise, nor but few of their friends', while behind the scenes the Guise brothers still manoeuvred to gain Catherine's ear and Catherine, who was too wise to antagonise them totally, kept them at arm's length. Mary was now isolated from the day-to-day running of the court.

One of Mary's most obvious immediate needs was to keep the lords in Scotland informed and, if possible, pacified. She sent an embassy to Scotland in January 1561, promising to return and offering an amnesty for all that had passed in her absence. She did not tie herself to any specific timetable but used the time-honoured formula of 'when affairs permit'. Meanwhile she seemed to Throckmorton to be 'content to be ruled by good counsel and wise men – which is a great virtue in a Prince or Princess and which argueth a great judgement and wisdom in her'. Unfortunately, Mary had neither wise men nor good counsel who could be relied on to act in anything but their own best interests, and so she left the French court to take up residence with her Guise relatives.

In March 1561, Cecil, guessing that Mary might return to Scotland and give him a Catholic kingdom as his northern neighbour, sent Thomas Randolph to Edinburgh to 'sound out the Protestant lords for the maintenance of amity and goodwill'. His instructions contained a veiled threat that this 'amity' might be forced on Scotland, but suggested that, while their queen was in France, they might like to make a formal alliance with England. Also, the Scottish lords were recommended to 'persuade their sovereign to marry at home or else not to marry without some great surety'. This was a recommendation which would be vehemently echoed by Elizabeth in the not-too-distant future.

Mary was also being treated, somewhat hopefully, as a queen regnant by Pope Pius IV, who wrote to her on 6 March 1561 in the first of many letters asking her to throw her weight behind the Council of Trent by sending ambassadors to it. This would have signalled her tacit support for the Counter-Reformation, and she avoided the issue by simply doing nothing. Nine months later, on 3 December, Pius wrote again, reminding her of her Catholic duty and promising his spiritual support and the mission of a legate, Nicholas de Gouda, to stiffen her resolve. Again, Mary did not reply.

By the end of March 1561 Mary was in Rheims, lodged with her aunt, Renée de Guise, the abbess of the Convent of St Pierre des Dames where her mother was now buried. She had stopped briefly in Paris to supervise the inventory of her personal jewellery and wardrobe, so she had definite plans for a withdrawal from the court.

Much has been made of Mary having been driven out of the court by Catherine, and fifteen years later Delbena, the Spanish ambassador 'made a long recital of many things past to persuade me that the Queen Mother never loved the Scottish Queen'.

James Melville of Halhill, a young Scots nobleman and page to Constable Montmorency, reported that 'the Queen Mother was content to be quit of the government of the house of Guise and for their cause [and] she had a great misliking of our Queen'. However, the truth seems much simpler. Mary was an eighteen-year-old widow with no close female relatives in the court. Her Maries still attended her, but they were an odd mixture of childhood friends and quasi-servants; what Mary needed, in simple terms, was a shoulder to cry on, and Renée fitted the bill exactly. In the convent she could find uninterrupted peace until her tears dried – at least for the moment.

Mary's intended destination was Joinville in Lorraine, the family castle of the Guises, thus throwing Throckmorton into a panic at the thought that she might continue her journey eastward to meet with Ferdinand I, the Archduke of Austria and Holy Roman Emperor, who had two marriageable sons. Throckmorton repeated to Elizabeth that as far as Mary was concerned, 'It is her religion chiefly that has made her amity so valued. At present she [Elizabeth] has peace with all the world and no war will arise from any place or person but by the Queen of Scotland.' Cecil vehemently echoed these views.

Mary's progress to Joinville was, however, halted by two visitors from Scotland. The first was John Leslie, later Bishop of Ross and the leader of the Catholic faction which was now more or less confined to the north-east of the country. Ross was a 33-year-old professional churchman and a 'supple diplomat' who would become Mary's ambassador during her imprisonment in England. He met Mary on 14 April and assured her that he was acting as an emissary from the earls of Huntly, Atholl and Crawford, as well as the bishops of Aberdeen, Moray and Ross. He told her she would be welcomed by all Catholics in Scotland as the restorer of the true religion and proposed that she make a sudden return, landing at Aberdeen, where he would guarantee a military force which would overthrow the Protestant parliament in Edinburgh. This dangerous proposal was accompanied by a mountain of flattery assuring her that Scotland was waiting for her like a new dawn. This, as usual, gave her a moment of cheer, although she wisely rejected the proposal.

This was doubly wise since the next day she met Lord James Stewart, who had been sent by a convention of the nobility to 'grope the young Queen's mind'. She assured him that she would rule with their freedoms at the forefront of her mind and asked him to make all preparations for her return after she had attended the coronation of Charles IX. Bizarre counter-offers were made between the two when Lord James was offered a cardinal's hat by the Guise brothers if he returned to Catholicism, while, in turn, Lord James attempted to convert Mary to Protestantism. Throckmorton had suggested this earlier and Mary had replied, 'I will be plain with you. The religion which I profess I take to be the most acceptable to God: and, indeed, neither do I know, nor desire to know, any other. Constancy becometh all folks well, and none better than princes, and such as have rule over realms and especially in matters of religion. I have been brought up in this religion, and who might credit me in anything if I show myself light in this case?'

Lord James also reminded her that the celebration of the Mass was now illegal in Scotland, but he gave her a loophole by saying that if she celebrated Mass privately he would assure her of her safety. Both parties ignored the uncomfortable but legally important point that since Mary had not summoned the parliament or signed its acts into law, the outlawing of the Mass had no legal validity. He ended by asking Mary to grant him the earldom of Moray and Lord James returned to Scotland, via Throckmorton in Paris and Cecil in London, giving each suitably edited versions of the interview. Mary distrusted Lord James's 'special devotion to the Queen of England'. And he had received no firm commitment from her as to whether she would return to Scotland or remain in France.

In reality Mary had several options, but most of them required the eating of some humble pie served up by Catherine which was, for a Guise, unthinkable. She knew she would not be welcome at the French court as a queen dowager with no political influence, while maintaining her own expensive rival royal court and so creating a drain on France's wildly over-extended finances.

She had already experienced a sterile marriage to a husband whom she had treated lovingly as a younger, retarded brother and who was hardly six months dead. To contemplate a second dynastic marriage would be to re-enter the troubled world of alliances, knowing that by marrying into one princedom she would immediately antagonise all the others. She could buy herself time to reflect by entering a convent, and with two cardinals, a grand prior, and an abbess as close relatives, a suitable situation with royal comforts and diversions would not be hard to find. However, Mary was young, beautiful and elegant, educated to be courteous and a focus for the adoration of gallant nobles. She also enjoyed dancing, riding, eating and the life of the châteaux of the Loire. As Duchesse de Touraine she could retire to that beautiful province, although unfortunately not to Chenonceau, where Catherine's masons were hard at work building her gallery across the river, and certainly not to Chambord, still a favourite choice of the court. Amboise still held blood-drenched memories, but a luxurious palace with suitable hunting grounds could easily be made available. Uncomfortably, on the Loire she would have frequent royal neighbours. However, she was still popular with the French people, for whom she was '*La Reine Blanche*' in her white mourning, and the golden life of the Duchesse de Touraine was undoubtedly attractive.

Her last remaining choice was a return to Scotland, a country of which she knew nothing, and had only heard of its struggles insofar as they affected her mother or the kingdom of France. Since her departure from Scotland, thirteen years previously, her interests had been entirely familial or personal. Nursing her boy-king, maintaining her own court and pleasing her uncles had happily coincided with hunting, dancing and receiving the extravagant praises of poets and musicians. It is unlikely that Mary could have named more than two towns in Scotland; she only spoke Scots as a secret game with her Maries, and she had no knowledge of the religious and political divisions she would have to rule over. As far as the impact of the Reformation on Scotland was concerned it was of no interest to her whatsoever, except that Huguenots were troublesome. During her mother's visit to France eleven years previously, we may be sure that Mary was told that her destiny was to fill the throne of Scotland, and her duty now lay firmly in that direction. At Joinville, there had been a Guise family conference at which Mary may have been advised to return and for the moment, at least, to accept the Reformation. To avoid that duty meant taking direct action, rejecting the advances of the Scots lords and making some kind of accommodation with Catherine, and, inevitably, Mary Stewart's enchantment with the path of least resistance took precedence over her only slight political acumen.

First she had to tie up some family loose ends in France, and she therefore went east to the city of Nancy where her sister-in-law, Claude, was the Duchesse de Lorraine. Here the old lights of festivity flickered again with family christenings and engagements followed by banquets, balls and, of course, hunting, as well as 'all kinds of honourable pastimes within the palace'. In spite of these relaxations Mary fell into a 'tertian ague'. This was a common form of malaria in which the fever would recur every three days while the bout lasted. During the gaps in the fever she travelled to Joinville, where her grandmother, Antoinette de Guise, nursed her in preparation for her expected return to Rheims for the coronation of Charles IX.

The coronation took place in Rheims Cathedral on 15 May 1561, but without the attendance of Mary, who was still in Joinville. Charles IX was even punier than his late brother, and the ceremony took place with the Guise cardinal and his brothers glaring at Catherine, who had only attended at the request of the Pope, and without much of the pomp seen eighteen months previously.

Mary returned to Paris on 10 June to be met by the Duc d'Orléans, the King of Navarre, the Prince of Condé and the Duc de Guise. This mixture of Huguenots and Catholics is a clear illustration of the power struggles at the heart of Charles's court, but they loyally joined together to escort Mary to the Palace of St Germain, where she had first met the French royal court, to be greeted by Charles and Catherine. On 24 July 1561, a fête of farewell began at St Germain which lasted four days and rekindled all her happier memories. At the fête she was celebrated by Ronsard:

> Like a beautiful field shorn of flowers,
> Like a picture drained of colour,
> Like heaven if it lost its stars,
> A tree its leaves, another its blossom,
> A great palace the pomp of its king,
> And a ring its precious pearl,
> So careworn France loses its greatest ornament,
> Its flower, its colour, its clarity.

On 29 June 1561, Mary put an end to the speculation over her future, writing to Lethington as her principal secretary and assuring him:

> If you employ yourself in my service and show the good will whereof you assure me, you need not fear calumniators or talebearers, for such have no part with me. I look to results before believing all that is told me . . . and nothing passes among my nobility without your knowledge and advice. I will not conceal from you that if anything goes wrong after I trust you, you are the first I shall blame. I wish to live henceforth in amity with the Queen of England and am on the point of leaving for my realm. On arriving I shall need some money for my household and other expenses. There must be a good year's profit from my mint . . .

Mary was setting out her intentions with such strident clarity that the instructions might have come from Elizabeth herself, and she was putting Lethington in the place of Cecil. Lethington certainly realised this when he had her letter copied and sent to Cecil.

There can be no doubt that the now-certain knowledge of Mary's intention to leave France must have been a great relief to all. It was also a relief to Throckmorton, who had been unable to reach Mary on her travels and had been told by Elizabeth not to return to England without having gained Mary's ratification of the Treaty of Edinburgh. He knew that Mary did not intend to give an answer until she had consulted her advisers in Scotland and, although Mary had told him that she would sail from Calais, he had received a rumour that she intended to sail from Nantes, landing in Scotland at Dumbarton, the port from which she had sailed to France as a child. Mary now played directly into Elizabeth's hands and sent d'Oysel as her ambassador to England to ask for a safe-conduct if she should have to land in England, and a guarantee of an untroubled time to rearrange a journey by land. Elizabeth was furious at what she saw as gross cheek, but assured d'Oysel that she would be glad to agree once Mary had ratified the treaty, and he was peremptorily sent back to France to get it. Elizabeth also confounded Mary's principal excuse by personally writing to the Scots lords, asking them what their advice to Mary would be – her letters contained threats and promises to them in equal measure. Before they could reply, Mary informed Throckmorton that she had no need of a safe-conduct and could sail untroubled directly to Scotland. She could not ratify the treaty without meeting with her advisers and, as to the quartering of her coat of arms, it had all been the idea of her father-in-law Henri II, and she had ceased to continue with the practice since her husband's death. Next day, probably 20 July, Throckmorton called again and received what was clearly a well-prepared speech:

Monsieur de l'Ambassadeur, if my preparations were not so much advanced as they are, peradventure the Queen your Mistress's unkindness might stay my voyage; but I am now determined to adventure the matter, whatsoever come of it: I trust the wind will be so favourable as I shall not need to come on the coast of England: and if I do, then, Monsieur de l'Ambassadeur, the Queen your mistress shall have me in her hands to do her will of me; and if she be so hard-hearted as to desire my end, she may then do her pleasure, and make sacrifice of me; peradventure that casualty might be better for me than to live; in this matter God's will be done.

Despite what Mary had told Throckmorton, she had, of course, continued the troublesome quartering and was childishly and light-heartedly brushing the matter aside, but the end of her address to Throckmorton belied her light heart. Not for the first time she was expressing the sentiment that death was a preferable option to making up her own mind, something she felt she had now been forced to do. She was returning to Scotland with no gladness in her heart or any wish to rule the country as its queen.

Mary now went to the Louvre to oversee the despatch of her furniture and wardrobe for Rouen and Newhaven, then she left Paris again for St Germain. She made her formal farewells to Charles, Catherine and the royal court on 25 July and with her six Guise uncles ensuring that she had remembered what had been discussed at Joinville, as well as a considerable retinue, travelled towards the English Channel. Her exact route and final port of embarkation were closely guarded secrets, but by 7 August she was at Abbeville, where she had her last interview with Throckmorton. The Lord of St Colme and one Arthur Erskine were sent to Elizabeth with one last appeal for a safe conduct, although, even if Elizabeth had granted it, the actual document could not have arrive until after Mary's departure. It was simply the crossing of a diplomatic 't'.

The day before she sailed, Mary sent Throckmorton two basins, two ewers, two salts and a standing cup, 368 ounces of silver-gilt in all, as her traditional present for his services. With René de Guise, Marquis d'Elbeuf; Claude de Guise, Duc d'Aumale; François de Guise, Grand Prior; the poets Brantôme and Chastelard; her four Maries; a doctor of theology and two doctors of medicine, Mary and her retinue embarked on 14 August. There were two galleys for the royal passengers, under the command of the same Villegaignon who had commanded the ships bringing her to France thirteen years previously. There was also a considerable flotilla of cargo ships carrying her furniture, plate, dresses and jewellery as well as 200 horses and mules. The final arrangements for this had been made by the high admiral of Scotland, James Hepburn, Earl of Bothwell, whose father had been a suitor to Mary's mother in her early widowhood. Mary had previously met Bothwell in France when he had appeared fleeing not only from creditors but also from a rash engagement to Anna Throndsen, his Norwegian mistress. Throckmorton thought Bothwell 'a glorious, rash and hazardous young man', and he was quite right.

As the royal galley left Calais harbour, a nearby ship sank and all hands drowned, to Mary's total horror and moans from her retinue that it was the worst of omens. Mary refused to go to her stateroom below, but had a bed made up on the poop deck, where she spent the night watching the shoreline of France recede. Mary, one of the great weepers of history, lay in floods of tears as the country she had loved disappeared, taking with it her youth. She was an eighteen-year-old virgin, a crowned queen and a widow for whom Scotland was a completely foreign country. Mary's nineteenth-century hagiographer, the Jesuit Joseph Stevenson, said of her new country, 'The Scotland which could admire Knox and submit to the dictation of Elizabeth was not the home for Mary Stuart [sic].' She was about to start a life that was totally alien to anything that she had ever dreamed of.

PART III

Scotland, 1561–68

CHAPTER SEVEN

We had landed in an obscure country

⸙

On Mary's sea journey north there had been no hostile intervention by Elizabeth, who had in fact sent the long-awaited safe-
conduct to France. English ships had been sighted in the breaks
in the fog, although they were England's normal anti-pirate
patrol, and the only inopportune event was a forced landing at
Tynemouth of one of the cargo vessels due to adverse winds.
Unfortunately it was the cargo ship carrying much of Mary's
furniture and prized horses – the finest horses that France could
supply – and since the animals carried no passports, the
surprised warden of the port promptly impounded them for a
month.

Mary's arrival in Scotland was not auspicious. Even though
she had forbidden the use of the lash on the rowers, her two
galleys arrived unexpectedly early, on the night of Monday, 18
August 1561, in the Firth of Forth, in the midst of torrential rain
and thick fog. When the poet Brantôme saw the sailors lighting
lanterns and braziers, he told them that their work would not be
necessary since 'One glance from the Queen's eyes will light up
the whole sea'. The crew was not convinced and anchored in the
firth for the night.

Next morning Brantôme could not see the main mast from the
poop, 'a sign that we had landed in an obscure country', but the
landing went ahead. Knox, who reported that 'scarce could any
man espy another the length of two pairs of boots', felt the
weather to be an omen: 'What comfort was brought into the
country with her, to wit, sorrow, dolour, darkness and all
impiety.'

123

Since the voyage had been so fast and the Scots lords had not thought to post look-outs, there was no one to meet the royal party and Mary, wearing her *deuil blanc* with her Maries in the more conventional black or grey, stepped ashore alone in the fog and the rain. Cannon were fired from her galley to notify the town and a messenger was sent into Edinburgh to fetch help – the horses were still in Tynemouth – while the royal party approached the most prosperous house they could discern in the fog. It belonged to an astonished merchant, Andrew Lamb, who managed to arrange a makeshift luncheon for his unexpected royal guests. Two hours later, the breathless Châtelherault arrived with apologies, followed shortly by the official welcoming party of Lord James, the Earl of Argyll and Erskine of Dun with horses and even more apologies. Messengers were sent to make hasty preparations at Holyrood, which was not yet entirely ready, so Mary and her dripping wet entourage set off on what was hardly an *entrée joyeuse*. It goes without saying that Mary wept at the squalor of her reception and Brantôme tells us that she felt she had exchanged Paradise for Hell, although he was probably speaking for himself.

Hardly had they set out when they were approached by a party of petitioners. A month previously a Feast of Misrule had taken place in Edinburgh and one John Gillon, a tailor, had played the part of Robin Hood, the 'Lord of Inobedience'. This was a festival of mischievous nonsense, and 'Robin Hood' was given licence to indulge in petty pilfering for the day – although most of the goods were returned. Heavy drinking and casual sex also played major roles and the festival had got out of hand. Gillon had been arrested and sentenced to death, expecting the sentence to be reduced to a judicial whipping in accordance with tradition, but Knox had forbidden the pardon. On the day of Mary's arrival a mob had broken into the Tolbooth – Edinburgh's civic jail – and rescued Gillon. He was now on his knees, as was the mob, before Mary and begging for his life. She had not the slightest idea of what was going on, or of what the condemned man was accused of, but was advised, probably by Lord

James, to grant the pardon, and the mob returned to Edinburgh shouting the praises of a beautiful and merciful queen. Politically this was the perfect start to her reign – today it would be a photo opportunity – and cannot have been a pure coincidence. By the time Mary arrived at Holyrood there were bonfires lit around the city to welcome the new and merciful queen who, the populace had been informed, had paid Scotland the compliment of landing without a bodyguard. Mary had only been in her kingdom for a few hours and, unknowingly, she had already been manipulated by her nobles. All of this, to say nothing of the laggard welcome and the weather, were completely unexpected and quite unlike anything she had ever experienced before; neither had any of the accounts of the political and religious changes in Scotland prepared her for it. She now faced an impossibly steep learning curve.

It is fair to say that any memories Mary retained from her infancy in Scotland would have been of no use whatsoever since during her absence the country had undergone one of the most profound changes in its history. Calls to Queen Regent Marie for greater tolerance toward the Protestant faith by such nobles as Lord James Stewart and Erskine of Dun had fallen on deaf ears; the Catholic Mary Tudor had ruled England with fierce intolerance; the absentee Queen Mary had become Queen of France, and Marie de Guise was firm in her resolve to contain, or even to reverse, the reforming movement. The exiled Knox had returned briefly in the winter of 1555/56 and dined with Erskine of Dun and Maitland of Lethington, but his presence was only tolerated provided he maintained a low profile. Since his profile was never low, he returned to Europe to bombard Scotland with the inspirational letters of an exiled leader. On 3 December 1557 the earls of Argyll, Glencairn and Morton, along with Lord Lorne and Lord Erskine, had signed the Band of Congregation, openly declaring their Protestant faith and, in so doing, becoming an alternative government to that of the queen regent. They were now the Lords of the Congregation and their reformed faith attracted growing support from the minor lairdry and some of the burgh elite – provided, of course, it did not interfere with trade.

In 1558 Christopher Goodman, a fellow minister of Knox in Geneva, had published 'How Superior Powers ought to be Obeyed', and in it he had argued that the people had the power and the moral authority to remove the government if it did not conform to their ideas of good administration and justice. This was totally revolutionary and highly suspicious to the nobility, but Marie had inflamed the majority of Scotland and reaffirmed the need for reform by the totally unnecessary burning of Walter Myln, a harmless eighty-year-old schoolmaster of 'decrepit age' who had been arrested for teaching a child its catechism. To the eternal credit of the town of St Andrews the civic authorities had flatly refused to take part in the martyrdom and the churchmen had had to perform the grisly deed themselves. Unfortunately they had bungled the affair, prolonging the old man's agonies unnecessarily.

On 17 November 1558 Mary Tudor had died, and the Protestant Elizabeth had become Queen of England. Then in early May of the following year Knox had returned to Scotland. Marie, her resolution hardening, had outlawed the Lords of the Congregation, who had gathered in Perth – then called St Johnston – where Knox preached against idolatry in the Church of the Holy Cross and St John the Baptist. The result had been a riot in which all the decorations of the church were destroyed by what Knox called the 'rascal multitude' – for whose acts he never took responsibility – and the fire of reform had burst into flame with a sporadic war breaking out between the Lords and the queen regent. Both sides had suffered changes of fortune and defections, but the end had been put beyond all doubt when Elizabeth had sent military help to her fellow Protestants. Marie's death on 11 June 1560 had marked the end of hostilities and paved the way for the Treaty of Edinburgh and the meeting on 8 August of the Reformation Parliament.

Technically, since the queen had not summoned the parliament, it had no validity, but the presence of the three estates of the nation in Edinburgh had given it all the authority it needed. Knox had preached for a religious settlement to be included –

according to Randolph, the English ambassador, 'Mr Knox spareth not to tell them' – and had begged that the Catholic clergy be excluded from the second estate. This did not happen, but, in the event, most of them stayed away. One of the first actions of the parliament had been for Speaker Lethington – he was called 'Harangue Maker' – to ask Knox to prepare a Confession of Faith. This endorsed the Protestant faith and could easily have been written in Geneva. Parliament had gone further by outlawing the Mass in Scotland and completely rejecting the authority of Rome. The celebration of Christmas and Easter had been banned as being Papist and idolatrous, but, perhaps wisely, the pagan festival of Hogmanay had been left untouched. Scotland had now become a totally Protestant country and a commission had been sent to France asking for Mary's endorsement of these sanctions as well as her signature to ratify the Treaty of Edinburgh. This was when Lord James Stewart had arrived 'to grope the young Queen's mind'. He wisely had not pressed the points of her endorsements. Her acceptance of the Acts of the Reformation Parliament was vital for the peace of mind of the Lords since, in 1555, an agreement had been reached in Augsburg, principally to end the various wars and skirmishes between Catholic and Protestant factions in Germany, but with an overriding clause allowing that a ruler could personally decide on the legal religion of his – or her – subjects. Although this Peace of Augsburg had no legal force in Scotland, it could have been used as a dangerous precedent since Scotland was not simply a small country on the northern fringes of civilisation, but was subject to the pull of European tides. Therefore, what was current practice in Augsburg could have soon become a bone of contention in Edinburgh. Unsurprisingly, no endorsement of either the treaty or the Acts of the Reformation Parliament had been received, although Mary had endorsed the principle of 'amity' with England. With both Scotland and England now in the Protestant camp, this 'amity' was more important to the Scots than the Auld Alliance had been.

Meanwhile, Knox had produced a draft of the *Book of Discipline* and had presented it to an assembly of the reformed church, which was, in effect, the first General Assembly of the Church of Scotland. This was rejected and the consultative committee was widened to redraft the book. This was a far-reaching proposal for the parishes – roughly equivalent to today's parliamentary constituencies. Each parish was to elect a committee, or 'session', which would appoint the minister and the schoolteacher, teaching a surprisingly liberal range of subjects. The sessions were answerable to synods, although including some laymen, and all were answerable to the annual General Assembly which now formed the clerical estate. Secondary schools and universities were included in Knox's proposal, with a range of fees making universal tertiary education available and, indeed, even obligatory to those who were 'docile' – in other words, of sufficient ability. The whole would be financed by the income from confiscated Catholic ecclesiastic revenues. Unfortunately most of the confiscated church revenues were already in the hands of the nobility, who were reluctant to give them up, so the book received praise but no financial support. Recently, a very senior Scottish political leader was asked what, in theory, he would do with such a document presented to him today as a green paper. His response was that he would sing its praises from the rooftops and then ask his civil servants quietly to bury it.

In Scotland there had by no means been an overwhelming call for Mary's return since many people saw her as a possible replica of her mother, and on 9 August Randolph reported to Cecil, 'Some care not though they never saw her face.' The Earl of Huntly's wife consulted her 'familiars' – she maintained a private coven of witches – and was assured that Mary would 'never set foot on Scottish ground'.

Mary's plans, however, had been made without regard to Scottish opinion; her relations with France had been severed, and, like it or not, Scotland now had a queen regnant whose actions would be closely watched for any signs of persecution or tolerance, and her choice of privy councillors would be examined as closely as the Roman augurs picked over the entrails of sacrificial animals – that is, unless Mary herself was that sacrificial animal. Whatever was to happen, the new queen had now arrived at the Palace of Holyroodhouse, which was to be her home for the next six years.

As she approached the palace from the hill of Abbeymount to the north, the sight lifted her spirits. A richly carved gateway, surmounted by James V's coat of arms, led into a wide forecourt beyond which was the west front, finished in the best French style, with a rectangular tower at the north-west corner and the old abbey church nestling against the north side. The abbey had been restored after the Rough Wooing, but it would, technically at least, be limited to members of the Protestant faith since a new royal chapel had been built by James V in the south quarter and would be Mary's private chapel. The entrance led into an inner courtyard, with the royal apartments on the west side and, to the east, a range of buildings providing accommodation for the court and the officers of state. The building was surrounded by a huge royal park with three lochs, dominated by the volcanic plug of Arthur's Seat with the spectacular crags to its west. In the forecourt there was space for a tiltyard to be constructed, and there were plentiful private gardens and stabling beyond the main building to the east. It was a far cry from the magnificence of Chambord or the charm of Chenonceau, but it was certainly not squalor and it represented a welcome shelter from the rain. Grooms rushed to take the horses and Mary was shown to her private quarters on the first floor: an audience chamber, measuring about fifty feet by twenty with a table and stools; a hastily lit warming fire; and a bed which would be disassembled during the day to provide a private chamber. Servants were unpacking what had been carried from the ships at Leith – the bulk of Mary's goods were still impounded at Tynemouth. Mary went on to inspect her private supper room, which was in fact a tiny twelve-foot square closet with a fireplace and windows opening from her bedroom. All the windows faced west and the quarters were still rather dingily decorated, although she had a clear view of

Edinburgh, half a mile distant and now ablaze with celebratory bonfires.

By dark, an impromptu band of musicians and singers had assembled in the forecourt below her windows. According to Knox, 'a company of the most honest, with instruments of music and musicians gave their salutations at her chamber window'. 'The melody', as she alleged, 'liked her well; and she willed the same to be continued for some nights after.' Knox was not present, but Brantôme was, and he gave a different view of the same event: 'Five or six hundred knaves of the town came under her window, with wretched fiddles and sung psalms so badly and out of tune that nothing could be worse.' Admittedly Brantôme was by now a convinced Scottophobe, but to one raised on the court music of Jannequin and de Sermisy the first contact with Protestant psalms chanted throughout the night must have been a considerable culture shock.

By the next day the nobility had made themselves ready and 'all men [were] welcome and well received, with good entertainment great cheer and fair words'. Even the most firmly Protestant knew that preferment sprang first from the crown, and a new queen, albeit a Catholic, might wish to ingratiate herself with her subjects by being lavish. These men were aristocrats and their first loyalty was to their newly arrived queen, so their immediate response was to visit and pay homage. Later they would make personal judgments as to the strength of their loyalty. They had all taken part in the Reformation Parliament and had dutifully listened to Knox's sermons, but he himself had said 'the belly hath no ears', and the nobility of Scotland had a very great regard for their bellies. The doors of Holyrood began to resemble the door of 21st-century No. 10 Downing Street with a Cabinet reshuffle in progress. The Reformation, which was still young, could easily now be reversed.

The first test came on Sunday, 24 August 1561, five days after Mary's arrival, when she celebrated Mass in her private chapel, as she had been promised by Lord James, who now guarded the door of the chapel, ostensibly to prevent any Scotsmen from entering, but in fact to prevent any attack on the priest. A mob led by Lord Lyndsay demanded that 'the idolater priest should die the death', the Earl of Montrose attended Mass, while according to the *Diurnal of Occurrents* 'the rest [of the nobility] were at Mr Knox's sermon'. The congregation included Randolph, who feared that Knox might 'mar all' with his inflexible attitude. The mob reappeared later in the day in the abbey and met some of Mary's court, including her uncles and female attendants. These attendants were habitually referred to by Knox as 'dontibours', an old Scots word, sadly translatable only as 'whores'. They all declared that they could not live without the Mass and without access to it they would return to France, an idea which Knox enthusiastically embraced, but which was, in fact, an empty threat. Mary felt, however, that some of the doubts of the Lords – especially over the Peace of Augsburg – should be put to rest, and on the following day, 25 August, the Register of the Privy Council of Scotland shows an undertaking by the queen and her council, 'For the contentment of the whole, that none of them take on hand privately or openly to make any alteration or innovation of the state of religion, or attempt anything against the form which her majesty found publickly and universally standing at her arrival in her realm under pain of death'. As a quid pro quo worthy of Catherine de Medici, permission to attend Mass was tacitly extended to all in Mary's personal household. Mary's charm was having its effect on the Lords, with the young Arran alone opposing the move.

It is significant that Mary's first direct intervention in government was to assure the Reformation supporters by an act of the Privy Council that they could expect no trouble from their Catholic sovereign. In other words, she had no religious, or political, zeal and would happily let the government be run by her advisers, without royal intervention, while she did what she did best – behave as a glittering jewel, sufficiently schooled in the arts – and used her charm to ensure a quiet reign, which may have suited her Guise advisers very well.

Nine days later, on 2 September, Mary turned that charm on

the notoriously fickle population of Edinburgh with an *entrée joyeuse*. The burgh council had had only a week to prepare for this and needed the co-operation of the craft guilds, but Mary's pardon granted to Gillon had ensured this. She left the palace early and rode up to the castle to have lunch with the nobility, except for Châtelherault and his son, Arran. The procession later that day was politically and religiously important in that Protestants were by no means in the majority in Edinburgh, and the possibility of the faint-hearted returning to Rome at the sight of their beautiful young queen was high. Then at one o'clock Mary left the castle as 'the artillery shot vehemently'. Crossing the drawbridge, she was met by fifty young men dressed as Moors in yellow taffeta. They had black painted legs and faces and black hats with precious rings in their mouths and gold chains on their arms and legs. During her progress down the High Street, 'sixteen most honest men held her pall of purple velvet lined with red taffeta, fringed with gold and silk', then, as the approach to the castle widened out, a cart with children offering silver plate – hastily purchased from the Earl of Morton and Maitland of Lethington – appeared. Mary graciously touched the plate and the cart then followed her to the palace. By now most of the population were lining the street and shouting themselves hoarse at their beautiful eighteen-year-old queen in her white silk, glittering with jewels. A gate had been built across the street at the West Bow, above which were children as if in heaven and a cloud which opened to reveal 'a bonny bairn' who descended with angel's wings and presented Mary with the keys of the town, a Bible and a book of psalms bound in purple velvet. Not only were the psalms Protestant psalms but both the psalms and the Bible were in the vernacular, a totally new experience for Mary. According to Knox, who was not present, she began to frown and handed the books to Arthur Erskine. The child 'made some small speeches and gave her three tracts the tenor of which are uncertain' but were designed to show her 'the perfect way unto the heavens high'. He then returned to his own cardboard heaven. The procession came to a halt at the Butter Cross just west of what was then called the High Kirk of St Giles. Knox's house was nearly opposite the great church, on the first floor, and the temptation for him to look at the embodiment of his greatest fear in all her royal glory must have been enormous; but he was nowhere to be seen. At the Tolbooth she was met by three virgins, one dressed as Fortune, the others as Justice and Policy; she then went down to the Mercat Cross where four more sumptuously dressed virgins greeted her at a fountain flowing with wine. At her next stop, the Salt Tron, or weighbridge, she received a stern lecture on the abolition of the Mass and a representation of the fiery fate of Korah, Dathan and Abiram, who were burnt for rebelling against Moses, was acted out on a scaffold in front of her. There had been a plan to have an effigy of a priest burnt, but Huntly 'stayed that plan'. However, the French courtiers in Mary's entourage thought the display 'derisive, contemptible and presumptuous'. At the Netherbow, Edinburgh's eastern gate, a dragon – the symbol of the Antichrist – was burnt and a psalm sung; then, finally, back at Holyrood another psalm was sung and the children with their cart made a plea for Mary to accept the cupboard of plate, worth 2,000 merks, as a gift from the burgesses. She had won the hearts of the populace as only a well-trained princess of France knew how and enough of the nobility were on her side to guarantee her support in the council. But the religious opposition had to be faced, and to do this she felt that she had to turn her charm on to Knox, blithely ignoring any advice that Knox was impervious to charm. After all, she had been constantly assured by poets and courtiers in France that her charm equalled that of the very goddesses of classical times. Thus, on Thursday, 5 September, only three days after her *entrée joyeuse* and with her memory of it still fresh, Mary, the sovereign queen, met John Knox, the subject preacher, for the first of their confrontations.

Before leaving France, Mary had told Throckmorton that she felt that Knox was the most dangerous man in her kingdom and she was prepared for a battle. Mary's resentment of Knox stemmed mainly from his pamphlet 'The First Blast of the

Trumpet against the Monstrous Regiment of Women', published in 1558. This often quoted and seldom read tract would be more properly entitled 'The First Blast of the Trumpet against the Impropriety of Women holding Royal Power' and was written as an attack on Mary Tudor. It was composed as a treatise full of Biblical precedents showing the disastrous results of female power. Knox's timing could not have been worse since Mary Tudor died almost immediately, and when Elizabeth succeeded to the throne the very mention of Knox turned her white with fury. Knox tried to calm her by casting her not as a Jezebel but as a Deborah, thus weakening his arguments and going no way to calm the Tudor rage. Mary, as a teenager and a Guise, would tolerate no criticism and would meet Knox head on.

Knox, on the other hand, had been largely ignored by Marie de Guise, whose quarrel was a temporal one with rebel nobles, and under her reign there had been very few martyrdoms compared to the bloodbaths of Mary Tudor. Knox had cast Mary as a Jezebel out to impose the Mass on Scotland and put the Reformation into reverse, neither of which were her intentions. In normal life, as his letters show, Knox was very sympathetic to women and was courteously polite to them, but in this instance he wanted Mary to be a symbol of everything he hated and he would use all his debating skills to crush her. Knox had been trained at the University of St Andrews by John Mair (or Major), one of the most brilliant minds of his time, and in subsequent life he had honed his debating technique across Europe. Mary's training in rhetoric had been suitable for a royal princess, not a theologian, and she had simply accepted the teachings of the Cardinal of Lorraine as a dutiful daughter of the Church. The confrontation would be one-sided, and since our only record of what was said is that written by Knox himself, our knowledge of it is equally one-sided.

They met in Mary's audience chamber, where she was attended by two of her ladies-in-waiting, and Knox was accompanied by Lord James, acting as a sort of umpire. Mary was seated throughout while Knox stood at a respectful distance, not, as some Marian apologists have suggested, 'towering accusingly over the Queen'. In fact, he was only of medium height, but broad-shouldered from his time as a galley slave, and in debate he spoke quietly with a pronounced English accent.

Mary started by referring to 'The First Blast', and how Knox had caused 'great slaughter in England', and, bizarrely, how he achieved all his fame by necromancy. These wild accusations were hardly worth answering, but Knox begged her patience to hear his 'simple answers'. If to teach people to follow the truth of God was to preach sedition then he pled guilty, and as to the book which 'seemeth so highly to offend your Majesty', he was content that 'all the learned of the world should judge of it'. Pointedly, he did not include Mary among the 'learned', and he knew she felt inferior and nervous without a Guise cardinal standing at her elbow. As a skilled debater he also knew that if she lost her temper he would win the argument. Nettling her further, he claimed that he was as content to live under her rule as Paul was to live under Nero.

Mary was forced to change tack and claimed that Knox had taught people to receive another religion than their princes could allow. Therefore, since God commands subjects to obey their princes, Knox's doctrine cannot be of God. Mary felt that this argument was decisive, but Knox replied that subjects were not bound to follow the religion of their princes, although they are commanded to give their princes their obedience. However, if the sovereigns are exceeding their bounds, and if the subjects have the means, they may then disobey their sovereign, as a child, who is bound to obey his father, may resist him if the father is 'stricken with a frenzy in which he would slay his own children'. This was rigorously logical but was running totally counter to everything Mary had ever been taught, and she 'stood as it were amazed more than the quarter of an hour'. It was probably the first time in her life that anyone, apart from her childhood nurse Janet Sinclair, lovingly, had ever contradicted her, and yet here she was, a crowned queen, used to the total obeisance of her courtiers, sitting under her cloth of state in her own palace, being told that she could be disobeyed, even removed, if she exceeded bounds drawn up, not by her, but by her subjects. She had no answer for Knox and the silence was broken by Lord James asking what had offended her. She replied in a mixture of girlish petulance and outrage: 'I perceive that my subjects shall obey you and not me . . . so I must be subject to them and not they to me'.

Knox now had a wide-open goal and could afford to give the ball the gentlest of taps, assuring her that he never sought to have anyone obey him since everyone should obey God, that kings should be foster fathers to His Kirk and queens should be nurses to His people. Mary retired into her own faith, telling Knox she would defend the true Kirk – the Kirk of Rome. Knox naturally denied this but Mary said that her conscience told her it was so. Knox chided her that conscience required knowledge and feared that she had none. Mary said, 'I have both heard and read' and clearly fervently wished that the Cardinal of Lorraine was still by her elbow and that she had listened more carefully to his teachings instead of merely accepting them blindly. In such a close argument Mary realised that she was losing heavily. Knox then struck a final blow, telling her that 'Christ Jesus neither said, nor yet commanded Mass to be said at his Last Supper, seeing that no such thing as their Mass is made mention of in the whole Scriptures.' Obviously Mary had not read the Scriptures in their entirety, but merely said that if her authorities were present they would be able to answer him. Knox pounced on this saying that he would be glad to answer them. Mary, now thoroughly rattled, threatened him that such an event might happen sooner than he thought, and Knox, as was his custom, got the final word by saying if it happened in his lifetime it would indeed be sooner than he thought. To her relief, Mary was then called in to dinner, probably since a prearranged period had passed, and Knox prayed that she would be as blessed in Scotland as Deborah was in Israel.

Mary managed to retire before the inevitable tears, but Randolph reported, 'Mr Knox spoke upon Thursday to the Queen, he knocked so hastily upon her heart that he made her weep.' She could not understand why, when she had made no attempt to impose Catholicism on her people, Knox should be so vehement. Mary had started by directly accusing Knox of stirring up dissent and of using necromancy, charges that she could not possibly maintain, but, having heard of his forceful style of argument, she had decided to attack from the start. Knox was polite, if not deferential, and argued from his base of total Protestant conviction. Defeated by this, Mary alternately hectored or retired into a 'little girl lost' attitude. Her faith had been part of her life since birth, while Knox had departed from the Church of Rome as a result of internal debate, giving him all the vehemence of the convert. Thus Knox could not believe that Mary's simplicity was genuine: 'If there be not in her a proud mind, a crafty wit, and an indurate heart against God and His truth, my judgement faileth me.' His judgment had failed him, since he could not believe that everyone was not a fanatical zealot cast in his own mould. Zealots see only faith or heresy, politicians see plots and conspiracies everywhere, lovers see devotion or betrayal in every action, and none of them can imagine a simple middle ground of stability or peace. Mary was no zealot, had no head for politics, and loved only physical pursuits and the calm contemplation of beauty. In her highly percipient essay, 'Godly Reformer, Godless Monarch', Dr Jenny Wormald says that 'Mary saw him [Knox] not as messenger of the Lord so much as a profound irritant, a huge and buzzing fly – a pest'.

On 6 September, the names of the members of Mary's Privy Council were published. The twelve names held no surprises, being: the Duc de Châtelherault, the earls of Arran, Huntly, Argyll, Bothwell, Errol, Atholl, Morton, Montrose and Glencairn, and lords James Stewart and John Erskine, Lord Keith. The Earl Marischal could attend, if requested by the council, and Maitland of Lethington, as the queen's secretary, was in constant attendance. This Council of Twelve had seven Protestant lords, all identified with the Lords of the Congregation who, as an all-powerful drafting committee, had previously dictated policy to an often supine parliament. Six of them would be in permanent attendance on the queen and the council met daily, from eight until ten in the morning and from one until four in the afternoon.

Privy Councils had existed often enough previously, often as a temporary measure in one of the frequent regencies, but this situation was new. The council had formed itself, based on the inherited rights of the nobility, and had been endorsed by the 1560 parliament although, in the strictest sense, that parliament, not having been summoned by the monarch, was itself illegal. While Mary was the undoubted queen regnant, she could not diminish their hereditary rights, and now she joined what was an already existing government, as its head. The Scottish historian Julian Goodare describes it as the start of 'corporate government'.

Of her council, Secretary Lethington was the perfect embodiment of a sixteenth-century politician. He had been born William Maitland at Lethington Tower, now renamed Lennoxlove, the seat of the dukes of Hamilton. Since William Maitlands were all too common in his home area, he was known, as were most Scots in his position, by the name of his estate, hence he was usually referred to as 'Lethington'. Mary's son James VI would comment, 'I would there were not a surname in Scotland, for they make all the trouble.' Lethington's father was Sir Richard Maitland, a gentleman devoted to gardening and literature, who would rise to the post of Lord Privy Seal under Mary until blindness forced him into a long retirement before his death in 1586. Lethington's education had followed a similar pattern to Knox's: the local school in Haddington followed by university at St Andrews, until money and position sent him to Europe, where he learned French and Italian. He was fluent in Latin and – a rarity for the time – also in Greek and Biblical studies. He rose through the ranks of the government as a civil servant under Marie, enjoying the patronage of fellow Protestants Lord James and the Earl of Cassilis. He joined the Lords of the Congregation, not out of religious fervour, nor with an eye to choosing the winning side, but rather because he felt that Marie's reliance on

France was distorting the legal basis for her rule. Lethington saw the proper order of the realm restored in her daughter and quickly became her chief counsellor, charming her by providing legal bases for her actions, as he had charmed Elizabeth on his many missions south with industrial quantities of flattery. In his portrait he is the perfect courtier, with lace at his throat and a scattering of pearls in his hat, but his gaze is unrelenting and his eyes are cold. The picture gives a true portrait of the man, but gives no hint of his terrible end.

Alongside Mary's bastard half-brother Lord James Stewart, Lethington was one of the two most influential men in the kingdom. As Thomas Randolph, Elizabeth's ambassador, said, 'Take these two out of Scotland and those that love their country shall soon feel the want of them.' Randolph also said of them, 'Lord James deals after his nature rudely, homely and bluntly – Lethington more delicately and finely'.

Thomas Randolph himself was 'of a dark intriguing spirit, full of cunning and void of conscience. He was a faithful servant of his mistress Elizabeth.' However, curiously, he and Mary formed a close friendship and shared an enthusiasm for horseback exercise, although Randolph always put Elizabeth's interests first. He had met Mary on 1 September 1561, and pressed her on the vexed question of ratification of the Treaty of Edinburgh, but she blithely said she was unacquainted with the matter, and would take counsel and then speak to him again. Mary clearly had an ease of manner when speaking to men like Randolph, at first in French, then, as her facility with the language improved, in Scots. Randolph treated her with the full court protocol of being in the royal presence and his manners held memories of St Germain and the Louvre. When the formalities were over she enjoyed a lack of ceremony, which, combined with her un-doubted beauty, was captivating. Diane de Poitiers's lessons were being put to good use, even if Mary had no substance beyond the sugar coating.

Randolph told Cecil, 'She herself finds three points necessary to maintain her state – first to make peace with England: second to be served with Protestants – which surprises her.' The third point was 'to enrich her crown with Abbey lands, which if she do, what shall there lack in her, saving a good husband, to lead a happy life.' It would have been more accurate if Randolph had said that the first twó points were the policy of the Privy Council and that the third was a financial stricture proposed by the Reformers. The political inevitability of Mary's marriage was her known and accepted destiny, but one which could be delayed for the present.

CHAPTER EIGHT

Dynastic entity

⁂

Mary, not entirely through her own efforts, had now set up a
Privy Council through which she could rule, established her right
to hear Mass in private and shown herself to the population of
Edinburgh. Amongst her nobility, her more obvious opponents
and allies had been identified and she felt that she could ignore
her opponents, at least for the present. Knox she had met out of
curiosity and had been baffled by his approach. He was the
spiritual leader of a growing part of the population, but his
religion was meaningless to her. For Mary, religion happened
daily at Mass and was meant to comfort and soothe, not to
disturb and provoke. She, therefore, classified the Reformation as
a movement of undoubted importance to those who followed it,
but, provided the reformers showed tolerance to those of her
faith, it could be ignored as something which, quite simply, as yet
required her to take no action.

Mary's next move was to show herself to the people outside
Edinburgh, and on 11 September 1561, before the coming
autumn gave notice of her first Scots winter, she set out for
Linlithgow. Having left the palace eighteen years previously as an
eight-month-old child to seek refuge in Stirling, she had no
memories of the place. But now her father's glorious fountain
ran with wine as she returned, and some of her tapestries and
wainscoting had already been sent ahead. The palace had been
largely remodelled by James Hamilton of Finnart, a bastard son
of Châtelherault. He had visited Blois and Amboise on the Loire
and would have been introduced to François I's prize guest,
Leonardo da Vinci. Returning to Scotland he brought the latest

in French Renaissance design with him. Care had been taken to ensure that French noses would not be turned up, and instead of grunts of scorn there were gasps of admiration at the height of the palace and murmurs of approval at the elaborate carvings surrounding the windows and, most of all, the palace's position on a low hill sweeping down to an extensive loch. Across the water and beyond the River Forth, the hills of Fife lay on the horizon, giving a hint of the more northerly mountains. It was a totally different location from the Loire and, importantly, demonstrated quite clearly that there was a Scottish Renaissance style of building, which, though deriving from the Franco-Italian style, had a separate, equally elegant manner of its own. Mary rode through the town and banqueted with the awe-struck local gentry while the court relaxed on the loch-side. After two days, the royal entourage travelled the same route as had the messenger with news of her birth nineteen years previously, and Mary arrived in Stirling to lodge in the castle which had once been her second home.

Marie de Guise had arranged for French masons and plasterers to carry out James V's wishes and Stirling owed more to the French style than Linlithgow. The layout of the buildings and the furnishings of the royal apartments here were very similar to the Guise stronghold of Joinville – so much so that her three uncles started to feel almost at home and began to believe that their niece's future life was probably acceptable. A particular feature of Stirling was the profusion of carved wooden heads looking down from the ceilings, and today the outside bays carry a wide variety of carved figures, possibly one of Finnart himself carrying a broken sword. Even Brantôme now thought that life in Scotland was not so barbaric after all.

However, Mary narrowly escaped death when a lighted candle set fire to the curtains and tester of her bed while she slept. Since the curtains of the bed were drawn for the night, she awoke panicking and surrounded by flames. Knox, typically, interpreted the incident as a presage of her time in Scotland being followed everywhere by fire. A few days later, on 14 September, her 'devout chaplains' were to sing Mass in the Chapel Royal, where she had been crowned, but they were prevented by Argyll and Lord James, who 'so disturbed the quire, that some, both priests and clerks, left their places with broken heads and bloody ears. It was a sport alone for those that were there to behold it'. Given that Lord James himself had negotiated her peaceful celebration of Mass at Holyrood, this eruption sounds very like drunken hooliganism.

The court travelled on to visit the Earl of Rothes, who claimed that he lost some plate during the visit, and Randolph reports that wherever the royal party lodged they 'paid little for their meat'. At Perth there was a familiar civic ceremony during which the queen was presented with a heart full of gold pieces, accompanied, however, by the obligatory Protestant sermon condemning the errors of the Catholic world. The result of this on top of the various admonitions she received in Edinburgh was too much. Mary, predictably, fainted and had to be carried from her horse to her lodgings. Recovered, she received an honourable reception in Dundee before passing on to St Andrews, where a false rumour began that a priest had been murdered, and the dangerously devout Earl of Huntly proudly announced that he would 'set up Mass in three shires' if Mary would only command him. She briskly refused this offer, which strengthened her view that, if she wanted to keep peace in her kingdom, or even make herself acceptable to Elizabeth, the Earl of Huntly was a serious liability.

Mary's last stop before returning to Edinburgh was at Falkland Palace, the very palace in which her father had died. They had never met, and Mary had only a dutiful respect for him, although one hopes the royal servants ensured that she did not sleep in the room in which he died. At Holyrood there are no accounts of a Mass being said for him at his grave in the abbey. Mary did not regard him as a part of her family; hers was the house of Guise by emotion and occasionally the house of Stewart by right of dynastic succession. Mary returned to Holyrood on 29 September and, without the careful orchestration of the Guise uncles to ensure smiling and cheering crowds everywhere and at all times, she realised that while the Scots liked their beautiful young queen well enough, her popularity was yet to be fully established. Knox thought that all these towns had been 'polluted with her idolatry'. Scotland was not France.

Her return to Edinburgh was slightly marred by a proclamation from the magistrates, town council and deacons of the crafts in her absence declaring that 'all monks, friars, priests, nuns, adulterers, fornicators and all such filthy persons' must leave town within twenty-four hours on pain of whipping, branding on the cheek and exile. Mary, as was her right, promptly removed the Provost and bailies from their offices. Knox ranted hysterically, but on the advice of Lord James and Lethington new officials were appointed and the matter was allowed to drop.

What was not allowed to drop was Elizabeth's insistence on the ratification of the Treaty of Edinburgh, removing Mary's direct claim to the English throne, and Lethington travelled to London with letters of undying friendship, hopes for eternal peace between the kingdoms and a request that Elizabeth recognise Mary as her rightful heir. This was a slight shift of ground, but Elizabeth was having none of it and insisted on a full and formal ratification. When Lethington visited Elizabeth with the offer she told him bluntly, 'I looked for another message from your queen . . . I have long enough been fed with words', and he was told to increase the pressure on Mary to ratify. Mary simply ignored the request, not realising the long-term implications of her inactivity. The English historian Camden said of her claim to the English crown that from it 'flowed as from a fountain all the calamities wherein she was afterwards wrapped'.

Thomas Randolph met Mary regularly and repeated the ratification request but was met with polite deafness. He wrote, 'Her grace at all times gave me good words and those nearest about her, as Lord James and Lethington, say they are meant as they are spoken', and Randolph was admitted to meetings of the council. On 24 October, he noted that 'In the council chamber . . . she ordinarily sits most part of the time sewing some work or other'. Mary's enthusiasm for embroidery was clearly greater than her enthusiasm for affairs of state.

On 1 November she celebrated All Hallows Day with a sung Mass, the music probably by Robert Carver, but afterwards a priest was beaten up and a repeat proclamation that Mary's Mass was strictly private was expected. None, however, was forthcoming. A policy of political inactivity seemed to have taken over at Holyrood. Mary had now made her first tour of at least some of her country, had been greeted by the people of Edinburgh and was settling into her palace at Holyroodhouse. Hangings and carpets were being put in place and cooks were adapting to the needs of French tastes. Her horses were still in Berwick. Apart from the Marquis d'Elbeuf, her Guise uncles returned to France, the Duc d'Aumale taking the royal galleys while the Grand Prior and M. Damville travelled overland, both men carrying safe-conducts from Elizabeth.

Mary did manage to manipulate events to her own ends when on 16 November she awakened the palace by 'taking a fray [fright] in her bed as if horsemen had been in the close and the palace had been closed about'. The alarm was raised and armed guards searched the grounds but nothing untoward was found and everyone returned to bed. Suspicion fell on Arran, who was now rumoured to be coming to Edinburgh with a body of his Hamilton kinsmen to seize the queen, although, again, no such event took place. The final result was that Mary now had a personal guard of twelve halberdiers, which she would shortly double. Randolph, properly suspicious, was of the opinion that Mary had engineered the entire affair.

A few nights later another fracas disturbed the sleep of Edinburgh's inhabitants. Bothwell, d'Elbeuf and Lord John Stewart, Lord James's brother, had been partying with one Alison Craik, 'a good handsome wench', and some of her female friends. Unfortunately Alison Craik was also known to be Arran's 'hoor', and the pleasure-bound trio were met on their next visit with an armed gang of Hamiltons. D'Elbeuf ran to fetch a halberd, declaring that ten men could not restrain him from the battle, the town guard was called out, and Randolph watched the riot from the safety of his lodging; 'I thought it as much wisdom for me to behold them out of a window as to be of their company.' The result of this fracas was that Bothwell went into another temporary exile from Edinburgh and Arran fell further from Mary's favour.

A problem that would have to be faced was still occupying gossipy minds in Europe. Monsignor Commendone, a papal representative in Louvain, wrote to Cardinal Borromeo on 23 November, 'The queen should quickly make up her mind to marry someone who could uproot heresy from that kingdom.' The contemporary historian Marcus Merriman has commented, scathingly, 'Mary was never as significant as a person as she was as a dynastic entity.'

Pope Pius IV wrote to Mary on 3 December with a reminder of her duty as a Catholic sovereign. 'Persevere with the utmost constancy – remember how good Mary was,' he counselled her, referring to the reign of Mary Tudor, during which more than 300 Protestants were burned to death. For the moment at least, Mary was content to postpone dealing with these problems; the court settled down to enjoy itself and Mary concentrated on doing what she knew best.

On Leith Sands, half of the male courtiers dressed as women while the others wore masks to 'run at the ring', a game in which mounted horsemen tried to spear a cloth ring suspended on a pole. Then, in complete contrast, shortly after, Mary ordered the court to wear mourning on the first anniversary of François II's death. None of the Scottish nobles observed the order. During the Requiem Mass Mary herself approached the altar and offered up a large wax candle covered in black velvet. She was an enthusiastic participant in the more theatrical rituals of the Church, and on the Feast of the Purification of the Virgin, or Candlemas, the queen carried more candles than all the rest of the court. On Maundy Thursday, during Easter Week, 1567, Mary duly appeared in a simple white apron and cap to wash the feet of twenty-four virgins – the number of years in her age. To perform this humble act of contrition Mary was attended by forty-six courtiers.

The Scottish nobility were taking a great interest in the redistribution of the incomes seized from the Catholic clergy, much of which was now in lay hands. It would be impossible for these funds to be reallocated without some pain, and in December a method had been devised which was, at least, less painful than other systems. No allocation had yet been made for the payment of ministers in the reformed system or for a subvention to the queen, and a system of 'thirds' was put in place whereby one third of the seized wealth was paid to Mary, while she, in turn, used half of these sums to pay the reformed clergy. Her direct income from customs was £2,155 Scots, her thirds varied wildly from £2,033 to £12,700 Scots and her French income, when it was paid, was £30,000 Scots. Knox was furious that she had been allowed any money at all from the public purse, while Lethington, on his mistress's behalf, complained, 'the Queen will not get at the year's end enough to buy a new pair of shoes'. But for the first time the Scots had a sovereign who needed no direct taxation for her upkeep. Mary built no palaces and indulged in no foreign wars – she could not have afforded them without crippling taxes – but her domestic household remained nearly at Valois level at no great cost to the people of Scotland.

This was not a meagre court in a broken-down palace, but a glittering presence. There were fireworks, equestrian displays, banquets and balls, with Knox decrying her 'dancing of the purpose', that is to say 'lasciviously' – 'more like to the brothel than to the comeliness of honest women'. Randolph reported that he never found himself so happy and that the merry ladies were lusty and fair. Knox also objected to the balls continuing late into the night, but, since he never attended them and had probably never seen the decorum of minuets and pavanes, his vehement ranting is totally unjustified.

The Scottish weather may have occasionally limited, but not prevented, hawking and hunting, but indoors Mary had a range of diversions and played billiards and backgammon with her Maries. She also continued her Latin studies with the scholar and poet George Buchanan, although whether she made any significant progress is not known. Holyrood filled with music, and Mary played both the lute and the virginals, although Sir James Melville of Halhill acknowledged that she was not as expert a musician as Elizabeth. Mary maintained a professional court orchestra and her courtiers played lutes and viols as well as singing as a choir. However, it was a choir which lacked a bass singer, and a young Piedmontese valet in the service of the Savoy ambassador joined Mary's household to fill the gap. His name was David Rizzio.

All of Mary's furniture had now arrived from England – the inventory shows 186 items – and Holyrood was transformed into a vibrant echo of the great Valois palaces. Situated neither on a river nor on a cliff top, its place in open parkland was ideal for a court that took such pleasure in outdoor activities. Inside, the palace was lavishly furnished with more than a hundred tapestries and thirty-six Turkey carpets. Significantly, Mary's favourite tapestry was a set showing the French victory over Spain at the Battle of Ravenna in 1512, and this tapestry travelled with her wherever she went. Ten cloths of state decorated her thrones; there was even a crimson satin cloth to be used especially when the queen dined out of doors. To the end of her life her cloth of state carried the arms of Scotland and Lorraine. There were twelve embroidered bed covers, some worked with gold or silver thread, and twenty-four table covers, two of which were fourteen yards long. Even the cupboard linings were of damask.

For travel there was a litter covered with velvet and fringed with gold and silk, which was carried by mules. She had a coach as a novelty, although it was hardly ever used. During Mary's stay in France there were only three coaches in the kingdom, belonging, predictably, to Henri, Diane and Catherine. However, by 1563 there was a petition to prevent the use of coaches in Paris since there were then so many of them that they blocked the narrow medieval streets. The traffic jam had arrived. For normal travel, the court preferred to ride on horseback.

All of this was under the control of Servais de Condé, Mary's French chamberlain. Personally, she was served by her ladies of honour, three ladies of the bedchamber under Margaret Carwood, grooms, butlers, cooks, upholsterers, furriers and jewellers. Usually by Mary's side was la Jardinière, one of her fools, whose piquant remarks were often as near to the truth as any Mary heard. Another favourite fool whom Mary had brought from France was simply known as Nicola la Folle, although poor Nicola was sadly forgotten when disaster struck, and two years after Mary had fled to England the poor lady was still haunting the corridors of Holyrood. Mercifully, the Earl of Lennox noticed her plight, gave Nicola a pension and arranged for her return to France.

Closest to Mary were her Maries, with Mary Seton still arranging the queen's hair, often twice a day. In 1568 Sir Francis Knollys told Cecil that Mary Seton was 'the finest busker, that is to say, dresser of a woman's head of hair that is to be seen in any country'. Since the queen's coiffure often had jewels entwined in it, Mary Seton was helped by Mary Livingston, who kept control of Mary's jewellery. The inventory of jewellery had 180 entries including, touchingly, a cross of gold set with diamonds and rubies which Marie de Guise had pawned for cash to pay her soldiers during her war with the Lords of the Congregation. Mary redeemed her mother's pledge for £1,000 Scots. Mary also possessed one of the finest collections of Scottish pearls. A hundred years earlier Aneas Sylvius, later Pope Pius II, had claimed that Scottish pearls were the best in Europe. In all, her jewels were valued at 490,914 Scots crowns, or £171,810 in English pounds sterling.

Jewellers and dressmakers were always on hand, since dresses were often remade, jewellery reset or pearls restrung. In the case of Mary's cousin Elizabeth, this was sometimes done overnight so that each day a fresh Gloriana would emerge. In Mary's case, her wardrobe inventory tells of 131 entries, with even her pet lapdogs having blue velvet collars.

The rooms in Holyrood were elaborately decorated. There

was a ballroom 'glowing with heraldry', and a dining-room draped in black velvet with embroidered table covers, some with gold fleurs-de-lis, for gold and silver plates and Venetian glass to glitter in the light from four gilt candle-holders.

Objets d'art stood on side tables. There was a priceless piece of amber carved into a life-size man's head, along with busts of heroes and gods alongside the busts of a priest and a nun. It was a lavish Renaissance palace to stand beside any in Europe.

One of its greatest treasures was Mary's own library, which replaced the royal library burned by the Earl of Hertford during the Rough Wooings. There were 240 works catalogued under 'Greek, Latin and Modern Tongues', although there were very few Greek works, with Latin and French dominating. The standard histories and commentaries on Scripture were in Latin, while Modern Tongues held a few works in Spanish and Italian. The bulk of the collection of Modern Tongues comprised works in French by Marot, whose songs Mary had listened to, and, inevitably, the poetry of du Bellay and Ronsard. Ronsard's *First Book of Poems* had pride of place and there is no doubt that he was Mary's favourite author. She once gave him a plate worth 2,000 crowns inscribed 'A Ronsard l'Apollon des Français'. In prose there were two editions of *Amadis de Gaul*, Boccaccio's *Decameron*, the *Heptameron* of Margaret of Navarre, Ariosto's *Orlando Furioso* – a continuation of the adventures of Roland – and Rabelais's *Pantagruel*, but, oddly enough, no *Gargantua*. There were very few works in English – no Chaucer or Thomas More, only *The Rules of Chesse*, a Catechism and a copy of the Acts of Parliament of Mary Tudor. Peculiarly to us today, Mary did not possess a single copy of the Bible, but as a devout Catholic relied on prayer books, books of hours and lives of the saints.

The extent of this library has given Mary a reputation for great learning and devotion to study that may well be unfounded. After all, in our own day, Deborah, Duchess of Devonshire, was chatelaine of one of the finest libraries in private hands, but there is no evidence that she ever used it. Indeed, she is reputed to have said, 'I did read a book once, but I didn't like it and never read another.'

Mary's time spent with George Buchanan reading Livy seems to have been no more than an attempt to continue her schoolgirl studies. Buchanan was important to Mary, however, since he was the deviser of many of her court masques. These were much-loved fantasies, often based on the Classics. Courtiers took part and the masques were designed to astonish by stage effects as well as to idolise the sovereign. One, with the whole court including Mary herself dressed in black and white – as an echo of Diane – lasted for three days. Later masques featured shepherds, dressed in white damask and playing silver flutes, or Highlandmen in goatskins with their women in other animal skins. Mary's 'Highland' dress consisted of a long black cloak embroidered with gold thread.

Mary was enjoying herself thoroughly. An example of the lavishness of court entertainment occurred in February 1562, when Lord James was married to Agnes Keith. There was a religious ceremony in St Giles with a sermon from Knox, after which the bridal party walked down the High Street to the palace – without Knox – where they were greeted by Mary. She created Lord James Earl of Mar and knighted twelve of his gentlemen, prior to a banquet which was followed by fireworks and a masque. On the following day the party moved to Cardinal Beaton's old town residence in Blackfriars Wynd for another masque and banquet. The climax came on the third day when they returned to Holyrood for a last banquet and another masque. Mary drank her cousin Elizabeth's health from a twenty-ounce gold cup which she then gave to Randolph, who reported in May that Mary's court 'did nothing but pass the time in feasts, banqueting, masquing and running at the ring'. By springtime the weather allowed for an outdoor masque half a mile from the palace, by St Margaret's Loch under the romantic ruins of St Anthony's chapel.

This was a high-spirited court headed by a nineteen-year-old girl, surrounded by her four best friends, all with similar tastes, and full of physical energy. The masques gave them a golden chance for dressing up and, led by the tall Mary, the ladies of the court on occasions disguised themselves as Edinburgh housewives and, with much giggling, went unescorted into the town. In this case half of the fun must have been escaping from the halberdiers, chamberlains and servants who watched their every move. When Mary was *en travestie*, with her long legs exposed, Brantôme confessed that he could not tell whether she was a beautiful woman or a handsome boy, and this mixture of freedom and flattery was a heady brew for royalty usually closely confined by strict convention. Even for Mary's middle-aged courtiers her behaviour and the atmosphere it engendered were a welcome breath of fresh air from the weightier matters of the court. The Privy Council sat on 29 February and did not meet again until 19 May; Mary – who was in Edinburgh at the time – attended neither session. It seemed a carefree existence.

Mary had created a replica of life in the Valois courts of her childhood, devoid of all political cares. Her private court did not involve itself in the affairs of Scotland, and, apart from her allowance of the thirds, she cost the country nothing at all, while providing a permanent party at Holyrood. Provided she ensured that her close courtiers, especially the foreign elements among them, took no part in Scottish affairs, Mary would be tolerated as a highly decorative figurehead.

In May one result of being a beautiful and unmarried monarch manifested itself grimly. Knox, who had a highly efficient intelligence service, was informed that Arran and Bothwell had conceived a plot to ride to Falkland Palace, where Mary was in residence, seize the queen and murder Mar and Lethington, Knox's enemies. Knox was a zealot, but he was no fool, and he set about defusing the danger by sending for Arran, who now told him that when the queen was taken she would undergo a forced marriage to himself [Arran]. Arran also told Knox that he knew that Mary was secretly in love with him. Knox realised that the man was totally mad and counselled him to wait, instead of which Arran fled to his father Châtelherault's house at Kinneil, near Bo'ness, where he confessed all to the duke. Acting with prompt good sense for once in his life, Châtelherault locked his mad son in his room, but he failed to mount a proper guard, whereupon Arran wrote a letter, of unknown content, to be given to Mar by Randolph. He then escaped by the traditional method of knotting sheets together and climbing down them into the garden. Randolph received the letter when he was riding in Holyrood Park with Mary and immediately sent the news on to Mar that Arran and Bothwell were plotting treason. Both were swiftly arrested, although, as normally happened, Bothwell escaped to his castle, Hermitage. Arran, now totally mad, was locked up in Edinburgh Castle, where he believed Mary was in bed with him. He was shackled, but he sent for a saw to cut off his legs, and, since he was now no danger to anyone, he was eventually released into the care of his family, who kept him in more or less benign imprisonment with occasional releases until his death in 1606. In this instance, Knox had acted as a useful alarm bell on Mary's behalf.

More distant warning bells came from France, where the freedom of Huguenots to worship in their own way had suffered a severe setback. There had been an attempt at reconciliation between Catholics and Huguenots in October 1561 at the Colloquy of Poissy, but little had been achieved except for a very uneasy truce. Then, on 1 March 1562 at Vassy, a Huguenot village in the Champagne region, the Duc de Guise had found the Protestant villagers holding a church service contrary to the agreements in force. According to one source – and there are many versions of what took place – he sent some armed men to stop what he considered to be blasphemy and the dispute grew to an armed conflict ending with thirty dead Huguenots. This was a sufficient spark for the Huguenot Louis de Condé to start the first of France's seven Wars of Religion. Randolph was inundated by requests for passage through England by Scots volunteers eager to join the Huguenot cause, and over 1,000 Scotsmen left from Mary's kingdom to take arms against her uncle. Catherine de

Medici was forced to support the Huguenot Condé to prevent the power of the Guises becoming all-powerful, thus putting politics and her family before the interests of the Catholic Church. This misfired badly when Condé announced Catherine's support as a call to arms for all Huguenots, and she was forced hastily to backtrack.

Mary herself was brought into contact with Catholic Europe in July when the promised papal nuncio, Nicholas de Gouda, arrived in Edinburgh. He had travelled in secret, but knowledge of his presence leaked out and the street cry was for true followers of the Reformed Kirk to make 'a noble sacrifice to God and wash their hands in his blood'. Having travelled from safe house to safe house, he entered the capital on foot with a Scots priest, Edmund Hay, and was admitted into Mary's presence, with, according to legend, the four Maries guarding the door, an hour before the time that Knox was due to start preaching in St Giles. De Gouda spoke in Latin, which Mary claimed to understand, but, in fact, she had to rely entirely on Hay as a translator. De Gouda delivered an appeal from Pope Pius IV begging Mary to accept letters once again inviting the Scottish bishops to attend the Council of Trent, where the Counter-Reformation was being put into motion. Mary, according to de Gouda, was nervous throughout the interview and kept glancing at clocks, but assured him that she would rather die than abandon her faith. She also refused him a safe conduct and advised him 'to keep in some secret chamber'.

Later she accepted the letters, but John Sinclair refused to meet de Gouda who commented, 'Hoc de illo!' ('So much for him!'). After a meeting with the Bishop of Dunkeld, which he had to attend disguised as a banker's clerk, de Gouda's final conclusion was one of despair: 'Et haec quidem de Episcopis' ('And so much for the bishops'). Of Mary he said, dismissively, 'She has been nurtured in princely luxury and numbers scarce twenty years.' He went on, 'Although religion is most dear to her, yet, as I have said before, she cannot execute the holy desires of her heart, because she is alone and well-nigh destitute of human aid.' Needless to say, by 'human aid' he meant Catholic doctrinal advice.

Mary's wish for a face-to-face meeting with Elizabeth had now grown urgent. She had written to Elizabeth on 5 January 1562 offering to create a new treaty in favour 'of you and the lawful issue of your body . . . we shall present to the world such an amity as has never been seen'. Her letter was backed up by Lethington on the same day, asking Cecil to 'push forward' with the plan, and again, on 29 January, saying that Mary 'is a great deal more bent on it than her councillors dare advise her'. In Scotland the Protestants favoured the meeting while the Catholics were wary of it, and in England the Privy Council was deeply suspicious. Lethington was in London petitioning Elizabeth directly, while Elizabeth objected on the grounds of seeming to ally herself with a niece of the anti-Huguenot faction. Then, on 29 May, Mary met with Randolph, who tried once more to delay a meeting, suggesting postponement for a year since Elizabeth could not travel far from London during the French crisis. Mary, while 'tears fell from her cheeks', avowed that she would rather forfeit her love for her uncles than lose 'amity' with her sister. By mid June Elizabeth wrote to Mary agreeing, in principle, to a meeting. Mary was so overjoyed that she sent Elizabeth a heart-shaped diamond, and melodramatically showed Randolph that she kept Elizabeth's letter next to her skin. 'If I could put it nearer to my heart, I would.'

The lengthy memorandum by Cecil agreed a suitable midway meeting place between York and the River Trent between 20 August and 20 September. The terms of the meeting were that Mary must ratify the Treaty of Edinburgh, while Elizabeth was not obliged to discuss any subject offensive to her. Mary would pay her own costs – Elizabeth had a cautious way with money – and would change her Scots currency for English at Berwick, where she was not allowed to pass with more than 200 people in her train, although her final court could number 1,000, all of whose names would be sent to Cecil at least ten days before their departure from Scotland. Mary could hear Mass privately. It was a supreme civil servant's agreement with every 'i' dotted and every 't' crossed. Elizabeth sent Mary a portrait and the latter asked Randolph if it was a true likeness, to which he replied that she would soon be able to judge for herself. By 8 July Cecil had, through gritted teeth, prepared a safe-conduct for Mary, who was preparing her council for the journey south. Cecil had even taken possession of an elephant, which would carry an effigy of Peace for the inevitable accompanying pageant. Châtelherault claimed he had a diseased arm and could not travel, while Huntly, his Catholic suspicion of Elizabeth coming to the fore, had a sore leg and had to remain at home. Randolph believed neither of these schoolboy excuses.

Four days later, on 12 July, Protestant England went to war with Catholic France as the Duc de Guise strengthened his hand by hiring more 'Switzers' [Swiss mercenaries], and Catholic troops started to pour into France from Spain, Savoy and the Papacy. Elizabeth wrote to Mary, 'Our good sister will well understand and consider how unmeet it is for us and our councils to be so careless of the time as to depart from these parts.' Everything was cancelled, with both sides protesting that this was only a temporary postponement, but with everyone, apart from Mary herself, foreseeing that such postponements would be a regular feature of the plans for future proposed meeting.

Mary's reasons for wanting the meeting were politically naïve. If she were to become legally established as Elizabeth's heir, in default of Elizabeth having children of her own – Elizabeth was thirty – then Mary's children would inherit the crown of England to add to that of Scotland. Ironically, this was exactly what would, in fact, take place. Mary was relying solely on her personal charm to achieve Elizabeth's acceptance, since Elizabeth would gain nothing by the arrangement except peace and 'amity' on her northern border. Mary's charm was legendary, honed by Diane de Poitiers and applauded by the French court, but courtiers are by nature sycophantic, and, in reality, her charm had failed totally with the politically minded Catherine de Medici. Mary's chances of success with Elizabeth, backed by

156

Cecil, one of the sharpest political intellects in Europe, whose Treaty of Edinburgh she resolutely refused to sign, were precisely nil.

What Mary could not understand was that raising the subject of the succession meant discussing two completely forbidden subjects: Elizabeth's marriage intentions and, more dangerously, the inevitability of her death, of which she had an unreasoning horror. She had a deeply seated fear that she was the result of a union condemned by the Pope and that she would join her father Henry VIII in Hell. She had no wish to look at her winding-sheet before her time. Admittedly this fear only arose at moments of extreme depression, but discussion of the succession could bring it boiling to the surface.

As to marriage, Elizabeth had often said privately, 'First there is love, then there is marriage and then there is death,' and such was, indeed, her mother's cruel experience. Realising that a marriage was thought to be a dynastic imperative, she agreed to accept the suits of all comers, thus pleasing everyone, and then confused everyone by refusing them all. Her policy of acceptance and postponement worked superbly, although it sometimes infuriated even Cecil. This situation was exacerbated by the fact that she had only a dynastic, and probably loveless, marriage to contemplate. She had, as a young queen, been romantically in love with Lord Robert Dudley, her master of horse. At the time, Dudley was married to Amy Robsart, whom he neglected disgracefully, and the court abounded in gossip of the affair which ended in tragedy on 8 September 1560. Amy, alone in Oxfordshire, had given her servants leave to attend a local fair, but on their return they found their mistress dead at the foot of the staircase with a broken neck. On hearing the news, Mary is reputed to have said, 'The Queen of England is going to marry her groom and he has killed his wife to make way for her.' After his inevitable exile, Dudley, whom she nicknamed 'My Eyes', remained at Elizabeth's side until his death on 4 September 1588 – for Elizabeth, a vivid example of love ending in death.

It was never Elizabeth's intention to meet a woman, reputedly more beautiful than herself and whose claim to the throne did not involve divorces, to hold negotiations involving talk of marriage and death, none of which would hold any great political advantage. Mary lacked the political skills to understand this, but by August she realised that the meeting would not take place in 1563. A relieved Cecil was able to return his performing elephant.

Mary's usual reaction to being thwarted was to burst into tears and take to her bed, but in this case she decided on physical activity as a distraction, and on 11 August she started on a tour of her northern provinces. North of Perth, Scotland was virtually a foreign country for her. In the north-west of the country the Earl of Argyll ruled Gaelic-speaking lands from north of Dumbarton to the Outer Hebrides, while in the north-east the Gordon earls of Huntly ruled from Aberdeen to Inverness. Both men held their own sheriff courts and each regarded their own areas as private fiefdoms, with the Highlanders themselves feeling more loyalty to their own chiefs than to a monarch in Edinburgh whom they had never seen. The Lowlanders regarded the Highlanders as almost subhuman; an Act of the Scottish parliament in 1600 defined them as 'a barbarous and evil disposed people'.

Establishing herself in her Guisian splendour among these people was an excellent reason for her journey, and Mary knew that making a royal progress was one of the aspects of queenship at which she excelled. However, Lord James and Lethington felt that there was another more pressing reason for her journey. Mary would be visiting Aberdeen, the centre of the Huntly dominions. After their meetings in France and St Andrews, she already distrusted Huntly as a loose cannon whose devotion to the Catholic faith was liable to cause as much trouble as Knox's Protestant zealotry. But while Knox's ranting might lead to civil disorder, Huntly commanded a large private army. He had been in and out of prison for most of his life, captured by the English at Pinkie, imprisoned by Marie de Guise, and then released, and after Marie's death he had suggested to Mary in

France that he would lead a Catholic rising if she landed at Aberdeen. He was fifty years old, an excessive eater and drinker, hugely fat, with a wife whom it was rumoured maintained a private coven of witches. George Buchanan said of her, 'she was a woman with the passions and purposes of a man'. Mary was easily persuaded that Huntly should be brought into line if a legal reason could be found.

Conveniently, Huntly's third son – he had nine – Sir John Gordon, had just escaped from prison and fled to the refuge of the Gordon lands in the north. Sir John was a handsome, if hot-headed, young man whose various exploits had been indulged by his father. He had been cynically encouraged by Lethington and Lord James to believe that he was a suitable prospective husband for Mary and that she would favour the match. This was, in fact, an early version of the honey trap so beloved by the 'cold warriors' of the 1950s. The hope was that his excesses would lead to the need for his arrest and the extirpation of the Catholic Gordons. He fell neatly into the trap when he was imprisoned for his part in a street brawl which was the result of a complex feud between the Gordons and the Ogilvies, and in which he wounded Lord Ogilvie.

Ogilvie of Findlater had disinherited his own son, James, in favour of Sir John Gordon, having been told by his second wife that his son, young James, had made sexual advances to her. The rumour-mongering wife then openly became the mistress of Sir John, but did not deliver the land he had expected her to bring with her, whereupon he shut her up in a form of house arrest and abandoned her. He had now fallen for the false information that Mary was enamoured of him – they had only met in the social circumstances of the court – and believed that her favour would protect him. When he met the disinherited James Ogilvie in the street, a brawl ensued. Sir John had escaped from prison, which provided the perfect excuse for Mary's progress to combine pleasure with a punitive expedition, accompanied by the disgruntled James Ogilvie, and ride north in pursuit of the miscreant.

Mary travelled with a considerable entourage, holding privy councils in Perth on 14 and 15 August and then travelling on to Aberdeen. Randolph was a reluctant member of her party: 'The journey is cumbersome, painful, and marvellous long, the weather extremely foul and cold, all victuals marvellous dear.' Huntly stayed at his house, some three miles outside the burgh, and refused to come to meet Mary, sending the countess with her train of servants in his place; likewise Mary refused to go to meet the earl. The countess pled for mercy for her son, Mary refused and Sir John gathered 1,000 horsemen to harry the royal party en route for Inverness. Randolph was certain that Sir John's treasonable rebellion was directly on his father's advice.

A further bone of contention was that Huntly, without any royal authority, had styled himself as Earl of Moray since 1549. When Mary elevated Lord James to the earldom of Mar, she forgot that Mar was the hereditary title of the Erskines. She had, therefore, been obliged to transfer the title to Lord Erskine and Lord James had then, to Huntly's fury, been created Earl of Moray.

Mary reached Inverness on 11 September and, since it was a royal castle, demanded its surrender. The commander of the castle, Alexander Gordon, refused, but the local people rallied in support of Mary, and the castle, which had only some twelve or fourteen men as a garrison, was taken. Randolph reported, 'The captain was hanged and his head set up on the castle, some others were condemned to perpetual prison, the rest received mercy.'

Mary spent five days in Inverness meeting loyal Highlanders, whom she regarded as rather quaint pets who spoke Gaelic and who wore plaid kilts and cloaks. They were every bit as entertaining as the Highlandmen who had appeared in masques at Chambord, and Mary was delighted with them. Randolph told Cecil on 18 September,

In all these garboils [adventures] I assure your honour I never saw her the merrier, never dismayed, nor never thought that stomach to be in her that I find! She repenteth nothing but, when the lords and others at Inverness came in the mornings from the watch, that she was not a man to know what life it was to lie all night in the fields, or to walk upon the causeway with a jack and knapskall [leather jerkin and helmet], a Glasgow buckler [small single-handed shield] and a broad sword.

For the tomboyish aspect of Mary this was total bliss. She could, while surrounded by a strong personal bodyguard, pretend that she was leading armed men into war; she could be a warrior queen; she could be a hero of the romances; and she was completely removed from the intellectual manoeuvring of politics. It was play-acting of the most satisfying sort.

On her return to Aberdeen she did come close to actual conflict when Sir John attempted an ambush as she passed the River Spey, but Mary's forces were now augmented by loyal Highlanders. Sir John's support therefore melted into the woods. She sent trumpeters to call for the surrender of two Gordon houses, but both refused, and she was glad to be welcomed back into Aberdeen, where she was presented with a silver-gilt cup holding 500 crowns. Unfortunately, the city was not equipped for such a large royal incursion and Randolph's growing enjoyment of the campaign was spoiled by finding that he had to share a bed with Lethington.

Events were now moving towards a final confrontation with Huntly who, on 25 September, was ordered to return the cannon he held on the queen's behalf. Captain Hay returned from Huntly's castle of Strathbogie with amazing news. Huntly claimed he was appalled at his son's behaviour, and 'with many tears and heavy sobs' assured Hay that the cannon would be returned within forty-eight hours. The countess took Hay into her chapel, 'all ornaments and Mass robes lying ready upon the altar with cross and candles standing on it', and explained that Huntly was being persecuted for his adherence to Rome by the evil counsellors surrounding Mary. When this was reported to Mary and the council, she declared that she believed not a word of it and they all had 'much good pastime'. There were skirmishes on both sides and, on 17 October, Huntly was 'put to the horn', that is to say he was outlawed and his property declared forfeit while he was under royal command to surrender himself 'to the Queen's mercy'. When Mary's men approached the front of Strathbogie, Huntly escaped without his boots or sword over a garden wall at the back of the house, leaving the countess alone with only a few servants. Huntly now took direct action and advanced on Aberdeen with about 700 men while Lord James with the Earls of Atholl and Morton marched against him on 28 October with over 2,000, including arquebusiers. This was the Battle of Corrichie, which was all over in a few minutes. Two of Huntly's sons, the reprobate Sir John and his younger brother Kenneth, were taken prisoner and Huntly himself was captured on foot. He was placed on horseback and 'without blow or stroke . . . suddenly [fell] from his horse stark dead'. The *Diurnal of Occurrents* said that he 'burst and swelled', but it is more likely the cause of death was a stroke. His corpse was taken to the Tolbooth in Aberdeen, where it was embalmed before being taken to Edinburgh, where the embalming was repeated. In the case of treason against the monarch, the corpse would have to appear in court.

The troublesome Sir John was tried in Aberdeen and speedily executed, while young Kenneth was pardoned on account of his youth, as was George, the next son, although he was placed under house arrest at Dunbar. Sir John was, according to Buchanan, 'A handsome young man in the very flower of youth, more worthy of a royal bed than to be cheated by the offer of it.' His execution was a grisly affair, however, as the executioner botched the job and several blows were needed to sever the head, Sir John all the while declaring his love for Mary. Since he was executed for treason against the crown, Mary was obliged to attend, but she fainted and had to be carried to her lodgings. Subsequently, Mary had to attend the equally grisly trial of Huntly's now strongly smelling corpse in Edinburgh on 18 May 1563, when the open coffin was stood upright to face her on the royal throne. He was found guilty and the name of the Earl of Huntly was declared extinct, all his titles passing officially to

Lord James as Earl of Moray. Bizarrely, for a Catholic queen, the result of the raid was the destruction of the most powerful Catholic family in Scotland.

Back in Edinburgh, Mary started to relax, especially when good news arrived from France.

CHAPTER NINE

The dancing grows hot

🪶

In what would become known as the French Wars of Religion, the Guise family were in the ascendancy, occupying Rouen on 26 October 1562 after a long and bitter siege. Elizabeth's forces, who had been supporting the Huguenots, were driven back to Le Havre. At Holyrood Mary celebrated her family's victory with a series of balls leading up to what would be a splendid celebration of Christmas. Knox, disgusted with what he saw as the celebration of Protestant deaths, commented, 'the dancing began to grow hot'.

Mary should have realised that in her Protestant country celebrating the Catholic victories of her family over the Huguenots was provocative in the extreme, and, instead of simply dismissing her antics as an example of a nineteen-year-old girl's insensitivity, Knox rose to the attack in a passionate sermon in St Giles. In mid December he preached on the text of 'Oh, understand, ye kings, and be learned, ye that judge the earth', focussing on Mary's having 'danced excessively until after midnight'. This was delivered in the presence of some of Mary's bodyguard, who promptly reported the import of the sermon to the queen. Mary could have ignored the outburst but decided to try to swat the fly, and Knox was sent for.

This interview was more formal, with Lethington, Moray, Morton and some of the witnesses from the guard also present. Mary started with a long, previously prepared, harangue accusing Knox of attempting to bring her into disrepute with her people. Knox simply, although inevitably at length, said that she had been misinformed and that he had only condemned dancing when pleasure in the dancing came before the vocation – that is the Christian faith – of the dancers. He also condemned dancing to celebrate the 'displeasure of God's people' – in this case the Huguenots. Mary backed down and acknowledged that he differed from her uncles but that, if he had any quarrel with her, 'come to myself and I shall hear you'. His answer was that he was sure that her uncles were the 'enemy of God' and that she could hear him any day in his pulpit. He was now waiting on the court and thus was absent from his book. Mary and the courtiers were astonished at his apparent rudeness, and she replied weakly, 'You will not always be at your book,' and swept out. Asked by some of the court if he was not afraid to behave in this way, he shrugged and asked, 'Why should the pleasing face of a gentlewoman frighten me?'

Mary now put a cautious foot into not only the politics of Scotland, but also that of England and France. In Scotland she realised that the downfall of Huntly had worked to the personal advantage of Moray, whose power base became stronger. She started to exclude him from her council, using Lethington as her chief adviser and appointing Morton as chancellor. Then, at the end of December 1562, she gave Lethington instructions to offer her services to Elizabeth as an arbitrator between Guise and Condé – 'to see the matter amicably compounded and taken up to the reasonable and honourable content of both parties . . . we would be glad to become a mediatrix' – and also to ensure that Mary's claim to the throne was brought before the English parliament. How Mary, a Catholic Guise, ever thought she could be acceptable either to Condé or to Catherine is unfathomable, and, on the second point, she and Lethington must have known that Cecil was manoeuvring to put a Bill to parliament specifically excluding her from the succession. Then, in January 1563, she fired off three letters. The first, on 29 January, was to Montmorency, the constable, who had been taken prisoner by Condé at the Battle of Dreux in December, sympathising with him on his imprisonment. Since she did not write to Condé, who had coincidentally also been taken prisoner at the same battle, her powers as a 'mediatrix' are seen to be limited. The second letter was to her uncle, the Cardinal of Lorraine, who was about to visit Pope Pius IV, asking him to assure His Holiness that she would rather die than change her faith and give protection to heresy, and that it was her determination to reintroduce the Catholic faith to Scotland and obey all the recommendations of the Council of Trent. The third letter was to Pope Pius IV himself, reiterating what she had told her uncle. The latter two letters were written in Italian, a tongue in which Mary was not fluent, although she would have learnt some of it when a child; the letters would have been polished by David Rizzio, now no longer just a singer in the Chapel Royal but Mary's Italian secretary and soon to replace Raulet, her private secretary. However, throughout her time in Scotland Mary made only token efforts to accommodate the Catholic faith, although she was properly protective of the Catholics in Scotland and did make efforts to prevent their persecution. Her letters to Pius were merely empty promises. Her confusion of loyalties is evident and any idea that she could involve herself in international, or even local, politics can be seen to be absurd.

The advancement of Rizzio and the continued maintenance of Mary's largely French personal household made it obvious that her heart was not wholly in Scotland. Her close family were all in France and she claimed to think in French, not Scots. She also favoured the courtliness of France, with its florid compliments and meaningless flirtations, habits which her Scots council found unnecessarily exotic in their sovereign, while Mary longed for the artificial elegance of Chenonceau.

A reminder of those days came in the person of Pierre de Bocosel, Sieur de Chastelard, who had accompanied her from France as a page to Damville, returning to France early in 1562, and had now rejoined her court as she travelled south from Aberdeen. He was twenty-two years old and a grandson of the Chevalier Bayard, who had died in 1524, a legend of heroic knighthood under Louis XII and Francis I. Chastelard claimed to have abandoned his wife in France out of love for Mary and when he delivered a letter from

Damville he also gave Mary what an informer described as 'a book of his own making, written in metre, I know not what matter'. Chastelard was a minor adherent of the Pléiade and memories of her adored Ronsard came flooding back.

This was enough to trigger a torrent of unwisdom from Mary and she took Chastelard under her wing, giving him a sorrel gelding, which itself had been a gift from Lord Robert Stewart, and choosing him as her favoured dance partner, to Knox's horror. Knox was never an eyewitness to this and Mary probably wanted no more than to learn the latest steps from fashionable France, but she was duly reported by the royal gossip-mongers as having kissed Chastelard on the neck. To the Scots nobility it seemed as if any foreign popinjay could claim the queen's favours with more success than their efforts to drag her mind from her embroidery in her now rare Privy Council attendances.

On 13 February 1563 Mary was, for once, working late with Moray and Lethington, and her grooms of the chamber were making their routine search of the tapestries and cupboards in her bedchamber. To their total surprise Chastelard was discovered hiding under the bed and was promptly seized and ejected. Some reports have him in boots and spurs, which seems unlikely, but all agree that he was carrying his sword, so his purpose is unclear. He had no accomplices and no horses made ready, so if he was in riding dress ready to carry the queen away he was totally ill prepared; if his aim was seduction, why was he still fully dressed and armed, unless he was intending to rape Mary at swordpoint? The most likely explanation is that he had gone out of his mind, as had Arran, and had presumed that he would be welcomed into the royal bed.

After discussing the breach of security – where were her halberdiers? – the news was kept from Mary until the next morning, when she ordered Chastelard from the court which was en route for St Andrews. There, on the next night – St Valentine's Day – he once again breached security in spite of his banishment and burst in on Mary, who was half undressed and on the point of getting into bed, attended by only two of her gentlewomen. He begged her forgiveness and gave the feeble excuse that he had been 'heavy for want of sleep' and that Mary's bedroom had been 'the nearest place of refuge.' The result was not forgiveness but hysterics, and the understandable screaming brought the Earl of Moray to the room at once. Mary besought him, 'As you love me, slay Chastelard, and let him never speak word!'

Moray, thinking fast with a sword in his hand, hesitated. 'Madam, I beseech your Grace, cause me not [to] take the blood of this man upon me. Your Grace has entreated him so familiarly before that you have offended all your nobility, and now if he be secretly slain at your own commandment, what shall the world judge of it? I shall bring him presently to the presence of justice, and let him suffer by law according to his deserving,' he replied.

Mary went on, 'Oh, you will never let him speak?'

'I shall do, madam, what in me lieth to save your honour.'

Chastelard was swiftly removed to St Andrews, tried, found guilty of treason and went to the executioner's block on 22 February, eight days later. During his examination he confessed that he had 'attempted that which by no persuasions he could attain to' and as he laid his head on the block he recited Ronsard's 'Hymn to Death' and his last words were 'Adieu, the most beautiful and the most cruel princess of the world!'

The rumour mill went to work at once with a vengeance. Chastelard was thought to be a Huguenot and the Venetian ambassador to France was told that he was in the pay of a Mme de Courcelles, an ally of the new religion, and had been sent to blacken Mary's name. If that was true, why did Mary want him kept silent? A confession of Huguenot perfidy would work in favour of the Guises and confessions to that end have always been all too brutally easy to obtain. Mary knew that she had over-indulged his attendance and he misinterpreted the 'familiar usage in a varlet' to the point of madness. Four months previously, Mary had witnessed the bloody execution of Sir John Gordon as he proclaimed his love for her, and Arran was still chained to the floor of his dungeon in Edinburgh Castle, raving of his passion for her. The death of another man driven to madness was too much and Mary did not want to hear his protestations, but since he had attempted the life of the sovereign she was duty-bound to watch his beheading. Mary Fleming slept in her royal mistress's bedchamber from then on until Mary's marriage.

The plight of these three men tells us more than the florid tributes to her beauty by her French courtiers and poets. Mary Stewart was clearly very beautiful and equipped with an attractive charm beyond any of her contemporaries. Diane de Poitiers had skilfully used this charm to ensure that she was eulogised as a divine beauty. This gave her influence and power. Mary's natural beauty had been honed by Diane into a sometimes-fatal allure, but Mary never managed to take the next step necessary to use her attractiveness as a basis for power in a man's world. In fact, she had little in the way of policy nor any concrete ambitions beyond enjoying her courtly life. Her duties as a queen were to ensure the safety and wellbeing of her subjects and to protect and enhance the state of her kingdom, but she had no deep-seated ambition to do any of these. Her Privy Council attended to political matters on her behalf, she was guided by Moray and Lethington, and, with the stupid exception of her loss of face with Knox, she avoided any confrontations. Lethington, however, appointed Ruthven to the Privy Council, to the displeasure of Moray, who accused Ruthven of sorcery, a charge believed by many.

In April, Mary tried again to mend fences with Knox. She was staying at the castle of Lochleven, which is on an island in the middle of the loch, and is in some respects an idyllic setting, the loch being the habitat of its own delicious species of trout. For Knox it meant a thirty-mile ride followed by a boat trip to meet Mary in time for her supper. Knox was not offered any food, and, instead, she pleaded with him to lessen the strictures against Catholics in view of some recent arrests, but Knox reminded her that the extirpation of the Catholic faith was the law of Scotland and that, without such a law, the people might well act on their

169

own behalf. She, at once, asked, 'Will you allow that they take the law into their own hands?' Knox told her that true justice was God-given and temporal powers had no monopoly on it. Her response was to retire for her supper. Since it was now dark, Knox was left to stay for the night only to be summoned to meet Mary, who was 'hawking' on the mainland, at half-past five. The meeting took place on horseback with Mary now trying her charm on the ill-fed and sleep-deprived cleric. She merely gossiped about her nobility and asked Knox to use his influence in the marital squabbles of the Earl of Argyll. Knox promised he would try and rode back to Edinburgh, leaving both sides as far apart as ever.

Her sense of isolation had already been increased when on 15 March she was told of the death of the Duc de Guise; 'our fair faces at the court are greatly impaired. The queen herself marvellous sad, her ladies shedding tears like showers of rain.' Mary's uncle had been attempting to lift the Huguenot siege of Orléans when, in February, he was shot by Jean de Poltrot, a Huguenot assassin. Under torture Poltrot implicated Coligny – he would have named anyone he had been asked to – and the Guises now set out for revenge. The duke's death and the resultant loss of power for the Guises did relieve some of the pressure on Catherine, who was now free to negotiate the Peace of Amboise. This treaty once again allowed some limited freedom of worship to the Huguenots, and, for the moment, both sides drew breath.

Mary's reaction to the news of her uncle's death was, once the immediate tears had dried, to indulge in physical exercise, and she moved constantly around the country hawking and hunting. The Duc de Guise had, after all, been her surrogate father, guiding all her political decisions, and his death severed a major link with France for her. Mary was still only twenty years of age and already she was losing her family. Her husband, who had been her childhood friend and had lived under her undoubtedly loving protection, was already dead, as was her mother, now buried in France. Her uncles had returned to France, no longer available at her elbow with advice, and now one of them had died. On 19 April she poured out her despair to Randolph, telling him how destitute she was of friends and how she could see no end to her sorrow. Randolph, remembering his post as an ambassador, reminded her that she would find no better friend than Elizabeth.

Another blow would fall soon – the death of another uncle – but for the moment this was kept from the queen. The gloom in Mary's household was temporarily dissipated when Randolph delivered a letter from Elizabeth. Mary was hunting at the time and, to the displeasure of the Maries as well as of the other hunters, called the hunt to a stop while she read it then and there. The letter – of condolence – caused her to weep, this time for joy at the comfort she felt from her cousin's words of sympathy, and she 'incontinent putteth it into her bosom next unto her skin'. This was in full view of the now-stationary hunt. Mary was making a public demonstration of her love for Elizabeth, since she could be sure that Cecil would have at least one informer among her close servants. Whether her love was true or false was of no importance; it was only the public demonstration that was of significance.

It fell to Mary Beaton – the 'hardiest and wisest' of the Maries – to break the news of the death of François, the Grand Prior, in March 1563, and with these tidings, combined with those of the capture of the Cardinal of Lorraine by the Huguenot forces, the entire court went into a state of depression. 'Here we have not a little ado . . . I never saw merrier hearts with heavier looks since I was born,' wrote Randolph.

Mary's unlikely offer to mediate between England and France was now, with the Peace of Amboise temporarily in force, unnecessary, but Lethington had other matters to attend to while in London and in France. Mary's increasing feeling of solitude at last sharpened her resolve to settle one of the most important matters she had to deal with: her marriage.

Mary was a widowed queen with a private fortune and no children, and her choice of husband would cement a powerful alliance. In particular, Mary carried with her everywhere the double infections of religion and politics, thus any alliance she made was inevitably going to antagonise the rest of Europe. Her normal method of ignoring any unpleasantness or difficulty would now no longer work, and she moved increasingly in an atmosphere of fevered rumour as the suitability of all the candidates who had been considered after the death of François was being reconsidered. Knox said, 'The marriage of our queen was in every man's mouth.' Hints of Mary's ambitions came from Moretta, the ambassador from Savoy, who told de Quadra, Bishop of Aquila and Spanish ambassador to Elizabeth, that Mary was determined 'to marry very highly' and that Don Carlos of Spain was a possible candidate. Lethington, who was in London, suggested to de Quadra, with skilful subtlety, that a marriage to Mary's brother-in-law Charles IX of France was being considered. This suggestion gave Catherine de Medici apoplexy and she would have opposed the match with every fibre of her being, but Lethington's ploy worked with de Quadra. The prospect of Mary marrying into the French royal family for a second time prompted Philip to send messages of support for a marriage to Don Carlos. Without any prompting, the Cardinal of Lorraine started negotiations with Archduke Charles of Austria, son of Emperor Ferdinand I. The archduke brought the Tyrol as a dowry but little else, and was ruled out on the grounds of poverty. Don Carlos, who, while dangerously disturbed, had not yet descended into complete madness, was still the leading contender. This alliance would have greatly strengthened Philip's position as a threat to France or England, and the promise of Spanish arms in Scotland gave Cecil and Elizabeth nightmares. The Scots, who had recent experience of 'friendly' foreign armies on their soil, were equally hostile. Scotland was also a recently reformed Protestant nation with all the fervour of the convert and had no wish for a Catholic union, although the possible prospect of Mary sitting on a throne in Madrid, thus leaving Moray and Lethington free to govern the country themselves, was certainly appealing. The rumours of a marriage with Don Carlos reached

Knox, and in May 1563 he made his feelings known in a sermon to the nobility: 'This I will say, my Lords – note the day and bear witness afterwards – whensoever the nobility of Scotland, professing the Lord Jesus, consent that an infidel (and all papists are infidels) shall be head to your sovereign, so far as in thee lieth, ye do banish Christ Jesus from this realm; ye bring God's vengeance upon the country, a plague upon yourselves, and perchance small comfort to your sovereign.' Knox admitted that this sermon managed to antagonise even his own supporters, and he was unsurprised to be summoned to Holyrood to meet with Mary, who was in a 'vehement fume'.

Mary was in the full fury of a wronged Guise: 'never prince was handled as she was . . . I offered you presence and audience whensover it pleased you to admonish me; and yet I cannot be quit of you. I vow to God, I shall be revenged!' At this point her chamber boy was sent for more napkins to dry her tears as 'the howling, beside womanly weeping, stayed her speech'. Knox told her that he was guided by God and was not master of himself, while Mary got quickly to the point. 'What have you to do with my marriage?' She repeated the question and, when Knox remained silent, then asked one question too many, 'Or what are you within this commonwealth?' Knox's answer to this has been taken as a cornerstone of Scottish democracy: 'A subject born within the same, Madam. And albeit I be neither Earl, Lord nor Baron within it, yet has God made me (how abject that ever I be in your eyes) a profitable member within the same.' This was too much altogether for Mary, who plunged into hysterical rage and was rendered unable to speak. John Erskine of Dun tried to calm her; Lord John of Coldingham offered his support but to no avail; and Knox was asked to withdraw and was eventually sent away.

By summoning Knox, Mary had exposed herself to insult and a lecture on the principles of democracy without achieving anything at all. It was a childish outburst, similar to her trial of strength with Mme de Parois – although in that case she won a petty victory – and an attempt to maintain her authority as a queen, resulting in a total loss of face. Neither Diane de Poitiers nor Catherine de Medici would have behaved so childishly.

On 24 June 1563 ambassadors arrived from Eric XIV of Sweden, a Protestant, but he was peremptorily rejected. Eric was the son of Gustavus Vasa, who had unified Sweden while driving out their Danish oppressors. He had declared the entire wealth of Sweden to be his personal fortune and had married Katarina of Sachsen-Lauenburg, thus founding a powerful Scandinavian dynasty, although one in search of Western European ties. The ambassadors were also keen to strengthen trade ties in the Baltic, where Swedish trade was under threat from Russia, and such formal ties would have meant increasing prosperity for Scottish merchants, already looking across the North Sea for more profitable Scandinavian links. However, Elizabeth had already rejected Eric, and Mary regarded him as an unsuitable cast-off from a distant and barbaric country. She had not the slightest interest in trade and the plight of merchants was of no concern to her. The ambassadors returned empty-handed. Eric's behaviour became erratic – he even attempted to murder a cabinet minister four years later – but he married a Swedish noblewoman, Karin Mansdotter, in 1568. The next year, he was deposed by his brother, Duke John of Finland, and Scotland's opportunity to reinvigorate the commercial opportunities of the Hanseatic League was lost.

Almost immediately after the departure of the Swedish ambassadors, Mary set about using the last of the summer weather before the Scottish winter set in to confine the court indoors. The most enjoyable form of outdoor exercise was a royal progress, so the entire court, including a reluctant Randolph, visited the west and south-west dressed up as their idea of Highlanders. Their activities followed the usual pattern: Mary showed herself to the admiring population, visited the local gentry and, of course, hunted and danced enthusiastically, freed from the cares of politics. She was making contact with parts of the population unknown to her, many of whom had never seen a monarch before. The personal loyalty of the lairds to their queen was never in question in spite of the religious differences between them, but this loyalty was no more than a formality and could be suspended at any time.

Lethington remained in London, where Elizabeth, with the help of her excellent intelligence service, watched the continuing marriage negotiations with close interest. Her own marriage plans were as vague as ever and so, without an heir to her throne, the question of the succession became paramount. If, as seemed likely, Elizabeth died childless, then the direct Tudor line would end. But, over a century earlier, after the death of James IV at Flodden, his widow, Margaret Tudor, sister of Henry VIII, had married the Earl of Angus and given birth to Margaret Douglas, who became the Countess of Lennox and mother of Henry, Lord Darnley. Darnley was, therefore, a Stewart descended from a Tudor. Margaret Douglas's husband, Matthew Stewart, Earl of Lennox, was descended, albeit by a female line, from Mary, daughter of James II, whose bloodline also included the house of Hamilton in the persons of the Duc de Châtelherault and the now intermittently insane Arran. But Queen Mary, as a Stewart descended from a Tudor, was Elizabeth's obvious heir, and her son, if she had one, would inherit the throne of England. If Mary married Don Carlos and had a son by him then Spain, Scotland and England would all be ruled from Madrid. Lethington was given a clear and forceful message from Elizabeth and Cecil that such a marriage would make an enemy of England, and instructions were sent to Randolph to tell Mary three things: first, that there should be love between husband and wife; second, that Mary's choice should be liked by the people; and, last, that her husband would not interfere with the amity between England and Scotland. This was no more than a gentle warning. Lethington was also asked to 'infer by consequence that no such mighty marriage [as Don Carlos] may be sought for'. Cecil and Elizabeth were now treating a sovereign monarch as a refractory child.

On 1 September 1563, Mary and her retinue arrived at the imposing castle of Craigmillar, just outside Edinburgh, where she could have had no idea that Elizabeth's instructions were waiting for her. The royal party dismounted inside the courtyard and walked up the steps to the great hall, Mary's servants turning left to prepare her accommodation, while she herself went to dine. After dinner Mary met Moray, Lethington and Randolph, who delivered his mistress's ultimatum. Mary at first appeared not to understand, but asked for a written memorandum clearly setting out Elizabeth's intentions. The marriage question now became a protracted game of who would blink first. In November Elizabeth showed a little more of her hand and recommended a further three things: Mary should marry 'some fit nobleman within the island', and declared that 'no child of France, Spain or Austria will be acceptable'. Finally, she now openly threatened that 'her [Mary's] right and title to the English Crown will depend much on her marriage'. In case Mary was veering towards him, Elizabeth let it be known that she would not reject a suit from Archduke Charles on her own behalf. She had no scruples over making promises that she had no intention of keeping.

Most of these machinations were of little or no interest to Mary, who hunted, hawked and rode through the beauties of her kingdom. She expected nothing from a marriage but a dynastic alliance sealed by her giving birth to a prince, and her first marriage had demonstrated that, had she been able to produce a dauphin, her usefulness would have been over. She was in no hurry to carry out what she knew all too well was her expected function as a broodmare. However, when she returned to Edinburgh, she found that Knox had been busy in her absence. He had composed a private prayer to be said after grace with his own family: 'Deliver us, O Lord, from the bondage of idolatry. Preserve and keep us from the tyranny of strangers.' There is no doubt that those of Mary's household remaining at Holyrood had breached the agreement made with Lord James when they celebrated Mass in her absence, not in the Chapel Royal but more openly in the abbey. A mob, led by Patrick Cranston and Andrew Armstrong, burst in and broke up the proceedings on 15 August. On receipt of this news Mary impetuously ordered their arrest for 'forethought, felony, hamesucken [showing violence to a householder in his own home], violent invasion of the palace and spoliation of the same'. Knox, equally impetuously, wrote to his principal supporters to 'make convocation' in Edinburgh and oppose Mary's continued celebration of the Mass. The trial of Cranston and Armstrong was adjourned and eventually forgotten, but Mary judged Knox's letter to be treasonous and he was again summoned to Holyrood on 21 December 1563 where he and Mary met for the last time.

On this occasion, Knox had arrived with so many supporters that they spilled out of the audience chamber, down two flights of stairs and filled the inner court of the palace, while the entire Privy Council took their seats across the table from the bare-headed Knox. They then rose and applauded as Mary came in with 'no little worldly pomp', flanked by Lethington and the Master of Maxwell, who sat on either side of her and offered advice into alternate royal ears. To everyone's astonishment she took one look at Knox and burst into laughter saying, 'That man made me weep and wept never [a] tear himself. I will see if I can make him weep.' Knox was shown one of his letters, confirmed his authorship and was asked to read it aloud. Mary then asked her council if they did not think it treasonous. To her horror, Ruthven pointed out that, since as minister of St Giles, Knox regularly summoned convocations to pray and hear his sermons, such a letter could not be held to be treason. Mary briskly overruled Ruthven and demanded that Knox answer the charge of accusing his sovereign of cruelty. Knox denied this but told her that the cruelty was done, not by her, by rather by the 'pestilent papist' who had inflamed her against pure men. Mary warned him that he was not now in the pulpit, but he replied that he was now in a place where he was obliged to speak the truth, thus placing Mary in the invidious position of having brought the forthcoming tirade on her own head. As Knox continued, citing lengthy Biblical examples of preachers being persecuted although God-inspired, Lethington shook his head and smiled in admiration of this virtuoso display of Knox's training in argument by medieval Schoolmen. He then whispered in Mary's ear that she had lost the argument. Mary blustered but Lethington told Knox, 'You may return to your house for this night.' A vote of the council was taken and, overwhelmingly, Knox was exonerated. Mary swept out of the room in a violent temper.

It had been foolish of Mary to attempt the trial, probably against the advice of Lethington, who was probably delighted for Mary to see the results of ignoring his counsel. There had never been any reason for Mary to instigate the confrontations, and had she carried out her policy of non-intervention in the affairs of Scotland more rigorously, she would not have caused the resultant hardening of reforming attitudes.

The year 1563 was one Mary probably wanted to forget, and immediately after her twenty-first birthday she took to her bed with a pain in her right side, remaining incommunicado over the Christmas and New Year celebrations. She claimed she had caught a cold 'being so long at divine service' but Randolph, supported inevitably by Knox, believed it came from over exertions in late-night dancing.

On the marriage question, Randolph reported the following private conversation on 21 February: 'Sometimes she likes to hear of marriage. Many times the widow's life is best; sometimes she may marry where she will, sometimes she is sought of nobody.' Randolph asked that 'at least she will have compassion on her four Maries, who for her sake have vowed never to marry if she be not the first'. In fact, Mary Livingston was already married and two other Maries would marry before their mistress.

Mary's comments here are revealing for a queen who had, so far, avoided any of the responsibilities of power. Mary lived in a time when women were largely defined by their condition as wives. There were, certainly, three outstanding exceptions in Catherine de Medici, Diane de Poitiers and Elizabeth I, but, by and large, unmarried women were only of interest as possible wives, and the relative importance of wives was directly related to the importance of their husbands. Widows, on the other hand, were presumed to have performed their duties to society and

178

could be left to lead their own lives. The fact that they were often financially independent and vigorously set about interfering in the lives of their younger relatives marks them out as being outside the normal strictures of society. Mary felt that she had no need to make any further effort to establish her own personality, but could simply enjoy the rest of her life dancing, eating and hawking.

In addition, Mary's wish to 'marry where she will' was strictly proscribed by her position and religion, but since she had from childhood accepted the advice of others she now had no real sense of her own will, except in a petty and wayward manner.

Mary's regret that she was 'sought of nobody' is no more than childish self-pity. At least three European rulers had offered themselves and she could have accepted any one of them. But Mary had seen many of her household marry for love. They had been wooed, courted and adored and their stolen kisses had led them to love and marriage. Mary had been scrupulous in attending their weddings and the christenings of their children, always enjoying these low-key domestic celebrations. Clearly she envied them their freedom to behave as private people; there have been very few monarchs who have not envied the lack of responsibility enjoyed by their subjects. It is always easy to envy the poor from the comfort of a velvet chair in a palace.

It is true that Mary did not choose to be a queen – few queens ever do – but she enjoyed the privileges that accompanied her position. There have been many queens who have acceded to the throne unexpectedly – both the Queen Elizabeths who came to rule in England and Great Britain are good examples – and have made brilliant monarchs, but they accepted the necessary sacrifices uncomplainingly. Mary avoided royal responsibilities but continued to enjoy her state and fondly attend the weddings of her ladies-in-waiting. She was still waiting for her Amadis, her knight errant, to spirit her away on his pure-white charger.

One marriage that did take place did not please her at all. Knox had been a widower since 1560, and on 1 March 1564 the banns of marriage between him and Margaret Stewart, the daughter of Lord Ochiltree, were read out. She was seventeen and Knox was fifty, and there was something of a scandal. More importantly, however, the young bride was distantly related to Mary – 'of the blood and name'. The queen 'stormed wonderfully'.

However, matters of her own marriage lay quiet until, later in March that year, Lethington told Randolph that a further offer for Mary's hand had been received from the emperor, who was prepared to finance his son, the archduke, to the tune of 2 million francs during his lifetime and 5 million after his death, to 'live with her in Scotland [bringing as personal retainers] as few in number as shall seem good to her council'. Lethington added that the emperor expected an answer by the end of May. This was confided to Randolph as 'a great secret', and Randolph suspected that this increased offer was no more than a gambit to force Elizabeth to make a decision.

It was a sufficient stimulus for Randolph to 'declare at good length what [he] had received in writing from her majesty'. It does seem possible that Randolph had been given his instructions some time before and had been told to judge when the time was right to deliver them. He carried them out on 30 March 1564, when Mary was at Perth, a town which she loathed because it was thought to have been Knox's sermon in St John's Church that had actively launched the Scottish Reformation. Here Mary broke off a Privy Council meeting to receive Elizabeth's ambassador. Elizabeth now openly recommended that Mary should marry Lord Robert Dudley.

Mary was stunned by the news, saying that Randolph had 'taken her at an advantage' since she had rather expected news of peace between Elizabeth and France. This was mere procrastination while Mary gathered her thoughts, at first insulted that her cousin should recommend marriage with a commoner – whom Mary had previously called 'Elizabeth's groom' – while Randolph speculated that such a union might bring about eventual possession of the throne of England. Mary brushed this aside, 'My respect is what presently be for my commodity, and for the contentment of friends, who I believe would hardly agree that I should imbase my state so far as that!' Mary then made Randolph repeat the offer to the few of the Privy Council who were still sitting. Formally, she then posed the question to him of what Elizabeth thought would happen to Mary if Elizabeth had children and Mary had made a commoner King of Scotland. Randolph could only reply weakly that these were matters he was sure Elizabeth had foreseen and would deal with correctly. Mary, now with Argyll, Moray and Lethington, went in to supper 'merry enough' and Moray asked Randolph if he could not persuade Elizabeth herself to marry rather than bother Mary when she was hungry for her supper. Privately, Moray favoured a marriage with Lord Robert, who was a personal friend, and being seen as the sponsor of Dudley's bid for the Scottish crown would be greatly to his advantage.

After supper Lethington told Randolph that all three statesmen had conferred and they would like to discuss the matter further with some suitable person – the Earl of Bedford was suggested – at a future conference at Berwick; 'Nothing shall be omitted in this sovereign's part towards amity.'

Why Elizabeth made such an offer is a mystery. There can be no doubt that she tended towards love for Dudley, though never physically, and she possibly thought that she could control Mary through him. Although Dudley would have obeyed Elizabeth as his queen, he was ambitious and arrogant, so as a puppet ruler in Scotland he would have been disastrous. Also, to offer Mary a husband who was not only a commoner but also a man many saw as a cast-off lover was insulting in the extreme. But he was an available Protestant and Elizabeth was now desperate to bring the matter to a conclusion. One of the great procrastinators of history, she was always very keen to tie up other people's loose ends.

Elizabeth did tie up one loose end, much to the horror of Cecil. The Earl of Lennox had been in exile in England for twenty years, and Elizabeth made approaches to Mary to allow his return. Cecil's horror was that Lennox's wife was a Catholic, only recently released from the Tower for stirring up disaffection, and, above all, that his son, the twenty-year-old Henry Darnley, was a prime candidate not only for Mary's hand but even for the crown of Scotland itself. Darnley's own religious beliefs are difficult to pin down, in that his father had worked for Henry VIII and Protector Somerset, while Margaret Douglas, his mother, was firmly Catholic and had carefully raised her son to be acceptable to English Catholics. Perhaps the best that can be said of Henry Darnley is that he swam with the tide of advantage. In April 1564 Elizabeth granted Lennox a passport to travel north.

Mary was now hinting that she was indifferent but would probably not marry Lord Robert. Instead she favoured Darnley, and to demonstrate her lack of concern, in July she left for another royal progress, this time to Argyll and the Gaelic-speaking north-west. It was also part of her personality that she did not react well to being criticised or being given instructions, and was very likely to rush impetuously in the other direction. Lethington did not accompany the royal party but remained in Edinburgh: 'In the place I occupy, I cannot be spared for voyages, nor do I like it (for it lacks not peril) unless to some good end.'

Elizabeth, realising that she may have set light to a trail of gunpowder, panicked and now refused to allow Lennox to travel, causing Lethington to write to her on 13 July assuring her that the rumours of hostility in Scotland towards Lennox were exaggerated – Lennox had been hated since his flight to England in 1544, and that, for his part, Lennox's return was 'no great matter up or down'. Elizabeth's fears extended to the dreadful possibility that if Mary predeceased Darnley, then his mother, Lady Lennox – Elizabeth's current bête noire – might succeed her.

Catherine de Medici now made two surprising offers: first, that Elizabeth should marry Charles IX; and second, that Mary should marry his brother, the Duc d'Anjou. Both offers were refused, but the French ambassador, Michel de Castelnau de la Mauvissière, was predictably enchanted by Mary, whom he found a 'woman in the flower of her youth'. Elizabeth was in despair as to how she could move events forward and wrote to Cecil on 23 September, 'I am in such a labyrinth that I do not know how to answer the Queen of Scotland . . . find something good that I may put in Randolph's instructions.' Mary now, atypically, took some action on her own behalf and despatched her own ambassador to Elizabeth to pour oil on the increasingly troubled waters. He was Sir James Melville of Halhill, a gentleman of her bedchamber.

Melville was twenty-eight years old and had served Mary as a page for four years when she was only six, passing into the service of the French constable, Anne de Montmorency, and then serving with Casimir, son of the Elector Palatine. Melville returned to Scotland on 5 May 1564 and met Mary at Perth, just after she had heard of Elizabeth's offer of Lord Robert Dudley. Needless to say, Melville was entranced by her: 'I thought her more worthy to be served for little profit than any other prince in Europe for great advantage.' She promptly sent him to England on 28 September 'with instructions out of the queen's own mouth'. His memoir gives verbatim accounts of conversations with Elizabeth, but the historian Gordon Donaldson warns that Melville probably reports 'not what they actually said but what they thought afterwards that they might have said'.

In his first conversation with Elizabeth, which took place in French, since Melville had been so long abroad, he 'could not speak [his] own language so readily', she told him that she was determined to end her life in virginity but was keen for Mary's marriage with Lord Robert, whom she was about to create Earl of Leicester and Baron Denbigh. Melville was asked to stay and witness the ceremony, which took place in Westminster Abbey with Elizabeth breaking from the solemn ceremony to tickle Leicester's neck. Melville acknowledged that he was a worthy subject, but Elizabeth pointed to Darnley, who, as the nearest prince of the blood, had carried the sword of state, and said, 'Yet you like better of yonder long lad.' Melville assured her that no woman of spirit would like such a person, more like a woman – beardless and lady-faced – than a man. Darnley was polished, urbane and effeminate beyond the point of fashion. His flagrant bisexuality had earned him the name of the 'great cock chick'. Melville did not tell Elizabeth that he had a secret instruction to procure from Lady Lennox permission for Darnley to visit Scotland, ostensibly to accompany his father south again.

Elizabeth reiterated her desire to stay a virgin, and Melville claimed that he told her, 'Madam, I know your stately stomach. You think, if you were married, you would be but Queen of England; and now you are King and Queen both. You may not endure a commander.'

Elizabeth continued to flatter Melville, showing him Mary's portrait in her private collection of miniatures. But Melville noticed that on the top of the pile was one wrapped in paper inscribed in Elizabeth's own hand 'My Lord's Picture' – it was a miniature of Leicester. She showed Melville a 'great ruby, as big as a tennis ball' and he suggested that she might send it as a token of her love. After a sharp intake of Tudor breath Elizabeth said that if Mary followed her wishes she might have the ruby and the man, but in the meantime she would send a diamond. Next day Melville was asked which woman was the fairest, and he replied that Elizabeth was the fairest queen in England and Mary was the fairest queen in Scotland. Asked to choose between them by a now increasingly acid Elizabeth, Melville admitted that Mary was lovely but Elizabeth was whiter, due to generous applications of poisonous white lead make-up. Mary was taller, so Elizabeth said that was too high. What were her favourite exercises? Melville was now improvising desperately and told Elizabeth truthfully that Mary had just come from hunting in the High-lands and, less truthfully, that she liked reading good books and histories. She also played on the lute and virginals. Elizabeth, who prided herself as a musician, demanded to know if Mary played well, and Melville risked everything by replying the she played reasonably well, for a queen. That night, after dinner, he was taken for a stroll by Lord Hunsdon whereby – quite accidentally, of course – he was able to overhear Elizabeth playing the virginals. Elizabeth summoned Melville and spoke to him in German, but since her German was not perfect she switched to Italian, which Melville did not speak. This late-night linguistic contest was a draw.

Melville's next engagement was to take a private boat trip with Leicester himself, who told him that the marriage proposal had first come from Cecil and thus had left him powerless, 'For if I had appeared desirous of that marriage I would have lost the favour of both queens.' He was clearly unhappy at being used as a marriageable chess piece by the woman he loved.

The following day Melville returned to Scotland showered with presents – a gold chain for himself from Cecil and Elizabeth's diamond for Mary, while Lady Lennox outdid both with a ring with a 'fair diamond' for Mary, an emerald for her husband, a diamond for Moray, a watch set with diamonds for Lethington and a ring with a ruby for his brother, Sir Robert. Melville concluded that Lady Lennox was a very wise and discreet matron. Randolph said she was 'more feared than beloved of any that know her'. In Scotland her husband had been welcomed to parliament and moves were afoot to restore his lands and incomes to him. Meanwhile he ingratiated himself with Mary, playing at dice with her and diplomatically losing a crystal set in gold.

As had been proposed, Lethington and Moray met Randolph and Bedford at Berwick, but the meeting achieved nothing. Cecil continued to push Leicester's case, while Mary dithered. She was simply waiting for events to catch up with her, but these were moving very slowly. From the politician's point of view, both sides hesitated for different reasons: if the marriage took place (and it was now clear to all that a marriage would take place) and then foundered, no one wanted to be seen as the architect of disaster. Lethington disliked the idea of Leicester because he was English and Moray disliked Darnley because he would favour the Catholics if it was to his advantage. The two lords were 'in great agonies and passions'.

Cecil still hoped for a marriage with Leicester and wrote himself a memorandum: 'Seeing they two [kingdoms] cannot be joined by marriage, the second degree to make them and their realms happy is that Mary marry whom Elizabeth favours and loves as her brother . . . she has already begun to advance him both to honour and livelihood and therein means not to deal sparingly with him.' Here there is a hint that Leicester's dowry might be lavish.

The log-jam showed signs of moving when, astonishingly, on 12 February 1565 Randolph noted that Cecil and Leicester had both encouraged the granting of a licence for Darnley to come to Scotland. He came first to Berwick, then by way of Dunbar and Haddington to Edinburgh. He was well spoken of, although ill equipped, and Randolph had to lend him a pair of horses.

When Melville described Darnley to Mary he differed from the opinion he gave so diplomatically to Elizabeth. Now he had told Mary that Darnley was 'the lustiest and best proportioned long man . . . of a high stature, long and small, even and erect, from his youth well instructed in all honest and comely exercises' and his physical attributes seem to bear this out. In his portrait, painted three years previously, he is certainly slim and elegant, but his face has a narcissistic look and his arched eyebrows look superciliously on viewers whom he seems barely to tolerate. He had been given the Renaissance education thought necessary by Margaret Lennox, and, with a royal marriage as a prospect, he undertook the role of suitor with great style.

Darnley crossed the Forth to lodge in the Laird of Wemyss's house in Fife, where on 17 February 1565 he met Mary and was 'well received of her'. Mary Stewart's second husband had arrived in Scotland.

CHAPTER TEN

Yonder long lad

≥₭

Darnley's arrival in Scotland set tongues wagging immediately: 'If she take fantasy to this new guest, then shall they be sure of mischief.' His father, Lennox, was to be reinvested with his lands in the west, especially the castle of Dumbarton, which had been taken from him during his English exile. Châtelherault was furious at his reinstatement. This had the effect of sealing Châtelherault's uneasy alliance with Moray, who now saw the possibility of a Lennox on the throne as king with heirs to succeed him, thus driving Moray's claim to the crown further away: 'If he match here in marriage it shall be the utter overthrow and subvention of them and their houses.' But, for the moment at least, Moray was friendly towards Darnley. Randolph continued to press Leicester's suit, but with no great hope of success. Mary had quite firmly rejected the idea of marrying Leicester, and, in order to calm some objections to Darnley, she reissued her proclamation of 1561 assuring the Scots that she had no intention of disturbing the religious status quo. Having heard that the Mass was 'planted again' in the north, Mary wrote to the participants asking them not 'to do any such thing as was feared by the Protestants'.

Mary may also have been influenced in this by a small but touching event which she experienced while in Fife, en route to meet Darnley.

At her coming to the Laird of Lundie's house, who is a grave ancient man, white head and white beard, he knelt down to her and said, 'Madame, this is your house, and the land belonging to the same, all my goods and gear is yours. These six boys . . . and myself will wear our bodies in your grace's service . . . but Madame, one humble petition I would make unto your grace in recompense of this – that your majesty will not have no Mass in this house as long as it pleased your grace to tarry in it.'

His request was granted and 'he thought himself twice happy to have the queen in his house, and that it should not be polluted with idolatry.' This was a vivid example of the obedience due – and freely given – by the common people to their sovereign, but not to the sovereign's religion.

As a continuation of the de-Frenchification of her court, Mary also sent her private secretary, Augustine Raulet, back to France with his wife, who had been mistress of Mary's household. Raulet is one of the shadowy figures who surrounded Mary. He had been in the service of the Cardinal of Lorraine and had come from France with the royal household, but had risen to hold the keys to Mary's private safe, and Mary, fearing that her private codes had been compromised, dismissed him. Prior to his departure, his own private papers were seized. He would later return to serve her again.

Mary's first meeting with Darnley was formal and strictly supervised, and Mary's first impressions were positive. She told Melville that he was 'the best proportioned long man that she ever saw'. Ten days later Mary was back in Holyrood, where David Rizzio was now her private secretary and was reputed to be 'he that works all', much to the discontent of the Privy Council.

The troublesome Earl of Bothwell had broken his exile and returned to Scotland, muttering insultingly against Mary that she was a 'Cardinal's whore' and that he would never receive favour at her hands. Darnley followed Mary to Edinburgh and attended a sermon by Knox before attending a ball at Holyrood, where he was invited by Moray to dance a galliard with the queen. For the first time in her life Mary danced with a man who was taller than herself, and the prancing display of 'yonder long lad' in the galliard delighted her, as did the quieter moments of formal greeting in the dance when she, at last, was able to look up to her partner. The first move in Darnley's mating game had been played successfully.

However, the elegance of his carriage and dancing was largely for the benefit of the male courtiers, although Darnley realised that if he married Mary he would, at some time, have to breed, and he was quite prepared to undergo the experience as a somewhat distasteful part of his necessary duty. He had, in fact, no interest in anything but his own personal pleasure, and, like Mary, had no wish to apply himself to the practicalities of government.

In April the court moved to Stirling, where Darnley fell ill with 'measles' and was, although kept in isolation, sent 'reversions' from Mary's table. His symptoms seem to have had few similarities with those of measles, and the word was probably used as a euphemism for something more serious. During remissions from 'measles', Darnley and Mary played bowls against Randolph and Mary Beaton; Randolph and Beaton won and Darnley paid the debts with a ring and a brooch set with agates 'worth fifty crowns'. Darnley, supported by his father, Lennox, was spending more than either could afford on his suit. By May, Lennox had run out of money and had to borrow 500 crowns from Lething-ton. He was not yet confirmed in his repossession of the stronghold of Dumbarton.

Cecil was becoming extremely anxious, and on 28 April he sent Nicholas Throckmorton, formerly the English ambassador to France and known to the Scottish queen, to Edinburgh with a long memorandum, the essence of which was, 'For pity's sake, try to find out what's going on.' From Stirling, Randolph reported that Mary's care for Darnley in his illness was causing great disquiet and that Moray was expected shortly to add his voice to the general discontent. This discontent spread to Edinburgh, where a priest was put in the pillory and pelted with eggs. A Catholic mob retaliated, and the Provost interrupted his supper to prevent riot spreading. The priest was clapped in irons in the Tolbooth and Mary was informed. She ordered his release to 'the great offence of the whole people', and a Privy Council was called to meet in Edinburgh and punish the Provost. Moray and Argyll refused to attend.

In London, Elizabeth was now panicking and informed her Privy Council that the Darnley marriage would be 'unmeet, unprofitable, and perilous to the sincere amity between the two queens'. Throckmorton was instructed to repeat this to Mary and to tell her that she could have the pick of the aristocracy, except Lord Darnley. Cecil added that if she were to marry Leicester, then the question of the succession could be arranged. There was now an open split in Mary's Privy Council, with Lethington, Atholl, Ruthven, and Rizzio supporting Mary's decision against Châtelherault, Moray and Argyll, who opposed the marriage. Moray's vehemence was such that Mary suspected that he 'would set the crown upon his own head'.

Since the nobility were totally preoccupied with the marriage question, the Border lairds took the opportunity to raid each other. On 3 May, Randolph reported 'daily slaughter between the Scotts and Elliots – stealing on all hands – justice nowhere'.

Mary's intransigence was simply the result of her obstinate refusal to accept the advice of her council or to read public opinion. Once she was told that the Darnley marriage was inadvisable she set her mind firmly – and childishly – to overrule everyone. After all, she was the queen, and a queen's wishes were not to be ignored, but rather to be instantly indulged. To marry Darnley was to thwart Elizabeth's desires for a greater unity between the nations and to reject the richest suitors in Europe – even the rejected Archduke Charles would have brought her a large chunk of Austria, plus his father's millions – to pursue a marriage with an unstable, but charming, pauper well below her in rank. To compound matters, on 8 May, Mary had a private audience with Moray and demanded his instant signature to an agreement to the marriage, although since he was not yet twenty-one, he could not yet be granted the crown matrimonial. 'Hereupon between them rose great altercation, she gave him many sore words.' She gained agreements to her marriage from Spain and France and sought the inevitable permission from Rome to marry her cousin. As a result of her own arrogance Mary now ruled a divided kingdom. Most of the nobility had tolerated her waywardness, but all were now forced to choose: for or against the marriage; for or against the queen.

Elizabeth had received reports from Randolph – 'the queen in her love is transported and Darnley grown so proud that to all honest men he is intolerable' – and she was putting on a brave face with regards to the proposed marriage. On 3 June, Paul de Foix, a French ambassador, found Elizabeth playing chess. She assured him that Darnley was of no more importance than a pawn on her board. This was bravado, as the following day her Privy Council resolved 'to establish the succession of both crowns in the issue of the marriage. The papists would devise all means within this realm to disturb the estate of the queen and consequently to achieve their purpose by force.' It was decided to fortify the frontier – 'forebearing breach of peace will suffer' – to put Lady Lennox in 'some place safe' – in other words, she went back into the Tower – and to recall both the Earl of Lennox and Darnley. There were even plans to enter Scotland 'with hostility' if these moves failed, and once again Elizabeth sent Throckmorton to sound out Mary's intentions and voice her own grave reservations. Two weeks later Throckmorton arrived at Stirling and, after a considerable amount of unsatisfactory delay, was admitted to Mary's presence with most of her Privy Council in attendance. He delivered Elizabeth's objections, which Mary brushed aside, saying that Elizabeth, having objected to any foreign suitors, had given her a free choice of any British nobleman. 'About this we had sundry disputes,' reported Throckmorton, and he was dismissed with a fifty-ounce gold chain to add to the plate he had received in August 1561. He afterwards said, 'I do find this queen so captiv'd either by love or cunning (or rather to say truly, by boasting and folly).' He added, 'The queen is so far passed in this matter with Lord Darnley that it is irrevocable and no place left to dissolve it except by violence.'

That Mary now had no intention of listening to anyone at all was made clear when, about an hour after Throckmorton's departure, she created Darnley Knight of Tarbolton, Lord Ardmannoch, Baron Rothesay and Earl of Ross. Darnley was in a foul temper throughout. His temper arose from the fact that Mary had promised him the dukedom of Albany, a purely royal title, and now withheld it until she heard how Elizabeth reacted to her rejection of Throckmorton's embassy. When Ruthven told Darnley of the delay, he went mad with petulant fury, launched himself at Ruthven, brandishing a dagger, and had to be physically restrained. After the ceremony the new earl took to his room in a sulk and began drinking himself into unconsciousness.

Mary, having boxed herself into a corner, behaved with more passion towards Darnley 'than is comely for any mean person' and 'all shame is laid aside'. Mary had abandoned all her regal state, her beauty had left her and her 'cheer and countenance had changed into I know not what'. Admittedly Randolph, the author of these statements, was totally opposed to the marriage, but he does present us with a recognisable picture of a spoilt 22-year-old girl experiencing her first love affair, knowing that she is infatuated with a totally unsuitable man who will alienate all her friends and eventually cause herself serious damage, yet determined to press ahead whatever the cost.

On 9 July 1565, Mary, now in the full knowledge of the damage her actions would cause, married Darnley secretly – with only about seven witnesses – and the couple went to bed in Lord Seton's house nearby. This was, in fact, no more than a formal betrothal or handfasting, and since Mary was rightly cautious as to public opinion, it probably took place in Rizzio's apartments in Stirling Castle.

Three days later, on 12 July, Mary did try to ameliorate the situation by issuing another proclamation to prevent the spreading of rumours among 'the wicked, ungodly and seditious', assuring her Protestant subjects that her non-interference with the Reformed religion would continue. In concentrating on reassuring the people about the security of their religion, she showed herself to be unaware of, or simply ignoring, a major point of objection to her alliance with Darnley and the house of Lennox. Any foreign marriage would have antagonised all the countries apart from that of her future husband, but could probably have been made acceptable to the Scottish nobility, if not to Elizabeth. But by marrying the heir to the earldom of Lennox she had, at a stroke, reawakened the bitter rivalry between Lennox and the house of Hamilton, headed by Châtelherault, as well as incurring the hatred of her half-brother and his Stewart line, who would now virtually be removed from the line of succession. None of the lords whose interests in any way conflicted with those of Lennox, and there were many – Argyll, Rothes, Glencairn – could tolerate such a match. Instead of sowing the seeds of discontent in the monarchies of Europe and grave disquiet in London, Mary was blindly preparing the ground for a general domestic uprising.

Religion was also the urgent concern of the General Assembly of the Church of Scotland which, on 26 July, besought Mary to suppress the Mass throughout the kingdom. Mary procrastinated, declaring that she would 'press the conscience of no man' and hoping that they would not 'press her to offend her own conscience'. The assembly was not happy with her answer but delayed any further action for the moment, which was all that could be hoped for in the now rapidly deteriorating situation. By 20 July Darnley had finally been created Duke of Albany, and the banns for the marriage were read in St Giles. On the same day, the Bishop of Dunblane arrived in Rome to seek the papal dispensation, but with it or, more likely, without it, the arrangements were made for the couple to marry in a public ceremony on 29 July 1565. The day before, letters patent were sent to the heralds telling them that from henceforth Darnley would be styled the 'King of this our kingdom'. This action, without the consent of parliament, 'was a ground for the people to repine, as though it infringed their liberties, to proclaim a king without their consent'. Sally Mapstone, in her essay 'Scotland's Stories', has said that in Scotland, 'kingly rule is predicated on the congruence of its interest with those of the political community'. Knox and his colleague Christopher Goodman had preached this philosophy with vigour, even to Mary in person, but the Valois kings held their power to be God-given and Mary followed their example blindly.

The wedding took place in the royal chapel at Holyrood, at the early hour of five in the morning of 29 July 1565, Mary wearing a mourning gown of black with a black hood. This did not signify grief, but the fact that Mary was a widow and dowager queen. Lennox and Atholl took her arms and led her to the altar, then left her there while they brought in Darnley. The ceremony then took place according to the Catholic rite, during which she received three rings, the middle one a 'rich diamond'. The couple then knelt and prayers were said over them by John Sinclair, Dean of Restalrig and Bishop of Brechin. Darnley did not stay to hear the nuptial Mass, but briefly kissed his wife and left to await her in her chamber. After the Mass, Mary was expected publicly to allow the congregation to undress her and to change her mourning dress for a more festive one to signify a happy life to come, but she curtailed this ceremony and only allowed every man near her to remove a pin from her dress, thus performing enough of the symbolic act. She then retired to her husband.

This was all a very far cry from the lavish ceremony of her marriage to the Dauphin. Neither Moray nor Randolph attended, and although there was dancing and largesse, many people present, including even some of the Maries, dreaded to imagine what the outcome might be. The next day, at nine o'clock in the morning, heralds proclaimed Darnley King of Scotland, and declared that the marriage – which had gone ahead long before the papal authorisation had been received – was fully 'solemnised and complete', and also that henceforth all royal correspondence should in the names of 'both their majesties'. Lennox called out, 'God save his grace,' but the rest of the nobility were silent and the country held its breath. Moray, rather glumly, hoped that the royal couple, being youthful, might be tractable.

Elizabeth sent one John Tamworth to intercede in the now-increasing split in the loyalty of the nobility, notwithstanding 'her strange proceedings in her own realm', and 'friendly and neighbourly to admonish her'. He was told to refuse to accept Darnley as Mary's husband and to remind him and his father that the Countess of Lennox's treatment in the Tower depended on their behaviour. Elizabeth was deeply regretting her endorsement of Darnley as a match for Mary.

Before Tamworth could arrive, Moray was summoned to appear before Mary within six days and to explain himself. The nobility were summoned to meet Mary at Linlithgow on 24 August with supplies for a fifteen-day military campaign. To no one's surprise Moray did not appear and was 'put to the horn'; meaning that he was now beyond the law, and could be apprehended or even killed by anyone in the queen's name, while his lands and possessions were forfeited to the crown. In quick succession Rothes and Kirkcaldy of Grange followed Moray as outlaws.

When Tamworth arrived – delayed by 'evil horses' on the way – he received a predictably chilly response – 'she was marvellous stout' – as well as the inevitable assurance that there would be no change in religion; he was also informed that the plight of the Earl of Moray was an internal matter for Scotland. Mary also issued a threat to Elizabeth: 'I am not so lowly born, nor yet have I such small alliances abroad, that if compelled by your mistress to enter into "practices" with foreign powers, she shall find them of such small account as she believes.' This was repeated more diplomatically in a letter by Darnley and Mary to Elizabeth, assuring her of their amity and asking for an Act of Parliament acknowledging their right of succession, after Elizabeth and her heirs, to the throne of England, as well as placing any further children of the Countess of Lennox third in line. It was an arrogant rebuff for Elizabeth's tampering in the affairs of Scotland. The unfortunate Tamworth, having been told to ignore Darnley, refused a passport signed by him and was captured at Dunbar by Lord Hume and locked up in his Border castle for two or three days. Mary and Darnley found this childishly amusing and endorsed Hume's action.

On 15 August, Moray, Châtelherault and Argyll summoned Glencairn, Rothes, Boyd and Ochiltree to join them at Ayr in the south-west to be armed and in the field within five days. The battle lines for civil war were being drawn up.

Possibly to reassure the burgesses of Edinburgh that their religion was in safe hands, Darnley let it be known that he would attend St Giles on 19 August, and a throne was specially built for him to sit head and shoulders above the congregation. The construction meant that he would be seated almost face to face with Knox, and when he preached a sermon based on Isaiah, Chapter 26 – 'O lord our God, other lords besides thee have visited thee . . . the Lord cometh out of this place to visit the iniquity of the inhabitants of the earth upon them' – it was clear that Knox was making a direct personal attack on Mary and Darnley. The whole congregation watched Darnley, on his throne, gritting his teeth harder and harder until, at the end of a long, though precisely argued, torrent of invective, he stormed out of the church in a white-faced fury. The *Diurnal of Occurrents* says he was 'crabbit', a virtually untranslatable Scots word that combines the sourness of the crab apple with the anger of a trodden-on crab. On his return to Holyrood he refused the meal that was awaiting him, leapt onto his horse and spent the afternoon hawking with his close companions.

One week later, Mary, with Darnley at her side, followed by 600 arquebusiers, 200 spearmen and towing six pieces of field artillery, rode out of Edinburgh towards the Hamilton strongholds in the west to 'dunt' Moray. Mary wore a steel cap, carried a 'pistolet' and was reputed to be wearing a 'secret defence on her body', probably a mail shirt under her bodice, while Darnley glittered in a decorative gilt breastplate. This was the start of what has been named the 'Chase-about Raid'. Since the two opposing forces never met, but marched and countermarched all over the southern Lowlands of Scotland, the campaign, if it can be called such, was more of a progress by both sides· than a serious conflict.

The Privy Council of 6 September guaranteed – unnecessarily, as it turned out – that all the families of the slain would be recompensed. Interestingly, at that council meeting, Darnley, who did not attend, is referred to not as king but as Lord Darnley.

He and Mary were enjoying themselves vastly. It was the same kind of autumnal weather she had experienced on her punitive expedition against Huntly, and all her chivalric fantasies were being fully fed.

Mary, having gone to Glasgow with her now-considerable force, allowed Moray and the disaffected lords to ride into Edinburgh on 30 August with 1,200 horse. They occupied the capital but not the castle, the governor of which fired off a salvo of artillery to announce his impregnability and loyalty to the queen. News came that Mary was now returning to Edinburgh and the artillery fired into the town, to the annoyance of Knox, who was preparing his sermon – 'the terrible roaring of the guns' – causing the rebels, who were now saying that all they wanted was an assurance as to the safety of the Reformed faith, to realise that the citizens would now shortly turn against them. Moray and his forces left hastily for Lanark at the extraordinary hour of three in the morning, before riding south-west again to Dumfries.

From Glasgow, Mary issued a call for total mobilisation and demanded that the rebels surrender to her at St Andrews on 11 September. Atholl was now appointed Lieutenant-General of the North, replacing Argyll; Lennox was given the western shires from Stirling to the Solway; and Bothwell, after a catalogue of adventures – trials, acquittals, exiles, and an escape from pirates – was appointed Lieutenant-General of the Middle Marches. Meanwhile, Mary wrote to Philip II of Spain assuring him as the champion of the Catholic faith that she was unbending in her devotion, and asked him to assure her of his support.

197

Shortly after her wedding Mary had freed Lord George Gordon from his house arrest at Dunbar and restored him to the title of Earl of Huntly. Since he saw Moray as having been responsible for the death of his father and brother, he was all too keen to join an avenging force. Mary now had three highly competent commanders in Atholl, Bothwell and Huntly. There was a dispute as to the position of commander-in-chief, with Lennox eventually becoming commander of the vanguard and Bothwell and Darnley uneasily sharing command of the main force. This had caused 'jars' between Mary and Darnley, and given such divisions, it is fortunate this force was never required to fight a battle. Mary and Darnley both felt that they could easily be the targets for a popular revolt and the French ambassador Mauvissière, was told that they feared that they might be killed. He was asked to transmit a plea for help to Elizabeth.

Ignoring Edinburgh, Mary progressed north-east into Fife, then across the Tay to Dundee, which refused to pledge its loyalty, and Mary, who was now seriously running out of money, had to pay the burgh £2,000 Scots for its support. She returned to Edinburgh, borrowed 10,000 merks – £6,667 Scots – and wrote to Elizabeth reaffirming her love and friendship. She also asked Elizabeth for 3,000 soldiers, a request which was politely ignored. The rebels were also writing to Elizabeth requesting men and money: to defend their religion, their lives and their heritages. Elizabeth, sensibly, suggested a cessation of hostility and a general pardon. With Bothwell and Huntly now united in their purpose – Bothwell would marry Lady Jean Gordon, Huntly's sister, in the Canongate Kirk, Edinburgh, on 22 February in the following year – the royal army marched south to face the rebels in Dumfries, arriving to find an empty town: the rebels had fled to Newcastle. On 18 October, Mary returned to Edinburgh from 'the said raid in which nothing was done'.

For Mary this had been an opportunity to make a royal progress and to show herself to her people, complete with breastplate and helmet. But instead of the obligatory cheering crowds, 'upon their approach the country people slipped from

198

them'. Royal popularity in Scotland was conditional; loyalty was something to be earned, and, once gained, its continuation had to be justified. Diane de Poitiers knew that a show of humility from time to time reaped rich rewards, but humility and Mary Stewart were strangers to each other.

Speculation now flourished as Europe wondered if Mary might use her seeming victory to reinstate the Catholic religion. Mary and Darnley had sent an embassy to Philip II asking for help to restore Catholicism and to supplant Elizabeth in England. Philip immediately informed the new Pope of what might be afoot. Both men realised that the request was simply to establish a position in the event of an all-out war with England breaking out. Pope Pius V, however, erroneously believed that the raid had been a Catholic–Protestant war, and he praised Mary on 10 January: 'We congratulate your Highness on having by this notable fact commenced to dispel the darkness which has brooded for so many years over that kingdom and to restore it to the light of true religion – complete what you have commenced.' Mary, wisely, for once, ignored the advice.

The satisfaction Mary felt at the end of this gallant fiasco reflected itself in a burst of affection for Darnley, who had acted the part of her chivalric companion with enthusiasm. By 31 October Randolph reported a rumour of royal pregnancy – 'upon tokens I know not what'.

The rebel lords were now gathered in Newcastle, hoping against hope for help to arrive from Elizabeth, and to this end Moray left for London, having written to Cecil that he would not have started the rising had it not been for Elizabeth's promise of support. The English Privy Council immediately wrote to Moray begging him not to come, but he was determined, and on 23 October he, with the Abbot of Kilwinning for moral support, met Elizabeth in person. He had committed an unforgivable sin in forcing Elizabeth to make a decision, and her response was predictably thorough.

On this occasion Moray had to address Elizabeth on his knees and be humbled before all of Elizabeth's court, as well as the representatives of France and Spain. Moray was told that the interview would take place in French as a gesture to the ambassadors. He said his French was not sufficiently good, but Elizabeth insisted. He was forced to admit that Elizabeth had never moved the lords to oppose Mary in her marriage or, even more damningly, to resist her by force of arms. After his confession he was allowed to stand while she told him bluntly, 'Now you have told the truth; for neither did I, nor any in my name, stir you up against your queen; for your abominable treason might serve for example for my own subjects to move against me. Therefore pack you out of my presence; you are but unworthy traitors.' She then told the penitent pair that she would intercede with Mary for mercy on their return and they left with their tails between their legs. They had narrowly escaped the Tower. The eighteenth-century historian Richard Keith described Elizabeth's behaviour as 'a piece of refined deceit as is likely to be met with in any age or court'.

Châtelherault agreed to go into exile for five years and left for his duchy in France. The other rebels were summoned to the market cross in Edinburgh on 18 and 19 December, where they were pardoned and told to appear before parliament on 12 March 1566 for final sentencing.

Mary was convinced that she had kept the affection of the common people – she always was convinced of it after a royal progress – and that she had won a victory over the nobility. But this sense of security was illusory since the nobility's resentment of her high-handedness in the case of her marriage grew and she now had to rely more and more on her own personal servants for advice. Lethington, who had maintained a very low profile during the Chase-about Raid, was sidelined in favour of David Rizzio. She was also forced to see that Darnley was beginning to behave with more and more arrogance, as well as abandoning the court in favour of the male brothels of Edinburgh, or 'hawking', 'having in his company gentlemen willing to satisfy his will and affections'. He had not yet been invested with the crown matrimonial, and although the Privy Council allowed his signature on documents, his name always came to the right of Mary's, thus giving her precedence. In spite of his demands to be treated as King of Scotland, eventually the council, despairing of his prolonged absences, had a facsimile signature made on an iron stamp, called a 'sign-manual' and the royal seals were given to Rizzio. Mary did travel to meet Darnley on 3 December 1565, and it was noticed that she had now abandoned riding for a horse litter, thus reinforcing the rumours of her pregnancy, although 'it was perceived that her love waxed cold towards him'. On Christmas Day 1565, Darnley attended Matins and Mass for the first time, 'devoutly upon his knees; though she herself the most part of the night sat up at cards and went to bed when it was almost day'.

Also on that day Randolph noted a change in the available currency. To celebrate the royal wedding a new silver coin had been introduced, a 'ryal' worth about thirty shillings Scots. It showed Darnley and Mary facing each other, with their names engraved around the rim – Henricus et Maria D(ei) Gra(tia) R(ex) et R(egina) Scotorum – giving precedence to Darnley. This coin was now withdrawn from circulation and the new ryal had the names reversed.

In early February 1566, the Seigneur de Rambouillet, an ambassador from France, arrived in Edinburgh and Darnley was invested with the Order of St Michel, France's highest order of chivalry. The embassy included one Thornton, who had been sent by Beaton, the Scots ambassador in France, with a private communication for Mary from her uncle, the Cardinal of Lorraine. Mary was told of a Catholic league formed by France, Spain and the Empire and advice from the Cardinal was for Mary to add her signature to it. She signed the bond 'in an evil hour', but she must have known that if knowledge of her endorsement of such a league became public then Elizabeth would have had to act and Mary's throne would have been in grave danger. Rizzio, wrongly assumed to be an agent for the Pope, was also enthusiastic about the Catholic League and, stupidly, let his support be known.

Lethington was now rightly fearful of the factions developing within the court, blaming Mary for her advancement of Rizzio in place of other of her council members. Lethington was also in love with Mary Fleming and Randolph chided him that, having been pushed aside by Rizzio, he now had the leisure to go mad with love.

Dissent among the nobility – 'to whom office but not fidelity was transmitted by birth' – was growing. George Douglas told the Earl of Ruthven that Darnley felt he had been abused by Rizzio and that it had been as a result of Rizzio's intervention that Mary had 'stayed her hand' in awarding him the crown matrimonial. Not having been crowned meant that there was no machinery for a royal succession 'in his body' if Mary were to die first. Darnley also felt, correctly as it happened, that Rizzio despised him as his intellectual inferior and as a king in name only, who had excluded himself from most of the affairs of state and had never attended the Privy Council. To some-one with Darnley's conceit and arrogance, this was fuel for passionate hatred, a hatred which fuelled a plot to assassinate Rizzio.

The principal plotter was Patrick Ruthven, who was forty-six years old, but rendered a virtual cripple by inflammation of the liver and kidneys. He was also a known necromancer and warlock. He agreed to join the plot to remove Rizzio, provided Darnley agreed to pardon the exiled rebels, who would then swear allegiance to him as King of Scotland. As king he would then use his influence with Elizabeth to free the Countess of Lennox from the Tower. Morton, with 'a head well turned for matters of cunning', planned to seize Rizzio in his quarters at the palace, but Darnley persuaded the plotters to take him as he attended a private supper with the queen – private suppers and games of cards from which Darnley, petulantly, felt excluded. Darnley, in a sadistic display of power, also wanted Mary to see that he was a principal in the murder and since the supper room was small she could not fail to notice his presence. A date of 8 or 9 March was agreed. Morton was convinced that only one way remained to extirpate the Catholic faith and put the Reformation on a secure footing. That one way was to murder Rizzio, forestall the meeting of parliament, imprison Mary until the birth of her child, entrust Darnley with the nominal sovereignty and restore Moray as head of the government. Lennox was sent to London to advise Moray to prepare for his return and, unbelievably, a 'bond' encompassing these plans was drawn up and signed by Darnley, Ruthven, Morton, George Douglas and Patrick Lindsay. The Chase-about exiles signed the bond in Newcastle on 2 March 1566. It quite precisely detailed the grim intention that the murder should be carried out in the palace 'in the presence of the queen's majesty'.

How word of this plot came to Mary's ears so late is a mystery since on 13 February Randolph wrote to the Earl of Leicester, 'I now know for certain that this queen repenteth her marriage; that she hateth him and all his kin. I know that he knoweth himself that he hath been a partaker in play and game with him; I know there are practices in hand contrived between father and son to come by the crown against her will. I know that if that take effect which is intended, David [Rizzio], with the consent of the king, shall have his throat cut within these ten days.' Leicester must have been glad Mary had chosen not to marry him.

On 19 February, however, Randolph was given three days notice by Mary to leave the country as a punishment for having lent Moray 3,000 crowns. Elizabeth was appalled at her 'strange and uncourteous usage of Randolph'. He left for Berwick and the Earl of Bedford, to whom he revealed the extent of the plot proposed by the exiled lords. They would return to Scotland immediately, grant Darnley the crown matrimonial and outlaw the Mass altogether. This, in spite of Darnley having attended Mass on 7 February. Bedford and Randolph also informed Elizabeth on 6 March that a 'matter of no small consequence was intended in Scotland' and that it would happen before 12 March.

The plotters were gathering in Edinburgh: Morton – who had seen his seals of office given to Rizzio – Boyd and Ruthven – awaiting the return of Moray. Clearly there was no chance of the plot remaining secret, but Mary had heard only rumours and defied the rebels: 'What can they do, and what dare they do?' Rizzio himself claimed that the Scots would brag but not fight: 'They are but ducks, strike one of them and the rest will fly.' But he took the precaution of raising a personal bodyguard of Italian mercenaries. Lethington, wisely, did not sign the bond but simply let events unfold.

The events of 9 March 1566 are among the best known in Scottish history. Mary was in her private supper-room with five other close friends: Lord Robert Stewart, her half-brother and Bishop of Orkney; Jane, Countess of Argyll, her half-sister, whose adulterous behaviour had made her marriage a public scandal; her equerry, Erskine; her page, Standen; and David Rizzio. The weather was still cold and a fire had been lit, but since the room was no more than a closet some twelve feet square, and given the voluminous costume of the time, the atmosphere must have been stifling, especially for Mary, who was now six months pregnant. Rizzio, who was a considerable dandy – after his death he was found to own eighteen pairs of velvet hose as well as a private cache of £2,000 sterling – was wearing only a damask night gown with a satin doublet. They were finishing their supper, which, although it was still Lent, contained some meat since the queen's pregnancy allowed her to break the fast, and were looking forward to music and cards after supper.

They were all surprised by the entry of Darnley, who now seldom met the queen and certainly was not one of her social circle. He had arrived in the queen's apartments by a private staircase from his rooms below, and now he left access to the staircase open because he knew that about 150 armed men had entered the building. He showed no affection to Mary, and made no apology to the company, but leant on the arm of the astonished queen's chair. He had accomplished all that was required of him: to open the private stair and to ensure that his wife remained in her supper-room to witness the forthcoming spectacle.

The company's astonishment grew as the Earl of Ruthven entered unsteadily. He was drunk, wearing armour under his robe with a dagger at his side, breathing heavily and red in the face. Mary asked him, 'What strange sight is this my Lord? Are you mad?' Ruthven replied blurrily, 'We have been too long mad. Let it please your Majesty that yonder man Davie come forth of your privy chamber where he hath been overlong.' Immediately the stifling atmosphere changed from one of embarrassment to one of terror. Mary pleaded for Rizzio to be tried if he had committed any offence, but Ruthven ignored her. Instead, he told Darnley, 'Sir, take the queen your sovereign and wife to you.' Mary asked her husband if he knew what was going on, although it was murderously clear, and Darnley mumbled that he had no idea. Rizzio, realising that his life was in danger, had retreated into the window recess and Ruthven made a drunken lunge towards him, causing Robert Stewart to move between them and push Ruthven away. Ruthven shouted, 'Lay not hands on me, for I will not be handled,' and drew his dagger.

This was the signal for the entry of the remaining conspirators – Kerr of Fawdonside, Patrick Bellenden, George Douglas, Thomas Scott and Henry Yair – who rushed into the already crowded room with drawn weapons, knocking over a table. Lady Argyll prevented a possible fire by catching and snuffing out a lighted candle, so that the macabre scene was lit only by firelight. There were now thirteen people in the tiny room and Rizzio had fallen to his knees, clutching the pleats of Mary's skirts and screaming with fear. Ker prised his fingers free of the fabric with one hand, while, in his other, he held a loaded and cocked pistol to Mary's pregnant belly. Rizzio ran behind Mary, but George Douglas seized Darnley's dagger from its sheath and 'struck him over our shoulders'. The conspirators then dragged the screaming Italian out of the supper-room, across the bedchamber and into the presence chamber, so that Mary was, at least, spared watching the ensuing butchery. Rizzio's screams of 'Sauvez ma vie, madame, sauvez ma vie!' quickly ceased as more blows rained down on the tiny body. Rizzio received over fifty dagger wounds before his butchered and bloody corpse was thrown down a public staircase to land on a chest, where one of the palace porters stripped him of chains, rings and even shoes. Darnley's dagger was still in the dead man's chest.

Back in the supper-room Mary and her guests feared that they would be the next to be murdered, but Ruthven righted one of the overturned chairs, sat on it, wiped his brow and asked for a drink to be brought to him before giving Mary a stern lecture on using favourites – especially foreign favourites – before her own nobility. Mary asked Darnley what he had to do with all this: 'I took you from a low estate and made you my husband. What offence have I made you that you should have done me such shame?' Darnley accused her of having cuckolded him with Rizzio, having denied him sexual favours, and of not making him master in his own house. He then launched into a long speech of self-justification, which, sadly, is still familiar in modern times.

How came ye to my chamber at the beginning, and ever, until within these few months that Davie fell into familiarity with you? Or am I failed in any sort with my body? Or what disdain have you at me? Or what offence have I made you, that you should not use me at all times alike? Seeing that I am willing to do all things that becometh a good husband to do to his wife . . . you promised me obedience at the day of our marriage and that I should be equal with you and participant in all things. I suppose you have used me other wise at the persuasions of Davie.

Mary turned on Ruthven, who had been a witness to this marital squabble, and called down the wrath of Europe: the King of France, the Cardinal of Lorraine, her uncles in France and even the Pope. Ruthven said he was too unimportant for such great men. Mary continued, 'If I or my child die, you will have the blame thereof.' Lamely Ruthven said they had only meant to hang Rizzio and had brought ropes for the purpose, but that now the queen was a prisoner and would be taken to Stirling until the birth of her child. If any attempt were made to rescue Mary, 'She would be cut into gobbets and thrown from the terrace.' Ruthven was fond of this threat. Mary asked Darnley where his dagger was, who answered that he knew 'not well'. 'Well', said she, 'it will be known afterwards.' She also assured Ruthven and Darnley that, 'it is within my belly that one day will revenge these cruelties and affronts.'

This family row could have continued except for the fact that the palace was now in uproar. One of the Maries rushed to Mary with news of the butchery in the presence chamber and Mary shouted, 'No more tears! I will now think of revenge!' The earls of Atholl, Bothwell and Huntly, who had quarters in the eastern range of the palace, escaped 'by leaping down out of a window toward a little garden where the lions were lodged'. Atholl and Lethington took refuge in Atholl's castle near Dunblane, while Huntly and Bothwell fled to Crichton, Bothwell's castle in East Lothian. The 'common bell' of Edinburgh was rung and the Provost arrived in the forecourt with some hastily summoned burgesses of Edinburgh, but was told by Darnley, leaning out of the window, that all was well.

Darnley then withdrew and Mary was left alone to consider her situation. By marrying Darnley she had alienated the Moray–Argyll faction to the point of an armed uprising. By relying on foreign Catholic advice from Rizzio she had moved the Morton–Ruthven faction to murder. She knew that Moray and Argyll were soon to be in Edinburgh, if not already present. If she could neutralise Darnley's influence and seem to be in control then she could forgive the Chase-about rebels and bring them to her side. With their help and the advice of Lethington – who wisely was nowhere to be seen – she could regain respect and, hopefully, present Scotland with an heir. But her first task was to control her erratic husband and escape from the physical control of the Morton–Ruthven faction.

Overnight, Darnley drew up orders for the prorogation of parliament, but he was forbidden to see Mary, who was now a virtual prisoner in her own quarters. Next morning, Sunday, 10 March, Melville persuaded the conspirators to allow him to leave the palace so that he could attend the morning service at

St Giles and as he did so, Mary shouted from her window for him to raise the town. Since the Provost had been assured by Darnley that all was well and the people 'were so discontent with the present government that they desired a change' this came to nothing.

An example of the lack of privacy enjoyed by royalty occurred later that day when Mary was on her *chaise percée*, or commode. Lady Huntly presented her with a covered dish, presumably of food, but Patrick Lindsay, who was also present, snatched off the cover to reveal a rope ladder. In the ensuing confusion Mary slipped a letter to Lady Huntly outlining her future plans. There was a suspicion that Mary might try to leave disguised as a servant – unlikely for the tallest woman in the palace – and a bizarrely worded order was given that 'no gentlewoman should pass forth undismuffled'.

Domestically the conspirators feared the queen's influence over Darnley – 'she will persuade you to follow her will and desire by reason that she has been trained up from her youth in the court of France' – but she did agree to lie with Darnley again, although he objected to the presence of her gentlewomen. The women were duly sent away, but that night Darnley fell asleep in his own chamber and Mary was spared the coupling. The conspirators noted that 'the king grew effeminate again' but they still held a trump card in having Mary as their prisoner.

Mary finally showed that she had learned some political skills while in France. Now with her own life and that of her child in grave danger, she put them to good use. Darnley had no idea what to do next and realised that he had put himself into the hands of Morton and the conspirators. If he were ever to be proclaimed king it would be as their puppet, but on that Sunday Mary had convinced him that together they could overcome their difficulties. Mary was well experienced in dealing with feeble-minded princes, and Darnley was easily persuaded by Mary, who appealed to his vanity and ambition.

Next day, Monday, 11 March, Mary summoned the conspirators and, to their astonishment, forgave them for their actions.

Moray had arrived in Edinburgh and was dining with Morton when a messenger came from Mary inviting him to receive her pardon; in a scene of high hypocrisy they drew each other into an embrace vowing eternal love. The conspirators realised that their fears of Mary's French-learned guile were justified but were powerless to act against her. The banished rebels of the Chase-about Raid had arrived in Edinburgh to hear their fate from the Lords of the Articles, but since Darnley had prorogued parliament no Lords of the Articles had been appointed and, in any case, their repentance was unnecessary. Mary met them and forgave them, but, before they could ask for recompense, she fell forward, crying out in pain as her labour started. The midwife, who was now in permanent attendance, was called and the gentlemen dismissed. She also convinced her captors that she could not move from Holyrood until the next day without putting her child in danger. They, being men and terrified of anything to do with childbirth, agreed out of embarrassment. Mary had, of course, been faking the labour pains.

However, before Mary could take any other action she needed her freedom, and it was a simple matter to persuade Darnley to accompany her, although he tried to get Mary to let his father Lennox accompany them. Mary refused, and sent for Stewart of Traquair, the captain of her guard, as well as Erskine and Standen, the latter two having been witnesses to Rizzio's murder, asking them to make arrangements for her escape that night. Darnley and she went down the private staircase which had allowed access for the conspirators and through the servants' quarters and wine cellar. The French ambassador reported that 'pregnant as she was, the queen escaped by climbing down a bell rope'. However romantic his story might have seemed, no one believed him. Ironically, they passed the small newly dug grave of Rizzio before collecting their horses. Mary was given a pillion seat behind Erskine, while Traquair had a Marie, probably Seton, on his horse. Other servants followed, mounting as best as they could. At Seton Castle, twelve miles east of Edinburgh, they were met with more horses and attendants, thanks to the arrangements made by Lady Huntly, as requested in Mary's smuggled letter. Darnley, at first, took fright on seeing the soldiers at Seton and attempted to ride on, callously ignoring his wife's condition. In spite of their increased escort, he insisted on galloping, cruelly flogging Mary's horse and was frequently out of sight of the pregnant queen and the rest of the fugitives. When he had to stop to allow them to catch up he was abusive and insulting towards Mary, saying, 'If this baby dies we can have more!' and then riding off alone. Mary well knew that the usual result of a miscarriage was the death of the mother, and any affection between her and Darnley was now quite definitely finished.

The detail of this journey is given by Claude Nau, secretary to Mary from March 1575. He was the author of *The History of Mary Stewart*, which is based on details given to him nine years after the events took place. These details inevitably reflect Mary's total hatred for her late husband, for which one must accept some exaggeration.

On arriving unexpectedly early at Dunbar Castle, Mary's party wakened the astonished servants. Mary herself cooked some eggs and the fugitives settled down to breakfast. Mary transferred the wardship of the castle from the Laird of Craig-millar, one of Rizzio's murderers, to the Earl of Bothwell. The rest of the nobility had now lost patience with Darnley. As Nau wrote: 'They found the king was a man without any constancy, and all complained of him. Some would not speak to him or associate with him; others (especially Lord Fleming) openly found fault with his conduct towards the queen, his wife . . . [none] of the nobility had accepted him or admitted him as their king.'

Morton and Ruthven fled to England, and the Chase-about rebels rallied to Mary's side so that by 18 March 1566 she was able to advance to Haddington, where 4,000 men came to her support. On the next day she rode to Musselburgh to meet the Hamiltons, Atholl, Huntly and Bothwell with further forces. On the same day she re-occupied Edinburgh, where she was carried in a litter by four arquebusiers. Recent events made Holyrood an unwelcome place and apartments in Edinburgh Castle were still in preparation, so Mary took lodgings in the High Street for the time being. On 28 March, she took up residence in the castle. One of the rooms being prepared for her was to be her lying-in room in which she would give birth to her child.

CHAPTER ELEVEN

She wished she had never been married

꽃

Stability was the most urgent need for the country and the Privy Council, led by Moray, Argyll and Glencairn, now included Bothwell and Huntly. Darnley tried to assert himself and advised the removal of Lethington – who was still under a form of loose house arrest – only to be peremptorily overruled by Mary. He threw a petulant fit and stormed out, saying that from now on he would sleep with two loaded and primed pistols by his bed. That night Mary went quietly to his bedroom, presuming correctly that he would be in a drunken stupor, and removed the pistols. She gave a final honour to her murdered servant Rizzio by having his corpse re-interred, according to the Catholic rite, in her chapel at Holyrood.

Retribution for Rizzio's death was surprisingly mild. Thomas Scott was hanged, drawn and quartered for the murder. Scott's bloody fate was shared by Henry Yair, who had killed a Dominican priest shortly after Rizzio's murder, thinking it had been a signal for a general slaughter. Two other small fry, Mowbray and Harlaw, were brought to the scaffold to watch these executions, but were pardoned at the last minute. Morton and Ruthven were now in exile in England – Morton in Alnwick and Ruthven in Newcastle. Ruthven died in May, totally insane, believing that he saw the gates of paradise opening and hosts of angels welcoming him to heaven. In the vain hope of reconciliation the rebel lords sent Mary the bond that Darnley had signed giving his support to the plot in return for the crown matrimonial. On receiving such concrete proof of her husband's treachery, Mary gave 'so many great sighs that it was a pity to hear'.

Darnley now lived in a court largely deserted by his familiars, who realised that any contact with him was poisonous; even his father blamed him for destroying all the Lennox plans. Bizarrely, he continued to hear Mass daily and even washed the feet of the poor on Maundy Thursday. Meanwhile he conceived mad schemes to invade England – or, at least, Scarborough – all of which amused Cecil, whose spies had easily penetrated Darnley's circle of incompetents.

Equally incompetent was Christopher Rokesby, sent to Scotland as a secret agent, pretending to be the leader of disaffected English Catholics, and pleading for Mary's support in a plot to depose Elizabeth. Rokesby was immediately arrested, and among the papers he was carrying were the instructions from Cecil himself in cipher. However, Mary now had to concentrate on giving birth and there the matter rested for the moment. Cecil may have been quite ready to sacrifice Rokesby to test Mary's intelligence's defences, and there would be other, more sophisticated, attempts to involve Mary in Catholic uprisings.

It was now crucial for Mary to see her nobles united and reconciled since she knew that Darnley, for all that he was politically isolated, would try to use the birth of an heir – should her child be male – to ease himself back into power. Perhaps more importantly, if she should die in childbirth – which was always a risk – a strong Privy Council could prevent Darnley claiming the crown for himself alone if the child were female, or appointing himself regent if the child were male.

Randolph, though *persona non grata* and officially replaced by Thomas Killigrew, reported the rumour that James Thornton, a chanter of the bishopric of Moray, had gone to Rome to start negotiations for a divorce between Mary and Darnley. It is difficult to see what grounds could have been found to grant such a divorce, except, of course, that Darnley was the grandson of Mary's grandmother, Margaret Tudor, by her second marriage to the Earl of Angus. Of course, the fact that Mary was also the niece of the Cardinal of Lorraine and a Catholic sovereign in her own right would not have been inconsequential for the Holy

See. Thornton had been given instructions to call on Mary's Guise relatives in France, which could have laid the foundations for an appeal to Rome. Such a divorce, if granted, would, however, call into doubt the legitimacy of Mary's child – a matter of vital importance if the child was a boy – so a delay in the papal decision would allow everyone time for reflection.

Mary had, for the moment, the united council she needed for a period of peace, and the nobility had moved either into the castle itself or into lodgings in Edinburgh. Darnley was isolated from power and Randolph reported that the troublesome consort was intending to go to Flanders 'to move his case to any prince who [would] pity him'. In fact, as well as plans to leave Scotland, Darnley was continuing to encourage a Spanish–Dutch landing at Scarborough, on the east coast of England. But, for the present, diplomatic breath was held, not only in Scotland, but also across Europe, as Mary established herself in her private quarters in the heart of the castle. Significantly, however, she had not dismissed her personal bodyguard of arquebusiers.

In spite of the seeming calm, Mary was now having one of her recurrent moods of depression. Most probably this arose from her realisation that her imminent childbirth emphasised her position simply as a dynastic breeding machine for the future of Scotland. On 18 May she voiced a wish to Mauvissière, the French ambassador, to return to France, either for three months' convalescence after the birth or even permanently, washing her hands of the affairs of Scotland for ever. Lethington fervently wished for the latter, with the country then coming under the control of a council of regency. The lack of firm government and the continual forming and reforming of the alliances among the nobility were becoming intolerable. Both Mauvissière and Cecil thought Mary's intention was an absurd passing whim.

The tiny room chosen for her 'travail' was in the south-west corner of what is now called Crown Square in the heart of the castle complex, with a single window looking south above the cliff of the castle rock. With a short corridor and two other rooms between it and the outside world, it assured her privacy. The extreme seriousness with which childbirth was viewed is exemplified by the fact that once she was installed with her female attendants as well as a midwife, Margaret Asteane, and a wet nurse, she made her will. There were three copies: one kept by herself, one sent to Joinville for safe keeping by the Guise family and one which would remain with whoever took control after her death. There were also rumours that three regents had already been appointed.

The will began conventionally enough by leaving everything in Mary's possession to her child. However, in the case of their joint deaths she gave precise instructions as to the dispersal of the jewels which were her own personal possessions. The document was simply an inventory of Mary's goods against which, piece by piece, she carefully indicated in the margin what she wished to happen to each item. Her annotations are in French, as is the inventory, and the pages are witnessed by Mary Livingston, who was in charge of the royal jewels, and by Margaret Carwood, Mary's most experienced bedchamber woman, who took charge of the linens and embroideries in Mary's cabinet. Margaret Carwood's signature is laboriously drawn and Carwood was probably illiterate. The Great Harry jewel, given to Mary by Henri II on the day of her wedding to François II, was to be included in the Scottish Crown Jewels, and seven of her largest diamonds were to be kept for the use of future queens. Her bequests to Darnley are interesting. There are twenty-six in all: a seemingly endless list of jewelled buttons, a diamond-set watch, a 'dial' she had received from Lennox and her red wedding ring. Mary wrote on the document, 'It was with this that I was married; I leave it to the king who gave it to me.' There were two rings of diamonds and rubies for her parents-in-law, the Earl and Countess of Lennox.

This ends the list of what was conventionally essential and the remainder of the bequests reflect more strongly her own personal wishes. There were many bequests of jewels for her extended Guise family, followed by bequests to various illegitimate Stewarts. There was jewellery to Lady Jane Stewart, Countess of

Argyll, who had caught the overturned candle during Rizzio's murder; to Lord John, another witness to the butchery, to her half-brother Lord James, now the Earl of Moray; and to the loyal nobility.

Her legacies to the four Maries seem trivial beside the mountain of jewellery – mostly embroidery and decorated linens. Only one of them had observed her vow of celibacy before Mary's own marriage. Mary Livingston had married John Sempill on 6 March 1564, and Mary had attended the wedding and provided her wedding dress. Mary Beaton had married Alexander Ogilvy of Boyne in May 1566, and she was bequeathed the queen's French, Italian and English books, while Mary Fleming would marry Lethington on 6 January 1567. However, Mary Seton, the hairdresser, never married but stayed loyal even during English exile and was only separated from Mary in 1584, when she went to the convent of St Pierre in Reims where Mary's aunt, Renée de Guise, was still the abbess. The ladies of honour – Countess of Atholl, Mme de Briante, Mme de Crie – were remembered, and a sapphire and pearl brooch was specified for Erskine of Blackgrange on whose horse Mary had ridden pillion on the midnight flight to Dunbar. Rizzio's brother, Joseph, was to get two jewels, and an emerald ring was to be given to a person whose name Mary had whispered into Joseph's ear. His identity is still a mystery. Margaret Carwood was left a miniature of Mary set with diamonds and a little silver box. Mary's linen was to be sold and shared among the three bedchamber women, while plate and furniture would be sold for ushers, valets, grooms, etc. Finally, her Greek and Latin books were destined for the University of St Andrews.

This will demonstrates two things very clearly. Firstly, Mary was a Guise princess and like all well-educated aristocrats put the care of her servants high on her list of priorities. Secondly, we can see from her behaviour at the weddings and christenings of her servants how much she enjoyed the easy informality of family gatherings as well as banqueting and dancing. Among her ladies she could behave as an equal, whether dressing up as a 'housewife' or, on a Twelfth Night feast when Mary Beaton found the 'bean' in the Twelfth Night cake, giving up her place as queen to Mary Beaton for the night – from then on Mary Beaton was 'Queen of the Bean'. With her male courtiers she enjoyed hunting and hawking, while indoors there were games of cards and dice, music and singing, as well as cautious flirting and intrigue. Her royal duties, to form alliances profitable to her country, to maintain peace according to the will of her people, and to increase the prosperity and wellbeing of her nation, never held any interst for her, but she had one unavoidable duty – to marry and produce an heir. Her disastrous choice of a husband had brought her country to the brink of civil war and now she had to perform her most dangerous dynastic duty.

The birthing chamber had been specially decorated, and on 3 June 1566, Mary moved into it and the waiting began. There was a false alarm on 15 June, with bonfires lighted and hastily extinguished, but the queen went into labour in earnest on 19 June. Bizarrely, Mary Fleming's sister, Margaret, Countess of Atholl, who was rumoured to be a practising witch, cast a protective spell on Margaret Beaton, who was also Lady Reres and an aunt to Mary Beaton, who lay in an adjacent room experiencing all the pains of labour. Lady Reres's simulated agonies did nothing to alleviate Mary's pains, which were 'severe and long lasting'. Mary prayed that if the worst happened she should be sacrificed to save the child. Mary was 'so handled that she wished she had never been married', and was not the last mother to voice this wish.

At about ten o'clock on the morning of 19 June 1566, Mary gave birth to a healthy and perfectly formed prince with a fine, thin caul stretched over his face. This was regarded as extremely lucky and prophesied that the child would not die by drowning. Mary Beaton immediately rushed from the apartments to give the news to James Melville, who set off for London. Perhaps to the chagrin of Mary, who would have been desperate for rest and restorative sleep, 'all the artillery of the castle shot and bonfires were set forth in all parts for joy'.

Melville spent his first night at Berwick – sixty miles in about six hours – and four days later was in London – roughly 100 miles a day – to give the news to Cecil. Elizabeth was at Greenwich Palace 'in great merriness and dancing after supper', and when she received the news all dancing stopped as she sat down with her hand on her cheek, saying, 'The Queen of Scots is lighter of a fair son while I am of barren stock!' Even for Elizabeth, one of the great dissemblers, this was an outrageous remark. Her barrenness had never been tested and, as one who vowed 'to live and die a virgin', was unlikely to be, but she did manipulate the situation to receive sympathy at someone else's good news. Elizabeth Tudor was never off-duty.

Melville formally asked Elizabeth to be a godmother, to which she agreed, and he then suggested that Elizabeth might have an occasion to see Mary, 'whereat she smiled'. Charles IX of France had also agreed to stand as a sponsor, although both monarchs would send proxies to the ceremony. Melville also saw Cecil and delivered Mary's forgiveness for the Rokesby affair.

Killigrew arrived in Edinburgh on 22 June as ambassador and was told that Mary welcomed him and would see him as 'soon as she might have ease of the pain in her breasts'. Meanwhile she ordered that a bed of her own of crimson velvet was to be set up in his rooms. The new ambassador then attended a sermon with Moray, Huntly, Argyll, Mar and Crawford. He noticed the split between Argyll, Moray, Atholl and Mar on one side and Bothwell, Huntly and the Master of Maxwell on the other. Bothwell seemed to have most credit with the queen, and with Lethington, still stained with suspicion of involvement in Rizzio's murder, was about to depart for Flanders. It did not take a diplomatic genius to see the beginnings of yet another split among the now-leaderless nobility.

Five days after the birth, on 24 June, Killigrew saw the prince with his wet-nurse and 'afterwards did see him as good as naked. His head, feet and hands, all well proportioned.' He spoke to Mary, who was still weak and replied faintly with a hollow cough. The worst was over for the queen. Scotland now had an heir, Darnley had moved further down the line of succession, and

Elizabeth had to realise that her successor was now alive and crying for milk in Edinburgh Castle. Needless to say, such an indelicate thought, presuming as it did her own death, was never put into words.

Darnley, with Sir William Stanley, was shown the infant prince, and Mary, knowing that Stanley would report her actions, acknowledged that he, Darnley, was the true father of the child who would, in time, unite the kingdoms of Scotland and England. Darnley realised that he was being left out of the equation and burst out, 'Is this your answer to forgive and forget all?'

Mary replied, 'I have forgiven but I shall never forget. What if Fawdonside's pistol had shot, what would have become of him and me both?' Darnley swept out of the room in speechless petulancy.

He now felt that he was excluded from any possibility of power in Scotland and was making alternative, and treasonable, arrangements. He had been in correspondence with Philip II, and he was in contact with disaffected Catholics in England. Darnley was investigating the possibility of preparing Scarborough as a landing point for forces invading from Holland and of laying claim to the ordnance in the Scilly Isles. On 5 July he received promises from his allies in the Scilly Isles, and from Scarborough he was assured by Sir Richard Semple that the town and its defences would be delivered to Darnley whenever he wished. At home he was behaving with total selfishness, 'vagabondising every night' and insisting that the gates of the castle be kept open to allow his drunken return, breaching security for Mary and the prince.

Mary recovered from her ordeal sufficiently to visit Newhaven, outside Edinburgh, in July, then travelled up the River Forth to Alloa, the seat of the Earl of Mar, where she started again to enjoy the outdoors. Darnley joined the party but stayed only a few hours. With Mary away from Edinburgh, rivalries inevitably broke out in the court. Bothwell's ascendancy as the royal favourite was beginning, and he quickly became 'the most hated man among the noblemen in Scotland'.

His power base in the Border country was as troublesome as ever. On 17 June the Abbot of Kelso had been murdered – it is said they smote off his arms and legs – by the Laird of Cessford and the brothers of the Laird of Ferniehurst. Since the Abbot had been under Bothwell's protection – and presumably had been paying well for it – this could not go unpunished, and on 28 July Bothwell was in Kelso. Here, he heard a rumour that Mary was to be in Jedburgh, nine miles distant, in eight days. By 8 August the journey to Jedburgh seemed to 'wax doubtful', yet by 14 August Mary was at Meggetland, south of Peebles, hunting with Bothwell, Moray and Mar and intending to return to Edinburgh via the house of John Stewart of Traquair.

The level of disagreement between Mary and Darnley increased and he petulantly decamped to Dunfermline, then unexpectedly appeared at Traquair House. Claude Nau gives us the following anecdote: 'While the party was at supper, the king, her husband, asked the queen to attend a stag hunt. Knowing that if she did so, she would be required to gallop her horse at a great pace, she whispered in his ear that she was *enceinte*. The king answered aloud, "Never mind, if we lose this one, we will make another," whereupon the laird of Traquair rebuked him sharply, and told him that he did not speak like a Christian. He answered, "What! Ought we not to work a mare well when she is with foal?" '

It is difficult to believe that the event took the course described in such detail, but it is clear that Darnley arrived unbidden and behaved boorishly. For Mary to have had certain knowledge of a pregnancy only two months after the birth of James by a husband she loathed is stretching the imagination, and if she was implying – more or less publicly – that the child was not his, she was behaving with more than her usual irresponsibility.

On her return to Edinburgh she did, however, give orders for the infant James to be sent to the total safety of Stirling Castle, her own nursery, and the traditional nursery for royal children. Thus on 22 August the two-month-old heir was carried in a careful litter with Lady Reres, and the royal party had an escort of 500

Mary of Guise, Queen of Scotland, wife of James V and mother
of Mary, Queen of Scots. She was, in truth, was always French at
heart. When widowed, for the second time, at 27 she lived on for
18 more years to rule Scotland with moderation and wisdom.
*Portrait of Mary of Guise, 1515–1560, Queen of James V attributed
to Corneille de Lyon © National Galleries of Scotland*

IACOBVS · 5 · D · GRA
REX · SCOTORVM

James V, King of Scotland and father to Mary, Queen of Scots. He died of, among other things, a broken heart, aged 30 without ever seeing his daughter. *Portrait of James V, 1512–1542, father of Mary, Queen of Scots by an unknown artist* © *National Galleries of Scotland*

Linlithgow Palace. Mary was probably born in the right-hand tower on the second floor. The palace was always a favourite of hers.

Stirling Castle. Mary spent the first six years of her life inside these carefully guarded walls as the centre of a Renaissance court while politics determined her future.

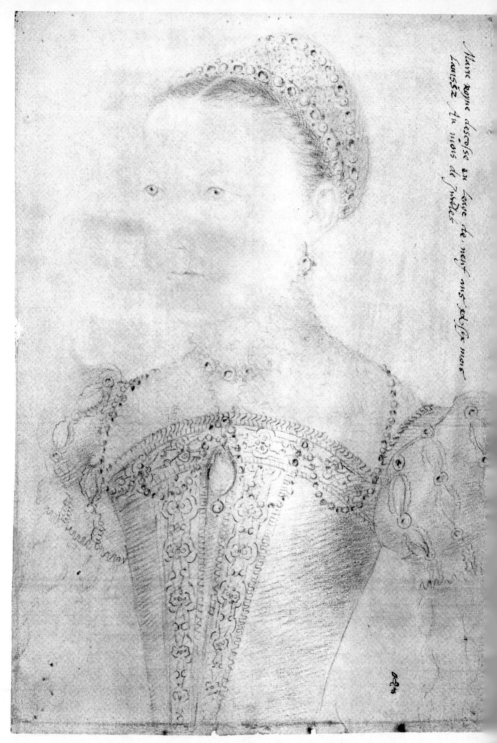

Mary, Queen of Scots aged nine years and six months. Already she is a bejewelled and tightly corseted
French princess. Her Scottish childhood was becoming a distant memory. *Portrait of Mary Stuart,
Queen of Scotland (1542–87) at the age of nine, July 1552 (pencil & sanguine on paper), Clouet, (16th century)
(studio of)/Musée Condé, Chantilly, France, Giraudon/The Bridgeman Art Library*

Henri II, King of France and father-in-law to Mary. He was enchanted by his little daughter-in-law and indulged her as a crowned queen. *Portrait of Henri II (1519–59) (oil on panel) by Primaticcio, Francesco (1504–70) (attr. to) © Chateau d'Anet, Eure-et-Loir, France/The Bridgeman Art Library*

...erine de Medici, Queen of France and ... to Henri II. Heavily built and clad in ...dark Italian fashion, she was a reluctant ...her-in-law to Mary. *Portrait of Catherine ...Medici (1519–89) (oil on panel), Clouet, ...çois (c.1510–72) (attr. to)/Musées de la Ville ...aris, Musée Carnavalet, Paris, France, ...os/Giraudon/The Bridgeman Art Library*

Diane de Poitiers, Duchesse de Valentinois and mistress of Henri II. She became a close friend and mentor to Mary. *Diane de Poitiers (1499–1566) mistress of Henri II, King of France (1519–59) by French School (16th century)* © *State Collection, France / The Bridgeman Art Library*

The chateau of Chenonceau. Only the right-hand towers existed when this was Diane and Henri's favourite chateau. On Henri's death Catherine took the chateau for herself and added the long gallery over the river. © *James L. Amos/CORBIS*

The chateau of Amboise. The heads of the rebels were impaled on the railings outside the long windows for Mary and the court to see as they dined. Leonardo da Vinci is buried in the chapel behind the trees. © *Kim Sayer/CORBIS*

The death of Henri II. The doctors in the foreground have ceased treating the still conscious king, but the priest has raised his hands in blessing. Beside the priest, Catherine is praying, while at the right of the group stands Mary with the Dauphin in front of her. A few moments later Mary became Queen of France. *The Death of Henri II (1519–59) 10 July 1559 (coloured engraving), Perrissin, J. J. (c.1536–c.1611) & Tortorel, J. (fl.1568–92)/Private Collection, Archives Charmet/The Bridgeman Art Library*

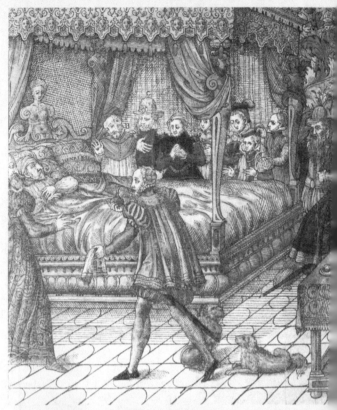

Mary in *Deuil Blanc*, the white mourning of France. She wore it so regularly that she became known as *la Reine Blanche* – the White Queen. *Portrait of Mary, Queen of Scots, 1542–1587, reigned 1542–1567 (in white mourning) by an unknown artist after Francois Clouet © National Galleries of Scotland*

Lord James Stewart, the illegitimate son of James and half-brother to Mary. He was sent to France to 'grope the young queen's mind' and became a leading member of her government. Mary created him first, Earl of Mar, then Earl of Moray. He led a revolt against Mary but was assassinated in 1570. *James Stewart, Earl of Moray, c.1531–1570, Regent of Scotland by Hugo Monro © National Galleries of Scotland*

William Maitland of Lethington, nicknamed 'Michael Wylie – Scotland's Machiavelli'. He was the complete Renaissance courtier, always putting expediency first. He was a loyal servant of Mary's and paid dearly for it.
Portrait of William Maitland of Lethington, 1528–1573, Secretary to Mary, Queen of Scots by 11th Earl of Buchan © National Galleries of Scotland

John Knox, the spiritual leader of the Scottish Reformation and an implacable enemy of Mary's way of life, both religious and social. Her wisest plan would have been to ignore him, instead of which she tried to debate with him. She lost the debates.

Henry Stuart, Lord Darnley and Mary's second husband. He was a vicious,
syphilitic bisexual who treated the Scottish nobility with arrogant disdain, and
Mary with cruel neglect. He was assassinated in 1567. *Portrait of Henry Stewart,
Lord Darnley, 1545–1567, Consort of Mary, Queen of Scots by an unknown artist*
© *National Galleries of Scotland*

The north wing of the Palace of Holyrood House. Mary's apartments were on the middle floor, and her supper-room was behind the left hand window.

Edinburgh Castle. James VI was born in the room behind the tiny window high on the extreme left.

James Hepburn, Earl of Bothwell, and Mary's third husband. 'A glorious rash and hazardous young man', Bothwell was an aristocratic bandit. After Mary's surrender at Carberry Hill he fled to Denmark, where he died insane after eleven years in grim solitary imprisonment. *Portrait of James Hepburn, 4th Earl of Bothwell, c.1535–1578 by an unknown artist © National Galleries of Scotland*

Craigmillar Castle, a few miles south of Edinburgh, where the
Confederate Lords plotted the murder of Darnley, almost certainly
with Mary's knowledge.

Hermitage Castle, Bothwell's implacable fortress in the Scottish
borders. Legend as it that anyone not locally born will go mad if
they attempt to spend the night within its walls.

The banner carried by the Confederate Lords at the battle of Carberry. It shows the murdered Darnley lying in a garden while a child holds a caption saying, 'Judge and avenge my cause O Lord.' *Reproduced by permission of the National Archives, HM Stationery Office.*

Lochleven Castle. The loch has risen since Mary's time here. Apart from the circumstances of her imprisonment, it is an idyllic spot.

ay grant leurs ages la nostre faysant prier dieu
pour une royne qui a esté nommee tres chrestienne
et meurt catholique desnuee de toutz ses biens
quant a mon filz ie le vous recommande autant
qu'il le meritera car ie n'en puis respondre
i'ay prins la hardiesse de vous envoier deulx
pierres rares pour la sante vous la desirant
parfaicte avec heureuse et longue vie vous les
recepverez comme de vostre tres affectionnee
belle sœur mourante en vous rendant tesmoignaige
de son bon cœur envers vous ie vous recommande
encore mes serviteurs vous ordonnerez s'il vous
plaict que pour mon ame ie soye payee de
partie de ce que me debvez et qu'en l'honneur
de Iesus Christ lequel ie prieray demayn a
ma mort pour vous me laisser de quoy fonder
un obit et faire les aumosnes requises
ce mercredy a deulx heures apres minuict

Vostre tres affectionnee et bien
bonne sœur MARI R

Mary's last letter, written to her brother-in-law, Henri III of France. She set out the circumstances surrounding her fate and asked for care to be taken of her servants. Mary wrote the letter at 2 a.m., and she knew that she would be beheaded in eight hours. Her writing is firm and legible. © *The Trustees of the National Library of Scotland*

LEFT. Elizabeth I of England, Mary's cousin. Here she wears pearls and has a pomander at her girdle, but she was politically implacable and intellectually brilliant. Nicknamed the 'Virgin Queen' she was, in fact, devotedly married to England. *Reproduced by permission of the National Portrait Gallery*

BELOW. The replica of Mary's Westminster tomb in the Museum of Scotland. The effigy has none of the royal pomp of other tombs but is devout and prayerful. Mary had asked to be buried in France beside her relatives, but instead of that, her son, James VI and I, had her buried in London beside Elizabeth Tudor. *Reproduced by permission of the National Museums of Scotland*

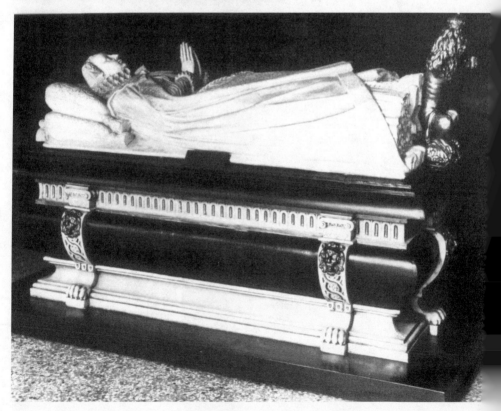

arquebusiers. Curiously, Mary's orders for the furnishings of the nursery were not issued until 5 September, but, when they were, they were lavish indeed: ten hanks of the finest gold thread and the same of silver, fourteen pounds of feathers for the pillow and twenty-eight pounds of wool for the mattress. There were fifteen ells* of blue plaiding to make a cover for the cradle, twelve ells of blanketing and two tapestries as well as a specially constructed bed. Special beds were to be built for Lady Reres and the 'mistress nurse'. The list was to be 'answered incontinently, because the same is requested and very needful to be had'.

Mary's council was becoming more united, if only in their hatred of Darnley, with Lethington now fully pardoned and partly reconciled to Bothwell. In fact, the only cloud on the horizon was the increasingly erratic behaviour of Darnley. He had refused to enter Holyroodhouse while Mary's council was in residence and dropped heavy hints about leaving the country, but she persuaded him to enter and gave him 'access to her bed'. Since they seem to have spent the night arguing over his intention to run into a self-imposed exile, neither party had much sleep. Next day he was summoned to appear before the Privy Council and was challenged by Mary and the members, in the presence of Philibert du Croc, the French ambassador, to declare his grievances in full. John Leslie, the Bishop of Ross asked him to confirm or deny that he had a ship fully manned and ready to leave. The result was a surprise. He confirmed the existence of the ship, announcing that he could no longer stay in Scotland and that he intended to leave the country and live abroad. The lords were appalled at the thought of such a loose cannon plotting unimagined intrigue abroad, and Mary took him by the hand again, asking him why. He muttered about not having been made king, and then, to everyone's horror, without asking for permission to withdraw, addressed Mary directly saying, 'Adieu, Madame, you shall not see my face in a long time.' Then, after turning to the astonished lords, he said, 'Gentlemen, adieu!' and strode out of the room.

*A Scots ell was 37.2 inches.

This behaviour would have been unforgivable anywhere, but to snub the queen in the presence of a foreign ambassador and before the assembled nobility – a nobility that already felt a deep-seated loathing for him – was to write his own death warrant. Mary was reassured immediately, 'It is vain to imagine that he shall be able to raise any disturbance, for there is not one person in this kingdom, from the highest to the lowest, that regards him.' Meanwhile the council contented itself with writing to Catherine de Medici to warn her that Lord Darnley was now thought to be mad.

Mary realised that it had been her petulant defiance of Elizabeth that had brought her to marry Darnley and that it was his arrogant behaviour which was tearing the country apart. She was incapable of firm action, and her council remained united – only just – out of self-interest and without any royal leadership to give it a common purpose. To deal with the problem of Darnley, their superior in the strict order of nobility, the council needed guidance and instruction from the queen, but none was forthcoming. Mary had no idea what to do and confided in du Croc that she was so miserable that she was seriously considering returning again to France, leaving Scotland in the control of a five-man regency consisting of Moray, Huntly, Mar, Atholl and Bothwell. This would have meant Mary abandoning her infant son and admitting that her decision to return to Scotland had been disastrous. The suggestion was emotional and irrational and no more than the desperate cry of someone who knows that she is personally to blame for the existing chaos and cannot find a way to impose order and good government.

As always, when surrounded by misfortunes, Mary found solace on horseback in the open air. A 'justice ayre' was due to be held in Jedburgh and Mary, with Moray, Lethington, Argyll and Huntly, rode south to attend. These 'ayres' were circuit courts held sporadically in royal boroughs, much like the English assize courts of comparatively recent times, and it would not have been uncommon for the monarch to attend. It was also an opportunity for the Privy Council to meet away from the capital. The court lasted for a week and adjourned on 15 October, when Mary, accompanied by Moray and a retinue of courtiers, rode to visit Bothwell, who was injured and in his castle of Hermitage.

Bothwell had led a punitive raid against the Elliots, under the outlaw John Elliot of Park. He had captured Elliot, who managed to escape on foot, but Bothwell stumbled after him in pursuit and was stabbed in the head, body and hand before he managed to shoot Elliot. He then passed out from loss of blood. His servants found him and dragged him back to Hermitage where he was now convalescing, having sent Elliot's head to Edinburgh.

Bothwell was now taking centre stage in Mary's affairs, having previously been told that he would never receive any favour from her. A totally self-serving opportunist, he was now one of her most senior courtiers, a bitter opponent of Darnley's and, since it was greatly to his advantage, fiercely loyal to Mary. He was one of the more interesting men in Mary's life and his portrait miniature gives us many clues. He was sturdily built, although of below-average height, and described as being 'of great bodily strength and beauty although vicious and dissolute in his habits'. His direct gaze in the portrait makes it quite clear that not only had he no fear of anything, he was also very easily roused. In short, not someone one should stand too close to if one wanted a peaceful life. The earl had not had a peaceful life, nor had his ancestors. His father, Patrick Hepburn, had vied with Darnley's father for the hand of Marie de Guise and other Hepburns had made 'suspicious connections' with the widow of James I as well as Mary of Gueldres, wife of James II. With the castles of Hermitage, which he held in trust as a royal castle, Crichton, and now Dunbar, the latter two both in the Lothians, he could control swathes of southern Scotland while harrying English advances, as well as exercising vigorous control over the Debatable Lands. Hermitage alone could hold a garrison of up to 1,000 men. The family's recourse was always to the sword first and to the negotiating table last.

Bothwell had been well educated, spoke French as well as Latin and had travelled widely across Europe, often only just keeping ahead of trouble. Mary had met him in France when he was fleeing a legal action for breach of promise brought by his Norwegian mistress, Anna Throndsen, and he had been imprisoned in both Edinburgh Castle and the Tower of London. One of his earliest mistresses was Janet Beaton, the 61-year-old aunt of the queen's Mary Beaton. She had had five husbands and was widely regarded as the most adept witch in Scotland. Whatever skills she had taught the 24-year-old Bothwell were more likely to have been in the dark arts than in courtly love. Now married to the fortunately rich Jean Gordon – fortunately since Bothwell was perennially short of money – he still had casual affairs, even consummating one with Bessie Crawford, a blacksmith's daughter, in the tower of Haddington Church. As the royal party rode over the Border hills, speculation as to the queen's motives for the sudden visit was at its height.

Hermitage was thirty miles distant from Jedburgh and Mary's party rode there and back in a single day. Mary, theatrical as usual, was mounted on a white palfrey, which unfortunately sank in a bog and had to be rescued. The bog is still called the Queen's Mire. A sixty-mile ride, plus a few hours at Bothwell's side, was a long day – Melville had travelled the distance from Edinburgh to Berwick in a day, but alone and over much better ground than the rough Border tracks – and such an adventure in dangerous country put the entire party at the risk of kidnapping or worse. However, an ad hoc Privy Council was held at Hermitage which lent some validity to the journey.

Disaster seemed about to strike when, back in Jedburgh, Mary fell gravely ill. A pain in her side which had been troubling her since her confinement developed rapidly and was accompanied by constant vomiting – over sixty times in three days – until on the third day she lost her sight. An immediate suspicion was that she had been poisoned, 'particularly as among the matter ejected from the stomach was found a lump of a green substance, very thick and hard'. Mary summoned the council and especially cautioned them to look after the prince and to ensure his succession, presuming that Darnley would try to claim the crown for himself. She asked du Croc to recommend the prince to his master, Charles IX. The Bishop of Ross then prayed over her, as Mary wished to die in the Catholic faith. She also made a second will, endorsing the one she had completed before the birth of the prince. However, Mary felt sure that if she could weather the next day she would not die. In the morning she lost the power of speech and suffered severe convulsions. By nightfall her limbs contracted, her face distorted and her temperature fell so far that her close servants presumed she was dead. 'The Earl of Moray began to lay his hands on the most precious articles, such as her silver plate and rings. The mourning dresses were ordered and arrangements made for the funeral. But Arnault, her surgeon, having observed that there were still some signs of life in one of her arms . . . used an extreme remedy in an extreme case.' He bound her tightly from her toes upwards including her arms and forced some wine into her mouth, which restored some feeling. He then administered a clyster – an enema – which produced 'suspicious results'. Since this account is based on a report by Nau, who had no reason to love Moray, the accusation of his seizing the rings and plate can be taken with the usual quantity of salt.

This attack of illness was the most severe Mary suffered, but she was prone to pain in her left side, 'below her small ribs' for most of her life. The attacks were frequently accompanied by vomiting, often of green slime, and could be eased by outdoor exercise. There have been many attempts to diagnose her illness. Gastric ulcers as a result of stress have been presumed, and the medical profession has rushed to a diagnosis of porphyria, connecting the ill-defined symptoms to Mary's royal blood, although there are no accounts of the vivid discolouration of the urine that is typical of the disease. The green colour of the vomiting indicates the ejection of bile, and the fact that the pain occurred in the region of her left kidney makes a diagnosis of recurrent kidney infections the most likely. At any rate, any diagnosis based on 500-year-old observations made by lay attendants is more speculative than clinically reliable.

Darnley arrived in Jedburgh in a foul temper since he had not been summoned to attend the council, and stayed only a few hours, lodging separately from Mary. He had to borrow the bed assigned to the Bishop of Orkney. Du Croc said of Darnley, 'His is such a fault that I know not how to apologise for it', and Lethington wrote to the ambassador in Paris, 'She has done him so great honour and he has recompensed her with such ingratitude, and misuses himself so far towards her, that it is a heartbreak for her to think that he should be her husband, and how to be free of him she sees no way out.' She was moving perilously close to the position of England's Henry II, who asked his knights if no one would rid him of 'this troublesome priest', or, in her case, husband.

Bothwell did appear, carried on a horse-litter, to attend another Privy Council before Mary left Jedburgh. Her departure was hastened by her lodging, in a fortified house near the abbey, catching fire. Before leaving Jedburgh Mary paid the lutenist John Hume 40 shillings, and for 'playing on pipe and whistle' John Heron became richer by £4 Scots.

Mary now demonstrated her remarkable powers of recovery by setting out on a progress across the Borders and up the east coast. It was not without incident since, when Sir John Forster, Warden of the English March, rode up to meet her, his horse bit hers on the neck and he struck her thigh with his stirrupped feet. He fell to his knees but she assured him that all was well. This royal courtesy was second nature to a Guise. The procession reached Dunbar, where Mary received news that Darnley was in close correspondence with Philip II of Spain and the Pope, claiming that Mary was being lax in forcing the Catholic religion on Scotland and that he, Darnley, with their support, would bring about a Catholic revolution. She confided to Moray, Huntly and Lethington that unless by some means or other she might be 'despatched of the king, she should never have a good day. And if by no other way she could obtain it, rather than she would abide to live in such sorrow she would slay herself.' With all this in mind she wrote to Elizabeth from Dunbar asking her to be the protector of the prince in the event of her death, since Darnley's fragile grasp on sanity made the assassination of Mary a very real possibility.

The result was that on 7 November 1566 Elizabeth instructed Bedford to tell Mary, 'We would never do or suffer anything to be done prejudicial to her right, and would earnestly prohibit and suppress all attempts, directly or indirectly, against the same, and that she might well assure herself of our amity.' A stumbling block to Mary's claim had always been the last will of Henry VIII, which disinherited the Scottish claimants, wishing instead that the English crown should pass to the house of Suffolk. But this will, made when the king was dying, was stamped only with a sign-manual, and Henry may never have seen it himself. Elizabeth certainly thought it should be ignored. She withdrew her requests for the ratification of the Treaty of Edinburgh and replaced it with a simple treaty of perpetual amity. This provided both parties with a suitable agreement. Elizabeth did not have to acknowledge the inevitability of her death without issue, while Mary became the heir apparent, with the prince as the next in line to both kingdoms. In effect, in 1566, the Union of the Crowns became a foregone conclusion.

The religious situation in Scotland was in a state of comparative equilibrium and in October Guzmán de Silva reported to his master Philip II, admittedly from the distance of London, 'Mass is said everywhere and the Catholics can attend it freely, whilst others may hold their services without any interference.' A statement filled more with hope than reality. However, he did report on 14 November,

I received today a letter dated the 1st inst from the queen of Scot by one of her servants who is on his way to France and Rome. He has been instructed to tell me that the queen had heard that her husband had written to your Majesty, the Pope, the king of France and the Cardinal of Lorraine that she was dubious in the faith and asked me to assure your

227

majesty that as regards religion she will never with God's help fail to uphold it with all the fervour and constancy which the Roman Catholic Christian religion demands.

Mary was refuting Darnley's accusations.

On 20 November Mary arrived outside Edinburgh to lodge at the castle of Craigmillar. Here the most controversial event of her short stay in Scotland was to take place.

Still not fully recovered, she 'vomited a great quantity of corrupt blood, and then the cure was complete', and another visit by Darnley to Craigmillar did nothing to improve her morale. She confided to du Croc, 'I could wish to be dead.' Du Croc, a thorough ambassador, talked with Darnley and concluded that the marriage was now in a terminal phase: 'The injury she has received is very great and her Majesty will never forgive it. I do not expect any good understanding between them, unless God effectually puts it to his hand.' The Scottish nobility agreed wholeheartedly.

As Mary pondered the problem of how to rid herself of her ill-chosen husband, her nobles took upon themselves the task of providing the solution. Early one morning towards the end of November, Moray and Lethington discussed how to persuade Mary to pardon Morton for Rizzio's murder and also how they could remove Darnley. The pair consulted with Argyll, who was still in bed, and while in general agreement they sent a servant to fetch Huntly. He agreed to their suggestion but, as a quid pro quo, insisted that his lands be restored to him. With this agreement the quartet visited Bothwell, who favoured Mary's divorcing Darnley since he was certain that a way might be found to legitimise Mary's son. His family had a long history of legitimising random offspring. They all drew a deep breath and took their plans to Mary, who was breakfasting before her morning ride. Lethington first proposed that if Mary pardoned Morton and the Rizzio assassins, their evidence against Darnley would be enough for a divorce to be sought. In any case, with Mary's powerful connections to the authority of Rome, a divorce on the grounds of consanguinity could be arranged. Mary grasped the point at once and said that it must be without prejudice to her son. In other words, the marriage could not be declared invalid since the prince would then be a bastard, but if Rome would agree to a dissolution of the union on other grounds, then she might approve. This course of action seemed fraught with difficulties and a more secular plan was discussed. However, all the parties realised that since Darnley was the king it was impossible to try him for treason; he had merely fulfilled his own expressed intention. He might accept going into a more-or-less enforced exile, but his unreliability made this unlikely. Lethington then suggested that there was a third solution of which they were all only too aware, although none of them dared name it. Lethington merely suggested 'other means', which Moray would object to but could be persuaded to 'look through his fingers'. Mary knew exactly what he meant and only said that she only hoped that nothing would 'be done against her honour'. Mary knew that these 'other means' meant a recourse to violence and, most probably, assassination, but now she simply asked that she should be declared blameless of the deed. With only this weak qualification coming from Mary, Lethington now knew that the decision could be put into effect. He assured Mary: 'Let us guide the matter among us, and your Grace shall see nothing but good, and approved by Parliament.' The council knew they now had carte blanche to murder the king, but had to be certain that Mary knew nothing whatsoever of the details of the plot. They also knew that their queen was a pastmaster of ignoring that which was inconvenient for her. Lethington, Bothwell, Argyll and Huntly, with Sir James Balfour, who was legally trained, drew up a careful document, later signed by Morton, vowing that 'he [Darnley] should be put off by one way or another; and whosoever should take the deed in hand, or do it, they should defend and fortify as themselves'. This was the infamous Craigmillar Bond. Not surprisingly, no copies of it now exist.

In the aftermath, Moray, who had not signed the bond, claimed that although he was present he gave no explicit consent, and Huntly and Atholl also vehemently confirmed that Mary had no knowledge of the details of the plan. Her ignorance was protected by Lethington and the others, but she knew full well that she would shortly be a widow for a second time. There is a quasi-legal phrase, 'qui tacet consentit' – he who is silent, consents – and Mary was indeed very silent.

In December arrangements for the baptism of the prince now dominated Mary's mind. The Earl of Bedford was despatched by Elizabeth with an escort of forty horsemen and by 25 November he had reached Doncaster; by 3 December he was at Berwick waiting to be invited to meet Mary. He brought with him an enamelled gold christening font weighing twenty-eight pounds and worth £1,000 sterling as Elizabeth's present to the infant, whose name was still a matter of speculation. Bedford's invitation arrived two days later, the ceremony having been delayed due to the late arrival of du Croc, now the Duke of Savoy's representative. France was represented by the Comte de Brienne, and Bothwell was given the task of receiving the foreign ambassadors. Charles IX sent a necklace of pearls and rubies and two magnificent earrings, while the Duke of Savoy contributed a jewelled fan, worth 4,000 crowns.

The baptism would be an ideal opportunity for Mary to demonstrate the supposed unity in her kingdom as well as the continuity of the Stewart line. It was also the last gasp of the Renaissance splendour she had witnessed as a girl at the court of Henri II. Mary planned the entire ceremony with all the thoroughness of a Guise, but, unfortunately, she did not have the income of a Guise and the baptism plunged her into debt to the merchants of Edinburgh for £12,000 Scots, causing her, for the first time in her reign, to raise a special tax.

On 17 December the actual ceremony took place in the Chapel Royal of Stirling Castle. At six months, the prince was older than was usual for a Catholic baptism, but the various tumults in the court had caused unavoidable delays. The infant was lying in his private chamber, where he had his own household, supervised by the Earl of Mar as his guardian with the countess as his governess. His wardrobe was in the care of Alison Sinclair, and there were five noble ladies who acted as James's 'rockers' as he lay in his cradle being soothed by his personal musician. There is no proof that Alison Sinclair was the daughter of the Janet Sinclair who had been Mary's nurse, but if she was it would create a charming symmetry. At five o'clock in the evening the young prince was carried to the chapel by the Comte de Brienne as Charles IX's proxy and was attended by the Countess of Argyll on behalf of Elizabeth. Barons and lesser nobility lined the passages from the prince's chamber to the chapel, all holding candles – directly reminiscent of François II's christening at Fontainbleau. They were met at the chapel door by the Archbishop of St Andrews flanked by the Bishop of Dunblane, William Chisholm; Robert Crichton, Bishop of Dunkeld, and John Leslie, Bishop of Ross, with the entire complement of the Chapel Royal in full clerical vestments. The prince was christened James Charles Stewart – 'James' for the continuity of the Stewart name and 'Charles' to please his godfather, the King of France. He was created Prince and Steward of Scotland, Earl of Carrick, Lord of the Isles and Baron Renfrew. At Mary's request the practice of the priest spitting into James's mouth was omitted, but in every other respect the ceremony was performed with the full pomp of the Catholic Church. In fact, it had been difficult to find Catholic nobles of sufficient rank to take part.

Huntly, Moray, Bothwell and Bedford – Protestants to a man – did not attend the service but stood outside the door of the chapel. They did, however, attend the state banquet afterwards during which Moray acted as carver and Huntly as butler, with the whole affair supervised by Bothwell. Even the banquet carried unmistakeable political overtones since care had been taken that Catholics served Protestants and vice versa. 'There was dancing and playing in abundance' and Bedford was persuaded that his male attendants should take part in the dancing, thus ensuring that England celebrated equally with Scotland. Next day there was a tournament, and on 19 December the climax came with another banquet. This was served at a round table by nymphs and satyrs on a movable stage. A child dressed as an angel was lowered from the ceiling and recited a Latin poem by Patrick Adamson ending with the triumphal statement that 'the crown of Mary awaits her grandsons'. Unfortunately, the machine controlling the moving table broke down halfway through the meal and the remaining courses were served more conventionally.

Later in the day the celebrations continued on the esplanade of the castle, where a mock fort had been built, representing Mary's position as queen. There were Highlanders dressed in goatskins who threw fire-balls, while demons and Moors in lambskins attacked with fire-spears. Soldiers defended against all comers, but the royal castle remained intact, and fireworks were launched. These had been hauled up the walls and crags under the supervision of the controller of artillery in secret and put in place over a period of seven days. Mary had arranged a similar, but smaller, display for the wedding of Lord Fleming in May 1562, when a sea battle was fought with fireworks and artillery on Dunsappie Loch beside Holyrood. This time Bedford could report that he had witnessed 'fireworks, artillery and all other things pleasant for the sight of man'. He had, however, been offended by one masque, devised by Sebastien Pagez, one of Mary's valets, in which men appeared as satyrs and deliberately shook their tails at the English, while the Scots roared with laughter. Since the English knew of the traditional Scots (and French) canard that Englishmen had tails, it was clearly designed to shock them and one courtier named Hatton, a member of the English ambassador's train, told Melville that 'if it were not for the Queen's presence, he would put a dagger to the heart of that French knave Sebastien'. But this was a trifling event during the triumphant three-day-long celebration.

The baptism had been a total success and Mary had 'behaved herself admirably well' and entertained 'all the goodly company in the best manner', although she was in pain most of the time, having had another riding accident and hurt one of her breasts, which was now swollen. What the fête celebrated may have been completely illusory, and the united loyalty of the nobility towards the Stewart crown was merely a propaganda dream, but in terms of splendour it certainly approached the *triomphes* of the Valois, and Mary knew that her uncles would have approved totally. The fact that it resulted in huge debts and an increase in taxation was of no relevance, and the loss of a flowered tapestry and a Turkey carpet, discovered when the inventories were made, was of no consequence.

Darnley had been absent from the proceedings entirely; 'His undecided mind had not determined whether to be present at the baptism of the child, or to remove to Glasgow, where he might enjoy the feeble communication of his father.' In fact he was sulking in his own apartments at Stirling and summoned du Croc to visit him, something that du Croc's master had expressly forbidden him to do. However, the ambassador did make the visit and reported one reason why Darnley did not wish to appear in public: 'His bad deportment is incurable nor can there ever be any good expected from him for several reasons which I might tell was I present with you.' In fact, Darnley was making the transition from secondary to tertiary syphilis, although his complaint was euphemistically referred to by the court as 'smallpox'.

The disease had been evident since his arrival in Scotland, when it had been called 'measles'. In this stage he would have had mucous lesions in his mouth and his breath would have smelled horrible. His 'measles' would have been suppurating pustules, or 'gammata', and it is a mark of Mary's devotion to duty that she allowed him to impregnate her. She was fortunate not to have caught the disease herself. When du Croc visited Darnley he was being treated with mercury and medicinal baths filled with sulphur water. Du Croc noticed that he had lost most of his hair and teeth and the mercury treatment was causing him to over-salivate – in other words he dribbled involuntarily. Should the infant James die there could now be no brother as a royal safety net.

CHAPTER TWELVE

Some evil turn

On Christmas Eve 1566 Mary granted a pardon – 'relaxation and dresse' – to Morton and the other Rizzio plotters, extending her clemency even to Kerr of Fawdonside, who had held the pistol to her belly. George Douglas and Andrew Mar were excluded from this pardon although at Craigmillar the lords had asked her for clemency for all. They had promised to rid her of Darnley by 'other means' on receipt of such clemency and now, even though the pardon had only been partial, they felt a solemn obligation to carry out their part of the bargain, although Mary probably did not understand that by pardoning the plotters she was activating the Craigmillar Bond. By 10 January, Morton was at Berwick and wrote to Cecil thanking him for his courteous behaviour while he had been in exile. His missive reads like the sort of bread-and-butter letter sent to one's hostess after a pleasant weekend in the country.

Mary wrote to Elizabeth on 3 January 1567 thanking her for examining the 'supposed' will of Henry VIII and promising to send some of her council to confer on these matters. Mary thanked Bedford for his attendance and gave him a chain set with diamonds worth 2,000 crowns, presumably treating du Croc and de Brienne with equal courtesy. She was well aware of Darnley's ineffectual plotting, including a mad scheme to seize power by raising a force in France, and, although he had now moved to his father's house in Glasgow, hysterically claiming he was being poisoned, he was still perilously near Stirling Castle and Prince James. So it was with some relief that on 14 January,

James's household arrived at Holyrood and into the safety of his mother's protection.

Darnley was now isolated and the queen seemed to move according to the will of the plotters as they began to implement their interpretation of the Craigmillar Bond.

Whittinghame Castle, just beyond Dunbar, belonged to Archibald Douglas, Morton's brother and a kinsman of Bothwell's, and it was there, on 14 January 1567, that Morton arrived to be met by Bothwell and Lethington. The fine details of Darnley's murder were then agreed. The lords also realised that Mary was soon to become twenty-five years old and, under the prevailing Scots law, could, on her birthday, revoke all the grants of land she had made previously. With Darnley's encouragement this could mean that Mary might impose a reversion on all grants made to Protestants, but now they had an opportunity to remove this threat to their fortunes by carrying out the unspoken wishes of their queen.

Mary had sent her own physician to treat Darnley but was well aware that a rival power base to her own was developing among the Lennoxes in the west. William Heigate, Provost of Glasgow, brought her information of a plot by Darnley to seize Prince James and declare himself regent, imprisoning Mary. It would therefore be to her advantage to have Darnley under a closer watch in Edinburgh, and, accompanied by Bothwell and Huntly, she left for Glasgow. The escort was necessary since Darnley, who was now in his ancestral lands of the Lennox where he could expect support, might attempt a coup d'état. Realising that the earls' presence in Glasgow would be interpreted as enemy action, the two noblemen took Mary as far as Callander and the final lap of the journey was made under the care of Châtelherault, whose Hamilton power base was nearby. Mary also took her own escort of halberdiers.

At Glasgow, Mary was met by Thomas Crawford, a servant of Darnley's, who told her that the Earl of Lennox was afraid to meet her in person because of 'sharp words' exchanged at Stirling. Mary replied, 'There is no medicine against fear', and

Darnley and she met on 25 January. He was now bedridden and his smell at close quarters was revolting. A taffeta mask hid his face where pieces of flesh had rotted away and most of his nose had gone. He made an unctuous and feeble plea to Mary: 'I am but young [twenty years old] and you will say you have forgiven me sundry times. May not a man of my age for lack of counsel, of which I am destitute, fall twice or thrice, and yet repent himself and be chastised by experience? . . . I desire no other thing but we may be together as husband and wife.' Mary questioned him over Heigate's allegations and he responded by telling her that he knew there had been some sort of agreement made at Craigmillar and that he was afraid he would be murdered in his sleep. Mary ignored this and promised that they would once again 'be at bed and board' when he was free of his sickness and that she would personally give him the sulphur baths when they were lodged at Craigmillar. Eventually, Darnley's vanity defeated any common sense and he agreed to Mary's proposal. Later, in private, Crawford told him that he would now be more like a prisoner than a free man.

Darnley arrived in Edinburgh on 31 January after a slow journey by horse litter and immediately complained that not only was Craigmillar too remote from the capital – it was three miles distant – but also that Holyrood was too damp. Immediately, Bothwell came up with a perfect alternative suggestion: a house in Kirk o' Field was vacant and Darnley could lodge there. Darnley, who knew that Châtelherault had a house in the Kirk o' Field area, and presumed that he would be lodged there, agreed at once. His presumption was wrong. The house in question was owned by Robert Balfour, brother to the Sir James Balfour who had drawn up the Craigmillar Bond and who was an employee of Bothwell's. Robert Balfour himself lodged in the house next door. The warden of the house was Hepburn of Bolton – a blood relative of Bothwell's – and having admitted Darnley and his party he immediately had all fourteen keys to the house and its rooms copied. Darnley was now, unwittingly,

236

in Bothwell's power, and the final stage of the plot could be put into action.

The events of the next few days have been examined, disputed and denied to an extent probably equalled only by those surrounding the assassination of President Kennedy in 1963. None of the evidence is impartial and the witnesses, many of whom only testified after torture, were all determined to avoid personal implication of any sort.

Kirk o' Field was the residence of the Provost of the Church of St Mary-in-the-Fields. The church was in a quadrangle with a small garden, and the Provost's house itself was in the south-west corner among the properties owned by Sir James Balfour. It was a two-storey building with a large reception room, or salle, on the ground floor giving on to a smaller room beyond, occasionally used as a bedroom. Beneath this was a cellar. On the first floor was a corridor reached by a turret stair with two small rooms used by servants as well as, at the eastern end, a larger room, some sixteen feet by twelve feet, with a small cabinet holding a velvet-covered *chaise percée* under a yellow silk canopy. This was the room occupied by Darnley, its window giving on to the town wall and an alleyway known as Thieves Row. Darnley's bed was against the far wall, with a bath placed under the window, and, to stifle the smell of sulphur, the bath was covered by a door which had been unhooked from its hinges elsewhere. A small Turkey carpet, some cushions, a chair and a table completed the furnishings. There were some tapestries, one of a rabbit hunter, and a few other hangings – loot from Strathbogie after the conquest of the Gordons at Corrichie – but it was all somewhat makeshift. On the ground floor, directly under Darnley's room, a small bed of yellow and green damask with a fur coverlet specially fetched by Nicholas Hubert on orders from Margaret Carwood had been installed, and Mary slept here on Friday, 7 and Saturday, 8 February. She spent her time with her husband or with Lady Reres, often singing to Darnley from the garden outside, presumably driven from the room by the combined smells of sulphur and the invalid himself. As long as Mary was

237

sleeping in Kirk o' Field, Darnley was unreachable and therefore safe, but the assassins knew that on 9 February Mary would attend the marriage celebrations of Sebastien Pagez, her valet, to Christina Hogg, one of Mary's gentlewomen. On that night, therefore, Darnley would have been comparatively unattended. His attendants, George Dalgleish, William Powrie, James and Hob Ormiston, along with Patrick Wilson, were all in Bothwell's pay, while John Hepburn and John Hay were blood relatives of Bothwell. In Darnley's room, his valet, William Taylor, slept on a mattress on the floor, while Thomas Nelson and Edward Symonds, Darnley's own servants, slept in the corridor outside, with only Taylor's boy attendant and his two grooms elsewhere in the house. Here Darnley would be at his most vulnerable before any remission in the disease allowed him to return to Holyrood. Anticipating such a window of opportunity, Sir James Balfour had bought £60 Scots-worth of gunpowder which was now stored in his brother's house next door. The choice of gunpowder provided the nearest thing to death by remote control that the technology of the time allowed, since it meant that no individual person could be identified at the scene of the murder.

On Saturday, 9 February, Darnley was in high spirits. His pustules had, in fact, subsided, and he considered his cure complete, although the syphilis had merely reached one of its many plateaux. However, he no longer had to take his sulphur baths and he was looking forward to returning to Holyrood. This was, therefore, the plotters' last chance of access to him. Mary was in a similar good state of mind since this was the last day before Lent began on Carnival Sunday. In the morning, Mary had attended Sebastien's wedding ceremony at which she had presented the bride with her wedding dress, leaving with a promise to return for the party later in the day. At four o'clock in the afternoon she attended a formal lunch given by the Bishop of Argyll for Moretta, the returning ambassador of Savoy, then, at about eight o'clock, Mary came to visit Darnley accompanied by Bothwell, Argyll and Huntly. She would later keep her promise to attend Sebastien's wedding party and some sources say that she came to Kirk o' Field in masquerade costume. Significantly, at this point Moray had to return urgently to his home in St Andrews to be with his wife, who had recently miscarried. While on the ferry crossing the River Forth, Moray remarked to Lord Herries and others who were standing beside him that 'this night the King shall lose his life'. Lethington had equally urgent work to attend to at the palace and Morton was still under a curfew as a condition of his pardon. Alibis were now being thoroughly established.

Mary spent the evening with Darnley while the nobles passed the time playing cards and dice. Below them, Mary's bed was moved out and William Powrie brought the gunpowder from Balfour's house to be tightly stacked directly below Darnley's room. To be effective, gunpowder needs to be ignited in a confined space and it seems that here the plotters used leather bags or 'polks'. This work was supervised by James Cullen, a mercenary soldier experienced in the use of explosives and now in the garrison of Edinburgh Castle. The work done, Mary was reminded of her promise to attend Sebastien's wedding masque and she prepared to leave. She reassured Darnley, who had grown affectionate during the evening and, to the horror of Bothwell and his friends, had begged her to stay. To their relief she bade him goodnight, giving him a ring and promising him access to her bed the next night. As she came out of the house into the quadrangle, Mary saw Nicholas Hubert, the page nicknamed 'French Paris', covered in black powder and called out, 'Jesu, Paris, how begrimed you are!' She was coming dangerously near to having to acknowledge that she was aware of what was taking place, but immediately rode to the wedding celebrations, herself taking part in the mildly bawdy ceremony of putting the bride to bed. Shortly after midnight Mary was safely asleep in Holyrood.

In Kirk o' Field Darnley continued to drink alone with William Taylor until he himself settled down to sleep. Taylor, as was normal, fell asleep on the floor of his room. The household was not entirely asleep, however, since Hay and Hepburn kept watch below beside the gunpowder.

What now took place can be pieced together from various reports, nearly all suspiciously similar in their incrimination of Bothwell. Just before two o'clock in the morning, Ker of Fawdonside, under orders from Morton and Bothwell, arrived beyond the walls of Kirk o' Field with a detachment of mounted and armed men. The garden of the house itself was already filled with Archibald Douglas and his men, all carrying torches – there was no moon that night – and heavily armed. These Douglases were kinsmen to Bothwell, and it had been at Archibald Douglas's castle at Whittinghame that the final details had been agreed. Their arrival was less than surreptitious and had wakened two local housewives, Barbara Martin and Margaret Crockett, who later testified that they had seen thirteen men arrive from the Cowgate. The noise also awakened Darnley and William Taylor, and, realising that danger was imminent, they made to escape. Hearing that going out by the front of the house would take them directly into the arms of Douglas and his men, they climbed out of their window, Darnley still in his nightshirt and covered with a fur wrap. The two men had used a contraption made from a rope and a chair to negotiate the drop of some sixteen feet, and then made for the garden wall, taking the chair and rope to help them climb over it. It was while attempting to scale the further garden wall of Thieves Row that the pair were spotted by Douglas's men. They were swiftly caught and strangled on the spot. Ironically, had they managed to escape through the garden and climb the next wall, they would have been trapped by Kerr of Fawdonside and his men. Their assailants probably did not know who they had murdered, although Darnley seems to have recognised the livery of the Whittinghame Douglases. Douglas himself did not know immediately that two escapees had been killed. In any case he might at first have presumed that both dead men were simply servants.

At about the same time, Bothwell and two friends left

Holyrood and walked up the High Street, which runs exactly parallel to the Cowgate. They then entered Edinburgh proper at the Netherbow Gate and descended by Blackfriars Wynd to cross the Cowgate and come to Kirk o' Field. They arrived just after Darnley had been strangled. Bothwell, coming directly to the house, found Hay and Hepburn by the door and the fuse lit. The men then locked the doors of the house and retired into the quadrangle. Bothwell felt that the fuse was taking so much time that it had probably gone out and was about to enter the house to check when Hepburn pulled him back – at that point the powder exploded under the now-empty room.

'There remains nothing, all being carried to a distance and reduced to dross, not only the roof and the floors but also the walls down to the foundations so that there rested not one stone on another.' Nothing was 'unruinated'. In fact, Douglas's men were lucky not to have been struck by falling masonry as they rode off, to be seen again by the two housewives who called them traitors and said that they had been at 'some evil turn'. As another part of their evidence the good ladies also claimed to have heard Darnley calling for mercy from his kinsmen (since the Douglases were related to him). When the two housewives, the only impartial witnesses, gave their evidence, 'some words escaped which the inquisitors expected not and they were dismissed as rash and foolish'.

As to the other occupants of the house, Nelson and Simmons, the two servants who were sleeping in the corridor, seem to have followed Darnley and Taylor out of the window, probably having heard the doors being locked, and Nelson himself was alive and well, halfway over the town wall when he was found later by the rescuing party. Two other servants were found dead in the rubble, but everyone else survived. Darnley was certainly dead but the explosion had been, in reality, unnecessary.

The explosion was compared to 'a volley of 25 or 30 cannon, arousing the whole town' and people rushed to the scene where the settling dust revealed total devastation. Captain William

Blackadder, a supporter of Bothwell's, was found wandering nearby and promptly arrested, only to be released when he was found to be no more than a late-night reveller returning home from an evening's drinking near the Tron, or public weighbridge. Bothwell, as sheriff of Edinburgh, was summoned to take charge. In a dubious statement made in 1568 he claimed to have been asleep in bed in Holyrood with his wife, 'his first Princess, the sister of the Earl of Huntly'. Antonia Fraser, in her biography of Mary, wisely points out that this alibi is time-honoured among the criminal fraternity. Bothwell arranged for Darnley's body to be duly inspected by those members of the Privy Council available in Edinburgh, most of whom had been involved in the plot – the foreign ambassadors who asked to see the body were refused access. It was then taken to Holyrood where Mary paid £42 6s Scots to have it embalmed. Although Mary looked at the corpse of her dead husband she 'gave no sign by which the secret emotions of her heart could be discovered'. On 15 February 1567, Darnley was buried in Holyrood Abbey beside James V and a solemn Requiem Mass and dirge was sung over him. A week later Mary entered on the formal forty days of mourning, and for safety's sake moved back into Edinburgh Castle.

Mary was, in fact, stunned by the all-too-evident result of the Craigmillar Bond and, apart from issuing a proclamation offering £2,000 Scots and a life pension for information, she had no idea what action to take. Almost in a trance she attended the marriage of her bedchamber woman Margaret Carwood on 12 February, the Tuesday after the murder. She then went to Seton, relaxing enough to take part in archery contests, partnered by Bothwell against Huntly and Seton. Huntly and Seton lost the contest and had to buy their opponents dinner in nearby Tranent.

There were no immediate arrests but rumours were rife, and the *Diurnal of Occurrents* reported, 'It was said that many great men gave consent to this treasonable deed, the like of which was never heard or seen in this realm. The Earl of Bothwell is more familiar with the queen than honesty requires.' Evidence was gathered in June 1567, when official statements were taken from the main protagonists. All had been tortured with great efficiency and all of their testimony now had a suspicious similarity. They claimed that Bothwell had brought the gunpowder from Dunbar and stored it in his apartments at Holyrood. In fact, Balfour had bought the powder and since his house was next to the Provost's lodging and since it had a perfectly good cellar, the explosive would have been stored there. Hay testified that Bothwell had warned him to be ready on 7 February, then that Powrie, Hepburn, Hay and the two Ormistons were briefed by Bothwell at four o'clock on 9 February, and that at ten o'clock the powder was transferred to Kirk o' Field in 'trunks' on horseback. Bothwell had returned to the palace having left Darnley and changed his silver-trimmed black clothes for more practical black velvet. He was seen entering Edinburgh at the Netherbow Port, so that fragment of the 'evidence', at least, is true. Bothwell was then said to have personally supervised the powder being carried in bags into the room below Darnley's, although one version has the powder being transported in barrels which were too wide for the door and then having to be carried loose into the building. However, Mary saw French Paris with a blackened face when she left the house with Bothwell on the night of 9 February, so the powder must have been in place already. All the versions agreed that the powder was heaped loosely in a 'mine' or 'bing' on the floor. However, gunpowder in this state is highly flammable but not explosive, and if a light had then been set to it, it would have flared briefly with a not-very-satisfying 'phutt'. To have caused an explosion of such destructive power it must have been tightly packed by James Cullen, the mercenary soldier. Darnley and Taylor presumably slept through all this activity, and one version has the plotters wearing slippers over their shoes to muffle the sound of their feet. Hepburn then lit the fuse, locked the door and joined Bothwell in the garden until the explosion took place and the conspirators scattered, Hepburn dropping the copied keys down the Quarry Hole, a nearby well, as he made his way home to Leith. Bothwell was challenged by the sentries at the palace but reassured them that he was 'a friend of Lord Bothwell' and then retired to bed in Holyrood. Half an hour later he was roused by George Hackett, a palace guard, with the news that 'The King is blown up. I trow the King is slain!' Testimony from French Paris on 9 August 1569 and Ormiston on 13 December 1573 confirmed these unlikely stories. The explosives expert Cullen was examined and confirmed everyone else's story, after which he was allowed to escape.

Veracity was actually of no importance since all the testimonies placed the blame firmly on Bothwell's shoulders and no other member of the nobility was mentioned. Clearly from the evidence obtained it could be stated that Bothwell had acted single-handedly and was solely to blame. Since all the others were under his direct command they were obliged to carry out his orders. It was a very satisfactory solution since, by the time the evidence was obtained, Bothwell himself had fled into exile.

Immediately after the assassination, the ripples of gossip as to Mary's involvement spread. Guzmán, the Spanish ambassador at Elizabeth's court, heard that Mary was at Dunbar with Argyll, Bothwell and Morton. He made the immediate presumption that Mary had had prior knowledge of the assassination and concluded, 'Even if the Queen clears herself from it the matter is still obscure.' Mary was not, in fact, at Dunbar, but Guzmán had already linked her with the principal conspirators.

When news reached Elizabeth, she reacted with customary practicality by having the doors leading to all her apartments locked, with the keys removed, leaving only one available, but closely guarded, entrance. Elizabeth also voiced her doubts as to the real culprits to Guzmán and the vexed question of a remarriage was raised. She sent Killigrew to investigate the state of affairs in Scotland with a strongly worded letter to Mary:

Madame, my ears have been so astounded and my heart so frightened to hear of the horrible and abominable murder . . . yet I cannot conceal that I grieve more for you than him. I should not do the office of a faithful cousin and friend if I did not urge you to preserve your honour, rather than look through your fingers at revenge at those who have done you such service . . . I counsel you to take this matter so far to heart that you will not fear to touch even those you have nearest to you and may show the world what a noble princess and loyal woman you are.

This letter shows Elizabeth's secret service at its most efficient. The repetition of the exact phrase 'look through your fingers' might be a coincidence, but it might also give a strong hint that an eavesdropping servant at Craigmillar had reported the substance of the Craigmillar Bond to Elizabeth. Also, as far as one sovereign queen could suggest to another, Mary was being told to arrest Bothwell – 'those you have nearest to you'. At the same time, the erroneous rumour in London was that Mary's nobility suggested to her that 'being a lone and solitary woman . . . she would do well to make him [Bothwell] partaker of her bed'. Killigrew was also told that all appearance of 'amity' would cease and that ratification of the Treaty of Edinburgh was once again paramount. In early March, Killigrew met with Mary 'in a dark chamber and could not see her face' but found her very doleful. The diplomatic clock had been put back seven years.

Moretta, the Savoy ambassador, also had suspicions of Mary's direct involvement and reported that a placard had been posted outside Holyrood saying, 'I, with the Earl of Bothwell and with others whose names shall shortly be declared, did this deed.' Bothwell reacted to this typically by declaring that when he discovered the authors of these calumnies he would 'wash his hands in their blood'. Drury said of him. 'His hand when he talks to any that is not assured to him, [is] upon his dagger, with a strange countenance'.

At the beginning of March another placard had appeared, making yet another accusation of guilt and linking Mary directly to Bothwell. It showed a naked mermaid wearing a crown (in this period a 'mermaid' was street slang for a prostitute). In its right hand was a sea anemone, representing the female genitalia, and in its left hand was the rolled-up net used to trap unwary seamen. Since the mermaid was framed with the royal initials 'MR', there could be no doubt as to who it represented. Below it was a hare – the crest of Bothwell as a Hepburn – with the letter 'H', surrounded with drawn swords. To the sixteenth-century mind, attuned to the niceties of heraldry, the implication was clear: the whore Mary had seduced the brute Bothwell.

At this point Mary had the opportunity to show her power as a ruling queen and could have acted decisively. Diane de Poitiers would have easily persuaded her monarch to undertake mass arrests; Catherine de Medici would have given the instructions herself and, after carefully focused torture, a scenario clearing her of all blame would have become the accepted truth; Elizabeth would have denied all knowledge of the Craigmillar Bond and turned her theatrical wrath on the signatories, despatching them to the Tower. But Mary, seemingly inert and under the control of Bothwell, did nothing at all. Not so inert was Sir James Balfour: he was accused, probably justly, of having had one of his servants killed to prevent him from turning informer. Moray, who had, of course, been in Fife on the fatal night, was now urgently requesting a passport for foreign travel. This was granted, and on 7 April he hastily undertook a five-year exile. The plotters were now isolated and ripe for arrest. But Mary had no trust-worthy allies to prompt her into unwilling action, and the only voice calling for justice was that of the Earl of Lennox, Darnley's father and a sworn enemy of Châtelherault and Moray. Mary had alienated herself from all the nobility except for the plotters, whom she had tacitly encouraged and who would have had no qualms about throwing her to the wolves. As so often happened in Mary's life, she had created a power vacuum, and into it stepped the Earl of Bothwell. By the end of March, Drury reported to Cecil that 'Bothwell does all' and that the rumour was that Mary would marry him.

Bothwell was a short-term opportunist with the philosophy of a Mafia boss. He had no far-sighted strategy to become King of Scotland; he merely seized whatever came to hand and was to his further advantage. Militarily he was an expert in the short, sharp attack coupled with surprise, a tactic which was most effective in ruling his turbulent Border lands. Diplomatically he applied force and, if that failed, he applied more force until his opponent decided to join him rather than be annihilated. Now he realised that no one was exerting any influence over the country and that the queen would never undertake any initiative on her own behalf. The plum of power was ripe for picking.

Catherine de Medici, who was amazed by Mary's inactivity, wrote that unless Mary revenged the death of her husband she would not only be dishonoured but would become the enemy of France. However, Mary continued to sleepwalk. After Darnley's murder 'she hath been for the most part either melancholy or sickly ever since'. J.P. Lawson, the nineteenth-century historian, said, 'The conduct of Queen Mary at this period evinces a fatality and imbecility which can only be explained by viewing her as under the influence of a strong, engrossing and ungovernable passion.' With the Privy Council now lacking Moray, and all of its other members lacking unity, Bothwell, whose wife was now ill, made his first move to gather power by supervising the removal of the prince back to his traditional nursery at Stirling under the governorship of Mar. This allowed him to appoint Sir James Balfour, a supposedly trusted ally, to be governor of Edinburgh Castle. This turned out to be a nearly fatal mistake.

Bothwell was now exercising more authority than Darnley had ever possessed and Lennox brought forth a formal petition that Bothwell be arraigned for the murder. On 21 March, while still at Seton, Mary did agree to summon a parliament, and five days later Lennox asked for Bothwell to be arrested. Nothing was done, but on 28 March a reluctant Privy Council did call Bothwell to appear before an assize on 12 April. Lennox, rather feebly, then claimed he had not enough time to prepare a case and asked for a deferment, also writing to Elizabeth and asking her to intercede.

Mary had been forced by public opinion to allow the move against 'those you have nearest to you', while Bothwell had his own way of dealing with an assize in Edinburgh. On the day of the assize Bothwell had brought 4,000 armed men into the city and posted 200 arquebusiers around the Tolbooth, where the assize was being held, totally controlling who was to be allowed entrance; 'no one had the courage to accost such a dangerous and unprincipled man.'

As Bothwell, accompanied by Lethington and Morton, were about to ride from Holyrood, Drury arrived with a letter from Elizabeth endorsing Lennox's request for a delay. He gave the letter to Lethington but was told that the queen was still asleep and the party rode off. Du Croc then pointed out to Drury that the 'sleeping' queen was, with Mary Fleming, Lethington's wife, standing at a window of the palace enthusiastically waving goodbye to Bothwell.

Bothwell passed 'with a merry and a lusty cheer' to the Tolbooth – the 'lusty cheer' being given by his 200 arquebusiers at the door. Lennox was allowed by law to present six supporters, but he claimed illness and sent only one, Robert Cunningham, while his advocates desired forty days for more perfect collection of his proofs, threatening that if the assize cleared Bothwell, they would lodge a formal protest for wilful error. 'The Earl Morton refused to be of that assize. It is affirmed that at this assize none were sworn. Bothwell has set up a cartel declaring himself clear of this murder, and offering to defend any challenge thereof with his body.' The charge was read and the court 'had long reasoning' but Bothwell, to no one's surprise, was 'made clean of the said slaughter, although it was heavily murmured that he was guilty thereof'. The court did not even notice that Bothwell had been accused of Darnley's murder on 9 February, the day before it actually took place. Less than three weeks later Lennox and his family left for England.

Bothwell, who had already been showered with gifts by the now totally entranced Mary, gilded the lily by appearing on Darnley's own horse, having had some of the dead man's clothes re-tailored for his own use. The tailor, taking his life in his hands, had remarked to Bothwell that this was right since 'according to the custom of the country the clothes of the deceased were given to the executioner'. After an uneasy pause Bothwell decided that this was a joke, and the tailor lived.

The war of the placards continued and two were attached to the Market Cross, one giving a detailed list of some of the conspirators and another, thinking ahead, claiming that no one could 'with upright conscience' part Bothwell and his wife even although he had murdered the husband of his intended new spouse, 'whose promise he had long before the murder'.

On 16 April, Mary rode to open parliament in the same Tolbooth. This was a ceremony she had always revelled in, glittering in jewels, assured of the cheers of an adoring crowd and surrounded by her nobility. Now Bothwell carried her sceptre, Argyll – in place of Moray – carrying the crown, and Crawford, the Sword of State. Her guard of honour, normally provided by the bailies of the Edinburgh Council, was now not ceremonial, but openly protective, and was formed by her own arquebusiers. The population of Edinburgh were no longer cheering their queen.

The parliament did not overtly ratify Bothwell's innocence but awarded him the lands which went with Dunbar Castle, as well as confirming Huntly and his relatives in their lands. It was altogether a more muted affair, and as Mary returned to Holyrood, she must have realised that she had lost the love of the people and passed whatever power she had – but had never used – into the hands of Bothwell. Her court was no longer the site of Renaissance celebration, dancing and masqueing, but a closely guarded military enclave of plotting and politics.

The power held by Bothwell was that of a victorious dictator on the morning after his coup d'état. He had reduced Mary to the position of puppet queen and she had acquiesced; the nobility, still amazed by his actions, were supporting him; he had used a servile legal process to clear himself of all illegalities and the inevitable backlash had not yet begun. His next move had to be to codify his support, which he made immediately on his return to Holyrood after the parliament.

On the evening of 19 April, Bothwell hosted a dinner at Ainslie's Tavern close by the palace, attended by Argyll, Huntly, Cassilis, Morton, Sutherland, Rothes, Glencairn and Caithness, among others, as guests. An official record of this meeting gives Moray as a participant, but since he was abroad this is impossible; he had left Scotland 'as out of discontent' and had left Morton, a man 'who knew well enough how to manage the business, for he was Moray's second self' in his place. Eglinton, who was present, 'slipped away' before signing the now inevitable bond. The signatories vowed to defend Bothwell's innocence and to support his marriage to Mary – 'if it should please her'.

Bothwell had, it seemed, ticked a very important box, but next day Kirkcaldy of Grange wrote to Bedford suggesting that support by Elizabeth for the pursuit of the murderers would win the hearts of all Scots. He also reported that Mary was now so infatuated with Bothwell that 'she care[d] not to lose France, England and her own country for him and [would] go to the world's end in a white petticoat ere she [left] him'. This was schoolgirl rhetoric even for an emotionally immature 24-year-old and contrasts interestingly with Elizabeth's claim that if she were cast out of her realm alone and in her petticoat she would, none the less, prosper.

Mary was clearly not prospering: her bodyguard, on the point of mutiny, demanded their back pay. Bothwell started to solve the problem in his own particular way by seizing the spokesman by the throat and drawing his dagger, but the man was rescued and Mary intervened immediately, paying the guards 400 crowns. Lethington, clearly prompted by Bothwell, implored Mary to marry for the stability of the kingdom, but she refused the plea. Given the history of her first two marriages this, at least, was sensible. Next day she left for Stirling to see her son, and Bothwell announced that he was gathering his forces to ride to Liddesdale. No one believed this and the common rumour was that he would seize the queen and take her to Dunbar. Meanwhile, Cecil wrote one of his many memoranda to himself to remind Elizabeth to seek out the murderers, to note that Mary's complicity in the murder was still widely believed, and to use all means to prevent her marriage to Bothwell.

Having seen that the infant James was fit and well, Mary left him with the Earl and Countess of Mar. Although she did not know it, this was to be the last time she would see her son. Mary set out with Lethington, Melville, Huntly and her normal armed bodyguard, resting overnight at Linlithgow. A few miles west of Edinburgh, where the Gogar Burn joins the River Almond at the village of Cramond, the royal party, having just been ferried across, were reassembling themselves when Bothwell sprang an ambush with 800 armed men. Mary's guards, hopelessly outnumbered, drew their swords, but she restrained them, saying that she would not have blood shed on her behalf. Bothwell took her bridle and told her there were hostile elements awaiting her in Edinburgh; he then escorted her by way of Granton and Leith to 'safety' in his castle at Dunbar, where the gates were locked on the entire royal party, including Lethington and Melville. The *Diurnal* reported, 'The Earl of Bothwell, being well accompanied, ravished the queen and took her that same night to his castle of Dunbar (not against her will).' Captain Blackadder, the nocturnal reveller and now one of Bothwell's men, alleged to Melville that the charade had been mounted with the queen's consent.

In fact, Mary did despatch a messenger to Edinburgh to mount a rescue, but he was a messenger who had just heard his queen order that no violence should be used, and his efforts were formal rather than effective. Bothwell knew that his star was only in the ascendant as long as he held the reins of power and that Mary was 'a feather for each wind that blows'. She had resisted Lethington's plea to marry and he had therefore decided to take the initiative by the means best suited to a Border bandit – kidnap. Mary had been genuinely taken by surprise but she had seen maidens being rescued and carried off by their knights from the terraces of Chambord and here, perhaps, at last was her Amadis. However, Bothwell's role as a knight in shining armour was more than a little tarnished.

The common presumption is that Bothwell's first action on his return to Dunbar was to rape Mary, but the *Diurnal* says quite precisely that he 'ravished her and took her to his castle'. Now, it is impossible that he raped her in front of the entire party at Cramond, but in the sixteenth century to 'ravish' simply meant to 'seize', and Mary, her head spinning with the romance of it all, may have consented easily to sexual intercourse at Dunbar. Whatever occurred, by the end of that month Mary was pregnant by Bothwell.

With Mary safely in Dunbar his next move was to marry her. Since she had been dishonoured by him she would have had no choice, but first he had to divorce Lady Jean Gordon. He rode to Edinburgh on 26 April to file for a divorce. With admirable thoroughness Bothwell cited his illicit rendezvous with Bessie Crawford in the church tower at Haddington as evidence of adultery, while at the same time lodging a request for an annulment on the grounds of consanguinity before the court of the Archbishop of St Andrews. Thus his divorce would have legality in both civil and canon law. No one contested the divorce and the decree annulling the marriage was granted on 7 May. The long-term effect of this cynical act would be to disengage Huntly, Lady Jean's brother, from Bothwell's supporters. Oddly enough, the Catholic Bishop of Ross, a one-time ally of the Huntlies, proved his skill as a diplomat by managing to remain a friend of Bothwell's, possibly since he was reputedly able to out-drink the Border lord.

On the day before the divorce was granted, Bothwell was

confident enough of his prize to return with Mary to Edinburgh. Accompanied by Lethington and the still-faithful Huntly, he entered by the West Port, rode through the Grassmarket and then up to the High Street and the castle. It was a shorter route and exposed the couple to less risk of public disapproval. This was a far cry from the *entrées joyeuses* of the past: with Bothwell now on foot leading Mary's horse by the bridle, she re-entered her capital more as a captive than as a sovereign queen. Bothwell had, however, disarmed his men and the royal escort looked comparatively peaceable. Bothwell immediately asked John Craig, as minister of St Giles, to declare the banns of marriage, which Craig refused to do, declaring in an open sermon that the marriage was adulterous and that Mary had been taken by force. Typically, Bothwell demanded that the town council hang the minister forthwith and the justice-clerk appeared with a letter from Mary declaring that she was 'neither ravished nor detained in captivity'. Craig, under protest, did reluctantly call the banns and on 12 May Mary declared to the Privy Council, '[she] stands content with the said earl and has forgiven him, all hatred conceived by her majesty for the taking and imprisoning of her at the time foresaid'.

Mary created Bothwell Duke of Orkney, reputedly placing the coronet on his head herself, and on 15 May the couple were married in the chapel at Holyrood by the Bishop of Orkney, Adam Bothwell, according to the Protestant rite, at ten o'clock in the evening with 'neither pleasure nor pastime'. One contemporary said that the marriage was 'huddled up in an unorderly way'. Lord Herries had begged her not to marry Bothwell, and du Croc warned her that the deed would lose her the friendship of France. Ironically, of Mary's first two marriages, one had been entirely dynastic and the other impetuous, if necessary for the continuation of the royal line, but both were celebrated with the utmost formal pomp. However, this third marriage at least appeared to be for her a romantic match and was, by contrast, a rather shoddy affair. She had been widowed by her first bridegroom, her second husband had been murdered only three months previously, and only fifteen months had passed since she herself had given Lady Jean Gordon a cloth-of-silver wedding dress for her marriage to Bothwell. Her careful Guise education had been of no use to her, and now she had isolated herself from even those of the Scots nobility who were still loyal. The popular view was made clear when placards appeared on the gates of Holyrood, now quoting Ovid: 'Mense malas maio nubere vulgus ait' ('As is common said, none but harlots marry in May'). David Hume, in his *History of England*, tells us that 'the Scots who resided abroad, met with such reproaches that they durst nowhere appear in public'. Mary wrote to Elizabeth, 'the factions and conspiracies that of long time continued herein, which, occurring so frequently had already in a manner so wearied and broken us that we ourselves were not able of any long continuance to sustain the pain and travail in our own person'. She does not declare Bothwell innocent, only that 'he was acquitted by our laws'. Elizabeth described her marriage 'hard to be digested by her or any other monarch'.

Following her abduction the enormity of her situation had started to be felt almost at once. On 1 May in Stirling a confederation of the nobility was formed to 'pursue the Queen's liberty, preserve the prince from his enemies in Mar's keeping, and purge the realm of the detestable murder of our king'. In hard political terms, what this meant was that the upstart Bothwell had become far too big for his boots and had to be cut down to size. This marked a reversal in the attitude of the nobility who had enthusiastically signed the Ainslie Tavern Bond, and demonstrates how quickly Bothwell had achieved his new status, with only one more step remaining between him and the crown.

Since the death of James V, Scotland had been ruled first by governors, then a queen regent, who was followed in turn by a French-educated girl who had imposed no firm government over the country. Now, with Prince James safely in their grasp under the governorship of the Earl of Mar, the nobility prepared themselves again for what had been commonplace over the last

130 years – a royal minority and a regency. Among others, the proposers of this action were Argyll, Atholl, Morton and Mar, three of whom had been signatories of the Craigmillar Bond, and they were to be joined in this new confederation by the earls of Glencairn, Cassilis, Eglinton, the new Earl of Ruthven and eleven others. With Châtelherault and Moray abroad, this confederacy of the nobility almost exactly mirrored those who had opposed Mary's marriage to Darnley during the Chase-about Raid.

They felt confident enough, while at Stirling, to commission a masque, 'The Murder of Darnley and the Fate of Bothwell', at the end of which the boy playing Bothwell was hanged amid uproarious applause. The hanging was slightly over-realistic and some anxious time elapsed before the boy actor recovered. Now the signatories departed to their own lands to raise levies.

Mary, who had never previously needed to raise an army, and whose income from the 'thirds' precluded such expenditure, had to face the first serious shortage of money in her reign. She had only raised taxes once before – to pay for her son's baptism. Now, she sold off plate and jewels and even tried to melt down Elizabeth's christening present of a gold font to mint coinage to pay her troops. The font was so large that it proved impossible to melt and Mary merely managed to deface the gift.

Mary's romantic notions were rapidly disappearing as her relationship with Bothwell disintegrated. She seemed unaware that his only previous female relationships had consisted of sexual conquest followed by virtual abandonment, and that he made no secret of his infidelities – 'there has been no end of Mary's tears and lamentations'. His divorced wife, Jean Gordon, still lived in Crichton Castle and was regularly visited by him, and du Croc reported that the earl still regarded Jean as his spouse, and the queen as a kind of legal concubine. The normal rules of society did not apply to Bothwell. His jealousy of Mary, his latest possession, was constant and she was allowed no male contact, being the victim of censure for the comparatively slight gesture of giving a horse to the unstable Earl of Arran. Bothwell also removed her female servants and replaced them with his own trusted retainers to keep her under constant watch. The depth of her unhappiness with the plight she had brought upon herself can be judged by her saying to du Croc on her wedding day that she 'wanted only death', and on another occasion, in the presence of Melville, asking for a knife to stab herself, 'Or else I shall drown myself.' This remark betrayed no real intention of suicide but was an impulsive cry of desperation which clearly showed the extent of her unhappiness. Extraordinarily, the once-loathed Darnley was now, on a placard, referred to as 'Gentle Henry', and when Mary was seen by some Edinburgh housewives they called out, 'God save your grace', but added, 'if you be guiltless of the king's death.' A ballad on the death of Darnley circulated beginning with the lines, 'Adieu, all gladness, sport and play, / Adieu, farewell both night and day.' Distance was lending enchantment to his memory.

In public, Mary tried to maintain a pretence of normality, riding with Bothwell and running at the ring together with him. Bothwell totally ignored court protocol, appearing in Mary's presence bareheaded, forcing her to try to make a joke of it by taking his cap and putting it on his head herself. He issued proclamations as if he were already either king or protector. Mary, needless to say, obediently trotted along, issuing yet another proclamation defending the Reformed religion, but courtiers noticed a coarsening in her language, echoing her normally foul-mouthed husband. Mary was rude about the lords: 'Atholl is but feeble, for Argyll, I know well how to stop his mouth, as for Morton, his boots are but new pulled off and still soiled, he shall be sent back to his old quarters', that is to say, back to exile.

The court itself was shorn of all gaiety. There were far fewer servants and many more soldiers, with Lethington and Huntly being the only advisers still loyal to Mary. In fact, Huntly was now an extremely reluctant ally of Bothwell's since the latter's cynical divorce from Huntly's sister, and he asked for permission to leave the court. Mary refused, telling him that she knew he was turning against her, as had his father at the Battle of Corrichie. This was not only petulant but also directly insolent and personally hurtful, and resulted in Huntly promptly defecting with his supporters to the safety of Edinburgh Castle. The castle was under the control of Sir James Balfour, who had secretly changed sides without the knowledge of Bothwell. Lethington felt his life was under threat from Bothwell, eventually quitting the court for the circle of the Confederate Lords and the King's Party. With these defections there was no longer any effective government in Scotland apart from that of Bothwell, who was seen as a usurper supported by his somnambulant wife.

The Lords made their first move to confront Mary and Bothwell while they were at Borthwick Castle, twelve miles south of Edinburgh. The hostile forces arrived on the night of 10 June and Bothwell, with his usual regard for his own welfare, escaped, leaving Mary to confront the Lords, who were now openly abusive outside the castle walls. On the next night Mary escaped in male disguise, riding astride on a servant's horse, and joined Bothwell at three in the morning. They then took refuge in Dunbar, while Bothwell hastily assembled an army: defensive action was not his kind of warfare.

On the following day the Privy Council declared that since Mary was a prisoner she could not govern, and therefore, for the sake of the nation, all means must be used to free her. The council went on to accuse Bothwell openly of murder, illegal marriage and 'ravishing and invading the princess's body', and called the burgesses to arms on three hours' notice. Sir William Drury reported to Cecil that even 'If there were no other quarrel or cause of choler than the evil speech that passed at Borthwick, it is like enough to cause the shedding of blood.' He was right.

The Privy Council on the same day accused Bothwell of having 'put violent hands on [Mary], and that he had seduced [her] into an unhonest marriage and murdered Darnley', whereupon the Lords occupied Edinburgh and summoned whatever levies they could to protect the prince. They also demanded that Bothwell be tried. The facts that the prince was safely in their power and that Bothwell had already been tried and acquitted were ignored in their legitimising of a call to civil war. In Edinburgh, Sir James Balfour, the probable author of the Craigmillar Bond, the purchaser of the gunpowder and a principal accessory to Darnley's murder, had been granted the governorship of Edinburgh Castle by Bothwell. He now asked the Confederates if he could remain in his post provided he put the castle at their disposal. This was an egregious act of treachery. John Knox had known Balfour when they had been fellow galley slaves and said of him, 'He has neither fear of God nor love of virtue, further than the present commodity persuadeth.' The Lords agreed at once, thus gaining the chief stronghold in Scotland and imprisoning Huntly without firing a shot. They also now controlled the mint and had possession of the gold christening font, Mary's last asset. Balfour proved his new loyalty by sending a message to Mary at Dunbar proposing that she and Bothwell return to Edinburgh, where they would find safety under the guns of the castle. Being unaware of his volte-face, they agreed and Mary called on her subjects to come to her aid at Musselburgh. She reached Haddington with 600 men, the country having largely ignored her call, and met Bothwell, who had summoned 2,000 more, as well as three pieces of artillery. The couple spent what would be their last night together in nearby Seton Castle.

The Lords rested at Musselburgh under the command of Morton and Argyll, having created a banner showing a drawing of Darnley dead below a tree, a child kneeling beside him with the motto 'Judge and revenge my cause, O lord!' This purported to justify their actions as not being against their lawful queen but only against Bothwell as murderer of Darnley.

By five o'clock on the morning of 15 June the royal forces were marching towards Edinburgh with Mary at their head, but not now sporting her one-time armour of the Chase-about Raid, a silver breastplate and a steel cap with a jaunty feather. Now, most of her clothes were in Holyrood, in the hands of the Lords, or abandoned in Dunbar, and she wore a simple red skirt, reaching only to mid-calf, over a red petticoat, her sleeves tied into points, a kerchief and muffler, and a velvet hat. Her choice of red, the traditional colour of Catholic martyrdom, is interesting. The legitimacy of her forces was simply established by the carrying of a flag with the national saltire of Scotland and a banner with the royal emblem of a lion rampant.

Two miles south of Musselburgh the two sides came face to face at Carberry Hill, near the village of Inveresk. Neither side wanted to fight a pitched battle since the Lords had only very dubious legality – in fact they were making war on their sovereign queen – and Bothwell knew that if he won a victory here he would still have to enter Edinburgh. By now he may have heard of Balfour's treachery and he knew he would be vulnerable under the guns of the castle. He had hopes that Huntly and the Hamiltons might appear to support him, but Huntly was a prisoner and the Hamiltons, wisely, remained in Edinburgh. Morton and Home took up a position with their mounted troops at the forefront, although Bothwell was well encamped on the crest of the hill with his artillery threatening any cavalry charge. Both sides waited nervously for the other to make a move.

Du Croc had followed the Lords from Edinburgh and, after an amount of bickering, he persuaded Morton to accept the surrender of Bothwell as enough to allow an honourable withdrawal. When he put this to Mary she responded furiously that the Lords were treasonably repudiating the Bond of Ainslie's Tavern, and that it was thanks to Bothwell that they were now confirmed in possession of their lands. Mary asked du Croc to tell the Lords that she would pardon any who begged for it, but she flatly rejected Morton's offer. Du Croc noted later that Bothwell's side was in greater order, 'One man in command, but the other side had too many counsellors, there was great disagreement amongst them. I took my leave of the Queen and left with tears in my eyes.' He also noticed that the queen was 'great' and was carrying Bothwell's child, the heir to the throne if anything were to happen to Prince James. The Earl of Glencairn received Mary's offer with scorn and repeated the demand for the surrender of Bothwell. Realising that he could broker no peace, du Croc returned to Edinburgh and the two sides continued to glare at each other in the summer heat.

By eleven o'clock the sun was well up and the temperature had soared. While the Lords could carry water from the River Esk, Bothwell's men had brought 'vin et viandes' and they fell out of line to eat lunch. As a result of wine and sun about 300 of them rode back to Dunbar with headaches.

Kirkcaldy of Grange appeared under a white flag and formally demanded the surrender of Bothwell. Before Mary could answer, Bothwell immediately ordered an arquebusier to shoot Grange – white flag or no – but Mary countermanded this. Bothwell then rode out in front of his troops on his black charger and offered to settle the affair by single combat, asking the Lords, 'What harm have I done?' The Lords immediately appointed Grange as their champion, but Mary, displaying a knowledge of the rules of chivalry, rejected him as being of too low a birth to fight with Bothwell. The Laird of Tullibardine offered himself and was rejected on the same grounds, although he sulkily complained that his blood was as noble as Bothwell's. Both Grange and Tullibardine instantly became the bitter personal enemies of Bothwell.

The farce of playground posturing continued as Bothwell now named the Earl of Morton as a suitable foe. This was admissible under the laws of chivalry but impractical since Morton was fifteen years older than Bothwell and without any battle experience. Bothwell was an experienced hand-to-hand warrior, a skilled swordsman with several killings already to his credit, and the much younger Lord Lindsay immediately offered himself as a surrogate. Morton gave Lindsay his own sword to carry. It was a two-handed six-foot-long weapon which had been Morton's father's and was completely unwieldy for use in a formal single combat, but Lindsay accepted – he could hardly refuse –

took off his armour, prayed for God's assistance, and then, re-armed, he mounted his horse with the giant sword at his waist. He would almost certainly be killed.

Surprisingly, Bothwell had not taken a favour from Mary to wear as her champion, and she now intervened in the contest by forbidding its continuance. Melville of Halhill reports that Mary then spoke again to Grange and offered to give up Bothwell in return for the Lords' obedience to her. As often with Melville, it is doubtful that this was the exact truth, but Bothwell would have seen his men melting away and recommended to Mary that they retreat to Dunbar to collect more forces. Mary, however, be-lieved in the Lord's promise of obedience and had previously spoken with Lethington and Atholl, who assured her of their loyalty. She now asked for a safe conduct for Bothwell, but was told by Grange that he had no authority to make such an agreement. However, Grange assured Bothwell that he would do his utmost to see that he was not pursued, and Mary decided to yield to the Lords, provided they promised to hold another parliamentary trial of Bothwell.

Bothwell and Mary then embraced in plain sight of everyone, pledging mutual loyalty. Bothwell, who liked to keep an ace up his sleeve, then gave Mary his copy of the Craigmillar Bond on which were the signatures of Lethington, Argyll, Huntly and Balfour and which also incriminated Morton. Bothwell had brought it with him should he be captured and openly accused of acting alone in the planning of Darnley's murder. He and Mary then parted and her last sight of the Earl of Bothwell was his horse galloping towards Dunbar.

The rest of his story is soon told. Failing to raise any support in Scotland, he sailed for France, but his ship was captured by Danish pirates and he was sold to the Danish king, Frederick II. Frederick's chancellor, Erik Rosencrantz, was a cousin of the Anna Throndsen who had pursued Bothwell across Europe in a breach-of-promise suit, and for this Bothwell was now brought to justice. At first he was confined in comparative luxury despite being an embarrassment to the Danes. Neither England nor

France wanted to take possession of the earl, and to return him to Scotland would mean antagonising Mary. Plots and counterplots surrounded him and eventually Rosencrantz, in a blood-chilling phrase, recommended that Frederick should send him 'where men may forget him'. This was the castle of Dragsholm, where he was chained to a pillar in a dungeon, in dark and solitary confinement. The man who had spent his life in the saddle among the Border hills of Scotland died, 'distracted of his wits and senses', in April 1578, nearly eleven years after the aborted Battle of Carberry Hill.

At Carberry, 'One was sent from the Queen's side with a long pike and cast it down before the horsemen of the other army in token that victory was theirs.' Grange was sent to receive the queen and he rode up and kissed her hand. She said, rather formally, 'Laird of Grange, I render myself unto you, upon the conditions you rehearsed unto me in the name of the Lords.' Part of this was an offer from Morton that this 'business [could] be wrought in a right posture'. Mary, out of impulse, managed to antagonise Morton immediately by riding up to him, with the faithful Mary Seton behind her on a pony, and asking, 'How is this, my Lord Morton? I am told that all this is done in order to get justice against the king's murderers. I am also told that you are one of the chief of them.' The arrogance of the Guises immediately took the place of any conciliatory guile.

Mary had expected to be greeted by penitent lords, if not on bended knee, then at least begging her pardon – which she would then graciously grant. Instead she was received by her rebellious nobility with courtesy enough, but the 'lesser sort' called out, 'Burn the murderess! Burn the whore!' Grange and others beat the mob into silence with the flat sides of their swords.

Her ordeal began as she was separated from her servant women and, with the banner showing Darnley's death held in front of her, she was ridden back to Edinburgh. It became clear that she was now a prisoner when she was taken not to Holyrood, but to a house belonging to the Provost, Sir Simon Preston. This was an old dilapidated building, called the Black Turnpike because of its narrow staircase, on the junction of what is now Hunter Square and the High Street, and when Mary arrived, about midnight, a dinner had been prepared for the Lords, who asked her to join them at their table. This was a complete reversal of etiquette that appalled the protocol-obsessed Mary. She replied that they had already provided her with food enough and now, having reduced her to her present state, she required rest. This was false bravado as she now feared the worst for her future, but the Lords, who had also had a hard day in the saddle, merely shrugged as if a servant had refused their largesse. Mary was thrust unceremoniously into a room thirteen feet square and eight feet high, furnished only with a small bed. Still trying to preserve some of her royal dignity, she waited for her serving women to arrive and undress her, but instead armed guards took up their posts outside. Some guards even lounged against the walls of what seemed to Mary to be her prison cell. It was now past midnight and Mary had not eaten since dawn at Seton. She was still in the clothes she had worn at Carberry – Mary who was so particular about her appearance – covered with the dust of the day, completely alone without servants and uncertain how long she would remain under these conditions. It was the first time in her life that she would spend the night alone. As a child there had always been an ever-present nurse, and from adolescence a lady-in-waiting had slept in Mary's room. She would have been dressed and undressed several times a day and never would a servant have been out of earshot. This was an entirely new and unpleasant experience for a woman of her rank, and it was not going to be the last.

She was allowed to write a letter to Grange complaining of her plight, and even this involved further indignity for her. She, Mary, Queen of Scots, had to address a guard directly, not through a court servant, and ask for writing materials, which would normally have been kept close at hand, and then write her letter while he watched her. The answer to her letter came back with suspicious speed, obviously never having reached Grange. Her loyal nobles, it read, fearing that she might fatally harm herself, were obliged to keep a close guard over her and dared not give her a key to her room. Exhaustion overcame her and she lay down, still fully dressed, on the bed, from where she could hear the chatter of the guards. But the mention of her possible death gave rise to the fear, that if she fell asleep, a pillow held over her face would give the rebels the opportunity to say she had taken poison and killed herself in the grief of parting from her murderous husband. After all, she knew that some of her captors had been party to Darnley's assassination, and although she was now in a state of complete exhaustion she was afraid to sleep.

By morning she was half mad with the unreasoning terror which had grown through the night. The window of the room gave onto the High Street and the placard showing the death of Darnley had been hung beneath it so that the Edinburgh mob had no difficulty in establishing the presence of their whore-queen. Indeed, they were shouting for her to face them. She screamed from the window that she was being imprisoned by her own subjects and the mob replied with jeers and calls of 'whore', 'adulteress' and 'murderer'. Now completely demented with sleeplessness, terror and impotence, she tore her already dusty and dishevelled hair down to 'hang about her lugs' and stripped to the waist exposing her breasts to the gaze of the crowd, who were now thoroughly enjoying the sight of a totally mad woman. She saw Lethington pass up the High Street to the council and shouted after him, but he 'drew down his hat and made as if [he had] neither seen nor heard her Majesty'. The crowd became angrier and started throwing the always dangerously available cobble stones, shouting for a ladder to be fetched, but her guards, wisely, pulled her away from the window and she was given some bread and a little water to drink.

The council spent all day debating the outcome of Carberry. The idea of keeping Mary captive while they ruled through the infant James had clearly been in their minds, but they were unprepared for the sudden reality of their imprisoned queen, half naked and screaming like a madwoman from a first-floor window in the capital. Lethington, having the coolest head and the greatest grasp of diplomacy, was sent to reason with her, while the council thought out their next move. Mary continued to scream treachery to Lethington until he managed calm her down and persuade her that he was the only friend she had left among the nobility. Morton came to visit her at nine o'clock in the evening and told her that she would be conveyed to Holyrood as soon as it was dark. As it was mid June, it was not until after eleven o'clock that she was taken to the palace where, at last, supper had been prepared and her female servants were assembled. Perhaps now she would be restored to her proper station, although the servants no longer knelt as they served her the food, and Morton stood behind her chair throughout the meal. She was given no chance to change her clothes and had to mend the damage to her bodice as best as she could. She was told that she would be given fresh clothes after she had slept.

This was, in fact, only a ruse. While she was still hungrily devouring her first food for two days, a servant confirmed to Morton that the second part of Mary's journey could be undertaken. On his orders the dishes were cleared – she had not finished eating – and she was told she could now be accompanied by two servants only, but would presently be taken to visit Prince James. She was not even allowed to take her nightdress, which led her to think her normal entourage would be following her, probably for an intermediate stop at Linlithgow. It was well after midnight, and, with a close guard, she was escorted to Leith, where she was put into the care of Ruthven and Lindsay, who saw her across the Forth to North Queensferry, where she expected to turn west for the ride to Stirling. To her complete surprise, however, they headed north towards Loch Leven, where Sir William Douglas had a castle on the island there. Mary had visited the castle many times and enjoyed the hunting grounds around the shore, but now she guessed that she was being taken as a prisoner. Hoping that she might be rescued as she travelled the ten miles or so to the loch, she tried to ride slowly – after all, she was three months pregnant – but her escort whipped her horse for her. On the shore she was met by Sir

William and his brothers, rowed across the lake to the island and shown into a room which formed part of the Douglas apartments on the ground floor, which had been roughly furnished by the laird with his own surplus furniture. The door was locked and Mary stood alone again, still in the clothes she had been wearing since she had left Seton two long days before.

CHAPTER THIRTEEN

It does not appertain to subjects to reform their prince

᪤

It had been determined by the council that Mary must not be allowed to 'follow her inordinate passion' and that she should be 'sequestered from all society of the said Earl of Bothwell', whose whereabouts were still unknown. Grange and Tullibardine, both of whom Bothwell had insulted at Carberry, were sent on what proved to be a fruitless pursuit of the earl. Meanwhile, Sir William Douglas received a formal commission to keep Mary 'without skaith [harm]' until 'further trial be taken about the cruel murder and treasonable slaughter of erstwhile Henry, King, spouse to the Queen'.

The other inhabitants of Lochleven Castle were Sir William's mother, the 'Old Lady'; she was none other than Margaret Erskine, also the mother of the illegitimate Earl of Moray by Mary's father, James V, and she heartily loathed Mary for her legitimacy. A handsome younger son, George Douglas, was the only other family member present. Ruthven and Lindsay were to act as her gaolers. The island was almost entirely occupied by the castle building, a fourteenth-century structure of four storeys with a single entrance on the second floor, adjoining a medieval round tower from which any view of the loch was blocked by the main building. It was in this bleak tower that Mary was eventually placed after a stay in the Gordons' apartments, its obscurity preventing her from signalling to the shore. She was now completely cut off from friends and totally at the mercy of the council who, on 16 June, issued a formal warrant for her imprisonment signed by Morton, Glencairn and Home. Lindsay and Ruthven were given the unwelcome duty of continuing on the island to supervise her close imprisonment. It was an ideal location for a covert assassination.

Argyll, Huntly, Arbroath and eight other minor lords swore to rescue Mary but were powerless to do more than declare their loyalty. The hostile lords now set about tying up loose ends by destroying the Catholic altars in the royal chapel at Holyrood, then seizing the plate and clothes in the palace, although the bulk of Mary's jewellery was still in Dunbar under the control of Patrick Wilson. Their most urgent need was to exonerate themselves from all guilt in the murder of Darnley, and, if they knew that Mary had a copy of the Craigmillar Bond – although it is difficult to see how she could have kept it in her possession through her experiences in Edinburgh – she was in no position to use it. For the rest they set about rounding up the men involved in the plot at Kirk o' Field, starting with the unfortunate Captain Blackadder, who, in spite of his most likely innocence, was hanged, eviscerated and quartered. Powrie, Hay, Hepburn and the rest were taken, and, after torture, produced the convenient confessions which totally incriminated Bothwell. They were summarily hanged. The two housewives, the only independent eyewitnesses, were never closely questioned and were probably told that their continued health depended on their silence. French Paris confessed to a confused version of the now-accepted story, and when Cecil asked to continue his interrogation in England the unfortunate page was swiftly hanged. Wilson and Ormiston fled successfully without trace. The truth was now satisfactorily established: Bothwell, with the connivance of the queen, and with the aid of a gang of personal thugs, had murdered Darnley with the intent of seizing the crown for himself. Everyone else was innocent. Some people actually believed it.

On 19 June an event may have occurred which has given rise to many volumes of debate. Morton claimed that on that evening he was dining with Lethington when a servant told him that Thomas Hepburn, John Cockburn and George Dalgleish had all been seen in Edinburgh. They were all Bothwell's men and on the wanted lists, so Morton despatched servants to arrest them. Thomas Hepburn made his escape, but left his horse behind;

John Cockburn was arrested. Dalgleish was found with 'divers evidences and parchments' but denied that he had any other documents. Morton disbelieved him and he was kept overnight in the Tolbooth in the 'jayne'* – a cage too small to stand up in and too short to lie down in. At the Tower of London a similar cage was called 'little ease', and as 'tiger cages' the same devices were used by both sides in the Vietnam War. After a night in the 'jayne' there was no need for further torture and the next day Dalgleish eagerly took Robert Douglas, Morton's agent, to his lodging where he pulled a silver casket from under his bed. It was taken to Morton at eight o'clock that night. The casket had belonged to Bothwell but had been in the keeping of Balfour at the castle. Bothwell had sent for it at the time of Carberry but the treacherous Balfour had let it come into the hands of Dalgleish. Next morning, in the presence of Atholl, Mar, Glencairn, Lethington and five other lords, the lock was forced. The casket was found to contain 'letters, contracts, sonnets, and other writings'. Morton kept it himself. He gives no account of these witnesses taking the trouble to read or even cursorily examine the contents, although they were all men desperate to blacken Mary and Bothwell's reputations, and they would all want to read the contents at length before making any statements about them. It was to become one of the most celebrated time bombs in the story of Mary Stewart, and by the time the casket's contents were made public, George Dalgleish, who alone could verify or deny Morton's story, had conveniently been executed.

These letters seemed to show Mary's complicity in her seizure by Bothwell and her guilty involvement in Darnley's murder, and they were now in the hands of her enemies. The opposition was, however, confused. On 1 July the Lords still maintained that Bothwell had forcibly ravished the queen when they might have claimed that they had equally damning evidence to the contrary.

On 23 June 1567, Elizabeth wrote to Mary, who was now allowed to receive mail in Loch Leven:

*A cynical corruption of the French 'gêner', meaning 'to cause distress'.

It has always been held in friendship that prosperity provideth but adversity proveth friends. We understand by your trusty servant Robert Melville of your estate, and as much as could be said for your marriage. To be plain with you our grief has not been small thereat; for how could a worse choice be made for your honour than in such haste to marry such a subject who, beside his other lacks, public fame has charged with the murder of your late husband, besides touching yourself in some part, though we trust on that behalf falsely!

She then commiserated with Mary's plight and assured her that she would do all in her power for her honour and safety, and to let Mary's nobility know that she had Elizabeth's backing. In other words, 'If you will be so stupid as to marry a murderer who incriminates you, what did you expect?'

She sent Throckmorton north with her careful instructions: 'He is to urge concord between their sovereign and them – also to declare that as a sister sovereign their queen cannot be detained prisoner or deprived of her princely state.' He was also to warn the Scots that it did 'not appertain to subjects to reform their prince, but to deal by advice and counsel'. He was given freedom, as an ambassador for Elizabeth, to reprove Mary for her faults, his embassy legitimising such *lèse-majesté*. Elizabeth was always careful to stress the inviolability of an anointed sovereign. The Scots were warned against forming an alliance with France.

Throckmorton – for whom one cannot but have sympathy in his task – was also given a memorandum by Cecil: the facts of Bothwell's guilt were to be established; Mary was to commission the nobility to proceed against Bothwell; parliament had to be recalled; all Bothwell's lands were to be given to Mary for Prince James's education; the succession was to be 'renovated and confirmed' – presumably according to the Treaty of Edinburgh; the Reformed religion was to be established – excepting 'none but the Queen's person'; and, finally, four or six councillors were to attend the queen monthly. Throckmorton was given no guidance as to how he was to persuade the rebel lords to undertake all this, but these instructions conform precisely with Cecil's passionate desire for a legitimate Protestant regime acting under the law. He then added, as a postscript to the memorandum, the Latin text 'Athalia 4 regum, interrempta par Joas Regem'. This is a reference to 2 Chronicles 22–3 in the Old Testament, in which Athaliah, Queen of Israel, was murdered by the high priests and nobility in the fourth year of her reign for her slaughter of the 'seed royal of Judah', rending her clothes and crying 'Treason, treason!' She was replaced with the boy-prince Joash under a regency until he took the throne on attaining his majority. So Throckmorton was to uphold the rigour of the law, but if anything else should happen to occur, Cecil would not be astonished and at least there was a biblical precedent.

Throckmorton replied, presumably in a private conversation, that he agreed with Cecil that Prince James would be better off in England, and that he was worried about the growing split of the nobility into Mary's partisans and the proponents of a possible regency. He added that he would accompany the French ambassador to 'see his countenance'. James Melville gave an account of how the sides were coalescing, with Morton, Hume, Atholl, Lethington and Sir James Balfour on one side – the King's Party – and their enemies, the Hamiltons and Huntly – the Queen's Party – on the other. 'The lords who were refused in friendship drew themselves together at Dumbarton, under the pretext to procure by force of arms their sovereign's liberty . . . which they would not have done if they could have been accepted in society with the rest'.

Another reason for Throckmorton wishing to keep close to the French ambassador was his knowledge that Moray, still in France, had been seeking help from the Cardinal of Lorraine and putting pressure on Catherine de Medici. Throckmorton, now at Ware, some twenty miles from London, and sending dispatches as he travelled, still defined Mary's liberty as the main 'mark to shoot at'. By Ferry Bridge in Yorkshire he noted that Argyll, Fleming, Seton and Boyd had joined with the Hamiltons and Huntly and that Dumbarton Castle was at the disposal of

Bothwell himself – should he ever return. Then in Berwick, where he complained that his lodging would make a better jail than a resting place, Throckmorton met Lethington. When asked how the Lords stood, Lethington smiled, shook his head and said, 'It were better for us you would let us alone, than neither to do us or your selves good, as I fear in the end it will prove.' Throckmorton had heard a rumour that Mary had been given the offer of a peaceful reclusion in a French abbey with her aunt, and that Prince James would accompany her 'at the French devotion', leaving Scotland to be governed by a council of regents. But since neither the French ambassador nor any other diplomat was to be allowed access to Mary, this was clearly nonsense. There was nothing for it but for Throckmorton 'to leap on horseback and go to Edinburgh'. Here he received another letter from Elizabeth telling him to assure Mary that her best course was to send Prince James to her in England, where he would be treated as her own child and 'become acquainted with her country'. Throckmorton also very quickly learned that 'no prince's ambassador, nor stranger, should speak with her [Mary] until the Earl of Bothwell be apprehended'. His task was indeed unenviable.

Meanwhile, Mary was recovering from the considerable trauma of her capture. On 14 July Throckmorton reported that she now had five or six ladies in attendance, that three or five gentlewomen and two of her serving women had been restored to her and that she was now taking what exercise she could on the confines of the island. She was still able to supervise her absent household and gave authority for Throckmorton to come to Edinburgh – he was, in fact, already there. It seems very likely that this information was false and that Throckmorton had been given a rosy picture in the hope of ameliorating Elizabeth's wrath – Mary still had only the two ladies she had brought from Holyrood. However, some of her seductive charm was returning and, coupled with close proximity to Mary's undoubted beauty, young Lord Ruthven proceeded to make a fool of himself.

One morning he burst into her bedchamber at four o'clock in the morning, threw himself on his knees and begged her to marry him in exchange for his organising her escape. This was not a surprise, since he had previously sent her a love letter, and this night Mary had concealed her chamber-women behind the tapestries to act as witnesses. This presupposes that Ruthven had told them of his intention and having summoned up his courage – probably with drink – he made his bid. Mary was four months pregnant, still married to Bothwell and with a very uncertain future, but Ruthven was young and stupidly impetuous. Mary indignantly refused him, reported his behaviour to Lady Douglas and Ruthven was recalled. This story was told to Nau by Mary during her captivity and may simply be a pathetic tale told by a prematurely ageing beauty nostalgically recalling, 'Of course they were all in love with me!' It does, however ring true of the Ruthven personality.

Throckmorton was not allowed access to Mary but duly reported the improvement in her condition, as well as her total intractability towards any abandonment of Bothwell. The women of Edinburgh were 'most furious and impudent against the Queen' and Throckmorton was fearful for his own safety among them. All were holding their breath while the Lords made up their minds as to what move to make next; some nobles were starting to consider what Mary's attitude to them might be if she gained her liberty. They all had an eye on the calendar, since Mary was only five months away from the age of twenty-five, when she could withdraw her grants of possession for their lands and, therefore, income. Throckmorton had given the Lords Elizabeth's requests for Mary's release and the prosecution of Bothwell, and they, in the best traditions of diplomacy, asked for time to consider.

Mary saw Robert Melville about 16 July, by which time Throckmorton had suspicions that Mary would be forced to abdicate. There is a quite believable story that he wrote to Mary telling her that a signature obtained under duress was legally invalid. Melville wrapped Throckmorton's letter around his sword and, thus hidden by the scabbard, delivered it to her. Mary, however, gave him her proposals to the Lords. Could she be moved to Stirling to be near her son? Could she have some more of her gentlewomen, an apothecary, a 'modest minister', an embroiderer and a page? She asked to be allowed to see ambassadors and said that if the Lords would not treat her as their queen, then would they please treat her as the late king's daughter and the young prince's mother? She refused to renounce Bothwell, since this would make her forthcoming child a bastard. She also claimed to be 'seven weeks gone with child'. This implies that she conceived the child safely after her marriage to Bothwell, but it is most likely that she was adjusting the dates forward – the reality being that the child was conceived out of wedlock at Dunbar, which would make her nearly three and a half months pregnant.

The problem of her child's legitimacy was brutally solved some time before 24 July, when she miscarried twins of an unknown sex. The fact that the two foetuses were large enough to be seen by her chamber-women – there was no midwife present – seems to make it clear that their conception had taken place at Dunbar.

Given her condition after this event – she suffered postnatal haemorrhage – the next move by the Lords was extremely unfeeling. They had finally decided to cut the Gordian knot and she was visited by Lindsay, accompanied by notaries, who was under precise instructions. Lindsay brought letters formally accusing her of being an accessory to Darnley's murder and of having had relations with Bothwell out of wedlock. There were also three documents which she was required to sign. The first was an instrument of abdication, declaring that she was 'so vexed, broken and unquiet' by the efforts of government that she could no longer continue, and of her own free will and 'out of motherly love' would place the crown and the power of government in the hands of her son. Since she would be admitting that governing had broken her, it would hardly seem a loving act to lay such a burden on James's infant shoulders, but the drafters of the document had no time for such niceties. The document would clear the way for James's coronation. The second document appointed Moray to the office of regent until James's seventeenth birthday, while in the third document, Mary was to appoint a council of regents – Châtelherault, Argyll, Morton, Glencairn and Mar – to await Moray's return to Scotland or to assist him if he so wished. The Lords had been thorough. Lindsay asked Mary to read the documents, but his attitude made it clear that it did not much matter whether she read them or not. Some sources claim that she did not, in fact, read them at all.

Mary, who was still in bed and very weak from loss of blood, quite naturally refused to sign and the atmosphere changed dramatically. It was hinted that if she did not sign she could be taken from the castle and drowned in the lake – echoing her fears when in the Provost's house in Edinburgh – or taken to 'some island in the middle of the sea, there to be kept unknown to the world, in close custody for the rest of her life'. Mary demanded 'very earnestly' to answer the points in the letters before a parliament. Lindsay said he had no power to negotiate, and the notaries read the instruments to her. They then asked her what her decision would be and she again refused to sign. However, Mary had now moved from her bed to a chair and realised that, in the world of realpolitik, the crown was no longer hers and that either her abdication would take it away legally, or her murder would take it away violently. With nowhere left to turn, she signed the papers, asking the notaries to witness that she had signed under duress. She was remembering Throckmorton's smuggled letter of advice. The long chain of conspiracies and of smuggled correspondence had started. It would continue until her death.

It was at this point that she was moved from the Douglas apartments into the medieval tower and was deprived of paper, pens and ink. As in the past in times of crisis, Mary fell ill. This appears to have been a form of jaundice or hepatitis, which caused a swelling, and 'a deep yellow tint spread over her whole body'. The swelling was probably a form of deep vein thrombosis occurring after childbirth. She was allowed a surgeon, who treated her with a heart stimulant and bleeding until she recovered. This illness and her now-stricter isolation cut her off from knowledge of events in Edinburgh and Stirling.

Throckmorton met first with Lethington, who immediately told him that any attempt by England to gather support for Mary would put her life in danger. Then he met the Lords – booted and spurred, ready to ride for Stirling – to whom he appealed for a delay in the coronation since it was not for the good of the state to put the government in the hands of a child. He was told, 'The realm could never be worse governed than it was, for either the Queen was advised by the worse counsel or by no counsel', and the Lords summarily departed. Throckmorton now suggested to Cecil, vainly as it turned out, that he return to London since there was now nothing for him to do. This would save him an embarrassment since the Lords had invited him to attend the coronation and his compliance with this invitation would seem to lend Elizabeth's endorsement of the event. His dilemma was solved on 26 July when he received a long letter from Elizabeth, bidding him to stay in Edinburgh and to continue insisting on Mary's freedom. He was to tell Mary how much 'we mislike their [the Lords'] doing'. In the letter Cecil crossed out 'their', and replaced it with 'her', thus altering the whole tone of the communication. Throckmorton was to tell the Lords 'we will take plain part against them, to revenge their sovereign, for example to all posterity . . . You may assure them we detest the murder of our cousin the king, and mislike the marriage of the queen with Bothwell as much as any of them. But think it not tolerable for them . . . to call her . . . to answer to their accusations by way of force; for we do not think it consonant in nature that the head should be subject to the foot.' Finally, he was expressly forbidden to attend the coronation 'by any means'.

Melville wrote to Elizabeth on 29 July 1567 and reported that Mary had said 'she would rather herself and the prince were in your realm than elsewhere in Christendom'. More importantly, on the same day in the parish church of Stirling the 13-month-old boy was crowned as James VI, and the Scottish nobility touched the crown as a sign of their fealty. The rebel, were firmly in control: Morton and Erskine of Dun took the oath for the boy, Ruthven and Lindsay affirmed Mary's abdication and Knox delivered a sermon on a text from 2 Kings verses 1 and 2, in which the eight-year-old Josiah was crowned and 'did what was right in the sight of the Lord'. The one point of dispute was that James was anointed by a priest, at which 'Knox and the other preachers repined', but the coronation party made a solemn procession to the castle with Atholl carrying the crown, Morton the sceptre, Glencairn the sword and Mar, as the royal governor, the new king. Knox, along with the justice clerk and Campbell of Kinzencleuch, were recorded as witnesses to the ceremony. In Edinburgh, James was proclaimed King of Scotland 'with joy, dancing and acclamations', and 'throughout Scotland there were widespread bonfires, shooting off of cannon and ringing of church bells'. Douglas of Loch Leven, with a vicious lack of tact, fired off cannon, lit bonfires and his whole household danced in the gardens. Mary, in her tower prison, fearfully asked the cause of the celebrations and some of the household unfeelingly told her that 'in her bravadoes her authority was abolished and she no longer had the power to avenge herself on them'. In turn Mary told them that they now had a king who would avenge her and, this time with considerable justification, fell on her knees and 'wept long and bitterly'. It could be said that she was no longer Queen of Scots, but when she wrote to Throckmorton in mid August from her 'prison en la tour de Locklivin' she signed herself 'Marie R'. Previously her signature had been simply 'MARIE' but from now on she asserted her position as queen.

She was, however, not without friends. In the west the Hamilton faction was rumoured to be gathering forces, hopefully without provoking the Lords to act against Mary. The Queen's Party did, however, prevent the heralds from declaring the abdication and the coronation of James. On the day of that coronation a formal bond was made at Dumbarton by Hamilton, Archbishop of St Andrews, Argyll, Huntly, Arbroath, Galloway, John Leslie, Bishop of Ross, Herries and others, demanding Mary's freedom. In England, Elizabeth's wrath was growing and

Cecil feared that she might take recourse to open war, although he confided to Throckmorton that her reasons were, firstly, that she wanted public opinion to realise that she could not condone the imprisonment of a monarch, and, secondly, that she did not want this to be a precedent which could be used against her.

As soon as Moray arrived in Edinburgh on 12 August, Throckmorton met him and Moray told him that he would accept the regency, albeit with diplomatic reluctance. With Moray came de Lignerolles as ambassador from France, who openly admitted that he was going through the motions of seeking Mary's liberty for the sake of diplomatic nicety. Mary was a sovereign queen, his king's sister-in-law, and there was a long tradition of amity between the two countries. He had no intention of seeking access to Mary, and as soon as he had delivered his message to the Lords he would immediately return to France.

Three days later, on 15 August, Moray, accompanied by Atholl, Morton and Lindsay, visited Mary. After supper Moray talked alone with his half-sister for two hours in a bizarre reversal of their meeting at Reims in March 1561, only six years previously. At that time Moray, still merely Lord James, had been sent out to 'grope the Queen's mind', and together they established the conditions under which Mary might return to rule as queen in Scotland. Now he was to demonstrate the reasons why she could not continue as queen and why he would replace her as regent. There are two widely differing accounts of the meeting.

The first version was given by Moray to Throckmorton: 'He [Moray] behaved himself rather like a ghostly father unto her than as a counsellor.' Mary was forced to confront the fact that she had taken charge of a reasonably prosperous country with good relations with France and England which had established a Reformed religion and was slowly accepting this Reformation; in which past divisions among the nobility were reluctantly closing as they became ready to accept a central rule from a strong monarch; and in which trade with England and Continental Europe was prospering. Instead of a strong monarch, Scotland got a beautiful girl who preferred her own courtly pleasures, who antagonised England by a wilful marriage and who was now being ignored by the French queen – appalled at Mary's possible involvement in a royal murder – and who, by negligence, had brought her country to the brink of civil war. Moray left her that night 'in the hope of nothing but God's mercy'. Unsurprisingly, Mary wept bitterly.

Next morning she sent for Moray, who told her that he would do all in his power to preserve her and begged her to keep the lowest of profiles and with the utmost modesty – not a virtue of which she had great stock – to assure the Lords that 'she harboured no thoughts of revenge towards those who had sought her reformation and preservation'. Her response was typically emotional, and she embraced and kissed Moray, begging him to accept the regency. Moray said somewhat hypocritically that this meeting had 'cut the thread of love betwixt the Queen and him for ever'.

An alternative account of the meeting was given to Nau by Mary some ten years later. Moray arrived on the shore of the loch arrogantly mounted on one of Mary's own horses, and to her delight fell off it into Loch Leven. How she saw this tumble from her close prison is a mystery. Moray behaved with less than the courtesy expected of one dining with his sovereign, and afterwards she had to remind him of the duty he owed to his queen. He asked her advice as to whether he should accept the regency, since other candidates might not treat Mary with such kindness. She reminded him that she held the only just authority under God and that those who were intent on usurping it would have no qualms over replacing him. She reminded Moray, 'He who does not keep faith where it is due, will hardly keep it where it is not due.' All his talk of protection for Mary she took to be dissimulation. Mary asked for the return of the rings she herself had purchased or had been given her by Henri II. Moray refused, saying that the Lords would need to keep the jewels in case she used them to finance a rescue. Nau commented: 'Here you may notice the impudence of this miserable creature, who did not hesitate to turn the queen's private property against herself.'

As always, the truth must lie between the two versions, with both people remembering only what they believed to have been said, and with what intent. Moray was understandably angry with his irresponsible half-sister and regretted ever going to France to fetch her, while Mary, with her fingers in her ears metaphorically, heard nothing but unjustified criticism of a monarch who was, by right of God, above criticism.

Six days later, on 22 August 1567, Moray was declared Regent of Scotland at the High Cross in Edinburgh 'by heralds and trumpets'. He swore, under the king, to maintain the true religion, to hold a parliament and not to have any contact with Mary without the advice of the Privy Council. De Lignerolles left for France with the usual collection of silverware, and Throckmorton duly reported the events to Elizabeth, who replied giving him permission to tell the Hamilton faction of her support. The Queen's Party once again refused to allow the heralds to make the declaration in the west of the country.

When Mary heard that Moray had summoned a parliament for 15 December she saw an opportunity to plead her case in public and wrote to Moray at length. She reminded him that she had treated him as a true brother, not as a bastard, and that she had entrusted him with the entire government of the realm since it had come under her authority. She demanded permission for a hearing before the parliament, promising that if that parliament required it she would 'resign the authority which God had given her over them'.

Moray refused the permission and the Privy Council of 4 December confirmed the existence of papers 'in her own hand' implicating Mary in Darnley's murder and even accusing her of plotting the death of the infant James. News of the Craigmillar Bond started to leak out and Lethington is reputed by Drury to have burnt all existing copies, except for the one which 'concerns the Queen's part, kept to be shown'. To tie up the now-rapidly unravelling ends of Mary's imprisonment and Moray's regency, the parliament of 15 December set about legitimising the actions of the rebel Lords. Darnley's murder, Bothwell's revolt at

Carberry and Mary's detention at Loch Leven were 'in the said queen's own default'. Bothwell was described as 'the chief executor of the said horrible murder', but this accusation was 'in no way prejudicial to the issue of our sovereign lord's mother, lawfully come from her body to the crown of the realm, nor their heirs'. A request was made to hear of the letters that had passed between Bothwell and Mary, but they were not produced, although parliament was assured that the letters proved 'she was privy art and part of the actual devise and deed of the fore-named murder of the king, her lawful husband'. Parliament also noted 'the demission and over giving of the crown and regiment of this realm made by the queen's grace, our sovereign lord's dearest mother, by virtue of her letters of commission and procuration signed with her hand, and under her Privy Seal of the date of 24 July'. The parliament wisely also ratified all the gifts of land made by Mary, thus avoiding the possibility that she might revoke them on her birthday. Mary was no longer Queen of Scots and she herself declared, 'we are so vexed and wearied that our body, spirit and fancies are altogether become unable to travail in that rowme [situation]. And therefore we have demitted and renounced the office of government of this our realm.'

Clumsily wishing to ensure that such things never happened again, the parliament moved against women in general: 'In no times coming any women shall be admitted to the public authority of the realm or function in public government within the same.'

Lord Herries objected to the letters of abdication, claiming them to be invalid, and he wanted to visit Mary to hear her wishes in person. He led a minority of members in refusing to sign the Act of Abdication. It was, however, passed, along with forty-one other acts stiffening the grip of the Reformation, a Confession of Faith re-affirming the belief in Calvinist doctrines and more extreme acts against the Catholics. The Hamilton faction did not attend the parliament.

Moray spent two days in Edinburgh Castle, where he gave the keepership to Grange, then set about his regency by seizing whatever had belonged to Bothwell, immediately forcing Patrick Wilson, now declared a regicide, to deliver up the castle of Dunbar after a brief siege. This act had more than territorial significance since it was at Dunbar that the bulk of Mary's jewellery was kept, and, as she had rightly suspected, Moray took possession of it all, including her rings. Mary had seen this happen before, to Diane de Poitiers at the death of Henri II and to herself at the death of François II. In those cases the gems became royal property, but now Moray gave some to his wife and kept the remainder for his own use.

In September Moray met with the Lords, who presented him with some gilt plate and questioned his intentions towards Bothwell, to which Moray replied that they 'could not merchandise for the bear's skin before they had him'. Throckmorton also noted that the Hamiltons had 'a convention in the west country' and on 5 September Bedford told Cecil that Moray meant to take up arms against them. However, by 15 September Moray had met Argyll with the Hamiltons for discussions. These must have been fruitless, since on 17 September the Hamiltons demanded the liberty of the queen and the bringing to justice of Darnley's murderers. They avowed their allegiance to James as prince but not as king, and pledged to seek 'the relief of the lords that took this in hand'. They had now levied 400 footmen and had the promise of 9,000 more. The battle lines were being drawn up, although on 14 October Moray assured Cecil, 'the state of the realm draws to a great quietness'. The undercurrent of the secret casket letters – rapidly becoming less and less secret – came to the surface on 16 September, when Moray signed a receipt before the Privy Council for the casket. Along with Morton he declared the letters to be genuine.

Moray also had to face one of the ever-present problems of government: he was now 'very bare of money' and undertook the disposition of Mary's jewels, selling some to the ever-acquisitive Elizabeth. Mary herself, however, was becoming reconciled to her imprisonment, 'wax[ing] fat'; 'instead of choler she makes show of mirth and has already drawn divers to pity her'. This seems to make clear that she always had a propensity to put on weight, which previously she had controlled by vigorous exercise, but now, deprived of that, she was gaining weight rapidly. From June onwards parcels of clothing and other goods started to arrive for the prisoner queen, now joined by Mary Seton, although it was clear that the luxury of her past wardrobe would never be matched again. There were the materials for her embroidery and lengths of material as well as new shoes, handkerchiefs, and underwear. She also received an alarm clock and, of practical importance, parcels of false hair for her coiffure. Like all prisoners, for Mary the hope of release was constant, but she was afraid of events which might be taking place outside her prison.

The confessions of the lesser Darnley plotters were extracted and they were barbarously executed. These confessions showed that Bothwell, now safely abroad and imprisoned, was the principal instigator and that his wife, the ex-queen, was his co-conspirator. It was all very satisfactory and the signatories to the Craigmillar Bond could sleep safely in their beds. The nobility even considered the possibility of Mary marrying again – she was still the wife of Bothwell, but that uncomfortable fact could easily be obviated – and several suitors among the nobility were considered, although it is unlikely that Mary herself was consulted.

She was still a close prisoner with thoughts of escape. However, Mary did not want to escape from Loch Leven to reclaim her power as a sovereign, but rather to be free to once again enjoy her life as a princess. She had written to Catherine de Medici and to Elizabeth asking both for help and had managed to get the letters smuggled out, but neither sovereign was inclined to risk a war to rescue a queen accused of murdering her husband. Mary's own resources for escape were slight, and even the writing of the letters involved her making ink with the soot from her chimney. She had beguiled a boatman to carry her letters, but everyone else was under close supervision and her captors were as much prisoners as Mary herself. She had, however, the willing assistance of George Douglas, the younger brother of Sir William, and when he was ordered off the island by his brother, as a result of one of the many Douglas family rows, he managed to contact Lord Seton, a close ally of Mary's.

Mary's first attempted escape, in late spring, involved disguising herself as a laundress while Mary Seton acted as a decoy on the island. However, one of the boatmen suspected the identity of the six-foot-tall servant and made to pull off the scarf hiding her face. Mary instinctively put her hands up to the scarf, giving herself away – a laundress's hands are red and roughened with continual washing, but these hands were pure white with elegantly long fingers. Although she was returned to captivity the boatmen did not reveal her attempted escape to anyone else.

Mary now used Willy Douglas, a young orphan, as a courier, but he was slipshod and even dropped secret letters meant for Mary, which were found by the laird's daughter. The girl promised to keep the matter quiet if Mary took her with her, but Mary, scenting a possible trap, told her that she had no plans to escape. Willy, who had been rewarded with gold pieces by Mary, was now accused of planning an escape and sent away from the island. Surprisingly, Sir William and Lady Douglas took no steps to increase security, but boasted to Mary's face that they would take good care of her. Meanwhile, George Douglas and Lord Seton had established a body of armed men in the shoreside village of Lochleven and waited for news. Young Willy was allowed to return, bringing Mary news that the escape was planned for 2 May.

There was an unplanned fracas when some servants raised a false alarm as a joke, which turned sour when one of Sir William's men grabbed an arquebus – which he claimed to have thought was loaded only with paper – and fired it into the crowd, injuring two bystanders. The actual plan involved Mary jumping from a seven- or eight-foot-high wall into a garden. One of her gentlewomen tried the jump first – 'for she thought it a matter of duty' – and seriously injured 'one of the joints of her foot'. This plan was promptly abandoned.

On 2 May 1568 Willy organised a Feast of Unreason at which he took the part of the Abbot of Unreason, insisting that Mary follow him wherever he went. With this he managed to disrupt all the routines on the island and to divert attention from behaviour that otherwise would have sent out serious alarm signals. A large troop of horsemen under James Hamilton of Ormiston was seen passing through the village on the shore, and Mary kept Lady Douglas in conversation until suppertime in order that she would not notice them. Sir William had seen Willy chaining and pegging all the island's boats – bar one – but Mary managed to divert his attention as well. Mary had received a pearl from George Douglas via a heavily bribed boatman as a signal that everything was now in place.

Sir William served Mary supper by himself and then left her in the charge of 'a person called Drysdale', who later absented himself for a game of handball. Mary withdrew from the two daughters of the house, telling them that she wished to pray, which she did 'very devoutly' before disguising herself with a hood, as did one of her domestics. Mary's ladies in waiting, in particular Mary Seton, Jane Kennedy and a Frenchwoman, Marie de Courcelles, were all privy to the plan. Meanwhile, Willy, while serving Sir William, pocketed the key to the great gate, and crossed the courtyard with Mary, in sight of several servants, then passed through the gate, which he locked behind him, throwing the key into a nearby cannon. Mary was seen by some washerwomen whom Willy cautioned to keep quiet, and she got into the boat. Here, the boatman advised her to lie on the bottom boards in case of gunshots. The crossing from imprisonment to freedom took only a very few minutes. She was met by George Douglas and John Beaton, who had horses for her and the loyal Willy Douglas. Two miles further on, Lord Seton and the Laird of Riccarton joined her escort and conveyed her across the River Forth at Queensferry. On the south side of the river she was greeted by Claude Hamilton, second son of Châtelherault, with twenty more horses, and arrived safely at Seton's palace in the village of Niddry about midnight.

For all the foregoing account we depend on Mary's reminiscences to Claude Nau and, typically, she recalls how waiting for her at Niddry was not news of the politics of Scotland but 'dresses and all other necessaries befitting her sex and dignity'. Since her personal wardrobe was in the hands of Moray and the Confederate Lords, these must have been borrowed clothes. From Niddry Castle she then travelled the twenty-five miles west to Hamilton, where she could be sure of safety from the Lords, although Throckmorton mistrusted the motives of the Hamilton faction: 'Those who provided the means of escape did so with no other intention than to seize the government of the realm.'

Meanwhile, at Lochleven Castle, the Douglas daughters quickly discovered that Mary was missing, and Sir William realised that the most important prisoner in Scotland had escaped from his personal care. His theatrical, though unsuccessful, attempt at suicide by stabbing himself was duly noted and no revenge was taken against him. He does not give the impression of being a man of great intelligence, but he had been in the difficult position of having to please his half-brother Moray while, at the same time, behaving honourably to Mary just in case she returned to power. Like so many men faced with the situation of a coup d'état, he was sensibly cautious about making his choice of sides too obvious. Three days later he sent Mary's belongings after her and she was once again reunited with some of her possessions.

Mary now had two new attendants with her in the persons of George and Willy Douglas, both of whom had fallen under her spell and willingly continued in her service. Also, her very presence as a free woman was acting as a magnet for her supporters, and on 8 May a bond was signed at Hamilton by nine earls, nine bishops, eighteen lords and many others, who promised 'to bind themselves to serve and obey her with their bodies, lands, good friends, etc.' However, 'Their force is not great and very evil frayed'.

Regent Moray had not been idle. On 3 May, when he was said to be 'fair amazed', he had summoned an army to convene at

Glasgow, while four days later a broadsheet was printed by Robert Leprevik outlawing any Marian supporters as traitors. Since Moray himself was at Glasgow only eight miles distant from Hamilton, the two sides could meet very rapidly, so the likelihood of another farcical Chase-about Raid was very slim. Mary had now repudiated her forced abdication and Drury told Throckmorton that he doubted if she had ever read the document. Mary now behaved as if she were restored to full power and sent Hepburn of Riccarton to Dunbar with instructions to seize the castle before proceeding to Denmark and recalling Bothwell. The journey was a sad failure and achieved neither of its ambitions.

Mary, however, had to decide how aggressively she should pursue her restoration, and Melville reported that 'she was not minded to fight, or hazard battle' – understandable after Carberry – but she was advised by the house of Hamilton, who realised that they had a numerical advantage over Moray's forces and recommended a move to a swift engagement. With this in mind letters were written on 5 and 6 May to 'all and sundry kings, princes, dukes, dominators, and magistrates, our friends . . . to all and sundry our lawful and well advised friends'. The contents were vitriolic in the extreme – she called Moray a 'spurious bastard', a 'bestial traitor' who murdered Darnley and incited Bothwell to ravish her. Châtelherault was now her 'father adoptive'; she revoked her abdication and appointed Châtelherault and his heirs as regents and tutors to James 'in the event of her absence in foreign countries'. In the event of her death, Châtelherault and the house of Hamilton would inherit the crown. Lethington and Balfour were condemned as traitors, as was the Laird of Craigmillar, while Cessford and Kerr of Fawdonside were soulless bloody tyrants. The list continued in this vein, but it is doubtful whether the letters were ever signed or delivered. Mary certainly saw and approved them, and she may even have had a hand in drafting them, but the historian Hay Fleming infers that the true author was Hamilton, the Archbishop of St Andrews.

Undoubtedly, Mary's best option was to reach a defensible strong point and from there summon a united army against Moray, some of whose forces were already bleeding away to join Mary's troops led by Argyll. A swift move north to encircle Glasgow from the east would open the path to Dumbarton, while her superiority in numbers could contain Moray. At Dumbarton Mary could draw breath and collect her forces – 'Little by little to draw home again unto her obedience the whole subjects.' It also provided a ready outlet to the sea should a flight to France become necessary – we have already heard her consider her 'absence in foreign countries'. Moreover, if she moved with enough speed she could reach Stirling, presently held by Mar, before he could join forces with Moray. Unfortunately the warlike counsels of Argyll and the Hamiltons prevailed, and Mary, rejecting her earlier plan 'not to hazard battle but to pass to the castle of Dumbarton', chose the worst option and marched north-west with 6,000 men. Moray was astonished at this move but marched south-east to the Gallowgate Port and drew up his much inferior forces on the hill overlooking the village of Langside. Mary expected no conflict and led her army as she was used to – in 'a sort of parade'.

Langside was a 'T'-shaped village with a long narrow street – Long Loan – only forty feet wide and running north to south. It was composed of cottages with gardens – kailyards – on either side in which Kirkcaldy of Grange placed arquebusiers to act as sharpshooters. He reserved his pikemen and cavalry on the western side of the village.

Mary's vanguard was led by Herries and his Border horsemen, who rode bravely into the village, but as he advanced up the confines of Long Loan – the worst tactic imaginable for mounted soldiers – he came under withering fire from Kirkcaldy's men. Cavalry are not meant for close-quarters house-to-house action, and Kirkcaldy's forces could now pick them off with ease. Even in spite of this, Herries was gaining ground, although at a terrible cost, and he desperately needed support from the main army at his rear, which was under the command of Argyll. At this crucial point in the battle the earl failed to order the advance. Charitable

288

chroniclers say that he was suddenly attacked with the 'stone', either kidney or bladder, and fainted from the pain, while the more sceptical point out that as Moray's brother-in-law, he might have hoped for personal advancement if Mary should lose the battle. One anonymous commentator claimed that he 'swooned as they were joining for want of courage'. In any case no orders were given to support Herries and Kirkcaldy now ordered his pikemen to attack the leaderless Highlanders of Argyll in a disciplined charge. Mary, on a nearby hill, saw the Highlanders drop their arms and run from the field. The pikemen met the main force in a savage encounter and, 'when spears were broken, they cast whingers [daggers], broken pieces of spears, stones or whatever came to hand in the faces of their enemies'. It was all over in under an hour with Moray losing only one man, while Mary's side had 100 killed and 300 taken prisoner.

Needless to say, Brantôme – who wasn't there – tells of Mary advancing personally to rally her troops, but the truth is more sombre, as it seemed as though the only route to freedom was to ride south into Galloway. For a moment Mary considered continuing northwards towards Dumbarton but soon turned south. Moray had no need to pursue her urgently since he believed she would now be a fugitive, her supporters scattered, and her appearance known to all – in spite of her having cut short her long auburn hair – with no effective hiding place.

The truth was different. Moray's support had been leaking away since April, when he had held a justice ayre in Glasgow and handed down excessively severe penalties. In spite of his moves in parliament his legitimacy as regent was being questioned and Mary's support was growing. De la Fôret, the French ambassador in London, believed that two thirds of the people of Scotland were for Mary rather than Moray. Even Moray's own supporters had advised him not to go south to Langside but to retire to Stirling, where Mar held the castle and the king. If Mary had continued with her plan to occupy Dumbarton she would have easily established a power base around which she could have gathered sufficient support for an effective restoration.

However, in the first of several disastrous decisions, accompanied by Lord Herries and with few personal servants, the royal party turned themselves unnecessarily into fugitives and rode down the valley of Loch Ken to cross the River Dee above the village of Tongland, where they burnt the bridge to delay their non-existent pursuers. All Mary had as sustenance was some bread moistened with spring water, and for rest she had some shelter in a nearby cottage while the bridge was being destroyed. Finally, they reached Lord Maxwell's castle at Terregles, a mile from Dumfries. Mary had travelled this country during the Chase-about Raid, but this journey had been no such chivalric progress and she gave an account of the journey to the Cardinal of Lorraine in a letter written three days later:

I have endured injuries, calumnies, imprisonment, famine, cold, heat, flight, not knowing whither, 92 miles across the country without stopping or alighting, and then I have had to sleep on the ground, and drink sour milk and eat oatmeal without bread, and have been three nights like the owls, without a female in this country, where to crown it all I am little else than a prisoner . . . it is all one for myself, but let not my subjects be deceived and ruined; for I have a son, whom it would be a pity to leave in the hands of these traitors.

It was six years since Randolph reported, 'She repenteth nothing that she was not a man to know what life it was to lie all night in the fields, or to walk upon the causeway with a jack and knapskall, a Glasgow buckler and a broad sword.' Mary Stewart's contacts with the reality of her romantic imagination were always unpleasant. Now her very existence seemed at stake and a decision as to her future had to be made.

The choices facing Mary at Terregles were varied. Her first option, and the one favoured by her supporters, was to rally her support in Dumfries and Galloway for a repeated journey north. Moray had left Glasgow and was earning himself greater

290

unpopularity by seizing the property of those who had supported Mary, thus causing royal support to grow. Remaining in Scotland and fighting the regent was more than just a viable option – it was the most sensible course of action.

The next possibility was of a flight to France, where Mary was not only Duchesse de Touraine but also Queen Dowager. In France, Catherine de Medici would ensure that Mary would have no political power – that was, in any case, the last thing Mary wanted – but Mary would have easily tolerated a rustic exile of considerable luxury. Mary, at twenty-six years old, was still marriageable and could, under Catherine's control, become a marriage pawn again, although now unable to indulge any headstrong ideas of her own. Also in France, an indefinite period in the lavish style of a rich convent was readily available.

The last option, and the least attractive, was flight into England and an appeal for help from her cousin Elizabeth. But Elizabeth would never support the expense of a war to restore Mary without some guarantee of advantage. The infant king's presence in London might be acceptable – but he was in the hands of Regent Moray. Perhaps Mary could simply live as a royal guest with her own court? Cecil would be quick to point out that as a focus for all Catholic interests, Mary would have to be closely watched and her irresponsible nature would make embracing mischief her first preference. Elizabeth would be delighted to see her cousin happily ensconced in a fairy château on the Loire with Cecil's spies somewhere in her retinue. Flight to England was the worst possible choice.

Herries, along with Mary's other noble supporters, was strong in his advocacy of remaining in Scotland. If she won back her throne – and there was a strong likelihood that she would – they could be sure of lavish gratitude, otherwise they would be left to the vengeance of Moray and his allies. The French option depended on Mary eating some humble pie at the table of her former mother-in-law, and humble pie was never a dish to the taste of a Guise princess. Elizabeth could hardly refuse the pleas of her cousin, another anointed queen. She had made her views known as to the horrifying impropriety of dethroning Mary, and Mary chose to ignore Elizabeth's guarded comments on her marriage to Bothwell. She would go to England. As when she chose to marry Darnley, she made the worst possible choice and, having made it, she petulantly closed the door to all contrary advice.

It is possible that Mary was now completely disillusioned with her native country. Since her arrival nearly seven years previously she had faced the enmity of Knox and the suspicion of the Protestant nobles, obligingly married a bisexual syphilitic, causing a minor revolt, seen her favourite counsellor stabbed to death at her feet and, having been given little option, been privy to the murder of her husband. Thereafter she had been abducted, remarried and delivered of still-born twins in prison, and had watched her forces flee in the face of her half-brother's rebels. Mary could be excused for wanting nothing more to do with Scotland. Thus Lord Herries reluctantly wrote to Richard Lowther, the deputy captain of Carlisle Castle, warning him of Mary's imminent arrival.

The decision was made to travel first to the abbey of Dundrennan, where Mary rested long enough to write a short letter to Elizabeth in which she hoped to meet the English queen soon in order to explain her plight. Then on Sunday, 16 May 1568 at three o'clock in the afternoon, with Herries, Maxwell, Fleming and Lord Claude Hamilton reluctantly attending, as well as some sixteen personal servants, Mary Stewart climbed aboard a small fishing smack and sailed for England. She would never see the country of her birth again.

PART IV

England, 1568–87

CHAPTER FOURTEEN

Whistling in the dark

❧

Claude Nau did the best he could to mythologise Mary's arrival in England: 'When the queen had crossed the sea and was getting out of the boat she fell to the ground, which many persons accepted as an augury of good success, interpreting it according to the common form, to mean that she had claim to England, to which she laid claim as of right.' An identical tale is told of William the Conqueror, so there is a solid precedent for the arrival of tumbling monarchs.

Mary landed near the small seaport of Workington – a village now called Maryport – at about seven o'clock in the evening of 16 May 1568. While she was being given supper, a messenger was sent by Lord Herries to Sir Henry Curwen of Workington Hall. In what turned out to be a completely vain attempt to conceal Mary's identity, Herries told Curwen that he was accompanying a young heiress, whom he had brought from Scotland, and who was keen to marry Curwen's son. Unfortunately, Curwen was not at home, but his house and servants were immediately put at Mary's disposal, whose identity had already been guessed by the local inhabitants, and confirmed by one of Curwen's servants, who had known Mary 'in better plight than now'. Mary's presence in England was now public knowledge.

The news of her flight from her kingdom astonished all who received it. Mary's fantasy was that she would shortly meet Elizabeth, then tell her of how she, a sovereign queen, had been defied by her nobility, threatened with death and forced to abdicate. Also, if she thought so far ahead, she would tell her cousin that she now wished to return to her kingdom and that

Elizabeth would promptly provide her with an army. The reality was very different. Mary had come to England against all advice and on a single impulse. It is doubtful if she had any cogent plan of action except to put her plight into someone else's care. To this end, while at Workington, she sent a second, longer, letter to Elizabeth setting out her case and delineating the various indignities her nobility had visited on her. It begins with the Chase-about Raid – her only mention of Darnley, 'le feu roy mon mari' – pointing out that her own forgiveness of the Chase-about rebels was at Elizabeth's advice, even though these men had murdered Rizzio in her presence. Mary pleaded not as a queen but as a destitute woman deprived of everything, who had just ridden sixty miles in a day and then not dared to travel except by night. She signed herself a 'good sister and cousin and escaped prisoner'. Elizabeth would have regarded such a letter as a formal opening of negotiations as to how she might help her Scots cousin, while gaining an advantage for England.

Both Cecil and Elizabeth would have closely examined the now totally changed situation. Scotland, under Moray's regency, could easily be dealt with and would willingly pay a high price for England's legitimisation of the new regime. But the return of Mary would jeopardise this. However, if Elizabeth refused help to Mary, then she might very well turn elsewhere and France would be her obvious first choice. France was still torn with the Wars of Religion, there was no united nobility to embrace a Catholic cause and the king, Charles IX, was desperately short of money. Charles had seized 1.8 million livres' worth of church property the previous year and it was still not enough for domestic purposes, so a military intervention by France in Scotland was unlikely. Mary was, however, still marriageable. Once set free on mainland Europe, the twice-widowed queen could turn into a sort of nubile loose cannon. So she should not be allowed to leave the country, although in England she would now provide a focus for Catholic elements, their ranks swollen by agitators from Europe. Elizabeth could not simply imprison Mary – the idea of taking such action against a sovereign queen made her blood run cold – but if Mary could be shown to have been an active participant in Darnley's murder, then further options opened up. Returning her to Scotland to be dealt with as a regicide was the most severe, while a gentle imprisonment in England was the kindest option. Elizabeth managed to achieve the best of both worlds by agreeing to nothing more than meeting Mary, but only after her innocence was proved. This was active procrastination at its best.

Immediate details had to be dealt with, since Mary, whose party had now increased to twenty people, clearly could not remain at Workington. Richard Lowther, the deputy governor of Carlisle, rode to greet her with an escort of 400 horsemen. He also wrote a puzzled note to Cecil, announcing that he would take Mary to Carlisle 'until I know by your honour the Queen's majesty's pleasure'. He desperately wanted to know if she was an honoured royal guest or a prisoner of the state. Elizabeth sent Thomas Leighton to Moray, instructing him to call on Mary first, setting out Elizabeth's conditions for Mary's as yet undefined stay in England.

Elizabeth began by expressing her joy at Mary's freedom and declared that all her subjects were charged to submit to her and that 'she shall not want the assistance of that power which God has given her. If she is content to stand to the Queen's order in componing the controversies with her subjects, without soliciting aid from France, she shall receive all aid from the Queen either to persuade or compel them.' Leighton 'shall move Moray to compromitt [sic] the whole controversies' to her decision. However, if Mary were to seek aid from France then 'she must conclude her principal object is to renew old quarrels' and Leighton would declare the queen's sorrow. Thus Mary could be assured of Elizabeth's unspecified help, provided there were no foreign interventions. Elizabeth, with Cecil at her elbow, was immediately aware that Mary could provoke foreign intervention in the shape of an attempted rescue from England.

Lowther, meanwhile, still with no definition of Mary's status, transported the royal party to the castle at Carlisle on 18 May.

The castle, founded by William II in 1092, had sufficient accommodation to allow for a modicum of royal state, but was not immediately defensible against cannon and was therefore unsuitable in the long term, if Elizabeth decided that Mary was indeed a prisoner and should be put beyond rescue. Lowther was afraid that Mary, who was lodged in the warden's apartments, might escape 'with devices of towels . . . at her chamber window or elsewhere in the night, a body of her agility and spirit may escape soon being so near the border'.

He wrote to Cecil, 'Her grace's attire is very mean', yet he was keen to report that he had paid all Mary's bills at Cockermouth and provided horses for her transport. Lowther was the first in a long line of Mary's unwilling hosts to send the bill for her expenses to Elizabeth. They were not always paid and seldom in full. Mary Stewart may have cost Scotland very little, but she was an expensive immigrant to England.

Lowther still had doubts as to Mary's position: 'If the Queen's Majesty will have her to court . . . how and in what manner?' Mary wept at the news that Moray was to execute some of her supporters and called for revenge from Elizabeth or, with the hint of a rather unwise threat, from her friends in France.

A mere two days after Mary's arrival at Carlisle her position became clearer, as can be seen in a letter from the English Privy Council: 'The Council commands the Sheriff, Justices of peace and gentlemen of Cumberland, to use the Scottish Queen and her company at Workington honourably, as the Earl of Northumberland shall appoint, and let none of them escape.' The word 'escape' indicated Mary was more of a prisoner than a guest.

By the end of the month, the situation had become even clearer. The Earl of Northumberland attempted to gain custody of Mary but was refused access by Lowther, while Elizabeth put Mary into the official care of Lord Scrope of Bolton. Scrope was warden of the West Marches and captain of Carlisle Castle. Elizabeth also despatched her vice-chancellor, Sir Francis Knollys, to become Mary's guardian. He was a 55-year-old courtier of great experience and a close friend of Elizabeth, with a vast family that connected him to most of the noble houses of England. His daughter, Lettice, had been widowed by the death of the Earl of Essex and had now remarried Robert Dudley, Earl of Leicester. Although a Puritan, Knollys became a friend of Mary's, but many others with Elizabeth's ear were sworn enemies. In London the Earl and Countess of Lennox met with Elizabeth and, more or less hysterically, demanded that Mary be tried for murder.

Meanwhile, Mary was now creating her own diplomatic network: she had sent Herries to London with letters for Elizabeth and Cecil, while Lord Fleming had been given instructions to visit France, carrying a letter assuring Catherine de Medici of Mary's undying love. Catherine, for her part, wrote to Elizabeth thanking her for looking after Mary's interests and sent a M. de Monmorin as an ambassador. Implicit in this was Catherine's heartfelt gratitude that Mary was Elizabeth's problem and not hers. Mary's instructions to Fleming were more inflammatory, however. Since Elizabeth would not use military force in Scotland to restore Mary to her throne and had moreover lent her support to Moray, Mary now asked France for 2,000 foot soldiers, money for 500 light cavalry with artillery and other munitions to be sent to Dumbarton. Her jewellery still in France could be used as a payment for this. Mary warned the French king against Scottish agitators travelling to France and advised him to admit no one without a passport from Mary herself. Fleming also carried a letter with similar demands to the Cardinal of Lorraine. In reality, Fleming never got further than London, where he was stopped by Cecil and Charles IX was saved the embarrassment of having to refuse. Mary sent Herries to London to quieten any doubts Elizabeth might have and began her letter with earnest pleading to meet Elizabeth in person. However, she added, 'If for any reason I cannot come to you, seeing I have freely come to throw myself into your arms, you will I am sure permit me to ask assistance of other allies – for, thank God, I am not destitute of some.' This was an ill-judged threat from a position of weakness which Elizabeth quietly ignored. Mary complained further: 'I have been kept as if a prisoner in your castle for 15 days, and on your councillors coming, not allowed to go to you only to declare the truth of my grievances.' Then, finally, she remembered her manners: 'I must not forget to thank you for my good reception . . . especially by the deputy warden Mr Lowther who did all courtesy without express command.'

On the same day, Scrope and Knollys met Herries, who was about to depart for London, and the three men got down to some realpolitik. There was no doubt that one of Elizabeth's greatest fears was the possibility, however remote, of a liberating French army in Scotland. This would have obliged Elizabeth to react with forces of her own; she had already come to the aid of the Reformation eight years previously. That action had been very expensive and Scotland had gained more than England. All parties agreed that there could be no possibility of Mary being allowed into Elizabeth's presence until she was cleared of all blame for Darnley's murder. Having agreed on this, Scrope and Knollys met Mary for the first time and expressed Elizabeth's sorrow for her 'lamentable misadventure and inconvenient arrival'. Atypically, these two men made no immediate comment on her beauty but 'found her to have an eloquent tongue and a discreet head and it seemeth by her doings she hath stout courage and liberal heart adjoined thereto'. When told of Elizabeth's conditions for a meeting, Mary burst into tears and immediately asked for safe passage through England since France and Spain would certainly help her. On the verge of hysterics she went on to accuse the Scottish Lords of taking by force the lands that she was about to reclaim at her birthday. Once again she threatened to seek French aid in Scotland and the interview was over. Scrope and Knollys thought that left alone she would not return to Scotland without French aid, but might try to pass through Scotland en route for France, although this could be stopped by putting good intelligence at the disposal of Moray. Also, they realised the dilemma that, while Mary could not be kept a close prisoner, her proximity to the Border made close guard essential.

However, to have her carried further into the realm was seen as 'the highway to a dangerous sedition'. Every option was dangerous and Mary was intractable. This was not what Elizabeth wanted to hear, and Cecil, as was his habit, wrote himself a long memorandum setting out the situation.

There would be no visitors without permission, and all secret letters would be seized. Anyone suspected of Darnley's murder or supporting Bothwell's marriage would, in a chilling phrase, be 'put in safety to answer'. France would be warned not to interfere. There should be incontrovertible proofs of Mary's culpability in Darnley's murder. If she were proved innocent then Elizabeth would restore her, but if she were found guilty, then Elizabeth would settle her in her realm secure from French tyranny. By no practice should she be conveyed out of the realm. 'It seems meet for her majesty to hear and decide any controversy for the crown of Scotland – for that of ancient right it appertaineth to the crown of England, as by multitudes of records, examples and precedents may be proved.' If Mary was to be acquitted, then the Treaty of Leith – Cecil made a rare error here as the treaty in question must have been the Treaty of Edinburgh, confirming Elizabeth's right to rule – should be ratified. If Mary were found guilty then she might be restored under limitations. However, the memorandum continued,

if the criminality be excessive to live in some convenient place without possessing her kingdom. If restored she and her son may reign jointly, the Regent retaining office till the son's majority. If she should go to France, then England would be surrounded by very powerful enemies and France is superior in force to us. If she stays she will embolden all the evil subjects here. If she returns to Scotland the friends of England shall be abased and those of France increased.

It is a long document in which every possibility is examined and every outcome projected. While Cecil did not state it explicitly, it is presumed that Mary would remain a close prisoner until some kind of trial took place, and while not prejudging the outcome, it was clear that Cecil's preference would be for Mary to be under close arrest in England. Cecil also feared a coup d'état in Scotland by the Hamiltons, which would result in England's frontiers being under constant threat – thus increasing the cost of defence. If Elizabeth read it – and it is very likely that she did – she would have been horrified at the thought of having to act against her cousin and at the possible expense. Cecil also issued orders that 'no access of English, Scottish or French be allowed to come to her . . . good heed to be taken to the apprehension of any letters that shall be sent secretly thither'.

Knollys directly confronted Mary about her implication in Darnley's murder after dinner on Sunday, 30 May and 'after her accustomed manner' she burst into tears. Three days later he discussed the likely places of confinement with Cecil – places where 'papistry is not so strong as it is in the north' – and earnestly hoped that he would not be Mary's 'settled gaoler'. Cecil's spies reported a suspicion that Mary was already in secret correspondence with France and the impasse continued, with Mary behaving as though she were a free woman and Knollys having to keep her under strict watch while both he and Cecil tried to prepare for her long-term imprisonment. Knollys complained to the Privy Council that he had a charge to see that the queen did not escape, 'yet we have no charge to abridge her, nor detain her as a prisoner'. Elizabeth let events develop, confident that Cecil would ensure her safety, while she sat on the royal fence, writing a long letter to Mary on 8 June. This assured Mary yet again of Elizabeth's undying love and care for her cousin, her care for her honour and her longing to see Mary cleared of 'these things people condemn you in'. This was delivered by Middlemore, a fresh envoy, but 'well known' to Mary.

Mary was now growing impatient at the lack of action from Elizabeth and was dropping hints to Knollys that she would use her dowry of £12,000 a year to hire mercenaries against Scotland and England and satisfy her 'bloody appetite to shed the blood of her enemies'.

Mary first met Middlemore on Sunday, 13 June at eight o'clock in the morning and she demanded to know how she could prove her innocence to Elizabeth when Elizabeth would not admit her. 'No one can compel me to accuse myself, and yet if I would say anything of my self, I would say of my self to her and to none other. But I see how things frame evil for me. I have many enemies about the Queen, my good sister.' Middlemore reported that this was done with great weeping and complaints of her evil usage. If Elizabeth would not help her would she 'suffer me to pass to other princes?' Mary also complained that Elizabeth favoured Moray against her and flatly refused to forbid the French to come to Dumbarton; 'She would go herself to the Grand Turk for help.' Middlemore, hoping that the news might calm the now-hysterical queen, told Mary that Elizabeth wanted her moved nearer to her, 'where she might have more pleasure and liberty and be utterly out of danger of her enemies'. 'She immediately asked if she was to go as a prisoner or at her own choice,' reported Middlemore. 'I said I was sure that her majesty meant no such thing as to imprison her . . . but thought she meant her a greater pleasure by bringing her nearer her.' Middlemore guessed that Mary did not relish a move further south since it made an escape more difficult, and the long interview ended with Mary, in a torrent of self-pity, as a prisoner in her cousin's hands, giving Middlemore a letter of complaint for Elizabeth. Mary never realised that threatening Elizabeth merely hardened her Tudor resolve and that complaining to a woman who had weathered the horrors of the Tower was interpreted as whining weakness and was instantly dismissed. What might touch the heart of a flattering courtier had no effect whatsoever on Mary's regal cousin.

However on the next day all this was forgotten as Knollys reported,

Yesterday she went out at a postern to walk on a playing green towards Scotland waited on by Scrope and himself [Knollys], with 24 of Read's halberdiers and some of her own gentlemen; where 20 of her retinue played football before her for 2 hours, very strongly, nimbly and without foul play – the smallness of the ball occasioning their fairer

303

play – and twice since coming she did the like in the same place and once rode out hare hunting, galloping so fast, and her retinue so well horsed, that they feared a rescue by her friends in Scotland and mean not to permit this in future.

This was Mary doing what she enjoyed most: vigorous physical exercise among her friends. She probably had no thought of escape or rescue, but merely enjoyed the summer sunshine and the wind in her hair. Mary and her ladies took exercise by walking the length of the southern walls of the castle to the great gatehouse. In spite of almost complete rebuilding, this area is still known as 'Lady's Walk'.

The negotiations concerning the conditions of Mary's stay at Carlisle were at a stalemate with minor annoyances – for example Mary objected to Moray being called 'Governor' when Herries, her ambassador and friend, returned from London. In London the Privy Council received Middlemore's account of his interview with alarm and immediately recommended that she be removed to Nottingham, Fotheringhay or Tutbury. Since she refused to be tried openly, the kings of France and Spain had to be informed of her intransigence.

Meanwhile, Moray was carrying out a campaign of punishment and retribution in the south-west of Scotland, hanging 'thieves', destroying property and starving the opposition into subservience. Nau called it 'an act of execrable and unprecedented cruelty'. Mary continued to write to Elizabeth urging that the two queens should settle the matter between themselves, and in a letter of 22 June Mary wrote of Moray's boasts 'at his table'. Moray was clearly boasting of the evidence he possessed which would implicate Mary in Darnley's murder and Mary complained of 'these letters so falsely invented'; the casket letters were always hovering in the background.

Mary's appeals to Elizabeth became even more pitiful a few days later: 'Assuring myself that you would either send for me to come to you or else allow me to depart elsewhere as freely as I came hither . . . I implore you, Queen, sister, and cousin, to have a fellow feeling for your equal.' Mary's letters to Elizabeth have a sad spontaneity and she clearly wrote as her emotions drove her with no thought either of strategy or of cohesive argument. Her first task – an almost impossible one – should have been to convince Cecil of her case and persuade him to unlock the door to Elizabeth, but Mary simply behaved as if Elizabeth were a nursery friend and would respond to childish nagging.

Knollys was now convinced that Mary had to be moved further south and made arrangements for her to go to Scrope's Castle Bolton in Yorkshire. Mary refused to agree to such a move, but welcomed the return of her servant, Mary Seton, since this meant that now 'every other day lightly she hath a new device of head dressing, without any cost and yet setteth forth a woman gaily well'.

Mary's gaiety ceased abruptly on 5 July, when Knollys formally announced to her that she would be moved to Bolton Castle. Mary flatly refused. He told her it was much pleasanter than this 'noisome and unsavoury place' but she continued to refuse, unless compelled, to move 'one whit' out of Carlisle without the queen's direct commandment. Knollys countered that if Mary refused a move, putting her only two or three days' ride nearer to Elizabeth, then he might 'presume some mystery'. Mary, again in floods of tears, said he need not fear that she would 'steal away'. She wrote again to Elizabeth, a long and rather tragic letter, agreeing to move to Bolton 'as a thing forced', but asking for the return of Lord Herries. Her plea for a personal interview was repeated: 'If Caesar had not disdained to hear or read the complaint of an advertiser, he had not so died . . . I am not of the nature of the basilisk . . . And though I should be so dangerous and cursed as men say, you are sufficiently armed with constance shows an undertaking shows an undertaking [sic] and with justice.' Mary realised she was losing the battle, and her gloom deepened when she received three trunks of clothing from Moray in which there was only one complete gown among saddle covers and 'such like trinkets'. Most of her clothing was still at Lochleven Castle.

As Mary's ambassador, Herries met with Middlemore in London in mid July and, according to Middlemore's letter to

Cecil, totally denounced Mary in an amazing volte-face. Middlemore claimed that Herries proposed that Elizabeth should rule Scotland, the French should be cast off, and Mary should never return home. In the light of Herries's continued support for Mary this letter seems to be pure slander. Middlemore's lack of subtlety had caused him to fail as an ambassador to Mary, although, as we shall see, he had had more success with Moray, and perhaps he wanted to creep further back into Cecil's favour by this rather clumsy deceit.

The first stage of Mary's reluctant journey to Bolton – escorted by Sir George Bowes and forty armed horsemen, ostensibly to protect her from her enemies – was to Lowther's house at Wharton, some twenty miles from Carlisle. Here, Knollys found Mary much more amenable. She was, after all, faced with a *fait accompli* and had no means of resisting, although Knollys still had no direct instruction from Elizabeth. Mary negotiated the right to send and receive messengers to and from her supporters in Scotland, also telling Knollys that she had given control of the government of Scotland to Châtelherault in her absence.

The royal party finally arrived at Bolton after dark on 15 July. Mary was 'very quiet, tractable and void of displeasant countenance', with an entourage which had risen to fifty-one people, of whom twenty-one were 'of the baser sort'. There were more people than Knollys had expected, and he was 'driven to hire 4 little cars, 20 carriage horses, and 23 saddle horses for her women and men – all to her satisfaction'. Mary was lodged on the second floor of the north-west tower, in a spacious room with a fireplace and extensive views across the Yorkshire Dales. Her bedchamber adjoined this room and she could now enjoy more comfort than at Carlisle.

The beautifully situated Bolton Castle had been completed in 1399 and was now a superb example of the mixture of stately home and fortress. Knollys reported, 'This house appears very strong, very fair and stately, after the old manner of building and is the highest walled house I have seen with but one entrance. Half the number of soldiers may better watch than the whole could do at Carlisle . . . The queen's chamber there [Carlisle] had a window looking to Scotland, the bars whereof being filed out of it she might have been let down, with plain ground before her to Scotland.'

Scotland was, in fact, some 150 miles distant and Mary was now well out of range of the sort of Border raiding party which had been feared at Carlisle. Moreover, alterations had been put in hand to improve the fortifications at Bolton. Five days after Mary's arrival, '5 light cart loads and 4 horse loads of apparel' arrived from Loch Leven. Sir George Bowes sent Mary carpets and tapestries, while a steady supply of venison came from the Earl of Northumberland. Finally, a consignment arrived bringing her cloths of state. So now Mary's court was established, but also established was her status in England. Although she did not accept the fact, Mary was a virtual prisoner.

Herries returned to Mary a few days later, on 24 July, with a proposal from Elizabeth. There was to be no question of Elizabeth sitting in judgment over Mary, nor could Mary, as a sovereign queen, be put to trial. Rather, Elizabeth would summon Moray to explain himself and his actions. If his explanation was satisfactory, which Elizabeth doubted, then Mary would be returned to Scotland in some yet-to-be-decided capacity and the nobles would retain their privileges. However, if their explanations were unsatisfactory, then Elizabeth would re-establish Mary by force, but on certain conditions: that she renounce her claim to the English throne and any league with France, and that she abandon the Mass and embrace the Book of Common Prayer. This proposal was an invitation for Mary to approve being tried, in fact if not in appearance, and in absentia. Further, she would be required to deny her religion and turn apostate. There was no possibility whatsoever of Mary accepting, but instead of being furious at the suggestions, Knollys reported, 'the Queen is merry and hunteth and passeth the time daily in pleasant manner'.

Elizabeth was able to make such an offer since a week earlier Middlemore had returned from his visit to Moray with the news that the lords of the Scottish council had in their possession 'such letters . . . that sufficiently in our opinion prove her consenting to the murder of the king her lawful husband'. The machinery for a trial was already under way, and Cecil and Elizabeth were becoming more and more confident of proving Mary's guilt. Mary was unaware that Moray had already assured Elizabeth that 'the noblemen of Scotland had not entered on it [the accusations against Mary] without good ground and occasion'.

Somewhat to Knollys's astonishment, Mary actually agreed to all of Elizabeth's suggestions, including the endorsement of the Book of Common Prayer. Mary had even received a Church of England chaplain and attended his services, though Knollys doubted if this was bona fide. He ended his despatch to Cecil with a further plea for money – but Cecil habitually ignored such pleas.

A mere three weeks later, on 16 August, Moray summoned a parliament during which he sold some of Mary's jewellery to pay his army. Parliament also formally forfeited the entire Hamilton family, in spite of which Mary commanded no retribution, to the fury of Herries, whose lands were also forfeited along with all those who supported the queen. He blamed Elizabeth for delaying Mary's restoration and so causing confusion in Scotland.

While Cecil, with the enthusiastic help of Moray, set about preparing the case against Mary, life was calm at Bolton. Mary convinced herself that the admonitory letters from Elizabeth were not, in fact, written by her but by 'one of her highness subjects' – undoubtedly she had Cecil in mind – and expressed her wish that her case be heard in Westminster Hall. Her plea for a one-to-one interview with Elizabeth now disappeared from her correspondence and she moved more towards appeasing her English hosts in Yorkshire, even attending Church of England services. It must be remembered that Elizabeth herself had asked her own Catholic sister, Queen Mary, if she could be given instruction in the Catholic faith and she even attended Mass – but this was for her own survival. It is unlikely that Mary was so skilled at dissimulation, but, like so many prisoners, she sought after novelty. Mary never, for a moment, wavered in her faith. Knollys's only complaint was that Mary's household continued to grow, even her pages and grooms now having servants. He was falling under the spell of Mary's charm and, when he was advised of a possible rescue bid by one George Herron, Knollys simply refused to believe that Mary would undertake 'such an uncertain adventure'.

At the end of August Mary paid Knollys a singular compliment and wrote to him in English promising a token for his wife – it was a pomander laced with gold wire. It was Mary's first attempt at writing in English and Scotticisms still occur: 'nicht' for 'night' and 'nocht bien' for 'not well'. She normally spoke French and, when necessity demanded it, used a version of Scots with a heavy French accent. One modern scholar, Dr Charles McKean, has called her speech 'Frécossais', and there is no doubt that Mary was only entirely at ease when speaking French. Elizabeth's letters to Mary – written in English – were translated into Scots for her.

During Mary's time in England, Moray had been busy with Anglo-Scottish affairs and his first and most important task was to make certain that Elizabeth knew that she was harbouring a regicide. Only five days after Langside, Moray sent John Wood to London with copies of what became known as the Casket Letters. Strangely these copies were a translation of the original French into Scots. Since Elizabeth only understood Scots with difficulty but spoke fluent French, why Moray made this translation is only the first puzzle in the bizarre and tangled story of the Casket Letters. Moray was, however, well aware that Elizabeth needed 'such evident reasons as her majesty may with conscience satisfy herself' and to this end on 27 May he had sent 'closed writings' to George Buchanan in St Andrews – where Moray had appointed him principal of St Leonard's College. These were presumably further copies, to be used by Buchanan in the preparation of an indictment. Buchanan was a 62-year-old scholar who had befriended Mary during her happier days at

Holyrood, writing masques and court entertainments for her, gently tutoring her in Latin, and behaving as scholar-in-residence to her court. From this position of profitable friendship, he would now to become her principal accuser, preparing his *Detectio Mariae Reginae*, a vituperative pamphlet directly accusing Mary of adultery with Bothwell. One episode Buchanan describes involved Lady Reres being lowered by a sash to Bothwell's apartments. The sash apparently broke but the good lady none the less plucked Bothwell out of his bed – where he was sleeping with his wife – and into Mary's lustful arms. This piece of nonsense was attested to by George Dalgleish immediately before his execution, at a time when memory of his recent torture would have inspired him to swear to anything. In any case, Lady Reres had been a mistress of Bothwell's and would hardly have acted as a bawd on the queen's behalf.

Before the publication of the grossly libellous *Detectio*, Buchanan prepared a formal 'Indictment', which he oxymoronically described as 'an information of probable and infallible conjectures and presumptions'. The manuscript of the first version of the *Detectio* was ready by 22 June. It was written in Latin but translated into Scots and sent to Lennox who, as Darnley's father, had been demanding a trial for some time. Moray was now proposing to Elizabeth that she should hold a trial 'with great ceremony and solemnity' to examine the situation. With diplomatic skill he suggested that what should be examined were his own actions as regent 'in hostility against . . . my own countrymen', thus allowing him to cite as justification the removal of an unjust queen – a murderess and adulteress. Thus all parties could claim that Mary would technically not be on trial herself.

This was important for Elizabeth, who was well aware that watchful eyes were being trained on her from the Louvre, the Escorial and the Vatican to see if she would dare to try a sovereign queen in public. Thus great care was taken to avoid the word 'trial' and to appear even-handed while a structure was put in place which would decide for Elizabeth what action to take. This structure consisted of the two sides pleading their respective cases before an unbiased commission appointed by Elizabeth. On 27 August Mary heard that the Duke of Norfolk was to lead Elizabeth's commission, which would then make its report; Cecil and Elizabeth could then reflect on their findings. Since Mary was not being tried, she would not be subjected to the indignity of appearing. At first it seemed that the examination would take place in Newcastle, but the venue was switched to York, and in mid September passports were applied for by Mary on behalf of the Earl of Cassilis, the bishops of Ross and of Galloway, lords Herries and Boyd, Sir John Gordon and Sir James Cockburn. Mary was so sure that she would be cleared of all blame by the commission that on 15 September she assured her brother-in-law, Charles IX of France, that Elizabeth had promised to restore her to her 'honour and grandeur in her country'. Moray, on the other hand, had passports for 100 persons in his train, plus the earls of Morton and Glencairn, Lord Lindsay, the Bishop of Orkney and the Commendator of Dunfermline, each with 100 persons in their trains.

Finally, on 24 September, Elizabeth sent a 'Memorial for the proceedings of Norfolk, Sussex and Sadler, with the Queen of Scots and her son's commissioners at the city of York' to her commissioners. Mary's involvement in the murder of Henry, Lord Darnley, as well as her adulterous relationship with Bothwell, would be examined, and after a complete vindication of these charges she would be restored to her throne by her cousin, Elizabeth. Moray, on the other hand, wanted nothing less than the condemnation of Mary and Elizabeth's endorsement of his rule. Elizabeth herself had issued precise instructions to her commissioners. They were to hear both sides apart from each other, with Mary's case heard first, and if there was to be no firm proof of the charges, then Mary must be restored. The proposals, that is to say, the rebuttals, were to come from Mary or from Moray and a treaty was to be agreed jointly by Elizabeth, Mary and Moray. The terms of this treaty would include an Act of Oblivion for past crimes, and a council to be appointed to assist Mary; her future marriage would be agreed by the three estates;

Bothwell was to be punished; the legal status of the Reformed Church would be ratified; the infant James would be kept in England and raised by Scots; and titles to the crown of England were to be clarified. Elizabeth was to be the umpire for all this, and if Mary were to break any part of the treaty, then James would immediately succeed as ruler. Inevitably the Treaty of Edinburgh was to be ratified and Mary was forbidden to enter into foreign leagues.

Elizabeth and Cecil saw this examination as a golden opportunity to tidy up old business, and they felt she could rely on her commissioners. Norfolk was England's only duke, and was recently widowed for the third time. Thin-faced and with a high forehead, he looked permanently worried, giving the impression that he was trying to look as if he understood what was going on around him. Nominally Protestant, he had many Catholic relations and would need Elizabeth's permission to remarry; he could, therefore, be relied on. Sadler, who had seen Mary as a naked baby twenty-six years previously, was, like the Earl of Sussex, a professional courtier and could be relied on to do his sovereign's bidding without too much thought. Mary would have to rely on reports from York being carried back to her at Bolton. Her life would be closely examined in public, but she would only be able to answer through proxies.

On 29 September Mary sent precise instructions to her commissioners in a document which was to be the sole authority for them to act on her behalf, since her great seal was still in Scotland. Like the quartering of her arms with England, the absence of her seal may seem trivial to us today, but to Mary it represented another petty reduction in her status. In her letter she rehearsed the offences of the Lords: her seizure after Carberry and imprisonment at Lochleven Castle. She pointed out that her abdication was invalid since it had been made under threat and had been ratified by a parliament she did not endorse. Similarly, the coronation of James without her permission had no validity. Now on slightly thinner ice, she denied any knowledge of the murder of Darnley and did 'nothing thereunto but by the advice of the nobility of the realm'. Mary obviously knew of the existence of the secret Casket Letters and insisted that if they were to be used in evidence against her, then she must be allowed to see the originals and 'make answer thereto'. She also pointed out that there were 'divers in Scotland' who could counterfeit her handwriting and copy her prose style. She did not ask for revenge against Moray, but promised to accept Elizabeth's judgment, maintaining the freedom of Protestantism, and assuring her of agreement in the matter of succession. There were no wild threats of foreign intervention and her case against the rebel lords was put reasonably and calmly. Mary was certain she would be vindicated and restored.

Five days earlier, on 24 September, Mary had written a long letter to her childhood friend Elisabeth, now Queen of Spain. She assured her that she was surrounded by adoring Catholics and, further, that Elizabeth of England was jealous of Mary's strength of faith, but would restore her in spite of the unjust accusations against her. Mary told Elisabeth of her plans to marry James to a Spanish princess, but could not have known that Elisabeth would die in childbirth before she could read this letter from her friend of the far-off days of tournaments at Chambord and of the nursery at St Germain. Mary Stewart was whistling in the dark and Cecil, who intercepted all her correspondence, knew it only too well. He would also know that his most Catholic Majesty Philip II of Spain was now free to remarry. With a satisfactory verdict from York, Cecil would be able to tie up a lot of the loose ends, which were starting to resemble a nest of writhing snakes.

CHAPTER FIFTEEN

A lawful prisoner?

By 7 October 1567 the three groups of commissioners had met in York and sworn oaths to deal only in truth, with each side showing a profound distrust of the other two. On the first day, 8 October, Mary's commissioners made a formal presentation of their case, and two days later Moray asked for a guarantee that if Mary was found guilty, she would be 'delivered in our hands', and declared that without such a guarantee he could not proceed. While Norfolk was considering this extravagant request an indictment arrived from Lennox. This was a compilation of Buchanan's fantasy with additions by Lennox himself and, according to John Hosack in his *Mary Queen of Scots and her Accusers*, 'the English commissioners were not greatly impressed by the taradiddles of Lennox and they wanted stronger stuff and they got it'.

On 11 October, Lethington, Buchanan, and James Macgill met with the commissioners without the knowledge of Mary's advisers. Macgill was clerk to the register of the Privy Council, described as a 'subtle chicaner and embroiler of the laws'. This group produced the various bonds they had signed agreeing to Bothwell's 'purgation' of the murder, the Ainslie Tavern Bond supporting him, and their agreement to his marrying the queen, claiming that all of this had been done under threat of violence from Bothwell's 200 arquebusiers. Since Bothwell was 'purged' of his treason in carrying off the queen, they claimed that by law he was also purged of all lesser crimes, including the murder of Darnley. This fantastic piece of legal logic-chopping – 'a fit policy for a detestable fact' – was followed by the Scots commissioners' trump card: they showed Elizabeth's commissioners the Casket Letters.

This action was completely invalid in legal terms and the letters would have been declared inadmissible in any court. They were 'closed in a little coffer of silver and gilt, heretofore given by her to Bothwell', but there was no forensic link with either Mary or Bothwell. There was no method of verification given to the commissioners. Neither Mary nor her commissioners had seen these letters or were given opportunity to confirm or deny their veracity. No comparisons of handwriting were made with known examples of her handwriting. Norfolk, who was making up the rules governing the commission as he went along, read the letters and was appalled to discover 'such inordinate love between her and Bothwell, her loathsomeness and abhorring of her husband that was murdered'. The letters were locked away again in their casket.

The Casket Letters which so appalled Norfolk have been the subject of intense debate and many books. They consisted of letters and other documents supposedly sent by Mary to Bothwell and kept by him in the celebrated silver casket, only to come into the hands of Morton on 19 June 1567. Thereafter they were the property of Moray. The originals no longer exist, having vanished from history in May 1584, and evidence based on copies translated from the French is extremely doubtful.

In the first letter – known as the Short Glasgow Letter and, like all the documents, undated and unsigned – the writer, presumably Mary, tells Bothwell that she is bringing Darnley to Craigmillar. It is an affectionate and chatty letter in which she gives good news of the infant James, but complains of the pain in her side. Mary must have written it in Stirling and the note at the foot of the document, 'from Glasgow, this Saturday morning' is a later addition, meant to add further veracity to what is almost certainly a genuine document.

The second letter, however – the Long Glasgow Letter – is altogether another matter. It recounts Mary's visit to Darnley in January 1567, just before he left for Craigmillar, and varies from the prosaic 'I thought I should have been killed with his breath', to the amorous 'God forgive me, and God knit us together for ever'. While this variance is possible for anyone writing while in love, Mary's other letters are normally as brisk and as business-like as she could manage. This reads like a genuine letter of Mary's but heavily 'salted' with interpolations of passion to increase the presumption of her guilt. She shows herself to be disenchanted with Darnley and besotted with Bothwell, but there is no evidence of, or even ambition for, adultery. It is clearly a forgery that uses fragments of truth to stitch together the whole.

This is followed by what seems to be a genuine love-letter in which the writer sends a locket and wishes to be 'bestowed under your regiment' during their forthcoming marriage. The style is hugely different from Mary's normal register – even in her informal letters to friends – and it has grammatical eccentricities which she always avoided. It may have been written to Bothwell by one of his many admirers, but it was certainly not written by Mary Stewart.

Next is another avowal of undying love which has so many mistranslations from the French that the original meaning is obscure. There are mistakes in French grammar – 'malheureuse' for 'malheureux' – and the page Bastiane changes sex to become Bastienne. It is a clumsy pastiche and reads as if a grown man was unsuccessfully imitating the style of a young girl, which is probably the case.

A fifth letter was claimed to have been found among the papers of Margaret Carwood and is an unashamed love letter by someone looking forward to marriage. Again it has the long involved sentences of a love-lorn teenager, this time the writer imagining herself becoming a countess. Since Mary was a queen and Bothwell stood to become a king, the claim that Mary wrote the letter to him is complete nonsense.

A clerk has endorsed the sixth letter 'From Stirling before her ravishing – it shows her mask of ravishing.' It was obviously written by another woman, who reproaches Bothwell for being slow in his advances: 'You had promised me that you would resolve all . . . You have done nothing thereof.' Huntly is described as 'your false brother-in-law', although at that time he and Bothwell were firm friends. The writer does say, 'I could never marry you seeing that being married you did carry me away', but ravishment of future brides continued at least to the eighteenth century in the Scottish Borders, and it is most likely that this letter was written by an earlier conquest of Bothwell's.

The seventh letter, however, reads exactly as one might expect from Mary. If it does refer to Bothwell's proposed abduction, then the opening is typically brisk: 'Of the place and time I remit myself to your brother and to you.' Bothwell is instructed, 'make yourself sure of the Lords and free to marry'. This is a sovereign writing to a subject. Last is a letter that was probably written by Mary after her marriage, during Bothwell's absence in Melrose. In it she voices her earliest fears of the likelihood of a rebellion by the nobility.

In addition to the eight letters there followed a sequence of twelve poems, incorrectly described as sonnets. Together they form, in fact, an interminable love poem, extremely badly written, often with faulty scansion. It is impossible to believe that a woman trained by du Bellay and a keen student of Ronsard could have produced such infantile versifying; Mary's natural inclination was to the high Renaissance style that she had learnt in her childhood. A crucial indicator of its falsity comes in line 17 when she describes Scotland as 'my country'. Elsewhere, it was always 'my kingdom', 'my realm', or 'this our land' since Mary's emotion towards Scotland was principally one of ownership.

The commissioners were also shown two marriage contracts and in each case the signature was a forgery. Mary's signature was very formal and would have been simple to forge, so why such an easy task was botched is difficult to understand.

To sum up the affair of these letters, it seems that some of them were genuine, while others were letters in Bothwell's possession adapted to read as if they came from Mary. There were no dates – at least up until the time the letters came into the hands of Morton – and, apart from the marriage contracts, no signatures.

The extant versions are all copies of translations, so errors will have occurred and handwriting comparisons are impossible.

In 1754 Walter Goodall published *An examination of the letters said to be written by Mary Queen of Scots to James, Earl of Bothwell: shewing by intrinsick and extrinsick evidence that they are forgeries*. In 1849 the barrister John Hosack was more cautious: 'If antecedent probabilities are rather in favour of the genuineness of the letters there is nevertheless a considerable amount of presumptive evidence that they are forgeries.'

Two questions remain. Who carried out the forgeries and why did the English commission take them so seriously? When Morton received the casket he had high hopes of finding incriminating documents, but the letters were not incriminating enough. Certainly Mary admitted to preferring Bothwell to Darnley and might be thought to have agreed to her abduction, but these admissions had to be strengthened. Further, once the chain of evidence was broken and the decision made to deal only in copies of the originals, then all of Bothwell's seized correspondence would have been available to Lethington, who was known to be able to initate the queen's hand and to create the desired effects. The commissioners, for their part, were told they were being shown 'secret' documents that would bring about a definite decision and, from then on, they were all-too-keen to believe them. Here was evidence of amorous passion in a female, loathsome to the macho culture of the nobility; there was evidence of Mary accompanying Darnley to Edinburgh, although no evidence that she knew that he would then be murdered; there was evidence of what was wrongly taken for unbridled lust in the writing of French love poetry, although it is unlikely that anyone ever read the verses; and all of this was enough for the commissioners immediately to refer the matter to higher authority.

The conclusive proof of Mary's complicity would have been found in the Craigmillar Bond – which Mary herself did not sign – but, since it would have incriminated most of the nobility, all copies had been burned and, at this stage, it was never mentioned. There was enough 'evidence' without it.

The English commissioners were also given a translation of *The Book of Articles* drawn up by Buchanan. This was a compilation of the 'evidence' contained in the Casket Letters, evidence from Lennox, and a summary of Buchanan's own *Detectio*. Mary and Bothwell were now also accused of an unsuccessful attempt to poison Darnley en route from Glasgow. In the face of this, Norfolk simply did what all good civil servants did when faced with a hard decision and referred the matter upstairs in a long letter to Elizabeth asking for a decision. Knowing that he was unlikely to receive one, Norfolk also wrote to Cecil advising him of the letters and that their effect would be to completely condemn Mary – if the letters were to be believed – or completely vindicate her – if they were thought to be false.

When news of the production of the letters arrived at Bolton Castle, Mary affected astonishment and assured Knollys that her commissioners would refute all charges. Her refutation was simple: the murder of Darnley was not mentioned at all while the treachery of the nobility was described in detail. The Lords claimed everything they had done had been done under duress; Mary maintained that they had done these things willingly. Bothwell had left the field at Carberry in order to prevent bloodshed and she had given herself willingly into the protection of the nobility. She had been unjustly imprisoned, forced to abdicate under threat 'of that present death which was prepared for her'. In the face of this revolt, it was 'therefore required that her grace may be supported by the Queen of England'.

To add to Norfolk's confusion, while the commission sat in York, Lethington met with the duke and suggested that a marriage between Norfolk and Mary might be arranged. Should Mary agree to ratify her abdication then Moray would be glad to accept Mary back in Scotland as the Duchess of Norfolk. Elizabeth would be delighted to have her troublesome cousin removed, with the possibility that she might even ratify the Treaty of Edinburgh, and, as the Duchess of Norfolk, she would technically be under the control of the English crown. Norfolk, who had been sent with a firm indication from Cecil that he was to establish Mary's guilt as an adulteress and murderer, was now being encouraged to marry her. It would not be difficult for Norfolk to come to some arrangement as to Mary's Catholic faith – his religious faith was a matter of convenience – and her guilt really depended on the somewhat flimsy evidence of the Casket Letters. Few knew better than Lethington how unreliable paperwork could be made to appear, and Norfolk was hardly the most intelligent courtier in England. Norfolk could return with her to Scotland. Lethington knew very well that any sort of evidence could be produced – a 'dodgy dossier' – so that Mary could appear pure as the driven snow. Mary unmarried was a threat, but Mary married to Norfolk was less dangerous. Norfolk would also believe anything he was told, and as an ambitious nobleman, he might have liked the idea of being married to a queen, even though her husbands had had a poor life expectancy.

On 15 October, Knollys, on his own initiative, tried to remove some of the dangers surrounding Mary and her marriageable state by suggesting that she might marry George Carey, his cousin, whom she had met in September. The suggestion was quietly ignored.

For all the careful instructions sent to Norfolk by Elizabeth, he was totally at a loss to determine what exactly Elizabeth and Cecil wanted as the outcome of the inquiry. While the marriage suggestion was still in the air, Norfolk had a long conference with Lethington on 16 October and both men agreed that the best conclusion would be a compromise in which Mary would have the suspicion of unproven guilt attached to her, thus allowing Elizabeth more time to confine her cousin and to refuse her a formal audience. With no firm conclusion, Elizabeth was also excused from giving her wholehearted support to Moray. This fog of indecision allowed Elizabeth to move in whatever direction she wished.

Elizabeth closed the inquiry at York, sent Norfolk to examine the defences of the Northern Marches and instructed Sussex to continue as President of the Council in the North. Sadler, Lethington, Macgill, Herries and the Abbot of Kilwinning were all summoned to London, where the investigation could continue under the watchful eye of Cecil and Elizabeth herself. Mary, naïvely, was delighted that her 'good sister would hear the matters herself'.

On 21 October, a few days after the inquiry in York had been closed, Moray wrote to Cecil telling him that as regent, or governor, he had to return to Scotland – he had not, in fact, been invited to London – to see to the safety of the king; he also told Cecil to ignore all arguments in favour of Châtelherault as the proper heir and successor to Mary. Moray strongly advised Cecil to support the establishment of his government in Scotland without delay 'or nourish faction, hurt her friends, maintain her enemies, endanger the state of religion and amity, and provoke the entry of strangers within the isle'. Mary's guilt or innocence was completely forgotten in the revival of the Stewart–Hamilton feud. Cecil would have filed the letter under 'background', although he had received a letter from Sussex suggesting that some kind of 'composition to save her honour if she were defaced and dishonoured' should be found to avert the possibility of a Hamilton coup d'état which might occur if Moray's plan of total condemnation was carried through. In the end, Sussex concluded it would be best if Moray could produce such evidence as to find Mary judicially guilty and then kept in England 'at the charges of Scotland'.

The ever-careful Knollys also wrote to Cecil, inevitably hoping he would soon be released from his task as gaoler and advising that the sooner Elizabeth made a decision the better, since, if Mary suspected she was to be kept permanently as a prisoner, she would 'leave no practise untried for escape'. She rode whenever the weather permitted and it would be simple for a rescue party to take her, since she could outride most of Knollys's household.

Meanwhile, Elizabeth was preparing to move Mary to Tutbury Castle near Derby, over 100 miles further south. Knollys pointed out that all the furnishings in Bolton were borrowed and could not be moved south. He ended his letter to Cecil, 'I beseech you let neither me nor my sons be longer troubled with this service.' Cecil ignored his plea.

Cecil also ignored a letter from Francis Walsingham on 20 November. Walsingham informed Cecil that if sufficient proof against Mary could not be found, one of his agents could readily supply it. Walsingham was a Puritan zealot and a member of Elizabeth's Privy Council. He ran the most efficient spy service in Europe, employing ciphers, agents and torture to further Elizabeth's cause. Walsingham adored the queen to the point of mania, while, for her part, Elizabeth distrusted the possibly expensive results of his obsessive zealotry.

A few days later, on 24 November, Elizabeth established a second commission to meet at Westminster and to conclude the matters begun at York. The original trio was increased by the Marquis of Northamptonshire, the Earls of Arundel, Pembroke and Leicester, lords Saye, Clinton and Howard, Sir William Cecil, Sir Walter Mildmay and Sir Nicholas Bacon. This formidable array of English nobility agreed that they would not meet judicially, but once again as commissioners. Moray was recalled, nominally to represent James VI, and Mary's team included the Bishop of Ross, Lord Herries and others to represent her side. Since James VI could not appear, there would equally be no need for Mary to appear in person, and Elizabeth herself would take no part in the proceedings. Elizabeth also claimed that the London meeting was to examine Moray for his effrontery in accusing Mary of such foul crimes. Elizabeth probably didn't believe a word of what she had said, but she was making sure that she could never be accused of putting her cousin and sister queen in jeopardy.

The hearing – great pains were taken to avoid the word 'trial' – opened on 25 November in the Painted Chamber, Westminster, with Elizabeth's commissioners seated at a long table on which lay the impressive royal commission. After swearing in the commissioners, the first move was made by Moray the next day in an 'eik', or addition, to their former accusation, that not only did Bothwell murder Darnley with the compliance of Mary but also that the adulterous pair planned to murder the infant James and so to 'transfer the crown from the right line to a bloody murderer and godless tyrant'. To this end the loyal nobility had forced Mary to abdicate, had crowned her son and then established Moray as regent.

Since plague had broken out in London, the commission transferred the whole proceedings to Hampton Court and, on hearing the 'eik', Mary's commissioners asked permission for her to appear and answer the charges directly. Elizabeth replied that the matter of Mary's guilt in Darnley's murder should be cleared up first, for 'I never could believe, nor yet will, that she ever did consent thereto', but that to appear before the commission might 'endanger her honour and estate'. Since this gave access only to Moray, Mary's commissioners refused to accept the decision and withdrew from the proceedings on 6 December.

In reply, Moray offered Buchanan's *Book of Articles* and produced the Act of the Scottish parliament ratifying his position as regent. The day after Mary's representatives withdrew, Moray once again produced 'a small gilt coffer, of not fully a foot long'. The Casket Letters were read and dutifully copied – with the occasional mistakes and mistranslations into English – by Cecil's clerks. Moray produced the depositions of Hay, Powry and Dalgleish and a 'writing signed by Macgill' in which Mary agreed to her abduction by Bothwell. The Bishop of Ross protested violently at this presentation of unsupported evidence, produced either by torture or, at least, the threat of torture, but Morton solemnly swore to his story of finding the casket. Moray, having agreed with this version, swore that the letters were genuine and in the 'said Queen's proper hand write'. Further verification was sought by comparing the letters with some of Mary's extant writings, but it proved inconclusive since there were no handwriting experts present. The commissioners had no intention of reaching a conclusion without firm guidance from Elizabeth, who would neither give a judgment, nor meet with Mary until she had heard Mary's case in full. Mary refused to declare herself or to meet anyone but Elizabeth in person. Elizabeth's Tudor temper was becoming overstretched and she insisted that either Mary responded herself in writing or 'answered some nobleman whom the Queen shall send or the Queen must deem her culpable'. The stalemate seemed unbreakable since Mary's intransigence meant that she could no longer appear to deny Moray's accusations, which would then be liable to acceptance. Elizabeth, however, would not accept them without more evidence and knew that since her cousin refused to appear before anyone but herself, the matter could not be resolved. And she herself could not be forced into taking any action.

Lethington and the Bishop of Ross continued to meet with Norfolk, ostensibly to go on hawking expeditions, occasionally pressing the idea of the marriage to Mary, even considering the espousal of Norfolk's daughter, Margaret, to the infant James VI. While they made efforts to keep the plan secret, especially from Elizabeth, 'a bruit ran among men of note' with Throckmorton and Leicester lending their weight to this scheme, while it seemed that no one bothered to consult Mary as to her next bedfellow.

Lethington made a subtle proposition to break the logjam, whereby Mary would acknowledge her abdication as only a demission of the throne in favour of James, so that she could still continue as queen while he was accepted as king, but should he predecease her then she would be restored to her full state. Sadly, nothing came of this elegant proposal. Mary's answer to Moray's 'eik' was, with more than a little reason behind it, to 'charge them [Mary's accusers] as authors, inventors and doers of the said crime that they would impute to us'. Cecil, meanwhile, wrote himself more lengthy memos of how Mary might be kept in England – 'a lawful prisoner'.

Knollys pleaded with Mary to yield to Elizabeth's requests that she appear before Moray and the English commissioners. Mary simply replied, 'I am not an equal to my rebels, neither will I submit myself to be weighed in equal balance with them.' This is almost a parallel to the defence put forward by her grandson Charles I, who stated that since he, as king, had no peers, no one could legally try him. The eventual outcome was the same in both cases.

Also in December 1568, Mary unwisely wrote to an unidentified correspondent to 'assemble our friends, my subjects – proclaim and hold a parliament, if you may'. This was unwise since the letter, like most of her private correspondence, was intercepted by Cecil and forwarded to Moray. On another occasion, on 10 January, her messenger Thomas Kerr was intercepted at Berwick by the commander Lord Hudson with 'matter worth the knowing', but his secrets remain a mystery.

Elizabeth had, in fact, grown weary of the stalemate, brought about, as she saw it, by her intractable cousin, and the court was rife with the gossip that Mary would face some kind of imprisonment in England. Although the commission was still sitting, the Earl of Shrewsbury wrote to his wife in mid December, 'Things fall out very evil against the Scots Queen . . . Now it is certain the Scots Queen comes to Tutbury to my charge.'

Elizabeth and Cecil had now managed to get all the accusations against Mary into the open, while Mary's non-appearance was taken as a confession of guilt. Early in the January of 1569, Huntly and Argyll approached the commission and spelt out the formation of the Craigmillar Bond in great detail, thus incriminating themselves along with Bothwell, Lethington, Sir James Balfour and Moray. Mary is cited as an accessory before the fact, and could not in any way deny her foreknowledge of a plot against Darnley, even allowing for her feeble desire that nothing be done 'to my hurt and displeasure'. If this statement was disputed, then the two noblemen challenged Moray and Lethington to single combat – Lethington was not of noble blood, but they were generously prepared to make an exception to the rules of chivalry and would allow him to fight. Moray's response to this was very simple: he flatly denied that he had been at Craigmillar on the relevant dates. Therefore, at least that part of the statement was fiction.

Before either of these declarations were made, however, on 7 January, Elizabeth let it be known that

The Queen of Scots must not in any sort understand, that the queen's majesty meaneth to deal any further in this matter, considering she doth not answer to the crime of murdering her husband, but that the Earl of Moray shall return to his government, and shall be by her majesty placed in no worse state than that she found him in at his calling from thence. The Queen of Scots would also be removed to Tutbury and no such free access of persons allowed to her as hath been. There should be a general restraint that none should come or send to her but by the queen's majesty's knowledge.

After this abrupt command there could be no further doubt but that Mary Stewart was now a prisoner of state. On 10 January Elizabeth wrote to the Scottish commissioners, 'forasmuch as there had been nothing declared against them [the commissioners], as yet that might impair their honour and allegiances, so, on the other part, there had been nothing sufficient produced nor shown by them against their sovereign, whereby the Queen of England should conceive or take any evil opinion of the Queen her good sister, for anything she had yet seen.' This was a perfect piece of Tudor prevarication, which in Scots law would be recorded as 'not proven'. It gave Elizabeth absolute freedom to deal with Mary as she wished, but presented her with the dilemma of deciding exactly what it was that she wished to do with Mary.

As realisation of her plight began to sink in, Mary's attitude began to change. A renewed approach had been made by Philip II of Spain for the marriage between Mary and Don John of Austria, but she wrote back telling Philip that, given her situation in the hands of Elizabeth, she could make no such commitment. Despite this, when Mary wrote to Elizabeth on 22 January, she made no concessions and proposed no action, but she did, unwisely, berate Elizabeth for her behaviour in the past. Elizabeth had not received her, Mary had not been shown copies of the Casket Letters, and, by allowing him to return with no more than a slap on the wrist, Elizabeth had tacitly appeared to find in Moray's favour and to condemn Mary. There were other 'petites rudesses'; Mary had had no news of her relatives in France and she was cut off from news of affairs in Scotland. Her letter no longer held neither cheerful optimism that a face-to-face meeting could put everything in order, nor Guise imperiousness, demanding the observance of her regal state. Now Mary had the whining tone of an imprisoned supplicant begging for favours.

Elizabeth, on the other hand, had cleared the decks with her accustomed efficiency. Reports that James was to come to England, that Edinburgh, Stirling and Dumbarton were to have English garrisons, and that Moray was to be declared legitimate and would hold Scotland on the death of James should he be 'without bairns' were declared to be totally false. Mary had not been tried, but in the court of public opinion she had been found guilty on the basis of unproven evidence and secret rumour. Elizabeth had now removed her to a safer and more comfortable place. And, at least for the moment, Elizabeth could forget about her troublesome Scottish cousin.

Mary's removal to Tutbury should have been simple. Cecil received a projected route from the Earl of Sussex: Bolton to Ripon (sixteen miles) then Ripon to Wetherby (ten miles) Pomfret [Pontefract] to Rotherham (sixteen miles) and so on by easy stages to Tutbury. As Tutbury was not at this time fully furnished it was planned that Mary would lodge first at another of Shrewsbury's houses at Sheffield. Confusion reigned, however, as Lady Shrewsbury, châtelaine of both houses, had already sent the furnishings from Sheffield to Tutbury. Logistical chaos was taking place as Mary, on the morning of 26 January 1569, was forced to leave Bolton. She had delayed for some days because of bad weather and ill health, but now the household had to move. Sixteen horses had been hired for Mary and her attendants, along with another sixteen for her guard, and thirty-six more for her servants, as well as six cartloads of baggage and eight carriage horses. Their breath steamed in the freezing air as Mary finally appeared, heavily wrapped against the freezing weather, and the cumbersome entourage lumbered out into the snow, to arrive at Ripon late that evening.

At Ripon, Mary had been met by Sir Robert Melville with instructions to discuss the possibilities of her marriage to Norfolk.

Since one of Moray's fears over Mary's liberty in Scotland was the possibility of her marrying a foreign prince, the idea of marriage to Norfolk was to be encouraged. Given Mary's ill humour and exhaustion, these discussions achieved nothing, although she did find time to write to Elizabeth complaining about her forced removal from Bolton and denying her authorship of the Casket Letters. She told Elizabeth she had written a long denial to Cecil, which she would spare her 'good sister and cousin' from reading. Doubtless Cecil had already communicated the relevant portions to his queen.

Knollys, 'much disquieted with this melancholy service in these strange countries, which melancholy humour groweth daily upon me since my wife's [recent] death', was still aiming to lodge his party at one of Shrewsbury's houses at Sheffield, but on 28 January he received the news that it was now uninhabitable and he should make directly for Tutbury. This was becoming more and more difficult as the rigours of such a winter journey began to take their toll. In Rotherham, Lady Livingston became so ill that she had to be left behind. At Chesterfield, Mary, who had been complaining of her recurrent pain in her side, refused to continue without her servant attending her. Lady Livingston was Agnes Fleming, Mary's cousin, and distantly related to two of the other Maries. Mary's stay at Chesterfield cannot have been made more cheerful by her receiving a reply from Elizabeth, who could not understand why Mary was upset and advised her, 'Quiet yourself in all things according to the princely good heart that God hath given you'.

Mary did not heed this patronising advice, given as though to a recalcitrant child, and at the end of January she wrote to Norfolk, 'Our fault were not shameful. You have promised to be mine and I yours; I believe the Queen of England and country should like of it. If you think the danger great do as you think best . . . I will ever be, for your sake, perpetual prisoner, or put my life in peril for your weal [health] or mine. Your own, faithful unto death, Queen of Scots, my Norfolk.' Mary, twenty-six years old, was behaving like an over-emotional thirteen-year-old schoolgirl.

Finally, on 3 February 1569, Mary arrived at Tutbury, there to be placed in the care of the Earl and Countess of Shrewsbury. A week earlier, Elizabeth had sent instructions to Shrewsbury, the highest ranking peer in England after the Duke of Norfolk, ratifying her earlier decision of December. The Earl and Countess were to treat Mary as a queen but not to let her overpower them or gain her freedom without Elizabeth's express consent, which she intended to give 'at time and in manner convenient'. Shrewsbury was instructed to limit Mary's retinue – the cost of maintaining them was prohibitive – and to let no one above the rank of 'mean servants' come to her out of Scotland. Since Elizabeth understood Tutbury to be in a poor state, Mary was to be lodged at Shrewsbury's own house in Sheffield. London obviously had no clear picture of Shrewsbury's domestic dilemma. Elizabeth, having made her wishes clear, broke off and the instructions then continued in Cecil's handwriting. If Mary were to make any complaint against Elizabeth, then all the charges made against her would be published. If she became ill or wished to speak to the countess, then contact should be limited and no gentlewoman apart from the countess should be allowed to attend Mary.

Her new host, who would have charge of her for fifteen years, was George Talbot, 4th Earl of Shrewsbury. Elizabeth, no doubt with Cecil nodding in approval, had chosen Shrewsbury as Mary's gaoler with considerable care. He was about forty years old, immensely rich and, more importantly, he owned seven great houses, not counting two of the greatest houses in England which were owned by his wife, and all of them were within easy reach of each other in the Midlands. He was a non-belligerent man, fussy to extremes and, like many rich people, very careful over unnecessary expenditure. His correspondence abounds with desperate appeals to Cecil over the high cost of accommodating Mary and her court. Needless to say, these appeals fell on deaf ears.

Equally important to Mary was her hostess, Elizabeth, the Countess of Shrewsbury. More often known as Bess of Hardwick, she was the earl's second wife, but he was her fourth husband. Robert Barlow, her first, died leaving her a property-rich widow, and she promptly married Sir William Cavendish, putting her determined foot on the first rung of the aristocratic ladder. Ten years later he died and she then married Sir William St Loe who, on his death, excluded his own family from his will in favour of Bess. She now owned Hardwick Hall and Chatsworth House and had become second only to the queen in wealth. Joseph Hunter, the antiquary, said of her that 'she had a mind admirably fitted for business, very ambitious, and withal overbearing, selfish, proud, treacherous and unfeeling'. This was the Bess of Hardwick who completely dominated George Talbot when he wasn't being dominated by Elizabeth Tudor. Into his household he now had to welcome Mary Stewart.

Tutbury was probably the most unsuitable of all Shrewsbury's houses: it was a medieval castle which he occasionally used as a hunting lodge and it was furnished for only one or two nights' stay at a time. The roof was missing in some places and the walls were only partially hung with tapestries. Some rooms had beds while others had only pallets on the stone floors. Gradually, some silverware arrived from the Tower of London and the main rooms were hung with tapestries; beds were erected and Mary's cloth of state arrived. To Shrewsbury's great relief Mary answered 'with temperate words and all passed without sign of offence', and she even accepted a reduction in her household from sixty to thirty people without demur. Many years later, however, Mary let her true opinion of Tutbury be known:

I am in a walled enclosure, on the top of a hill, exposed to all the winds and inclemencies of heaven. Within the said enclosure, resembling the wood of Vincennes, there is a very old hunting lodge, built of timber and plaster, cracked in all parts, the plaster adhering nowhere to the woodwork, and broken in numerous places; the said lodge distant three fathoms of thereabouts from the wall, and situated so low, that the rampart of earth which is behind the wall is on a

330

level with the highest part of the building, so that the sun can never shine upon it on that side, nor any fresh air come to it; for which reason it is so damp, that you cannot put any piece of furniture in that part without its being in four days covered in mould. I leave you to think how this must act on the human body; and, in short, the greater part of it is rather a dungeon for base and abject criminals than a habitation for any person of quality . . . the only apartments that I have for my own person consist – and for the truth of this I can appeal to all those who have been here – of two little miserable rooms, so excessively cold, especially at night, that but for the ramparts and entrenchments of curtains and tapestry that I have made, it would not be possible for me to stay in them in the day time; and out of those who have sat up with me at night during my illnesses, scarcely one has escaped without fluxion, cold or some disorder. [The grounds are] place to look at fitter to keep pigs in than to bear the name of a garden . . . This house having no privies, is subject to a continual stench; and every Saturday they are obliged to empty them, and the one beneath my windows from which I receive a perfume not the most agreeable.

Tutbury did, however, suit Elizabeth's purposes extremely well. It was far enough away from Scotland to make any escape attempt unlikely, while communication with London was easier than it had been at Bolton. Elizabeth could say with honesty that her cousin and sister queen, having not been found guilty by the investigation, was not, therefore, lodged in a prison. Yet Mary was under the strict control of a trusted courtier – a courtier who, moreover, owned several other houses nearby, an asset which was essential while considering Mary's long-term confinement in England. These great houses had little in the way of sanitation; their stone or wooden floors were laid with either rushes or, in the case of the more luxurious, a few rugs; and at least once a year they had to be 'sweetened'. The floors and walls were swept and washed down; vermin were expelled from the roof spaces and ceilings; the stables and privies were dug out and the excrement carted away; kitchen fires were extinguished and chimneys swept – so that for a period each year the houses were uninhabitable. Therefore, while Mary and her court would have to be moved, they did not need to move far and Shrewsbury could easily continue as host, or gaoler.

On 9 February Nicholas White, a messenger from Cecil to Moray, broke his northbound journey at Tutbury. He witnessed Mary attending a Church of England service with a book of Psalms in her hands. When invited to join her for a private conversation she admitted to him that her English was poor and she often used translations of the service. They discussed art, comparing carving, painting and needlework. White knew that she had a passion for needlework but they both agreed that painting was the most commendable of the arts. Mary told White that she embroidered in bad weather, although the recurring pain in her side made all kinds of activity difficult. White noticed that her chair of state carried an embroidery with the words *en ma fin est ma commencement* which was 'a riddle he understands not'. Predictably, he thought 'she is a goodly personage, an alluring grace, a pretty Scottish speech, a searching wit, clouded by mildness', and he admired her raven-black hair, although Knollys told him that it was most probably false. Mary admitted that she felt Cecil to be her implacable foe. Clearly, Nicholas White joined the long list of men who fell under her charm. Even in her discomfort and despondency, Mary Stewart could still display the elegant politesse of her upbringing, although there were now fewer and fewer people on which to practise it.

Mary now had to accept that her circumstances had changed drastically. She was no longer merely a visitor in the realm of her cousin, waiting there while Elizabeth prepared the military support needed to drive Regent Moray from power in Scotland. Her personal court was now limited to thirty persons, although this rule was applied by Shrewsbury with great elasticity and she often had double that number in attendance. Shrewsbury also maintained her stables – at his own personal cost – and he encouraged her embroidery parties with Bess, with Livingston and Seton in attendance. Masques and balls were now a thing of the past, and hunting and conversation filled her days. This was no longer the Valois-inspired court of Holyrood, but rather a 'mimic court': her cloth of gold and crimson chair stood on a dais beneath her cloth of state. Here Mary sat surrounded by her maids on their embroidered stools. She ate pre-tasted food off silver dishes, served to her by kneeling servants, and her bed had fresh linen sheets daily. Sir John Morton attended her as her personal priest and, in all, she was allowed all the ceremony that a queen was entitled to. She had no necessity to involve herself in politics apart from appointing Châtelherault, Huntly and Argyll as her lieutenants in Scotland. The only discordant note was struck by the fact that the increased household was stripping the countryside surrounding Tutbury of coal and wood, and on 20 April 1569, scarcely two and a half months after their arrival, the household moved to Shrewsbury's house at Wingfield.

Mary still maintained a correspondence with France through the ambassador Bertrand de Salignac de la Mothe Fénélon, although her codes, established in March, were quickly broken and her letters read by Cecil. She asked Fénélon to congratulate Catherine de Medici on the victory of King Charles IX at the Battle of Jarnac when the Huguenot Condé, who had been captured, was assassinated. In fact, Coligny assumed command and withdrew the Huguenot forces without great loss. Mary's praise for the murder of a Huguenot leader made unpleasant reading for Cecil and simply reinforced his view that she must be summarily dealt with as soon as possible. It was also to Fénélon that Mary complained, quite correctly, that Moray had imprisoned Châtelherault and Herries in Edinburgh Castle. When her much-delayed envoy, Sandy Bog, gave Mary the news of their imprisonment, she burst into tears and Bog was sent, with the Bishop of Ross, to London. Elizabeth feigned fury at these events, and Mary was alone in believing her theatrical protestations.

Elizabeth also spelt out her proposals for Mary's return to

Scotland: ratification of the Treaty of Edinburgh, James's education in England and Moray's continued regency, all of which would be considered in July. It seems probable that Elizabeth would have been happy to see her uninvited guest return to Scotland, but in 1615 William Camden hinted at more personal reasons for Elizabeth wishing her cousin could find a more comfortable settlement. Camden believed that Elizabeth 'found some conflict in her self, on the one side out of fear grown from an inveterate emulation, which among Princesses never dieth, and on the other side out of commiseration and compassion arising from often calling to mind of human compassion'. Thus he established the idea of Elizbeth's reign as a *Via Media*.

CHAPTER SIXTEEN

My fortune has been so evil

⚘

The possibility of Mary's marriage to Norfolk had already been raised and was now being urged on her by the Bishop of Ross. Moray endorsed the possibility – once Mary was divorced from Bothwell – since it would put an end to rumours of foreign alliances. Norfolk was a 33-year-old widower of impeccable lineage, if somewhat dull and unromantic. To his mind, continuing to live as a single man was unacceptable and a marriage to the queen of Scotland would improve his standing within the aristocracy. For her part, Mary was willing to accept his suit if it meant an end to her captivity. She said, 'My fortune has been so evil in the progress of my life, and specially in my marriages, as hardly I can be brought to have any mind to like of an husband.' Her first marriage had been as the price of French support against England's Rough Wooing, her second had been – she had thought – to please Elizabeth and her nobility, and her third had been as a result of what she claimed to be ravishment and capture. She had never met Norfolk, but the descriptions given to her by the Bishop of Ross were pleasing enough and the inevitable exchanges of jewels and portraits went ahead. The only person unaware of the proposal was Elizabeth, and even Cecil chose his moment with care before mentioning the idea of any sort of dynastic marriage.

In May Mary fell ill again and was prescribed pills for her spleen, but 'fell several times into convulsions', vomiting and experiencing a return of the illness that she suffered at Jedburgh, but the following day she had recovered enough to accost Shrewsbury at eleven o'clock at night, weeping, with complaints that George Bartly, one of her servants, was being detained at Berwick.

Elizabeth, ever practical, sent two doctors – Caldwell and Francis – to attend on Mary, and Mary took the opportunity to thank her cousin through them, assuring them that 'no physic was so good as that comfort [Elizabeth's continuing love] in adversity'. Shrewsbury wrote that Mary 'wished to God her [Elizabeth's] true heart and meaning were known to her and that it might please Him she might see her; and therewith appeared her tears'. Even the indulgent Shrewsbury was coming to accept the fact that epic bouts of weeping were inevitable adjuncts to Mary's behaviour.

The doctors pointed out that, in the next room to Mary's bedchamber, even in comfortable Wingfield, was 'a very unpleasant and fulsome savour, hurtful to her health' and Shrewsbury arranged for Mary's removal to Bess's palatial house at Chatsworth, some eight miles away, so that Wingfield could be 'sweetened'. Mary's visit to Chatsworth was a short one and within the month she was back at Wingfield.

Mary had kept up her appeals for help from France or Spain and a communication from Philip II to his ambassador in London gives us a glimpse of some of the wild stratagems she proposed: 'The Queen of Scots has not sufficient power over her son to be able to send him to Spain to be brought up.' Had Mary suggested that she send James to Spain as a token of goodwill while Alva, Philip II's general in the Netherlands, invaded England? To all prisoners the outside world quickly loses reality and what are really only hopeful fantasies seem to them possibilities.

On 28 July 1569 Moray held a convention at Perth at which Elizabeth's proposals for Mary's restoration were debated and, by forty votes to nine, were rejected. Mary would remain in England and Elizabeth would have to think of some way of dealing with her. Shrewsbury was now in great pain with gout, and the poor man was the recipient of a severe reprimand from Elizabeth for having left Wingfield in order to take the curative waters at Buxton. He had left Mary in the care of the redoubtable Bess and pointed out that his house at Wingfield, with 240 inhabitants, 'waxes unsavoury'. He suggested that Mary should be moved to Sheffield, where he had two houses, and she could then be shuttled between them without the need for long caravans proceeding across England. Elizabeth was determined that Mary should stay under the personal care of Shrewsbury – on 14 August he had been refused permission to visit the baths at Buxton seeking further treatment for his gout, so on 29 August Mary was removed to Sheffield with 'no pomp or assembly of strangers'. Mary was now, more than ever, a millstone around George Talbot's neck.

Five days earlier, however, Mary had been writing to 'My Norfolk', refusing his requests to command him, since she would rather show her wifely duty to him. Pamphlets were appearing with opinions on the marriage. 'A discourse touching the pretended match between the Duke of Norfolk and the Queen of Scots' stated, 'The safety of our sovereign should depend upon a match between the Duke of Norfolk and the Queen of Scots, for that otherwise the marrying a foreign prince might grow to that strength, as our sovereign's forces should not be able to countervail the same (a thing most dangerous considering her aspiring mind). If she falsify her faith, no pleading will serve, the sword must be the remedy.' This was reputed to have been written by 'one Sampson, a preacher'.

John Leslie, Bishop of Ross entered the debate publicly with 'A Defence of Queen Mary's Honour'. The printer, Alexander Harvey, claimed it was a joint work by the bishop, Herries and Boyd. It asserted that Mary was the lawful heir of Elizabeth, had had no involvement in Darnley's murder and, astonishingly, that the English commissioners were convinced of her total innocence and the guilt of Moray and his supporters: 'I say fie, and double fie, upon the impudence of these mischievous traitors . . . The nobles of England that were appointed to hear and examine all such matters as the rebels should lay against the Queen hath not only found the said queen innocent and guiltless of the death of

337

her husband, but do fully understand that her accusers were the very contrivers, devisers, practitioners and workers of the said murder.'

Given all this, the bishop claimed that Mary was free to marry Norfolk if she chose. The rumour of the proposed marriage came more clearly to Elizabeth's ears 'by means of the women of the court who do quickly smell out love matters', and at Farnham in Surrey, the country seat of the Bishop of Winchester, while walking in a garden, Elizabeth warned Norfolk in a 'nip' bidding him 'to beware upon what pillow he leaned his head'. Norfolk realised that he was liable to fall into deep disfavour and promptly answered, 'What! Should I seek to marry her, being so wicked a woman, such a notorious adulteress and murderer? I love to sleep upon a safe pillow.' Elizabeth commanded him to end the relationship and he, rather sulkily, retired from the court. The Scots ambassadors were instructed to tell Mary 'to bear herself quietly, lest she saw ere long those on whom she most leaned hop headless'. The rumours persisted with pamphlets for and against Mary's marriage flooding the streets.

Elizabeth was now in a spectacular Tudor rage and commanded Mary back to Tutbury under closer confinement, with the Earl of Huntingdon, whom Mary loathed, as an additional gaoler; the pretence was that Shrewsbury was ill, though, apart from the gout, he was in perfect health. Mary's loathing of Huntingdon was based on his continued claim to a right of inheritance to the throne since he was descended from a daughter of the Duke of Clarence. This was the duke who was a brother of Edward IV and whom Shakespeare had fancifully described as being drowned in a butt of Malmsey wine in 1478.

Mary and Huntingdon met on 21 September 1569, and he found her despairing of help from Elizabeth and once again threatening to seek help from 'other princes'. Four days later Elizabeth ordered that Mary should not be allowed to leave the castle, that her servants should be reduced and that searches of her own, and her servants', coffers should be made. Mary's response four days later was a tragic complaint to Elizabeth. The

338

searches had been violently carried out by men armed with 'pistolets', her servants had been driven out of the house and she was now being held a close prisoner. She begged that Elizabeth might grant her an interview, send her back to Scotland, or to France, and, finally, that Elizabeth 'put [her] to ransom' and not let her 'waste away in tears and vain regrets'. Elizabeth ensured Norfolk's compliance by sending him into the Tower on 11 October, while John Leslie was confined by the Bishop of London.

On 9 November Mary once again fell ill – 'Her colour and complexion is presently much decayed' – and Shrewsbury sent anxious reports to London while he and Bess took turns in watching by the bedside. Mary had always made decisions after hearing the advice of her advisers, the Guise brothers, or Lethington and Moray. Now she had no advisers, was prevented from applying her charm to anyone with power, and had no idea what to do. She realised, although she never admitted it, that her flight to England had been a hideous mistake and, as her confinement became stricter and her household was reduced, her position as a prisoner became clearer and clearer. Mary's current suitor, whom she had never sought, but had thoughtlessly encouraged – such flirtations were second nature to her – was now suffering royal disfavour in the Tower. Her only recourse was to illness and her body duly obliged.

Yet in the middle of November Mary became, unwittingly, a more potent danger to Elizabeth. The northern earls of Westmoreland and Northumberland were determined to restore the Catholic faith and, with a disorganised army of around 1,000 infantrymen and 1,500 cavalry, they marched south. In Durham Cathedral they heard Mass, re-established the altars and holy water stoups and burned all the Protestant prayer books. Sussex, as guardian of the Northern Marches, did not dare to engage the numerically superior rebels and they quickly seized Barnard Castle while aiming for York. By 23 November the rebels were at Tadcaster, just over fifty miles from Tutbury, and the possibility that they could, in the course of a very few days, free Mary and proclaim her Queen of England was becoming very real. The Bishop of Ross wrote to them urging them to capture Hartlepool as a port of entry for forces from Alva in the Netherlands. This, needless to say, provoked panic at Tutbury, with Mary herself fearing that Huntingdon might have secret orders to murder her, should her rescue seem likely. On Elizabeth's direct orders, Mary was hastily moved to Coventry.

Since, to Elizabeth's council in London, Coventry was no more than a conveniently placed dot on their map, they had no idea that there was no convenient castle or aristocratic house in which Mary could stay. In desperation, Shrewsbury lodged her first in the Bull Inn, where she arrived after dark and was confined to her room to avoid 'fond gazing and confluence of the people'. Elizabeth was apoplectic that the presumed focus of the Northern Rising was lodged in a common inn and demanded that Mary be sent to 'some convenient house'.

The rebel forces melted away on the continued journey south and, by 20 December, the remnants had turned back and were seeking refuge in Scotland. Six hundred were hanged, Northumberland was captured by Moray who, after ironically imprisoning him in the castle of Lochleven, sent him south for beheading. The few remaining survivors fled to the Spanish Netherlands as permanent exiles. Not for the last time, a misplaced love for an exiled Stewart was to end in death or exile.

Both earls, Northumberland and Westmoreland, had attempted to implicate Norfolk in their abortive rising, which he flatly denied in a long letter to Elizabeth. In it he also denied asking Mary to marry him. By the start of 1570 Mary was back in Tutbury and the panic started to subside.

However, one of the Earl of Arundel's men – Arundel was one of Norfolk's many relatives – planned that 'if she could be gotten away out of Tutbury, she might be conveyed to Arundel in Sussex, and then there take ship and go into France'. When they signified this to the Scots queen, she made answer, 'if the Duke or the Earl of Arundel or Pembroke would appoint a knight to take it in hand, she would adventure, otherwise she durst not'. In late December 1569 Mary had written to Norfolk accepting a diamond he had sent, swearing to wear it 'unseen about her neck'. She pledged her love to him 'faithfully until death' and warned him against Huntingdon, now returned to London. On 15 January 1570 she begged him to 'trust none that shall say I ever mind to leave you'. In spite of writing in codes, Mary must have known that her correspondence was being read by Cecil and that by encouraging Norfolk, still in the Tower, she was winding a noose around the poor besotted man's neck. The fact that they had never met makes her girlish behaviour even more reprehensible, but to Mary Stewart, the Earl of Norfolk represented a possibility of release, and when that was combined with the romantic notion of being rescued by a noble lord, what little sense of realpolitik she possessed flew out of the window.

During this time of turmoil Mary did find an opportunity to send some clothing to her son, the three-year-old James, along with 'two little ambling nags', or ponies, and John Leslie, the Bishop of Ross, duly begged for passports for the accompanying servants. As in the past, her Guise training ensured that Mary was always meticulous in her social and familial obligations, although this maternal duty had more than a touch of tragedy for the imprisoned mother. The passports were granted but delayed until 29 December 1569. Almost a month later, on 22 January, Mary wrote to James reminding him that he had 'a loving mother that wishes you to learn in time to love know and fear God', but whether or not he ever received the gifts is doubtful since his education was in the hands of George Buchanan, author of the most violent anti-Marian vitriol. Mary also sent clothing and an ABC – an 'example how to form his letters' – to her son via the Countess of Mar, begging her not to let James forget that he still had a loving mother.

With Moray in seemingly firm control of Scotland, a terrified Norfolk eager to do Elizabeth's bidding, the Northern Rising crushed and Mary being closely watched – the locks were removed from her servants' doors so that they could be subject to random checks, even when asleep – there appeared to be a period of calm at the beginning of 1570.

Diplomatic manoeuvres continued unabated as Guerau de Spes, the Spanish ambassador, was assured that, given support from Alva and Philip, the Catholics in England would 'rise in a day and persevere until this country is again Catholic and the accession is assured to the Queen of Scotland'. Somewhat confusingly, Philip was solemnly told that it had always been Mary's wish 'to take refuge in [his] dominions'. The English Catholics would be encouraged by support from Rome in the form of a Bull, excommunicating Elizabeth. Philip, who was short of money, had no intention of doing more than giving letters of reassurance and playing the waiting game. Montluc, the French ambassador, formally added his voice to the pleas for Mary's freedom.

It is difficult to believe that these machinations were more than polite responses to Mary's pleas through the Bishop of Ross. Neither France nor Spain had the slightest intention of provoking a certain war with England over the restoration of the Scottish queen. They made suitably devout noises towards Rome – itself now almost powerless – and kept the pot from boiling over by giving bland promises which nobody believed.

This calm was broken, however, on 23 January, when, despite numerous warnings as to his safety, Regent Moray was riding slowly through the streets of Linlithgow. A shot rang out from the direction of the house belonging to the Archbishop of St Andrews, where James Hamilton of Bothwellhaugh was concealed behind some drying laundry. A fresh horse hidden within a mile carried the assassin to safety. The bullet had struck the regent 'a little below the navel' and he was able to dismount and walk back to his lodging. However, his condition declined throughout the day and, at eleven o'clock that night, he died.

Moray was Mary's half-brother and had, of course, been one of Mary's most trusted advisers on her return from France. He had, with Lethington, stood at her elbow during her short reign; he was close to the throne itself by blood and had been given the power of the regency by the nobility. But he had never used political pathways to appease the Hamilton claim to the throne and had, instead, plunged Scotland into an intermittent civil war. Hamilton himself, with the vacillation that was typical of his family, did not seize the opportunity presented by Moray's death, and disputes that verged on another civil war raged throughout the spring. It was not until the summer of 1570 that Lennox was appointed as the new regent, with the Hamilton faction breathing down his neck. As Darnley's father, Lennox was a sworn enemy of Mary, and he was also hostile towards the Hamilton faction, but Elizabeth felt his regency could be useful to England. Once her support became known, Elizabeth received a long begging letter from Margaret, Countess of Lennox: 'I cannot see how his purse can be able to take that chargeable journey in hand . . . I have been forced to lay my jewels in gage.'

Although the Northern Rising had been crushed, there was still a lingering threat in the person of Leonard Dacres, Northumberland's cousin, 'one of the wildest of men' and one who had plotted Mary's rescue. On 19 February, Henry, Lord Scrope, as Warden of the West Marches, issued a warning to the populace against the continued threat of Dacres. Back in January, Cecil had been warned against him: 'if the Queen's majesty understood truly Mr Leonard Dacres part from the beginning of this woeful enterprise [the Northern Rising] to the end she would hang him above all the rest'. The difference between Dacres and the rebellious earls lay in the fact that the Northern Rising was a political movement which planned to restore the Catholic faith and use Mary to replace Elizabeth, while Dacres' plan was simply to free Mary from her cruel imprisonment. In his own mind, he was a knight errant riding to free a beautiful captive princess from her 'durance vile' at the hands of a cruel tyrant. Mary, who already had a somewhat lumbering knight errant in the person of Norfolk, dissuaded him, as did Norfolk himself, who feared that Dacres' intervention would ruin his own suit. The Bishop of Ross claimed that Dacres had met Mary 'on the leads at Wingfield and had put his plan of escape to her, but, on Norfolk's advice, she decided to ignore it'. Mary's encouragement of Norfolk was simply part of the same game, and once her mind had been fed with the fantasy of escaping into the arms of her loyal champion knight, her sense of reality was quickly abandoned and she readily accepted her new role as the embattled princess imprisoned in a dark tower. Dacres, with such men as he had gathered, met with Hunsdon's forces near Carlisle on 20 February and was soundly defeated, although he escaped and managed to send an apology to Elizabeth via Shrewsbury. The apology was not accepted.

In March, Mary wrote to the Countess of Mar, complaining, justly, that all her presents – ponies, books and clothing – to the infant James had been stopped. They were never delivered, and, thanks to the careful education of George Buchanan, James grew up with a distorted picture of his mother as neglectful and uncaring.

European monarchs continued to watch events in Britain with interest as Mary wrote, unavailingly, to Catherine de Medici and Charles IX. Equally ineffectual was the action of Pope Pius V on 15 May, when he issued the Bull so desired by the English Catholics. Entitled 'Regnans in Excelsis', it excommunicated Elizabeth but it did not trigger the rising 'in a day' promised earlier. De Spes thought that 'his Holiness allowed himself to be carried away by his zeal [the Bull] [and] will drive the Queen and her friends the more to oppress and persecute the few good Catholics still remaining in England'. Legend has it that one John Felton nailed a copy of the Bull to the door of the Bishop of London as a challenge to his authority, and on 9 August the ambassador watched Felton being executed 'with great cruelty' for his effrontery. The Bull had been issued in February against the advice of Philip and Alva, and also in the teeth of Catherine de Medici's opposition; she flatly refused to have it published in France. It marked a harking back to the days when the papacy possessed some temporal power, but now it simply signified papal acknowledgement of Elizabeth's presumed illegitimacy. It did, however, lend spiritual authority to any campaign to see Mary sitting on the English throne, thus sharpening Catholic opposition to her continued existence. It also meant that Elizabeth's Catholic subjects were no longer bound to her by oath and opposition to her reign was no longer treasonable. If its immediate effect was minimal, its long-term effect would be enormous.

Elizabeth took the opportunity of pursuing the remnants of the Northern Rising, sending Hunsdon into Scotland with a punitive force. He was eminently successful in pillage and destruction, ending the campaign with a confrontation with Dacres. Reputedly Elizabeth herself burst into verse:

No foreign banished wight shall anchor in this port.
Our realm it brooks no strangers' force; let them elsewhere resort.
Our rusty sword with rest, shall first his edge employ
To poll their tops that seek such change, and gape for joy.

The quality of this verse is well below what she was capable of achieving. Hunsdon's campaign did, however, let Scotland know that it would be wise to give whole-hearted support to a Regent acceptable to Elizabeth. Unfortunately, by June, Scotland was once again on the brink of civil war between supporters of Lennox – the King's Party – and those of Mary – the Queen's Party.

Leslie was released from the Bishop of London's care to visit Mary in the hope that he might travel on to Rome to start proceedings to annul Mary's marriage to Bothwell. He was instructed to meet with the Spanish ambassador and tell him that 'if his master will help me I shall be Queen of England in three months and Mass shall be said all over the country'. She also recommended Leslie to Norfolk as a useful servant. Mary herself was moved to the more comfortable Chatsworth at the end of May, where she hunted in good weather and embroidered in bad. In July the first physical effects of Mary's enforced lack of exercise were starting to appear: she complained that the pain in her side had reappeared as a result of a new gown being 'over straight'. In other words, Mary Stewart was putting on weight again.

Mary was still not free of the plots made by mad romantics and next in line as knight errant was John Hall. Hall was a Warwickshire man, educated at the Inns of Court, who served as a clerk in Shrewsbury's household. Totally without the knowledge of Shrewsbury or even Mary – whom he never met – Hall travelled to the Isle of Man and even as far as Whithorn and Dumbarton to sound out the possibility of a rescue. In every place he was met with cautious support in principle if not in practice. When he met with Francis Rolleston and his son George they were enthusiastic about his enterprise, and on 28 July Sir Thomas Gerard, a local Catholic landowner, joined the plot, in spite of warnings that Gerard might be 'over liberal in his speech'. The plot now involved taking Mary to the Isle of Man via Liverpool and then to an unspecified location. Gerard, in his turn, recruited Sir Thomas and Sir Edward Stanley. It should now have been clear to anyone that too many people, some of them of doubtful reliability, were involved, but Rolleston and Hall were too romantic in spirit to let such practical details bother them, and on 3 August at five o'clock in the morning they met with John Beaton, master of Mary's household, on the high moor near Chatsworth. Sir Thomas Stanley had a plot to take Mary out of Chatsworth through the windows and off into the surrounding woods. Mary was very properly cautious about the entire lunatic affair and through Beaton she asked for the names of the plotters and details of their plans, what ciphers were to be used and where she would be taken. Above all, she wanted an assurance of her own safety, which clearly could not be given, but all the details were duly enciphered and given to Beaton at another moorland meeting some two weeks later.

Two days later Rolleston gave the details of the plot to Thomas Stanley, who 'not so much as read the letter, but presently rent in pieces both letter and cipher saying that we are all undone'. The conspirators went into hiding before fleeing unsuccessfully.

Rolleston fled to the Isle of Man on 2 March 1571 then by way of Dumbarton to London on 27 May, while Hall was taken at Dumbarton on 2 April 1571. The other plotters were finally all arrested, and on 15 July, Stanley denied everything but begged the queen's pardon for not taking action against Hall. On 20 July, Francis Rolleston admitted that he had delivered ciphers, had met Beaton and knew some details, but stated that he had never met the Bishop of Ross and 'craved pardon, pleading his age, infirmity and poverty; and also his inability to stand the rigour of his imprisonment'. Hall himself revealed the disorganised state of the plot: 'he never heard of any determinate order or manner of the Queen of Scots delivery; howbeit it was thought that she might be taken away, either as she was shooting, or otherwise riding abroad to take the air'. Beaton, 'as from the queen his mistress', claimed that he begged them to 'desist . . . and willed the matter off'. Stanley 'was not the first beginner or deviser for the delivery of the Scottish Queen, nor ever had any such intent'. They were all liable to meet a traitor's death and Hall was executed, but, probably because of their complete incompetence, the others were given light sentences, with Thomas Gerard spending only two years in the Tower.

On 17 July 1570 Lennox was finally confirmed as the new regent of Scotland. He was 'burdened with the weighty and dangerous charge of regiment'. Lethington gave Mary a summary of affairs in Scotland, where her supporters were in a state of confusion. Mary had promised Elizabeth that they would not form an armed opposition, yet the opposing parties were, rightly, afraid to meet with each other unarmed. Lethington and Argyll were 'in great pain how to behave [them]selves'. Kirkcaldy of Grange still held Edinburgh Castle, with the bulk of Mary's jewels, such 'gold and silver work' and her gowns and furniture kept safely in store. Lethington had sent Lord Seton with Thomas Maitland, Lethington's brother, to Alva in the Netherlands and then onwards to France. He hoped for help to retake Dumbarton, which had been taken by Hunsdon on Elizabeth's behalf.

347

Norfolk had abjured all contact with Mary and had been released from the Tower, where plague had broken out, to go into house arrest in August 1570. Lethington, in a letter to John Leslie, Bishop of Ross, thought this the best news he could have hoped for, apart from Mary's restitution or 'that the Queen of England had been gone ad patres'. He also referred to the bishop having written to him about Mary's possible escape – there had been plans to take her to the 'West Seas' but with no final destination in mind – and Norfolk prayed that he would be wary: 'I fear "deadly" the craft of her enemies, who will not stick to make offers to convoy her away, and then, being privy to it, to trap her into a snare, and so to execute against her person their wicked intention.' He was quite right to be cautious.

Elizabeth made another attempt to solve the problem of Mary's position by negotiation. In October Cecil and Sir Walter Mildmay travelled to Chatsworth with a draft Treaty of Accommodation. It contained no fresh concessions by Elizabeth but proposed that Scotland be returned to the state of affairs on the eve of the Battle of Carberry on 15 June 1567. Inevitably Mary was asked to ratify the Treaty of Edinburgh and to send James to England for his education. Needless to say, although the discussions continued at Chatsworth and then in London with commissioners from both sides attending well into 1571, they reached no conclusion. They did, however, give the appearance that Elizabeth was willing to negotiate peacefully, and she could claim that she was having her friendly overtures rebuffed by her ungrateful cousin. However, Cecil did meet his archenemy Mary face to face and found that she was of 'clement and gentle nature, and was disposed to be governed by those in whom she reposed her trust'. Leslie, reporting to Norfolk, claimed that Cecil would 'travaile' to arrange a meeting of the two queens. Cecil seemed to favour the Norfolk marriage but reported that Elizabeth herself felt that, if married, the couple would 'wax over great'.

By 26 October Cecil and Mildmay were back in Windsor thanking Shrewsbury, on Elizabeth's behalf, for his hospitality, and advising him not to let Mary ride further than a mile or two from his house 'except it be on the moors' – in other words, safe from outside contact.

Outdoor exercise was still vital to Mary, and on 27 November she wrote 'of truth we are not in great health . . . there is one rheum that troubles our head greatly with an extreme pain and descends in the stomach so that it makes us lately to lack appetite of eating'. Shrewsbury did allow Mary as much exercise and fresh air as he felt to be prudent, and she wrote again that when 'we walked forth a little on horse back, and so long as we was abroad felt ourselves in a very good state, but that since then [we] find our sickness no thing slaked [eased]'. Shrewsbury moved the household to Sheffield Castle and the Bishop of Ross arrived there on 11 December with two doctors. Mary was still gravely ill, vomiting frequently and severely lacking in appetite; the pain in her left side was under her 'short ribs, and she has had no proper sleep for 10 or 12 days, giving rise to fits of hysteria'. The doctors treated her with medicines which she promptly regurgitated and the bishop wrote to Cecil and Elizabeth, convinced that her illnesses were brought on by her continued imprisonment. Since these complaints had troubled Mary since late childhood, it may be a reduced amount of exercise had exacerbated the symptoms. They would remain with her for the rest of her life.

Shrewsbury continued his surveillance of Mary, receiving information from Hunsdon that there would be a boy coming from Edinburgh, identifiable by a cut on his left cheek, with secret letters sewn into the seams of his coat. He was promptly arrested and the letters sent to Cecil. The commissioners from both sides continued to advance the well-tried arguments from past negotiations to Mary with no success. Mary sent long letters to Elizabeth begging for a face-to-face meeting, but they produced no change of attitude.

At the start of 1571, on 25 February, Elizabeth raised her faithful Sir William Cecil to the peerage as Baron Burghley. Among his many activities, reaching back into the previous reign of Mary Tudor, had been the arranging of financial affairs not only for the crown, but also for various noblemen. One of the many foreign financiers in London he had used in these affairs was one Roberto Ridolfi, a Florentine whose brother also ran a bank in Rome. Burghley also used Ridolfi as a banker on his own behalf and, like all foreigners in Britain, he was closely watched, his dealings with Norfolk being noted in particular.

In early March Shrewsbury found letters under a stone and sent them onwards to Burghley, who managed to decipher them. They were, firstly, from Mary to Alva, endorsing her support for Ridolfi, and, secondly, from Mary to Grange and Lethington, who were holding Edinburgh Castle for the queen, telling them to expect money to be sent to them soon. In the same month Mary had given a long letter, written in Italian, to Ridolfi with information for the Pope, the Duke of Alva and the King of Spain. In the letter she complained bitterly of her treatment by Elizabeth, of the persecution of Catholics in England and Scotland, and of the plots on her life. The Duke of Norfolk was named as the head of a movement to restore the Catholic faith to England and Ridolfi was instructed to assure the Pope of Norfolk's devotion to Rome. Mary went on to assure Ridolfi that she had severed all links with France and that, when she was established as Queen of England, she would form an alliance between England and the Netherlands, and that she wished King James to marry a Spanish infanta. Furthermore, she declared that she would personally lead an army to take Dumbarton and Edinburgh castles and that she had been raped by Bothwell and her marriage had taken place under duress.

This hugely incriminating letter was almost certainly not intercepted by Burghley, since the original now resides in the Secret Archives of the Vatican with a similar letter from Norfolk, written at the same time. In his letter, Norfolk asked Ridolfi to assure the Pope and the King of Spain of his devotion to the Catholic faith and of the number of noblemen in a similar position to his own who were prevented from making a public declaration of their faith. He asked for the approbation of Philip II for his marriage to Mary. Then he issued a shopping list for his military needs, consisting of 20,000 infantry and 3,000 cavalry under an experienced commander, 6,000 arquebusiers, then, curiously, only 4,000 arquebuses, 2,000 breastplates, 25 pieces of light artillery, and, of course, money. Of these forces, 2,000 men were to be sent to Ireland and 2,000 to Scotland, with the main force landing either at Harwich or at Portsmouth; Philip was to bear the total expense of the venture. This enterprise would prevent the marriage of Elizabeth to the French Duc d'Anjou – Norfolk believed that this marriage was being negotiated by French Protestants! – and furthermore it would re-establish Catholicism and place Mary on the thrones of Scotland and England. All of this was to be carried out with great urgency.

Certainly Norfolk's letter was treasonable and Mary's would have made her the implacable enemy of Elizabeth. In spite of her protestations that she had broken off correspondence with France, by the end of the same month she was writing to Fénélon vowing her complete confidence in French support. It was clear, however, that if Elizabeth did marry the Duc d'Anjou – a very unlikely circumstance – then all of Mary's support in France would be gone. This support had already been weakened by the Treaty of Blois in April 1571, which cemented an Anglo-French defensive agreement; both sides were being prudently cautious of the manoeuvres of Philip and Alva in the Netherlands.

Ridolfi carried both letters to their addressees, and nothing untoward was detected until March 1571 when Thomas Craw-ford of Jordanhill, one of the King's Party, seized Dumbarton Castle – under control of the queen's man, John, Lord Fleming – in a midnight raid. Not only did he capture the castle, he also captured documents belonging to Claude Hamilton of the Queen's Party giving details of the state of negotiations with Alva. Burghley immediately put the channel ports on full alert and, later that month, one Charles Bailly was arrested at Dover as he entered England from the Netherlands.

Charles Bailly, a 29-year old Fleming who had been a courier for John Leslie, Bishop of Ross for seven years, was carrying a copy of *A Defence of Queen Mary's Honour*. This book had been printed at Liege in 1571 giving Morgan Philips as the author, although it was, in fact, a version of the bishop's original pamphlet rewritten to seem more acceptable to Elizabeth. He was also carrying letters from Ridolfi for Norfolk, the Spanish ambassador and the bishop himself. Bailly was swiftly removed to the Marshalsea prison where, astoundingly, he managed to communicate with the outside world. Under his window was the roof of the house of some poor person with a hole in it 'wherein', he reported, 'I may easily thrust my hand'. Bailly told his informant that he would be at his window at seven o'clock in the morning, noon, three o'clock and between seven and eight daily. Bailly also allowed himself to be befriended by William Herle, a fellow prisoner, unaware that Herle was a double agent working for Burghley. Herle reported that Bailly was the Scottish Queen's man, a servant of Leslie from whom 'great things might be drawn', a man 'given to the cup and easily read'.

Almost as a diversion to these incriminating actions, on 11 May 1571 Shrewsbury wrote to Burghley asking for the wardship of young Sir Anthony Babington, since his father, a near neighbour of Shrewsbury's, had just died. The request was granted and Babington met Mary, probably falling in teenage love with her. Fifteen years later this love would cause Sir Anthony to be disembowelled.

Burghley had, by now, a bulky file giving details of various plans for Mary's escape, some sent to him from the Earl of Mar, who had become Regent of Scotland after the death of Lennox in August 1571, and some from the ever-nervous Shrewsbury. In all probability Mary knew nothing of them but merely used what diplomatic sources she could summon to promise anything to anyone who might help. In the Marshalsea, Bailly was interrogated by Burghley on 26 April and frightened in the extreme by threats of ear-lopping. Bailly was visited by his employer, the Bishop of Ross, who asked for the cipher and told him not to be afraid and that Burghley was 'only words'. After an unproductive interrogation at five in the morning on 29 April, Bailly was given into the care of William Hampton, Lieutenant of the Tower, to whom he revealed that he had met Westmoreland, the Countess of Northumberland and Dacres in Mechlin – near present-day Maastricht – and that they had given him the letters. He claimed that he had no idea of their content and had never heard of Ridolfi. He said to his torturer, 'Ils me mettent sur la gehenne.' (Gehenna was a place of human sacrifice dedicated to Moloch and also called the Valley of Slaughter.) In other words, he was to be racked to reveal the ciphers of his letters.

The rack was an instrument of torture where the victim was laid on his back – 'his' since only one woman was ever racked. His ankles were then strapped to a stationary bar while his wrists were strapped above his head to a large roller. When the roller was turned his limbs would be stretched to the point where his joints would dislocate – usually the shoulders, but wrists, elbows and hips could also suffer. The pain was extreme, and the instrument had the advantage, for the torturer, that, unlike a blow or burn, the agony could be constantly maintained. The pain could be prolonged, without risk of death, and the victim could have the dislocations brutally reduced and be 'rested' before continued sessions.

Bailly survived the initial session on the rack but was tricked by another of Burghley's double agents, a man called Story, into revealing the ciphers: the person '40' was Mary, and '30' was the Spanish ambassador. With this information Burghley slackened his grip on Bailly, and the bishop visited him again and told him not to worry. In fact, Bailly was freed in 1573 and died near Brussels at the ripe old age of eighty-five.

Shrewsbury now tightened his grip on Mary, demanding that her servants leave her at nine in the evening and not return until six in the morning, that none of them wear a sword, that, except when accompanied by Mary, none of them carry bows or arrows, that no expeditions be made unless he was given an hour's notice, and finally that, if an alarm was sounded, all of Mary's household be confined to their quarters. Stable doors were being bolted across the kingdom.

Mary swiftly asked the Bishop of Ross to petition Elizabeth that she be allowed to take the waters at Buxton for her sickness and 'vomisement', that physicians be brought from France 'that knoweth my sickness better', and that 'since . . . the Queen is minded to hold me perpetually in this country' she be allowed to ride out hawking and hunting. Mary assured Elizabeth that she would not try to escape, but she asked for the number of her servants to be increased, as well as for the payment of her Scottish revenues to be paid. Mary was here setting out the conditions for what she saw as the life in captivity that would be her lot if her various plots failed and no rescue came. There were various attempts either to free her by substituting another woman in her place, or to seize her by force. Secret letters arrived concealed in a walking stick but, thanks to the much-stretched vigilance of Shrewsbury, all failed and the investigations into the Ridolfi plot in London continued.

The third addressee of the intercepted letters was the Bishop of Ross and on 13 May 1571 he was promptly arrested and confined in the house of the Bishop of Ely in Holborn. His imprisonment was light: he travelled as part of the Bishop of Ely's entourage, receiving gifts of venison and even perfumed gloves. Leslie confessed that Ridolfi had carried letters written in March from Mary to Alva, to the Pope and to Philip II. Money was to be paid to one noted as '40' in the cipher and 'after some long pause' he confirmed that '40' was Mary. On Mary's behalf Ridolfi was to solicit Alva to land at Dumbarton or Leith, with money from the Pope. Ridolfi recommended a man called Johnson to Herries and Fleming in Dumbarton as 'a mete man for the wars'. He also suggested a Spanish landing on the east coast, possibly at Harwich, which he wrongly described as being in Norfolk.

Leslie, in a lengthy confession, told Burghley that back in August of 1570 Ridolfi, while at Arundel, had suggested that Norfolk, Arundel and Pembroke might seize the treasury in the Tower, and he also gave details of what Ridolfi had done in past embassies. Burghley was told that Mary believed that with the Pope and Philip on her side, her friends in England would readily assist her deliverance and she had asked the bishop to find out Norfolk's views. She had also asked the Pope to give 12,000 crowns to Ridolfi, and since his brother was a banker in Rome this could easily be arranged. Ridolfi was to give some to Westmoreland and some to Lady Northumberland, and to keep the rest for his own purposes. Norfolk now asked for fewer men than he had asked for in March, and Leslie was now almost certainly pulling numbers out of the air. Ridolfi had persuaded the bishop to solicit Norfolk to write personal letters of credence for him, although 'The duke was very loath', and Leslie, now bent entirely on survival, told Burghley that Norfolk must soon openly declare himself a Catholic. He also claimed that Norfolk liked the Treaty of Accommodation but was wary of having King James in England and had suggested that perhaps Shrewsbury could look after the child.

Shrewsbury, for his part, had questioned Mary, who flatly denied any correspondence with Ridolfi or any cipher with '30' or '40'; she admitted that she had written to all foreign princes for aid against the Scottish rebels, but vehemently denied sending for aid against Elizabeth.

The results of the bishop's examination and of Bailly's betrayal provided more than enough evidence, and on 4 August 1571 Norfolk was arrested at Howard Place, his London house, by Sir Ralph Sadler. Norfolk had 'two men in his chamber, four or five to dress his meat no one else'. Sir Henry Neville, with half a dozen guards in attendance, kept watch over the duke. Norfolk had received £600 in gold from the French ambassador and had sent it by messenger to Scotland. En route the messenger opened the bag and found the gold as well as a letter in cipher which was immediately passed to Burghley.

One sign of lack of total support for Elizabeth appeared in the county of Norfolk, where Protestant refugees from Alva's strict rule in the Netherlands had settled. Local Catholics under three local landowners – Throckmorton, a distant relative of the ambassador, Appleyard and Redman – were arrested and confessed to fomenting a revolt to free the Duke of Norfolk and remove Elizabeth from the throne. Mary was never mentioned in the confessions and was probably not aware of the rising, but her planned enthronement in Elizabeth's place was implicit. On 30 August the three ringleaders were hanged, drawn and quartered, while one Hobert and eleven others were sentenced to life imprisonment. On the scaffold Throckmorton said, 'They be full merry now that will be as sorry within these few days.' This caused another shiver of fear to run through Elizabeth, and Burghley's worried frown deepened. First the Northern Rising, now this display of revolt, and always the Scots queen waiting in the wings, albeit passively. Messages were immediately sent to Shrewsbury to tighten his security even further.

A month after his arrest, on 7 September, Norfolk was returned to the Tower 'without any difficulty and with such servants as were our friends'. The following day Sadler reported, '[he] very humbly behaved himself, on his knees submitting himself, with tears, to her highness's mercy, declaring great sorrow that he hath offended her highness and great will to make amends'.

At first Norfolk claimed to know nothing of the plot since he had read none of the letters and did not know where the cipher was kept. This was clearly nonsense since a few days earlier Robert Higford, Norfolk's servant, revealed that 'the "Alphabet" was 'under the mat by the window in the entry to my Lord's chamber'.

Norfolk then wrote a long and rambling apology to Elizabeth on 10 September and three weeks later he revealed that the code for Roberto Ridolfi was 'RR' but claimed he had only met the Italian once. There was, he had thought, great good will towards Mary's claim to the throne and he had intended to write to Alva. He knew of no actual commission to Alva, nor of any list of conspirators, and he had never spoken of any ports of entry. Since his 'last trouble' he never had any talk of marriage or of aid to Mary by speech, letters or messengers. He had only talked to John Leslie, the Bishop of Ross, about 'Articles of Deliverance' for Mary and he had had no knowledge of Ridolfi since he had left the country. The duke was now simply tidying up loose ends, and since he presumed that he would soon be executed, he had no regard for the truth.

Norfolk's imprisonment in the Tower was so relaxed that he was smuggling messages out and gold in, and ciphers for new communications were found hidden in his Bible. On 13 October he gave his views on the Treaty of Accommodation, believing that James should be sent south and that the Scottish castles should remain in the hands of Mary's friends. He also said that he had no knowledge of correspondence to and from Scotland and, although he had been told by Hugh Owen, Arundel's man, of an escape plan, and also of Stanley's plan, he had told Owen that he disliked all these plans and had taken no part in them. He had told Ridolfi that he would not deal with any foreign prince or subject. Otherwise he knew nothing. He had refused the offer of marriage to Mary made by Lethington at York and he knew that Mary had been upset by his previous promise to have no more to do with her, but it had been necessary to make the statement to ensure his previous release from the Tower.

In September Shrewsbury had been told by Burghley to 'Let her [Mary] know that her letters and discourses in articles being in cipher to the duke of Norfolk are found, and he hath confessed the same, and delivered the alphabet, so as she may not now find it strange that her Majesty uses her in this sort, but rather think it strange that it is no worse. Indeed we have the Scottish Queen's writing and the ciphers.' This initiative may have been intended to prepare Mary for what would come if Elizabeth were persuaded to try her cousin for an apparent treason.

Norfolk was formally tried, with Shrewsbury as Lord High Steward presiding. The outcome was a foregone conclusion, and on 16 January 1572 he was found guilty and sentenced to beheading. On 6 February he made a will of sorts in which Sussex got his Garter, George and chain – these were the very valuable gold collar, of the Order of the Garter as well as the jewelled pendant of St George – and Burghley was to inherit a piece of cloth of gold and a ruby ring. He made his last confession on 26 February, saying that he had always been a Protestant and was now truly sorry that he was thought to favour papists. He accepted that he 'did arrogantly presume, without her Highness's privity to enter into dealing with the Queen of Scots' even after he had promised Elizabeth to desist. Norfolk also admitted that he had dealt with Ridolfi more than he had confessed, and the long and tragic document was duly signed by 'The woeful and repentant hand, now too late, of Thomas Howard'.

Ridolfi wrote to Mary on 30 September reporting on his European travels. He had travelled to Rome – 'after stopping some days at my house in Florence to look after my own affairs' – where he gained Pius V's approval and sympathy for Mary's plight, travelling on to Madrid, but by the time he had persuaded the cautious Philip II it was too late. The Bishop of Ross and Norfolk were in the Tower, and Ridolfi was forced to retire 'to some place where there can be no jealousy of me'. He never returned to England. He died at the age of fifty and was buried in his native Florence.

Norfolk was never in love with Mary, as so many other suitors who had suffered under the headsman's axe had been, but as a member of one of the great families of England he was a dynast, taking as much care over the Norfolk bloodline as he did over the mating of his dogs and horses. To marry an anointed queen, a royal Stewart with Tudor blood, as his fourth wife was an attractive ambition. He was too stupid to understand that it was also treasonable to the queen from whom his power derived, and the combination of stupidity and arrogance led him to the block. It is hard not to have a scintilla of sympathy for Thomas Howard.

Elizabeth sent orders to the Sheriff of London on 9 April 'to proceed to the execution and judgement of the late Duke of Norfolk'. Elizabeth then cancelled the warrant and, as she did so frequently, hesitated before spilling blood; but the duke was finally beheaded on 2 June 1572, being guilty of 'Imagination and device to deprive the Queen from her crown and royal style, name and dignity, and consequently from her life. Comforting and relieving of the English Rebels that stirred the rebellion in the North since they have fled out of the realm. Comforting and relieving of the Queen's enemies in Scotland that have succoured and maintained the said English Rebels. His seeking of the Scottish Queen's marriage. He also sought to obtain this marriage by force.'

Since Mary had made no vows of fidelity to Elizabeth as her sovereign, she could not, technically, be guilty of treason, although, from now on, public opinion in England turned more vigorously against Mary. Her waning popularity received another blow when Buchanan's *Detectio* was published in England. Although it made no reference to the Ridolfi plot, the inferences of Mary's involvement in Darnley's death reappeared, further damaging her in public opinion. It was the last direct attack made by George Buchanan on his erstwhile patron. The historian Alastair Cherry in his *Princes, Poets and Patrons*, said of it, 'It is now widely agreed that his history is untrustworthy as an account of Mary's personal reign, being based on insinuation, half-truth and blatant falsehood, all inextricably woven together.' It is a disgusting example of vitriol for hire.

Demands were made by Elizabeth's council for the execution of Mary but, for the moment, she resisted them. As 1572 ended, John Leslie, Bishop of Ross, ordered his cook to prepare a lavish feast for his Christmas celebrations.

CHAPTER SEVENTEEN

Stranger, papist and enemy

꙰

While Shrewsbury was in London attending to Norfolk's trial, his place at Sheffield was taken by Sir Ralph Sadler, whose turn it was to receive Mary's complaints against her imprisonment. She displayed a certain arrogance when she said of Norfolk and the other conspirators, 'let them answer for themselves', and told him that she never knew Ridolfi. As for her ambassador, the Bishop of Ross, he 'will say whatever you will have him say'. Sadler and Bess oversaw the delivery of some medicines sent from France accompanied by a letter with a seemingly innocent content, but with a quantity of blank paper. Sadler tried to heat the paper – invisible writing with lemon juice would turn brown and reveal itself when heated – but found nothing. Next morning Mary, accompanied by Bess, walked in the gardens of the castle and Sadler delivered the letter, overriding her complaints that it had been opened. He noted Mary's lack of exercise, walking some-times on the 'leads', and her bitter weeping at the news of Norfolk's sentence. She plunged into grief and fasted, on alter-nate days sending vitriolic letters to Elizabeth, who responded by sending an answer with the returning Shrewsbury. Mary was reminded, inevitably, of her failure to endorse the Treaty of Edinburgh, and then, in a long list, of her rejection of Elizabeth's friendship, of Mary's defiance in marrying Darnley against Elizabeth's wishes, of her plotting with Norfolk and Ridolfi to seize the throne and of her plans to use foreign aid to invade England. Shrewsbury was commanded to read the document to Mary 'once or twice, or oftener, as she shall require it'. The days of Elizabeth as 'dearest sister' were over.

The year 1572 was also one that saw Mary's hopes of release fade further and further away. Once again Shrewsbury had to reduce Mary's entourage, partly for reasons of security as she became a focus for all disaffected Catholics and, more practically, for reasons of cost.

Elizabeth allowed the earl £52 per week, but the system of payment was erratic, to say the least. By February 1570 Shrewsbury had been due £2,808 but had only been paid £2,500 with no prospect of gaining the missing £300. His allowance was based on Mary maintaining a court of thirty people, but when it rose above this, as it frequently did, he had to find the balance himself. The allowance had not provided for Mary's waiting gentlemen to be served eight dishes at each meal while the ladies-in-waiting were given five. A mark of the height of state maintained by nobles was the lavishness with which they treated their servants and Mary had been trained as a Valois sovereign. Added to this, as escape attempts were discovered, Shrewsbury had to increase the number of guards. Elizabeth was keen that Mary used her dowager's pension from France, coupled with her revenues from Scotland, to pay for her own keep, but the French allowance was irregular in the extreme and the Scottish Regent had stopped all payments. Shrewsbury also complained, justifiably, that even his immense wealth was being drained by maintaining a household that, apart from anything else, consumed 500 gallons of wine each month. Shrewsbury was a decent man and tried to make Mary's imprisonment as comfortable as possible, but he was in a cruel financial vice. Although his wife, Bess, was herself independently wealthy, she was also one of the most ambitious builders in England, and he couldn't rely on her income.

On 26 May 1572, a letter was sent to Elizabeth by 'the clergy of the higher house' (the bishops in the House of Lords) demanding that Mary be punished 'even unto death', and shortly afterwards Elizabeth wrote to Mary telling her that parliament was forcing her to ask Mary to answer thirteen charges of disloyalty in a Bill of Attainder. A deputation came to Sheffield and Mary answered these charges by repeating the old justifications for quartering her arms at her ex-father-in-law's insistence and denying any knowledge of new activities – especially the Ridolfi plot. She had no knowledge of what her friends might be doing but 'there is no affirmation or publication that she is or ought to be Queen of England by her means procurement or knowledge'. Elizabeth had no wish to see a sister queen tried before parliament and possibly sentenced to death for a treason of which she was technically not guilty, and she used her considerable powers of persuasion to have the Bill of Attainder defeated.

Mary's status in England suffered a more serious blow in August thanks to affairs in France. Admiral Coligny, the Huguenot leader, had been gaining more and more in power and popularity, with the result that on the evening of 23 August 1572, St Bartholomew's Eve, Henri de Guise, the son of Mary's assassinated uncle, marched a squad of soldiers to Coligny's house in Paris. Coligny was murdered and word spread, erroneously, through Paris that a general slaughter of Protestants had been ordered. Over the next three days an orgy of violence against Protestants took place with up to 3,000 killed, often mutilated and thrown into the Seine. Needless to say, the houses of the dead were looted before being burned. In the countryside there were erratic outbursts until October. In all, about 12,000 Protestants were slaughtered across France.

Given the Northern Rising and the recent events in East Anglia, it was clear that militant Catholicism was still bubbling just under the surface in England, so the news of such a bloodbath and the possibility of it happening in England was Elizabeth and Burghley's worst nightmare. Both of them had only just managed to survive the reign of Mary Tudor, which had ended a mere fourteen years previously. In some village churches which had moved from the Protestant rite observed under Henry VIII to the Catholic Mass under Mary – sometimes with the same incumbent – altar cloths and vessels had simply been hidden when Elizabeth came to the throne, as people waited to see if orthodoxy would revert to Rome. In the main, English public opinion did not anticipate a return to the martyrdoms of Mary Tudor with any enthusiasm and linked the continued existence of Mary as a Catholic claimant to the throne with the possibility of an event similar to the Massacre of St Bartholomew occurring in England. The populace had never been overly friendly to Mary before, but it now became violently anti-Catholic. Mary had previously been a royal nuisance, but now she was seen as a malignant sore on the Protestant body politic.

The anti-Marian campaign continued with the Bishop of London suggesting to Burghley that she be beheaded, and a long anonymous letter was sent to Leicester declaring that 'there is no remedy for our Queen, for our realm, for Christendom, but the due execution of the Scottish Queen. The botch of the world must be lanced'. The tone of this letter is similar to the one of 26 May by 'the higher clergy'.

Mary's servants were reduced to sixteen and Elizabeth ordered that Mary be 'kept very straightly from all conference'. No one was allowed to enter Shrewsbury's properties without an express warrant from Elizabeth. And Shrewsbury wrote, 'She is meetly quiet, saying that she mislikes she cannot go hunting on the fields upon horseback, which I trust the Queen's Majesty will not assent to.' Shrewsbury made sure that the malignancy did not spread by ordering frequent searches of Mary's apartments and papers, and sending all correspondence immediately to Burghley for deciphering. Burghley, in his turn, asked Shrewsbury to 'tempt her patience and provoke her to answer'; in other words to act as an agent provocateur and encourage her to make disloyal statements. But Shrewsbury drew the line at that sort of behaviour. Mary was kept close within the walls of Sheffield Castle, but on 10 October Shrewsbury reported, 'This lady complains of sickness by reason of her restraint of liberty in walking abroad, that I am forced to walk with her near unto my castle, which partly stays her from troubling the Queen's Majesty with her frivolous letters.' For all this care and worry, Elizabeth created Shrewsbury Earl Marshal of England. The post had been held in heredity by the Dukes of Norfolk, and the new creation brought Shrewsbury no further income but did involve him in occasional extra expense. It cost Elizabeth nothing.

Throughout England there was great concern in October 1572 when Elizabeth contracted smallpox. Since the probability was that she would die, Shrewsbury was now acting as gaoler of the next Queen of England; he could expect either news that Elizabeth had recovered, or he might see the approach of a party of, probably Catholic, horsemen come to carry the new queen to Westminster – a queen who might reflect vindictively on the behaviour of her erstwhile gaoler. He wrote anxiously to London and on 22 October was rewarded with a touching letter: 'My faithful Shrewsbury, let no grief touch your heart for fear of my disease; for I assure you, if my credit were not greater than my show, there is no beholder would believe that ever I had been touched with such a malady, Your faithful loving sovereign, Elizabeth R.' Shrewsbury vowed to keep the letter – 'far above the order used to a subject' – 'for a perpetual memory'.

Mary too had been ill and had sent a letter to Elizabeth that she had a 'cold' in one arm which made it impossible for her to write, but 'if I did not fear it would importune you too much, I would make a request to you to allow me to go to Buxton well . . . which I think would give ease to it and to my side with which I am very much tormented'. Shrewsbury, who had visited the spa at Buxton for his gout, did not think it would cure her maladies and nothing came of Mary's request. However, he did become more sympathetic, but wished to delay her going there until 1573, 'when the house there shall be in readiness, and which, not being finished now, is nothing meet for that purpose'.

The Well of St Anne at Buxton had been a popular curative spring in the Middle Ages and the walls were festooned with the obligatory crutches and sticks, abandoned by the miraculously cured, when it came into the hands of the Talbot family in the fifteenth century. This popularity continued until the reign of Henry VIII – who might have done well himself to take the cure. But on Henry's behalf Sir William Bassett came to Buxton, suspecting the well to be a centre of Popish superstition, and sealed the 'baths and wells of Buxton that none shall enter and wash there until your Lordship's pleasure be further known'. However, by the 1570s the reputation of Buxton was once again high. Shrewsbury had built a four-storey house, adjacent to the chief spring, with thirty rooms as well as a 'great chamber' around the spring, with seats around the baths and chimneys for 'fire to air your garments in the bath's side'. Bowling alleys and archery butts vied with a game of Troule in Madame in which balls of various sizes were thrown at holes worth differing scores. Buxton was starting to attract a fashionable clientele and Bess made plans to become even richer with a scale of charges: 12d for a yeoman, through £3 10s for a duke and up to £5 for an archbishop.

Shrewsbury wrote to Walsingham in July 1573: 'Mary seems more healthful now, and all the last year past, than before. What need she have of Buxton Well I know not.' He asked for direct guidance from London, and in August 1573 Elizabeth granted permission for Mary to visit the spa, but with an increased guard. There was to be no contact with strangers and strict orders that the visit was to be medicinal and not social. Elizabeth was not a cruel woman and she was sympathetic towards a younger woman in poor health, but she had to balance this with the ever-present suspicion that Mary might be in the midst of some new plot – her new chancellor, de Vergé, had just left for France; was he carrying secret messages? – and with Burghley at her elbow feeding her disquiet she had genuine concern. Power has always brought the suspicion that others are plotting to remove it, and such paranoia has existed from Egypt's pharaohs to contemporary presidents and prime ministers.

The visit to Buxton was a success, not only from the point of view of relieving Mary's pain in her side, but also providing a much-needed break with the undoubted monotony of Chatsworth or Sheffield. Since Mary's furniture and wall hangings travelled with her, the interiors of these places were very similar, with the obvious exception of the loathed Tutbury, and her limited exercise gave her little relief. Mary was a very social lady, revelling in new acquaintances and gossip, but when every visitor

365

was closely watched and regarded as a possible spy, her entertainments were severely curtailed. Buxton was a very different matter. Here was a fashionable town, now with an exiled queen – a queen with a very racy reputation and renowned as one of the age's great beauties – visiting the baths under intriguing circumstances of secrecy. Everyone would be eager to catch a glimpse of her, and even the strictest security could not wholly prevent Mary from having some contact with the outside world.

In the 1950s Estoril in Portugal became the *refuge du goût* for exiled royalty from Europe and the Middle East and the fashion-conscious flocked to catch a glimpse of an erstwhile monarch on the beach or at the casino. Four hundred years earlier, Buxton necks were craned for a similar glimpse of the dangerous queen. Although Mary was now thirty-one – middle-aged in her times – and becoming stooped and overweight, she still retained her allure, and Buxton profited from it as Brighton would later profit from the visits of the prince regent.

Mary found relief at Buxton and believed, 'If in the coming year, it should please her [Elizabeth], at a better season, to grant me the same permission, and to give me a rather longer time, I believe that will quite cure me.' Mary now seemed to accept that her imprisonment would continue with periodic transfers to and from Shrewsbury's various houses, hopefully interspersed with occasional trips to Buxton.

What fragile hope there had been of Mary's restoration in Scotland died when Regent Mar died on 29 October 1573 and his place was taken by Morton, who was firmly determined to bring the chaos of recurring civil wars to an end. There was now no hope of Mary being restored to her throne in Scotland, and a peace treaty of February 1573 left only Lethington, Kirkcaldy of Grange and a few others embattled in Edinburgh Castle as the rump of the Queen's Party. Elizabeth sent 1,500 men to Leith, and on 16 June the garrison of 164 men, 34 women and 10 boys surrendered. Most, including Kirkcaldy of Grange, were hanged, while on 9 July, Mary's last supporter, Maitland of Lethington, the 'Machiavelli ' of Scotland, took poison and died, his body being found some days later as a feasting ground for maggots. Mary Stewart was now Queen of Scots in name only.

Mary also realised about this time that the Cardinal of Lorraine was withholding the bulk of her French pension for his own use. She had high hopes, alas unfounded, that de Vergé might manage to stop this plunder by her own family, but since she was of no further political use to the Guises they felt that they could rob her with impunity. Her brother-in-law Charles IX dismissed her summarily: 'The poor fool will never cease until she lose her head. In faith, they will put her to death. I see it is her own fault and folly. I see no remedy for it.'

The facts of her isolation and imprisonment were further brought home to her during this time as any news of the enormous changes in her kingdom arrived second-hand and at the discretion of Burghley. It was no longer felt important that she knew anything of Scotland; as a focus for plots, the less information she had, the better.

In December, an informer, W. Hayworth, warned Leicester of a plot by the papists of Lancashire to convey the Scottish queen to France, Spain or Scotland. The warning was vague in the extreme, giving no specific details, and could have actually been true at any moment of Mary's captivity. The letter reads like a plea from a bigoted and aggrieved citizen against his Catholic neighbours, but Mary was a focus for even petty disputes at the most local level. William Wharton suggested that counterfeit letters be sent to Mary, giving her false news and drawing her and her friends into a conspiracy so that they could all be arrested. The scheme was rejected, but Walsingham noted the idea as worthy of improvement.

The year 1574 started with a letter of reassurance from the Cardinal of Lorraine but advising her, 'dissimulate still a little and do not embitter anything', and vowing, unconvincingly, to work for her 'greatness and liberty'. Mary wrote yet again to Elizabeth expressing her concern at her cousin's long silence, and begging to be told, through Fénélon, how to please her, while 'waiting for God to inspire you to put an end to my long troubles'. She received no reply. Shrewsbury's policy of being strict but sympathetic drew criticism, and in April two men, Corker and Haworth, accused Shrewsbury of undue kindness to Mary and alleged that he favoured her claim to the throne. The result was a letter from the earl to Burghley: 'I doubt not, of God's mighty goodness, of her Majesty's long and happy reign to be many years after I am gone . . . how can it be imagined I should be disposed to favour this Queen for her claim to succeed the Queen's Majesty? I know her to be a stranger, a papist and my enemy.' The rumour, which arose out of petty jealousies rather than fact, since Shrewsbury was the most meticulous gaoler, refused to go away, and a year later, on 24 December 1575, he wrote again denying the rumour that he had become Mary's ally at Buxton. He was very sharply rebuked by Elizabeth 'with plain charging of me favouring the Queen of Scots'. He replied, 'As for the Queen of Scots, truly I have no spot of evil meaning to her: Neither do I mean to deal with any titles to the crown: if she shall intend any evil to the Queen's Majesty, my sovereign, for her sake I must and will mean to impeach her: and therein I may be her unfriend or worse.' In other words, he had no personal animosity towards Mary, unless she posed any threat to Elizabeth.

Another of Mary's links with France parted when her brother-in-law King Charles IX died of tuberculosis in May 1574, to be succeeded by his brother, the Duc d'Anjou, as Henri III. Europe held its collective breath to see what alliances the new king would make – he was already King of Poland and had to be hastily recalled to take the French throne, and he was already accused of incest with his sister, homosexuality and black magic. He faced a disastrous economy, growing Huguenot strength under their leader Henri de Navarre and a resentful aristocracy. This left Elizabeth free to attempt negotiations with Philip over the troublesome Netherlands. Mary wrote, no longer to Catherine de Medici, but to James Beaton, Archbishop of Glasgow and her ambassador in Paris, expressing her sorrow at the death of Charles and wishing Henri III well.

All long-term prisoners search out any form of diversion, some often keeping, and even becoming an expert on, caged birds. In July 1574 Mary wrote to the Archbishop of Glasgow, asking him to send her some turtle doves and 'Barbary chickens' so that she might raise them; 'This is the pastime of the prisoner.' She also made further requests for cloth of gold, silver thread and head-dresses, and also for her uncles to be reminded of their promises to send more caged birds. Some small dogs came from the Cardinal later in the year, and Mary wrote, 'the little animals are the only pleasure I have.' Mary had started to manufacture gifts for various people, especially Elizabeth, and in May, Fénélon had presented Elizabeth with a skirt of red satin embroidered with silver thread, 'to whom the present was very agreeable'.

She wrote again to the archbishop in mid August, and it is clear from her style that she was, at last, aware that her letters were being read by Burghley and Walsingham. She mentioned the rumours that she might be proposed as a wife for Henri III, the Earl of Leicester and Don John of Austria, and she stressed that all the rumours were untrue. There was a chance that the alliance with Don John might come to fruition since he was the illegitimate half-brother of Philip and, in March 1576, he became governor of the Netherlands, an appointment he accepted on the understanding that it would be a platform for the reconversion of England and rescue and marriage to the captive Queen of Scots. The situation was complicated by the fact that Mary was technically still married to Bothwell, but in April 1578 Bothwell mercifully died, blind and insane in Denmark. In October Don John of Austria himself died during a siege in the Netherlands, thus removing another possible, if unlikely, suitor. He was at least romantic, but his proximity to the Spanish throne made him dangerous. Burghley, who knew he was lying when he said it, loudly proclaimed Don John's death as being due to venereal disease. It was probably typhus. Walsingham wrote, 'God dealeth most lovingly with her Majesty in taking away her enemies.' In fact, back in 1574, Mary's correspondence with France was suffering greatly as a result of the prolonged illness of her French

369

secretary, Augustine Raulet, first noted on 20 February. He had been nominated as Mary's secretary in Scotland by the Duc de Guise in 1560 but had been sent back to France as a result of the xenophobia surrounding Rizzio. Now he had returned and had served Mary faithfully in exile, but he died on the morning of 30 August 1574, allowing the eager Shrewsbury an opportunity to search Mary's papers. The search was fruitless, but Raulet's death gave the Guise clan the chance to place another candidate close to their wayward relative. He was Claude Nau de la Boiselière and he arrived in early summer 1575. Nau had been a protégé of the Cardinal of Guise, who had arranged for him to study law. In some respects he was similar to Rizzio in that he dressed extravagantly and had the manners of the French court, which Shrewsbury, who spoke little or no French, found objection-able, but Mary found refreshing. Walsingham, a more objective witness, found Nau quick-spirited in Italian, Latin, and English. He merely smiled at Nau's protestation that if his mistress failed for want of any help, 'her Majesty [Elizabeth] would be answerable for the same before all the princes of Christendom'. Mary was so enamoured of Nau that she dictated a sort of memoir of her days in Scotland to him. In his turn he was so dazzled by her that he reported as fact her subjective account.

By September 1574 Mary was showing her usual care for her servants in asking the archbishop to find a watch – with an alarm – for Mary Seton. She was the last of the Maries to remain unmarried and was the object of devotion for Andrew Beaton, who had succeeded his father, John, as master of Mary's house-hold. But Mary Seton claimed a vow of perpetual chastity, presumably made while she was a child with her mistress in France. Beaton, obviously a man of some determination, went to France in 1577 to obtain an annulment for Mary. Whether it was successful or not is a mystery, since, on his return journey, the unfortunate Beaton drowned, and six years later the still-virginal Mary Seton retired to France and lived out her days in the convent of St Pierre in Reims, where, Renée de Guise, was abbess.

On 22 September Mary asked the archbishop to buy her some dogs, in addition to the pretty little pair she was sure her uncle the cardinal was sending her, since besides reading and necessary work she had no other pleasures. She ended her sad letter by reminding the archbishop to make sure the puppies were warmly packed for the journey.

Mary may have been concerned only with her growing menagerie, but Bess, her hostess, had a close eye on dynastic advantage. For some time she had been negotiating for her daughter, Elizabeth, to marry the Earl of Suffolk, but when she heard that the recently widowed Countess of Lennox and her son, Charles Stuart, the new earl, were to journey north, an invitation immediately went out for a meeting. Elizabeth had forbidden the countess to visit Chatsworth. The idea of Darnley's mother, an inveterate plotter and regular resident of the Tower, coming anywhere near Mary made her blood run cold, but Rufford Abbey was a property of the Shrewsbury's and on the countess's route north, so a visit was planned. It lasted five days, with the two mothers locked in pre-nuptial tête-a-têtes while the nineteen-year-old children were left to each other's company. Charles Stuart was the great grandson of Margaret Tudor and therefore had a direct claim on the crown of England, albeit through the female line, and if their marriage produced a son, he would in his turn become Earl of Lennox, with debateably a stronger claim to the English throne than that of James VI. For his peace of mind, if nothing else, Shrewsbury looked forward to the outcome: 'This taking effect I shall be well at quiet, for there is few noblemen's sons in England that she hath not prayed me to deal for at one time or another.' The marriage did 'take effect' with great promptitude.

Elizabeth was hysterical with rage and both countesses were immediately summoned to London to be thrown into the Tower. Both of these formidable women had offended Elizabeth so often that it is not over-fanciful to imagine that they had their own regular accommodation in that grim fortress, but, thanks to the intercession of friends, they suffered no more than house arrest.

Everyone except for Bess breathed a sigh of relief when, in the autumn of 1575, a girl, Lady Arabella, was born to the couple. For Bess, this meant that Mary and her son James VI stood in the way of her becoming queen mother of a united kingdom, and Bess did not like obstacles.

Logic had nothing to do with Elizabeth's paranoia and she hysterically included Shrewsbury and Mary in her rages, convinced that they had conspired with Bess to bring about the marriage. Mary was terrified that, at best, she might be transferred into the care of Huntingdon or, at worst, simply poisoned. She wrote to Henri III pleading for either a rescue, or the avenging of her death, and her sense of isolation increased when, on 26 December, the Cardinal of Lorraine died at Avignon. He was the last of her close advisers, and although he had embezzled large amounts of her income and had used her as a pawn in the political games of the Guise family, he represented a link with the golden days of her youth among the palaces of the Loire. She was willing to accept his death as the will of God, like all the other adversities visited upon her.

As yet unaware of the cardinal's death, Mary was writing to the Archbishop of Glasgow on the same day, explaining why she would reject all attempts to have James acknowledged as King of Scotland. He had been crowned aged thirteen months, as soon as had been possible after she had abdicated, but she had subsequently renounced the abdication and therefore she was, in her eyes, the true ruler of Scotland. Mary wished her ambassador to make clear that the treaties of friendship between France and Scotland were treaties with herself and no one else.

One of the long-term effects of the excommunication of Elizabeth had been an increase in the persecution of the Catholics, and Mary had been no exception. Ninian Winzet had been acting as her confessor while employed ostensibly as a secretary, but he had been exiled with John Leslie, Bishop of Ross and so, for some time, Mary had been deprived of her religious observances. They had been so much a part of her life that, as a result of their absence she wrote to Pope Gregory XIII in

October 1575 asking for various concessions. Mary wanted her chaplain, a Jesuit priest called Samerie, who visited secretly, to be authorised to grant her absolution after hearing her confession. She wanted absolution also to be granted to twenty-five Catholics who had attended Protestant services only in order to avoid detection; she asked for papal forgiveness for not having refuted the insults of heretics; and, finally, she wanted to obtain *indulgentiam in articulo mortis ore dicendo Jesus Maria*, an absolute forgiveness of her sins at the moment of death simply by utterance or thought of the words '*Jesus Maria*'. The possibility of a violent death, either by assassination or judicial process, was very real.

At about this time Mary inscribed some lines of verse in a Book of Hours which she had kept with her since her time in France. She seems to have used this priceless medieval devotional work as a scribbling pad to pass the time during her moments of depression, and the comments are depressing in the extreme. Many of the scribblings, such as 'was ever known a fate more sad than mine?', are desolate and may have been written over a long period. She now accepted her fate – 'I am no longer what I once have been!' – and appeared to think of life as something to be endured while awaiting death. Mary was not a deep thinker, but these lines show the dark side of her character. The flashing smiles and chivalric charm had gone and imprisonment had started to crush her optimism. Five years later, in 1580, she was presumed to have written an 'Essay on Adversity', a collection of loose jottings on the subject of her imprisonment without any real focus, which read as if she had started to assemble her thoughts and then to fortify them with examples. Being prevented from carrying out the duty to which 'God called me in the cradle', Mary sought to illustrate the misfortunes of life – 'a subject so familiar to me' – since she felt that no one else ever had greater experience of them, certainly no one of such royal quality.

Thus she began by establishing her God-given right to rule and the uniqueness of her plight. She spelt out a plan, which she failed to follow, of examining inner torment and then physical, showing how God will finally forgive all sinners. The inevitable

373

examples from Scripture followed with a diversion to the classics and celebrated suicides. She accused 'a noble and virtuous prince to whom I feel honoured to be related' who brought his 'illustrious name' into disrepute by failing to confess to a small dishonour. Mary did not tell us which of her relatives did this, but the choice was wide. She ended by warning that, while humility is a great virtue, those who have been called to greatness must not avoid their divinely attributed duty. The entire work, with its many erasures, omissions and alterations, was a teenager's version of a learned sermon delivered by a prince of the church, but at the time of composition Mary was thirty-eight years old and might have been expected to show greater maturity. The possibility of escape and restitution were no longer thought of and her only hopes for the future were an unquestioning belief in her God and the little ameliorations and relaxations accorded to life-sentenced prisoners.

Chief among those relaxations were, of course, her visits to Buxton, which she found relieved her painful joints, and, towards the end of May 1577, Nau hints at some hopeful rumour. Mary and he had received 'very secret' information that Elizabeth was to visit Buxton from where she would travel in disguise to Chatsworth to meet Mary. Nau was not entirely convinced of this, but Mary was certain that at last she would meet her cousin. It was an illusion and the information was completely wrong. Elizabeth had never had, from the time of Mary's arrival in England, any intention of meeting Mary. It was a meeting from which nothing could be gained except verbal expressions of love and amity, and one which might very well lead to unflattering physical comparisons between the two women. Elizabeth has been accused of being afraid that she might have been swayed by Mary's undoubted charm, but Mary's was a charm which was most effective on men, while Elizabeth was susceptible only to compliments from men. If Elizabeth had any doubts as to how to act, she prevaricated brilliantly, and if there was any possibility of being put into a situation where action was essential, she deftly avoided the trap. The two queens would never meet and in fictional portrayals of such an encounter the dramatic effect has been, at best, feeble, contributing nothing to the play.

Perhaps reflecting her mood at the time, in February 1577 Mary drew up a draft of her last will and testament. Should she die in prison, which she now expected, she asked that her body should be taken to the cathedral of St Denis to be buried beside François II, her first husband, and that, provided he converted to Catholicism, James was to be heir to all her property and to her rights to the crown of England. If he did not convert, then Mary left everything to Philip of Spain to dispose of as he wished on the advice of the Pope. If James should predecease her, she left the throne of Scotland to the Earl of Lennox or Lord Claude Hamilton, either to be selected by the house of Lorraine on condition that the selected one then married into the house of Lorraine. Lady Arabella was to be created Countess of Lennox. History cannot but be grateful that this will was never put into effect, since the result could have been war between Spain and England, coupled with a renewed civil war in Scotland.

In June 1577 Leicester paid a visit to Buxton as a guest of Shrewsbury. He was presumably overweight and Elizabeth sent Shrewsbury a comic diet to be served to the earl. Two ounces of meat, washed down with the twentieth part of a pint of wine and as much of 'St Anne's sacred water as he listeth to drink'. On feast days his diet would be augmented by the shoulder of a wren for dinner and the leg at supper. Elizabeth could still play silly schoolgirl jokes. Mary, with her Valois antennae finely attuned to smell out a plot, if lacking judgment as to the plot's chances of success, suspected that Leicester had come to Buxton to sound out the nobility as to the feasibility of his marriage to Elizabeth. Since Leicester had secretly married Lettice Knollys, the daughter of Mary's former gaoler, Sir Francis Knollys, in 1575, this was unlikely. Mary herself may have been at Buxton at the same time since on 25 June Elizabeth thanked Shrewsbury for looking after Leicester so well and, only two days later, Walsingham noted that Tutbury – his favoured prison – was unsuitable and Mary should be returned to Sheffield.

Burghley himself came to Buxton with as much speed as his 'old creased body' would allow him, and it is tempting to speculate that during all this coming and going Mary may have renewed her acquaintanceship with Burghley and may finally have met her quondam suitor Leicester. Either circumstance would have needed the connivance of Shrewsbury, and both men were more powerful than the earl. But both men were also well aware that the wrath of Elizabeth would be terrible in the extreme should they be discovered. Although, like all Elizabethan politicians, both men controlled a network of spies, they also knew that many of these spies were double agents, and that arching over all was the great spymaster, Sir Francis Walsingham, one of whose most sinister agents, Sir Richard Topcliffe, was in Buxton at this time.

Topcliffe was a psychopathic anti-Catholic frequently employed by Walsingham to administer the rack in the Tower, a task he greatly enjoyed. Should the torture of the rack fail to produce results, prisoners would then be taken to Topcliffe's own house – the windows of which were painted black – for more elaborate tortures. He enjoyed the total confidence of Walsingham and claimed – probably unjustifiably – to have seen Elizabeth 'naked above the knee'. He wrote to Shrewsbury on 30 August 1577 about 'Popish beasts' at Buxton – 'One Dyrham, as I remember, at the bath or lurking in those parts after the ladies' – and he asked Shrewsbury to arrest Dyrham. With the close presence of such a man under the patronage of Walsingham, even Burghley would be cautious. Inevitably there were rumours of rescues, and Burghley consoled himself that near Chatsworth there was 'no town or resort where ambushes may lie'.

The smaller pieces on the political chessboard started to move again, with indirect results for Mary. A new arrival in Scotland from the troublesome Stuart family arrived in 1579 in the handsome form of the 37-year-old Esmé Stewart, Seigneur d'Aubigny. He had been sent by the Duc de Guise to ingratiate himself with James and to clip the wings of Morton. In this he was partially successful, the fifteen-year-old James creating him

Duke of Lennox in 1581. Thanks in some part to Esmé's influence, Morton was beheaded in June 1581, which was followed by an official abjuration of Catholicism. Mary had once been the most powerful card in the Guise hand, but now she took carefully guarded walks in the gardens at Chatsworth while she was informed at third or fourth hand of their newest machinations.

Finally, in London, the Duc d'Alençon arrived, albeit in secret. He had previously been considered as a suitor for Elizabeth when he had held the title of Duc d'Anjou. As the youngest of Mary's brothers-in-law, he was over twenty years younger than Elizabeth, heavily pockmarked and below average height. He was, however, more than prepared to play marriage games and the couple, being careful not to appear together in public, exchanged intimate love tokens through Jean de Simier, Alençon's ambassador. Elizabeth, hugely flattered by the elaborate attentions of a much younger man, called Alençon her 'frog' while Simier was her 'monkey'. Alençon had shown distinct Huguenot leanings in France – to the horror of Catherine de Medici – and had befriended Condé.

For Mary the possibility of the Alençon marriage was terrifying for several reasons. Firstly, the marriage threatened that, even allowing for what was regarded as Elizabeth's advanced age, it might produce an heir and all Mary's dynastic dreams for James and herself would crash irrevocably to the ground. Secondly, Mary's only realistic source of foreign aid would then be from Spain where, so far, Philip had shown extreme caution in offering anything more than moral support. The Pope would fulminate, but, having already excommunicated Elizabeth, there was nothing more he could do. Mary let some of her feelings be known in conversation, and Elizabeth inevitably heard that Mary Stewart was criticising her marriage plans. When Mary heard that she had fuelled Elizabeth's fury, she wrote to de Mauvissière, the French ambassador, denying everything: 'Whosoever has told this to the Queen of England, my good sister, has wickedly and villainously lied . . . ask Shrewsbury and his wife in what terms I spoke of the Duke'. Perhaps with more honesty Mary wrote to the Archbishop of Glasgow, hoping that the marriage might improve the lot of the English Catholics. Elizabeth and Alençon's marriage dalliance continued with the young man trying to escape from the political clutches of his family and the older woman acting out the teenage romance she had never been allowed until, with finance from Elizabeth, Alençon undertook a campaign in the Netherlands where, on 10 June 1584, he died after an attack of fever. It was now inevitable that Elizabeth would die childless.

Mary's hope for better treatment for English Catholics had suffered a heavy blow in June 1580, when the first Jesuit missionaries had begun to arrive from the seminaries in Rome and Douai. The hope in Rome was that they could unify and strengthen Catholic support for Mary's seizure of the throne and the deposition, bloody or otherwise, of Elizabeth. The effect was exactly the opposite, since, almost without exception, they fell into the merciless hands of Walsingham and Topcliffe, to end their days in the cruellest of deaths, portrayed as traitors intent on delivering England into the hands of Spain to rekindle the fires of Mary Tudor. Also, the intensity of belief displayed by these agents at their deaths helped to strengthen the siege mentality in the country. And Burghley found it easy to identify the principal enemy within the walls as Mary Stewart.

Mary had now been the unwelcome guest of Shrewsbury for eleven years and his financial complaints were becoming more and more extreme. The consumption of wine, spices and fuel were costing him £1,000 annually, on top of which 'The loss of plate, the buying of pewter and all manner of household stuff which by them is exceedingly spoiled and wilfully wasted, standeth in me one thousand pounds by the year.' In August 1580 he asked if he had in some way offended Elizabeth and if her refusal to pay him was some kind of punishment, to which he got a sharp reply reminding him of his duty. Although he had reduced Mary's expenses almost to a starvation level, Shrewsbury was quietly warned by Leicester that rumours of his over-romantic liaisons with Mary were circulating.

James angered Elizabeth by rebuffing an embassy at Berwick – most probably an administrative error of which he knew nothing – and the incident was used by Elizabeth, in association with Robert Beale, the secretary for the 'Northern Parts' and clerk to the Privy Council, a bitter anti-papist, to impose more restrictions on Mary. She would be allowed to write to James only on the condition that she made an open demonstration that 'she would have no dealings with papists, rebels, fugitives, Jesuits or others which might go about to trouble that estate of the policy and religion now established, or would seek alteration of the same'. She was to cease all dealings with foreign princes and to persuade James that Elizabeth was his best friend, 'being herself diseased and not like to continue long'. This demand was too crude and was quietly dropped.

What was not dropped was a proposed association whereby Mary and James would rule Scotland jointly, Mary would renounce all her claims to the English throne, would join a league against France, renounce the Papal Bull of excommunication, give amnesties in England and Scotland for all misdeeds, and even consent to remain in England as a sort of hostage, 'in some honourable sort'. In other words, under twenty-eight different clauses, Mary would have to agree to a total rejection of everything she had claimed in exchange for a limited freedom. However, Mary had been secretly advised to agree to anything at all if it bought her freedom, and, in any case, it had been suggested to her in confidence by the Spanish ambassador that she remain in England. Should Philip, in alliance with the Duc de Guise, manage to launch the 'Enterprise' – an invasion of England – then Mary was already in place to stand at the head of the army. Unfortunately, Elizabeth realised that she could rely on James's loyalty without granting his mother anything at all and the matter was not pursued.

The miasma of intrigue continued to surround Mary and she took a captive's delight in watching the machinations from her prison. A Spanish agent, disguised as a dentist, was arrested in May 1582. Mary gave detailed instructions on how to use secret writing methods to her own agents. Plots to assassinate Elizabeth were still formed by English Catholics – a gentleman of Warwickshire announced to his friends that he was going to London to shoot Elizabeth, only to be met on arrival and escorted to the Tower – and in November of 1583 Francis Throckmorton, another Catholic member of the ambassador's troublesome family, was arrested. He possessed lists of Catholic conspirators as well as details of possible landing places for an invading army. Clearly he was a man of exceptional courage: not until after he had suffered seventy-two hours on the rack did he confess and 'disclose the secrets of she who was the dearest thing to me in the world'. In fact, since Mary knew nothing of his plot, the 'secrets' were invented under torture.

William of Orange, the leading Protestant in Europe after Elizabeth, was assassinated in June 1584 and anti-Catholic passions reached boiling point. The Privy Council drew up a Bond of Association, whereby in the event of an attempt, or even a planned or inferred attempt, on Elizabeth's life, anyone even remotely associated with the plot was to be executed. Voicing disloyalty, however weakly expressed, was now treason. The Bond simply formalised the view that England was under permanent threat from Catholicism, and the embodiment of that threat was Mary Stewart. On 5 January 1585, Mary, loyally if hypocritically, made a public declaration of her personal support of the Bond. Elsewhere, support for the Bond was overwhelming, but Elizabeth supervised a redrafting to require that there must at least be some proof of a third party's involvement. Parliament passed the Bond into law as the Act of Association.

What was now being spoken of was the revived rumour of a romantic intrigue between Mary and Shrewsbury, to the extent of Mary having borne his child. This ludicrous rumour was probably started by Bess of Hardwick, who was in a bitter dispute over property with her husband, who was now living apart from his formidable countess. Mary was furious and wrote at once to Elizabeth, asking, inevitably, for an interview in which she would explain everything. Mary was quite capable of defending herself and, when her request for an interview was, equally inevitably, refused, she wrote a letter to Elizabeth giving an account of Bess's privately expressed opinions of her queen. Bess had told Mary that Elizabeth was Leicester's lover, had enjoyed troilism with Sir Christopher Hatton and another, and was the lover of Simier, to whom she gave state secrets as pillow talk; Mary also told Elizabeth how Bess had advised her to encourage the young James to try to feed Elizabeth's nymphomaniac passions. The letter was never sent, but Bess knew that it existed and would only sharpen Elizabeth's already bitter hatred for her. Thus Mary had let Bess know that she had her finger on the trigger of an explosive charge. The situation was a very uneasy stalemate. Elizabeth had sense enough to realise that Mary's position as a pawn in the vicious chess game of hatred between Shrewsbury and Bess was untenable, and on 1 April 1584 draft orders were prepared to release Shrewsbury from his charge as gaoler. Mary realised that she was unlikely to be released into greater freedom – there had been another attempt to free her in the previous year – and in July she said farewell to Buxton and its healing waters.

In early September 1584, Mary travelled to Wingfield, and by the middle of the month Shrewsbury was relieved of his charge by the Privy Council. Mary passed into the care of Sir Ralph Sadler, whose life had touched hers at so many points. He had forty-three men with him as guards and he set about cleansing Shrewsbury's household of possible Marian spies. What Mary did not know was that her final destination was not to be Wingfield, but the hated Tutbury. There, 150 men would guard her, forty or fifty of whom were to be mounted soldiers. Sadler drew up an inventory and described her requirements. She had four coach horses and her gentlemen had six. Her household numbered forty-seven: 'five gentlemen, fourteen servitors, three cooks, four boys, three gentlemen's men, six gentlewomen, two wives, ten wenches and children'. She had no furniture, hangings, tableware or napery of her own and had used Shrewsbury's, which was now worn out. She was served sixteen dishes at both courses, more or less. Beer could be brought from Burton 'three miles off' and she and her household drank an astonishing 10 tuns of wine, or 2,500 gallons, annually. Her bedchamber was twenty-seven feet long with a private chamber within and her dining chamber was thirty-six feet long with a private cabinet and chimney. 'Thus in my opinion, she shall be very well lodged and accommodated in all things', Sadler concluded. Sir Amyas Paulet was to be Mary's gaoler once Sadler had delivered her, and on 1 January 1585 he did just that.

Shrewsbury, separated from Bess, lived on until 1590, when he died aged sixty-two, and the formidable Bess outlived him until 1608, when she died aged ninety. Bess and Mary were chalk and cheese, Bess using violent frontal attacks which were countered by guile and subtlety from Mary, and her bounding ambition and greed were contrasted by Mary's passivity and acceptance. Their embroidery sessions were no more than convenient pastimes for Bess, and if Mary had stood in the way of Bess's advancement she would have been crushed without another thought. Shrewsbury disliked Mary as a Catholic and a threat to his monarch, but he had been given a duty to perform and he performed it with as much courtesy as was possible. He was more at home with horses and dogs than with women, and he was heartily glad to be quit of Mary in 1585.

CHAPTER EIGHTEEN

To trap her in a snare

꙳

The terms under which Mary was now confined were much more severe than under the benign rule of Shrewsbury, and Sir Amyas Paulet was a total contrast to George Talbot. Coming from West Country squirearchy rather than high aristocracy, Paulet had no reverence for Mary's rank and rigorously carried out his instructions from Elizabeth to the letter. He had been appointed Lieutenant of Jersey in 1559 when he was twenty-three years old – his father was hereditary captain of the island – and seventeen years later had been knighted and sent to France as ambassador. He married Catherine Harvey, the daughter of a Devonshire landowner, and the couple had six children, five of whom survived them. Paulet's was not a glittering career; rather it was one of an unimaginative plodder who could be relied on to carry out instructions meticulously. He was a zealous Puritan of the strictest honesty with a bitter hatred of all things Catholic; he possessed no sense of humour and rejected everything not strictly necessary to a spartan existence. Mary's charm he found to be a shallow representation of an insincere personality and he was deaf to all her complaints. His total loyalty to Elizabeth is shown in a letter of 1586 in which he refers to his queen, 'whom God in his mercy long preserve from the dangerous snares of this lady under my charge and her adherents.' Paulet had been personally selected by Walsingham for the task, and he represented the first step on the road to a goal all of England knew to be necessary but which no one dared to contemplate seriously. That goal was the eventual removal of Mary.

Elizabeth flatly refused to consider taking such a drastic step.

Her natural gift for procrastination – the direct opposite to her father's impetuosity – combined with her political sense told her that to make Mary a martyr for the Catholic faith might easily make herself a martyr for Protestantism. There were no precedents for executing exiled queens, and Elizabeth was determined not to provide one. Burghley and her Council knew very well that any mention of legal actions to be brought against Mary would earn severe disfavour, and they all regarded their own positions too carefully to risk the royal wrath. Walsingham, however, had never enjoyed royal favour and his fellow courtiers were only too happy to encourage him in his anti-Marian attitudes.

Even in parliament there were plots against Elizabeth. One Dr Parry was discovered to be part of such a plan and under questioning he implicated Thomas Morgan, cipher clerk to Mary's French ambassador. Morgan was suspected by the Jesuits, with some justification, of being a double agent for Walsingham. The French obligingly imprisoned Morgan in the Bastille, but parliament was so shocked by Parry's revelations that it petitioned Elizabeth to allow a more exemplary form of execution than the law allowed. Their requests were summarily rejected and Dr Parry was castrated and disembowelled in the normal manner.

Mary herself had been able to wait in the wings, keeping all her options open, antagonising no one directly and showing herself willing to agree to almost anything to achieve her freedom. It would have been difficult to bring her to justice under the Act of Association, even allowing for what was known of her encouragement of Ridolfi and Norfolk, since there was no concrete proof that she had agreed to seize the throne after Elizabeth's murder. It was not treasonous to seek one's freedom, nor to pledge friendship to one's relatives, but Catholicism had been driven into dark corners and the Jesuit missionaries had been converted in the public mind into political agitators and possible assassins.

In August 1584 a Jesuit, Creighton, was stopped at sea by the

Dutch authorities. He tore up his documents and made to throw them overboard, but knowing more Scripture than seamanship, he threw the scraps into the wind and they came back on board. Pieced together, they were another version of the plans for the Enterprise of the invasion of England, and Creighton was handed over to Walsingham's men. Inevitably he confessed everything, revealing his contacts in England. The tide of hatred for Mary rose.

In Tutbury, Paulet enforced the letter of the law. Mary was forbidden to go out of doors and her servants were not allowed to walk on the walls of the castle in case they attempted to signal to sympathisers, although there were no bystanders since the area surrounding the castle for miles around had been cleared of any but the most trusted people. The effect of this close confinement on Mary was devastating and her claustrophobia increased, leaving her with only receding memories of long gallops through the forests of Fontainebleau. She was allowed no correspondence with the outside world and could only receive letters from her ambassador in London after they had been opened and read by Paulet. She was forbidden to give alms, in case they contained secret messages or were used as bribes. Her gifts of cloth to the poor were stopped – a year earlier Walsingham had intercepted a letter from her giving precise instructions on how to use alum for invisible writing in all sorts of ways, including on cloth, so this stricture was hardly surprising. In any case, Paulet disapproved of such charitable affairs as merely encouraging idleness among the poor. Walsingham had been more precise on this point: 'Under colour of giving of alms and other extraordinary courses used by her, she hath won the hearts of the people that habit about those places where she hath heretofore lain.' Rosaries, crucifixes, devotional pictures and embroideries were all regarded by Paulet as 'Catholic toys', and when some were sent to Mary as presents he attempted to have them all burnt.

Any one of these restrictions in isolation might have seemed reasonable from a security standpoint, but taken together they bordered on the brutal, and Mary complained to Elizabeth.

Elizabeth's response was unhelpful. Mary had, in the past, said that she was willing to accept whatever Elizabeth wished to give her, and she was now to accept Sir Amyas Paulet as Elizabeth's unquestioned representative: 'You need not doubt that a man that reverenceth God, loveth his Prince, and is no less by calling honourable than by birth noble, will ever do anything unworthy of himself.'

Paulet had started as he intended to continue, and one of his earliest acts was savagely hurtful to Mary. He removed her dais and the cloth of state with her heraldic arms which had hung above her chair. These were the tangible symbols of her royalty and had been with her for over forty years. Mary had been bred to believe that her total identity was contained in the arms which hung above her head, and some of her bitterest conflicts with Elizabeth had been over the quarterings of these arms. Sir Amyas considered that there was only one queen in England and, therefore, that only her cloth of state should hang anywhere. In his view Mary was quite simply Mary Stewart, murderess, adulteress, probable plotter against his sovereign and his prisoner. Mary then insisted on dining alone on a rigorous diet which she maintained for six weeks until finally Paulet conceded that when she next dined in public her cloth would be restored.

By 10 July 1585 Mary wrote to Mauvissière, the French ambassador, complaining of lack of communication from Elizabeth and of her dread of spending the winter in Tutbury. There were gaps in the ceiling allowing the wind to blow through her bedchamber and her doctor despaired of her health in such surroundings. Even in summer there were stoves burning indoors, and the hundred or so peasants in the wretched village below the castle were better lodged than she was – even their lavatories were superior to her arrangements. Mary had never been so badly housed since she came to England. James was being subjected to 'sinister and damnable' counsels designed to portray her as 'ungrateful disobedient and unnatural'. Mary hoped that Mauvissière might persuade Catherine and Henri to appeal to Elizabeth. Two months later, in September, she

386

repeated her requests adding that, bizarrely, the body of a tortured priest had been found hanging outside her windows and, a few days later, another corpse had been found to have been thrown into the well. In his regular reports to Walsingham, Paulet mentioned neither of these events.

For outdoor exercise Mary claimed she was confined to about a quarter of an acre around a pigsty – her gaolers called it a garden – where she could walk, or be carried in a chair, and she was everywhere accompanied by arquebusiers with their weapons primed ready to fire. We can presume that a significant part of their orders included instructions that, if a rescue were to be attempted, their first action would be to shoot her. Paulet had assured Walsingham that he would carry out this instruction himself rather than risk her being rescued – as Shrewsbury and Sadler had promised to do before him.

He was, however, prepared to allow 'soft' riding inside the limits of two miles and let Mary watch her greyhound course a deer, although her priest was not allowed to attend the hunt. Bemused by Paulet's seemingly random changes to the terms of her confinement, Mary remarked, 'Well, I find innovations every day.'

Paulet did, however, agree that Tutbury was unsuitable and, after several alternatives were rejected – not all noblemen wanted to give their houses as prisons for Mary – Chartley Hall was selected. It belonged to the Earl of Essex, who objected that all his trees would be cut down to provide wood for Mary's household, but he was assured that his timber would be spared. As an alternative, Essex had suggested the nearby house of one Robert Gifford, a 'recusant' living at Chillington, but the idea was rejected, and so Essex was persuaded to give up his house and leave his furniture and hangings for the prisoner. Paulet approved of Chartley since the house had a moat, which was not only a useful defence, but also meant that Mary's laundresses need not leave the house to draw water – these girls had been a constant headache for Paulet at Tutbury where he suspected that during their outings with laundry they were being used as couriers. Chartley was only twelve miles west of Tutbury – just beyond Uttoxeter – so Mary's removal could be made in a single day. The windows of Mary's chamber gave directly on to the park, but there was no danger she would attempt to use them as a means of escape, since she was now 'too infirm to run away on her own feet'. Her now grossly swollen and painful legs may have been a symptom of water retention due to poor circulation. Her mother was 'dropsical' from the same complaint. In addition, Mary's heart may have been in decline. Paulet tried to persuade Mary to remain at Tutbury until the start of the next year, but she insisted on making the move as quickly as possible, and on 24 December 1585 she was installed in her new prison.

In spite of her various moves and privations, Mary still maintained a considerable wardrobe, with twenty-seven robes, twelve of which were black, in varying materials, velvet and silk being the principals. Skirts, outer mantles, doublets and petticoats in scarlet were now worn under her habitual black, while on her head she wore her white lace widow's cap. Eleven tapestries, four carpets, and, most questionably, three daises ranked beside her three beds, two covered in velvet. The crucifix without which she was never seen was of solid gold. Mary had lost her freedom but she was hardly shivering in rags in a dungeon.

In France dangerous moves had been afoot. On 15 October Thomas Morgan, who was still under comparatively light incarceration in the Bastille, had received a visitor by the name of Gilbert Gifford. Morgan said that Gifford was 'a Catholic gentleman to me well known for that he has been brought up in learning on this side of the seas this many years past'. His uncle, Robert Gifford, was the 'recusant' who lived near Chartley, and the family were kinsmen to the Throckmortons. Gilbert had studied for the priesthood in Rome, but had been expelled before renewing his Catholic contacts in Douai in 1585. In Paris he had presented himself to ambassador Mauvissière and his replacement, Guillaume de l'Aubespine, Baron de Châteauneuf; he was now suggesting himself to Thomas Morgan as a possible courier for Mary's correspondence. Gifford was also in touch with Thomas Paget, a member of Archbishop Beaton's household, who was himself Mary's French ambassador. Paget was a close friend of Morgan's and a devoted agent of Francis Walsingham. Mary's network in France was thoroughly penetrated by double agents.

Robert Gifford was arrested immediately on his arrival at Rye and given the option of torture or of turning double agent to work for Walsingham. He agreed at once and with an appalling disregard for security he lodged in London with Thomas Philips – or Phellipes – Walsingham's cipher clerk and principal assistant. Morgan was still totally convinced of Gifford's honesty and wrote him a letter of warm commendation to show to Mary. Gifford also carried several months' worth of correspondence from the Paris embassy and Philips visited Paulet to arrange for Gifford's arrival and for the easy transmission of letters back and forth.

Philips had provided Gifford with a secret code for Mary's exclusive use – in fact, most of the letters she received were, unknown to her, in Philips's handwriting. Walsingham made sure that Elizabeth was kept informed, so in April she told the French ambassador, 'I know everything that is done in my kingdom . . . I know what artifices prisoners use.'

Mary met Gifford on 16 January 1586 and, in a state of delight, read her first letters for over a year. Apart from the official correspondence between embassies and their queen, Morgan wrote long and gossipy letters of the doings of the royal families of Europe, opening a window on the world she had once inhabited and from which she was now cut off. Gifford also explained to Mary and her secretaries the system by which she now could have secure communication with the outside world. Mary would dictate her letters to Nau or to Gilbert Curle, her master of horse and sometime secretary, who would present them to her as a 'minute' or fair copy. After her approval the secretaries would encrypt them in the code provided by Philips. The letters were then wrapped in a leather satchel and placed in an empty beer barrel which was taken to Burton for refilling. In Burton the satchel was given to Gifford, who either passed the contents to Philips at Chartley or rode with them to London, where they were decoded and given to Walsingham before being resealed and passed to the French embassy for onwards transmission to Morgan in Paris. The process would be repeated in reverse for letters written to Mary. The carter was always referred to as 'the honest man', but, since his wife dealt with the satchel in his absence without any knowledge of her husband's rewards, he was only slightly honest. Gifford said of him, 'There never was so fortunate a knave.' The system was very simple and Mary now believed that all the correspondence she received by this route was genuine and totally secure. Gifford felt that Mary trusted him to the extent of asking her to provide him with a pension for his efforts.

Mary was completely deceived by the ruse and wrote immediately to Morgan, 'I thank you heartily for this bringer [Gifford] whom I perceive very willing to acquit himself honestly.' Philips would have been delighted to read this letter. Mary described him: 'This Phellipes is of low stature, slender every way, dark yellow haired on the head and clear yellow bearded, eated in the face with pocks, of short sight, thirty years of age by appearance, and, it is said, Secretary Walsingham's man.' He had not only successfully set up the communication system with the brewers and the carter – both of whom were being paid by Paulet as well as Mary – but also operated as an intelligence gatherer for his master, Walsingham. Walsingham, in turn, had only to wait for Mary to implicate herself in a plot which could be reasonably thought of as treasonous under the catch-all Act of Association. There is no evidence that Walsingham encouraged such a plot directly – he had no need to do so – but if any such plot appeared he would know of it almost before Mary herself. The trap was set, the alarm bells were ready to sound; all Walsingham had to do was to wait for the bait to arrive.

In February 1586 Mary was given a new bed. Paulet thought it 'uncharitable to refuse' and late in the month she received

M. Arnault from the French embassy in London. Their conversation was supervised by the ever-vigilant Paulet, but Paulet panicked when Arnault offered a girdle with silver lace for Mary and books of tables, presumably almanacs of some sort, as a present for Nau. Mary gave Arnault 500 crowns and Paulet was so terrified by the last letters he had received from Philips that he feared 'to handle the girdle, the books of tables or any such thing' and promptly sent the presents to Walsingham.

His vigilance was necessary, since on 16 March Mary suggested to Châteauneuf that secret letters could be sent in the cork soles of shoes. The ambassador wisely rejected the idea since he probably knew that all correspondence was being read and the long letters from Morgan and the Bishop of Ross were all in Philips's hand. Mary did use an unbroken code for communication with the exiled Spanish ambassador Mendoza, but he reported that neither Catherine nor Henri III wanted the 'speedy reduction of England and chastisement of the Queen'. Philip of Spain agreed, in principle, with Mary's restoration, as did the Pope, but neither man offered anything tangible.

We have seen that in the past there were enough romantic young men willing to risk their lives to release Mary and see her on the throne of England. By 1586 the focus had changed. Now the plots only involved Mary insofar as she would stabilise the situation politically and reward the plotters after the assassination of Elizabeth. Elizabeth's death would be a master-stroke against heresy, sanctioned, it was erroneously believed, by the Bull of excommunication and endorsed by Catholic interests on mainland Europe. Mendoza burned with bitter hatred for the disgrace of his exile and promised military support from Spain, although without the authority of Philip II. Mendoza told Philip on 12 May, 'I am advised from England by four men of position who have the entry into the Queen's house, that they have discussed for at least three months the intention of killing her.' Mary had assured Mendoza that if James continued to embrace Protestantism, she would will all her rights in the English crown to Spain. Around Mendoza circled John Ballard, sometimes known as Fortescue, a priest with the fanatical belief that his God-given mission was to achieve the assassination of Elizabeth. Burghley said of him that he was 'a man vainglorious and desirous of his own praise and to be meddling in things above his own reach'. All of these plotters were in constant touch with Morgan and Paget, and all of their correspondence with Mary was read by Walsingham. Father J.H. Pollen, the Jesuit historian, said of these schemes: 'A lunatic was at the helm. Shipwreck was certain.'

Ballard made his way secretly to England and contacted Sir Anthony Babington. Babington was a rich 25-year-old Catholic from Derbyshire who had spent some time with Shrewsbury as his ward, and at that time he undoubtedly formed a romantic passion for the imprisoned queen. He had visited France and met Morgan but was now the centre of a circle of Catholic friends in London. They were attracted not only by his religious fidelity but also by the generous use of his wealth. One of Babington's fellow conspirators was John Savage, a zealot of limited intelligence who told Babington that he was ready at any time to kill Elizabeth. When Babington suggested that he go to court and carry out his intention that very day, Savage replied that he could not attend court 'for lack of apparel'! Babington and his plotters lacked the ruthless efficiency needed for success; their fanaticism clouded their judgment to the extent that they even posed for a group portrait to be painted.

Mary did hear that Babington was holding some letters for her, and on 25 June she wrote to him asking for any correspondence he might have to be sent on to her via Gifford. Walsingham was watching both Ballard and Babington closely and was keen to read his reply. Babington fell straight into the trap and replied at once giving details of a rescue of Mary, a plot to assassinate Elizabeth by six men and a plan for a foreign invasion followed by a Catholic hegemony. He told her that he was determined to go abroad but he assured Mary of foreign support: 'Ballard, a man of virtue and learning . . . informed me of great preparation by Christian princes for the deliverance of the country from the extreme and miserable state wherein it hath long remained.' He assured Mary of the deliverance of herself and the despatch of the 'usurping competitor': 'there be six noble gentlemen, all my private friends, who for the zeal they bear to the Catholic cause and your Majesty's service will undertake the tragical execution.' He 'with ten gentlemen and 100 followers [would] undertake her deliverance'. He would wait in Lichfield for Mary's reaction to his plan.

Before Mary could reply, Gifford told Walsingham that he had been contacted by Ballard who complained about inactivity by Morgan and Paget. Walsingham made notes as to how to deal with 'practitioners and conspirators' since he now had ample evidence to undertake the arrest and conviction of Babington, Ballard, Savage and his group. By her inaction – not immediately informing Paulet of Babington's intentions – Mary could already be seen to be guilty of treason under the terms of the Act of Association, but Walsingham waited to see if she would actually put an endorsement in writing. Philips merely said, 'We await her very heart with the next.'

Finally, Mary replied to Babington on 17 July, and of all her doubtful actions writing this letter was without question the least wise. Her previous decisions to return to Scotland and subsequently to flee into England both led to disasters, her involvement with the Craigmillar Bond was rash in the extreme, as was her marriage to Bothwell, but now she had put her head firmly on the block. It was a very long letter, dictated first to Nau as a minute in French, translated by Curle and then encrypted.

It began,

Write to me as often as you can of all occurrences which you may judge important to the good of my affairs, whereto I shall not fail to correspond with all the care that is in my power . . . In the meantime the Catholics here, exposed to all sorts of persecution and cruelty, daily diminish in number force means and power . . . in respect of the public good of this state, I shall always be ready to employ my life and all I have or may ever look for in this world therein.

393

Mary then addressed the points of logistics raised by Babington:

[W]hat forces on foot and horse may be raised amongst you all? What towns, ports and havens may you assure yourselves to receive succour from the Low Countries, Spain and France? What place you esteem fittest to assemble the principal company of your forces? What foreign forces you intend to use and for how long would they be paid? What munitions and forts are fittest for their landing in this realm? What provision will be made for armour and money?

So far in her reply Mary had condoned open revolt by endorsing Babington's plans to put herself at the head of an invading army. But then the most contentious passage in the letter appeared. When all the foregoing was in place, then, 'Set the six gentlemen to work, taking order upon the accomplishment of their designs [that] I may be suddenly transported out of this place.' Or, in another version which would be revealed later, 'Let the six gentlemen who have undertaken to assassinate Elizabeth proceed to their work and when she is dead come and set me free.' Mary wanted to know 'The manner of my getting from this hold.' Mendoza was to be kept informed, and Mary's code for letters to him was still unbroken. She besought Babington to make sure everything was in place before he made his move. She asked for military support – 'Set me in the midst of a good army' – and voiced her fear that if Elizabeth caught her she would 'enclose me forever in some hole from which I should never escape, if she used me no worse'. Mary promised to try to make the Catholics of Scotland rise and to put her son in their hands. 'I would also see some stirring in Ireland were laboured for.'

Then she settled to details: 'That at a certain day appointed in my walking abroad on horseback on the moors between this and Stafford, where ordinarily you know very few people pass, fifty or three score men well horsed and armed come and take me there, as they easily may, my keeper having with him ordinarily but eighteen or twenty horsemen with daggers only.' A second method suggested was to set fire to the barns and stables and in the confusion to rescue her. As a third option, Babington could use carts to get men into Chartley before the garrison was summoned. Wisely she wrote, 'Fail not to burn this present quickly.' The letter ends with a postscript asking for the names of the 'six noble gentlemen', although this is now generally regarded as a forgery inserted by Walsingham to improve his chances of arresting them. The letter is written in Philips's hand and endorsed 'This is a copy of the letters the Queen of Scotland.' Before sending the decrypted version to Walsingham, Philips drew a gallows on the outside of the letter. He was sure that this letter was the document that would send Mary to the scaffold. On 29 July – twelve days after Mary had sent it – the letter was delivered to Babington and decrypted by him and his ally, Chidiock Tichborne.

Was Mary now directly endorsing a plot to assassinate her cousin? If the second alternative version is to be believed, then there is no doubt. But what exists is Philips's copy – and he had the letter for some days before sending it on to Walsingham. The original minute and any notes were presumably destroyed at Chartley. If the original phrase – 'set the six gentlemen to work' – was the intended one then there is a little room to wriggle. Did Mary not question the 'designs' the six gentlemen were to accomplish? Babington's letter to her had made that clear – he talked openly of 'execution'. Was Mary now presuming that they would seize Elizabeth and convey her to some secure prison, so that Mary and she would reverse their roles? This could be maintained since Mary insisted that her rescue must be achieved, even though Elizabeth was still alive and able to commit her to 'some hole'. What is very possible is that Mary simply entered into a state of denial as to what the task of the 'six gentlemen' would be, just as she never questioned why French Paris was so 'begrimed' before Darnley's murder. That she should try to escape is perfectly understandable. Mary was a sovereign queen imprisoned on very doubtful grounds, but now, consciously or

395

not, she was endorsing a royal assassination followed by a total revolution, both political and religious.

Philips would understand that the original version was quite sufficient for a verdict of treason, but he knew the difficulties that arose when it was not only the Privy Council, but also Elizabeth who had to be convinced, and so he probably added some extra salt to the mixture. Even without it, the inference is fatally clear.

On the same busy day Mary wrote five other long letters to Mendoza, Morgan, Châteauneuf, the Archbishop of Glasgow, and Sir Francis Englefield, thanking them for their promised help and informing them that she embraced Babington's intentions. She noticed that Philips had arrived at Chartley but suspected nothing. She was now ready for rescue and installation on the English throne. On 19 July, however, Philips had written to Walsingham about Babington: 'I look for your honour's speedy resolution touching his apprehension.' He hoped that Elizabeth would hang Nau and Curle and was sorry to hear that Ballard had not been taken. On 2 August, Babington and others were proclaimed traitors, although before his arrest Babington wrote to Mary not to be dismayed: 'What they have vowed to do they will perform or die.' Walsingham hoped that Babington would reply to Mary in detail but decided 'it is better to lack the answer than to lack the man' and gave the orders for mass arrests. Gifford fled to France on 21 July, writing to Walsingham on 3 September asking him to pay a bill for £40, and was ordained priest the next year. He was subsequently arrested in a brothel for disorderly conduct and he later died in prison in November 1590.

Ballard was taken on 4 August to be 'committed to the Tower and forced by torture to utter that which otherwise he will not disclose'. A detailed list of what he would confess to was drawn up. Savage was arrested on 8 August with one Robert Poley, whose confession ran to twelve pages and implicated someone called Parsons and George Gifford, as well as men in Sir Walter Raleigh's service. Poley would have confessed to anything else he could think of and after Babington's execution, Raleigh was given part of Babington's estate as a recompense for the libel.

Babington fled to the north of London and was arrested, with his fellow conspirators, hiding in St John's Wood on 14 August. He was interrogated, but not tortured, and between 18 August and 8 September he confessed in detail to the entire plot, including Mary's acceptance; 'I wrote to her touching every particular of this plot unto which she answered.' Finally he tried to plead innocence and feebly admitted that he thought no one would believe him. 'He saith also and protests earnestly upon salvation of his soul, that to his remembrance he never moved or dealt with any touching the act against her Majesty's person, or the invasion of the realm, or the delivery of the Scottish Queen, but with such and in such manner as he hath before declared. Yet he saith that he must needs confess that his letters to the Scottish Queen do import great probability to the contrary.'

Babington may have escaped the terrors of the rack, but his execution on 20 September was horrifying even by Tudor standards. Elizabeth 'became more cruel as a result of the terror and danger she had gone through' and asked that the executions be more savage, and therefore more memorable, than usual. They were to take place over two days. Babington and six of his fellow conspirators were executed first, and after being cut down from hanging before death, their torsos were scarified with 'sinister looking pitch forks' before their hands and feet were cut off. Then the castration, disembowelling and quartering were carried out. On the second day, Elizabeth ordered that the remaining prisoners should be allowed to die by hanging before dismemberment.

A month previously Walsingham had had to deal with the problem of proving Mary's guilt, and to this end he needed to have a thorough search of her apartments and papers. He especially wanted to see the drafts or minutes of her letter to Babington, possibly with the intention of destroying them. Mary was unaware of the arrests and the collapse of the plot and was now in high spirits, her mood improving when Paulet suggested that she and her household attend a stag hunt on 11 August. She was delighted to accept, not knowing that Paulet had received precise orders to 'with all convenient speed as you may, under the colour of going a hunting and taking the air, remove the Queen your charge to some house near to the place where she remaineth as you shall think meet for her to stay in for a time, until you shall understand our further pleasure for the placing of her'. He was also to arrest Nau and Curle, sending them incommunicado to London.

By coincidence Mary had asked Paulet if she could be allowed to take the air, probably by being carried in a chair, and to her delight Paulet, who knew that she could still ride, suggested the hunting expedition. On the day of the false outing Mary dressed with special care in a long-unused but still-pretty riding habit in the hope that she might meet other gentry. Paulet, who was rheumatic, had fallen back from the main party and Mary was solicitous during the ride, riding back to help him. For the hunt Mary was accompanied by Nau and Curle, Melville, Dominique Bourgoing, her physician, and her page, Bastien, while one of Mary's grooms, Hannibal Stuart, performed an almost-forgotten task and carried her crossbow and arrows. 'Open air, the howling of the dogs, the hunting horns made her forget her present plight and undoubtedly recall the distant memories of the great hunts of St Germain and Fontainebleau.'

A few miles from Chartley Mary saw a company of horsemen approaching at speed and, for a moment, she must have thought they would be Babington's 'ten men' riding to her rescue. Paulet, however, was unalarmed at their approach, although Mary could now see that they were armed. Her hopes vanished when their leader, splendidly dressed in green serge, dismounted and approached Mary. He was the fifty-year-old Sir Thomas Gorges, a rising courtier, recently appointed keeper of the Royal Wardrobe and determined that he would be seen to carry out his task with utmost efficiency. He now gave direct orders for the arrest of Nau and Curle, whom Mary never saw again. Gorges, clearly speaking from precise instruction said, 'Madam, the queen my mistress finds it very strange that you, contrary to your agreement with her, conspire against her and her estate, something that she never thought to see. She believes that one of your servants is guilty. He will be taken separately and Sir Amyas will tell you the rest.' Mary called up Nau but was forbidden to speak to him. When she realised that they were not returning to Chartley, she dismounted and, supported by Curle's sister, Elizabeth, asked where they were going. Paulet showed her Queen Elizabeth's warrant 'to remove the said Queen unto some place as shall by you be thought meet'. Mary stumbled away and knelt on a tussock of grass some thirty paces distant and prayed, asking forgiveness for her sins, certain that she was to be executed there and then. The entire party was frozen in disbelief, Gorges's men nervously handling their weapons, unsure of what was taking place. Mary, certain that her guilt had been discovered, was making her last confession, without a priest. She declared that she was totally worthless and that her only liberty was in the Holy Catholic Church. Finally, Bourgoing, in fear for his own life, went to her and gently lifted her upright. He then supported her back to her horse and she was helped back into her saddle. Bourgoing told Paulet that he was behaving with unnecessary savagery towards an ageing and sick woman, to which Paulet did not reply but merely rode on stone-faced.

They rode to Tixall, a beautiful house belonging to Sir Walter Aston, but Mary enjoyed none of its pleasures, keeping to her room the entire two weeks of her imprisonment there. Paulet did not allow Mary to write to Elizabeth but did permit two ladies to join her, and she was allowed at least one change of clothing, since she was still wearing the pretty riding habit in which she had hoped to enjoy the hunt.

Meanwhile, Chartley was being ransacked with the help of Sir William Waad, and three strongboxes of papers as well as chests and boxes of loose documents were taken, although the crucial minutes were not found. A list of the jewellery that was taken out of the care of Jane Kennedy was drawn up – a list which contrasts sadly with those composed when Mary was widowed in France – but for a prisoner it was lavish enough. There were diamond and ruby rings as well as votary objects: the story of the Passion of Christ engraved on a gold crucifix as well as on painted panels, and Mary's much-annotated Book of Hours. There were little gold animals, bears, cows and parrots. More private was the collection of portraits: an ivory portrait of Elizabeth, one of James VI framed in gold, and small framed portraits of the French royal family as well as of Mary's Guise relatives. There was a double miniature of Mary backed by one of Elizabeth, a little chest garnished with diamonds, rubies and pearls, six little jewels and a chain enamelled in white and red – Mary had owned such a chain when a child in France. The sumptuous treasures of the past were all gone and what remained was a sad summary of Mary's personal life.

Prospects of her future life came in a letter from Elizabeth to Paulet: 'God reward thee treblefold in three double for thy most troublesome charge so well discharged. Let your wicked murderess know how with hearty sorrow her vile deserts compelleth these orders; and bid her from me ask God forgiveness for her treacherous dealings towards the saver of her life many a year.' There was now no pretence that Elizabeth was a sister queen, filled with sympathy for her cousin's plight. Elizabeth had been terrified by the Babington plot and by what seemed to her to be Mary's endorsement of her murder. From now on her principal problem would be how to dispose safely of her Scottish cousin without creating a Catholic backlash.

After the search and removal of documents was completed, Mary was returned to Chartley, although not without some dramatics on leaving Tixall. Paulet said, 'When she left Sir Walter Aston's gate she said in a loud voice, weeping, to some poor folks there assembled, "I have nothing for you. I am a beggar as well as you. All is taken from me." And when she came to the gentlemen, she said, weeping, "Good gentlemen, I am not witting or privy to anything intended against the Queen." ' She visited Curle's wife, Barbara Mowbray, who had had a baby daughter in Mary's absence, but, with no priest available, it was still unchristened, so Mary took the baby on her knee and named it Mary, baptising the child herself. It was typical of Mary to show what kindness she could to her servants and equally typical of her to miss no opportunity for a public show of histrionics.

Back at Chartley, Mary, now realising that a legal case against her was being drawn up, confined herself to bed, but even there she was not secure from the attentions of Paulet, who questioned her closely over the identities of the 'six men'. Paulet, realising that Mary's resistance was at a low level, tried hard to get his ailing prisoner to confess to her participation in the plot, but she denied all knowledge of Babington's plans. She only faintly remembered him when he had been Shrewsbury's ward; 'I have often received letters offering help but have never involved myself in their schemes.' Paulet also wanted access to a cupboard in her bedroom containing Mary's remaining money. The cupboard was locked so Paulet sent for crowbars and axes. Mary, still in her nightclothes and in bed, sent Elizabeth Curle for the key, and 'without slippers or shoes', under the watchful eyes of armed guards, she unlocked the cupboard for Paulet. It contained five rolls of canvas wrapping over 5,000 French crowns and two leather bags, one with £104 in gold the other with £3 in silver. Mary said the money was to pay for her funeral and to pay her servants after her death. The money was all sent to London with Sir William Waad, along with Mary's private seals. Paulet made a marginal note, 'This lady hath good store of money at present in the French Ambassador's hands.'

Meanwhile Nau and Curle were being interrogated about the content of Mary's letter to Babington. Curle read Babington's letter and testified, 'I do confess to have deciphered the like of the whole above written, coming written in one sheet of paper, as from Mr Babington. And the answer thereto, being written in French by Mr Nau, to have been translated in English and ciphered by me.' To which Walsingham replied, 'I would to God, these minutes were found.'

The interrogation of the two secretaries continued as they

were shown the very letters they had sent to Babington. Nau then claimed that he had taken direct dictation from Mary and Curle admitted that he had burnt the English copy. It was the familiar story of servants who had loyally followed orders now trying to save their own skins by placing the blame on Mary. Nau returned to France shortly afterwards, and Curle, since he was an Englishman, was imprisoned for a year.

In London, Walsingham was now in the position of having to bring Mary to a trial, even without the 'minutes', and he told Elizabeth that the documents no longer existed. Chartley would not serve as a location for Mary's trial, and Walsingham first suggested the Tower, only to be overruled by Elizabeth, who was displaying a sharply divided purpose. She would not allow the imprisonment of a sister queen in the Tower, but insisted that Mary be separated from her servants and that her money be seized. She also rejected Hertford, Grafton, Woodstock, Northampton, Coventry and Huntingdon as locations for the trial before finally accepting Fotheringhay Castle, near Peterborough. Elizabeth was bitterly afraid of Mary as a focus for revolt but was equally determined that she should be treated with some kind of formal respect. Burghley pointed out that, since Mary had signed articles of abdication in Lochleven Castle, she was no longer a queen regnant, but this did not sway Elizabeth's opinion. Walsingham was angry with Elizabeth, fearing that her treatment of the invalid Mary might accelerate her death – she was already known to be very ill and moving her again might prove the last straw – and let her escape the public trial he had in mind. More directly, Leicester wrote to Walsingham suggesting that Mary be quietly poisoned – and, in case Walsingham had any religious scruples against murder, recommending an Anglican priest who was willing to justify such an act from Scripture. The suggestion was rejected. Some members of parliament felt that, given the reported state of Mary's health, all these machinations were a waste of time, since the woman would die soon in any case.

On 5 September 1586, Elizabeth established a special tribunal to hear the case against Mary, its findings to be examined in the court of the Star Chamber and then ratified by parliament. To ensure a rapid conclusion, Burghley recalled parliament, saying, 'Thus the responsibility is spread and everybody is content.'

Mary realised that another, possibly final, move was about to take place and asked permission to pay off her servants, but Paulet, unreasonably, forbade this. In any case, Mary's money was now in London. She gave her servants receipts and told them to apply to the French embassy for back pay or for passage to France. On the day of departure Paulet locked the nineteen servants who were not going to Fotheringhay in their rooms and put guards outside their windows. Walsingham had chosen his gaoler well.

Mary was now too ill to ride and was led by heavily armed men into a coach which was escorted by 200 cavalry under Sir Thomas Gorges, himself carrying a pistol in his belt. During the journey – Mary was not told of the destination – she sat as upright in the coach as she could, watching the armed escort and questioning Roger Sharp, her coachman. 'The unfortunate princess feared that her throat would be cut.' She was not afraid of death, but did fear dying without a public confession and having her murder concealed as suicide.

The party left Chartley on 21 September and passed the night at Burton. They then proceeded in easy stages of seven to fifteen miles and arrived at Fotheringhay on 25 September. The only approach to this grim castle was by a path called Perryho Lane and Mary took one look at Fotheringhay and said, 'Perio! I am lost!'

Fotheringhay was a huge fortress in the unfamiliar flat Northamptonshire countryside surrounded by a double ditch, making access deliberately difficult: the exterior ditch was seventy-five yards across and the interior ditch stretched for sixty-six yards. The entrance to the castle itself was on the north side with a drawbridge and staircase leading to a vast courtyard with the Great Hall on the first floor. A chapel lay to the left, with a dining hall and tapestried staterooms, and the royal apartments were on the upper floors. It was a forbidding castle used solely as a state prison, its sinister aspects being emphasised for Mary by her currently being the only inhabitant, apart from a mere five or six servants. It seemed the ideal place for a secret assassination, although Mary correctly guessed that since many of the other rooms were being prepared for habitation others were expected.

Mary could have been tried under a statute of Edward III – even though she was not an English citizen – which made it treason to conspire against the sovereign, execute war within the kingdom or communicate with the sovereign's enemies. But it was decided that the Act of Association would suffice, since under this legislation anyone found guilty would have all claims to the English throne denied and could be lawfully sentenced to death. Since it was, in fact, a trial for treason, the rules applying to that charge were to be applied, and Mary would have no counsel nor could she call witnesses. The form of the trial was not explained to her in advance. Mary spoke and thought in French, had learned enough Scots for reasonable fluency, but still spoke and wrote English with difficulty. Armed thus with only her native wit and the knowledge that she was arguing for her life, she prepared to debate with the finest forensic brains in Tudor England.

On 1 October Paulet, armed no doubt with instructions from Burghley, asked Mary to confess her guilt, assuring her of Elizabeth's mercy. Mary replied that she was aware of 'no fault or offence for which I have to render account to anyone here below'. Mary could now be in no doubt that she was to be on trial for her life. Her plight increased when, on 12 October, Sir Walter Mildmay, Paulet and Edward Barker, a notary, gave her a letter from Elizabeth. It was one of the most savage letters ever written.

You have in various ways and manners attempted to take my life and to bring my kingdom to destruction by bloodshed. I have never proceeded so harshly against you but have, on the contrary, protected and maintained you like myself. These treasons will be proved to you and all made manifest. Yet it is my will, that you answer the nobles and peers of the kingdom as if I were myself present. I therefore require, charge, and command that you make answer for I have been well informed of your arrogance.

Act plainly and without reserve, and you will sooner be able to obtain favour of me.

Elizabeth R.

There cannot have been any doubt as to which verdict of the court would satisfy Elizabeth. Elizabeth also let it be known privately that she had made an offer to Mary that if she confessed, a royal pardon and confinement in comfort awaited her, but there is no evidence that such a letter ever existed.

The next day, Mary argued that she had never enjoyed the protection of the laws of England, under which she was being tried, and in the afternoon she met Burghley; Sir Thomas Bromley, the Lord Chancellor; and the Lord President. She told them she was no subject but would answer only before a full parliament or directly to Elizabeth herself. Since Mary was well aware that the commission might simply try her in absentia with the verdict a foregone conclusion, she cautioned them, 'The theatre of the whole world is much wider than the kingdom of England.'

Mary denied that the Act of Association constituted legal grounds for her trial and asked for experts in law from Pavia or Poitiers to be brought. This request was ignored. She was reminded of Elizabeth's letter but claimed that she could only remember the letter in snatches – 'it stood not with her royal dignity to play the scrivener'. Mary was told that Elizabeth 'would be much affected with joy if you are proved innocent', but replied that she would not answer 'to the judgement of mine adversaries . . . I will not submit myself . . . I am myself a Queen, the daughter of a King, a stranger and the true kinswoman of the Queen of England . . . As an absolute Queen I cannot submit to orders, nor can I submit to the laws of the land without injury to myself, the King my son, and all other princes.'

Burghley told Mary that Elizabeth had already protected her

from a trial for treason along with Norfolk and had 'protected [her] from the fury of [her] own subjects'. Mary smiled. Hatton interceded, 'If you be innocent you wrong your reputation in avoiding a trial. Lay aside the bootless privilege of royal dignity, which now can be of no use unto you, appear in judgement, and show your innocency.' This argument weighed with her, and on 14 October Mary agreed to appear before the commission. In reality she had no option. Her attempt to include her international allies was no more than a feeble hope, but on 21 November Henri III wrote to his ambassador, de Courcelles, 'Now I desire that you will excite the king of Scotland . . . to take up the defence and protection of his mother.'

The trial took place in a large room above the Great Hall, a cold and forbidding place that overwhelmed the hastily installed temporary furniture. At one end of the room was a dais with an empty chair of state under a cloth bearing Elizabeth's arms. On backless benches on one side of the hall the Lord Chancellor Bromley, Burghley, nine earls and a viscount were seated. One of these earls was her previous gaoler, Shrewsbury, who had done everything he could to be excused, including offering to send his verdict of guilty before the trial took place. He was firmly reminded of his duty by Burghley. On a bench facing them were thirteen barons. Nearby were Hatton, Walsingham, Sadler, Mildmay and Paulet. Chief justices and lesser legal lights were scattered around. All of these had tables covered with documents. In the centre of all of these was a chair for Mary with a cushion for her feet. She had no table. She was to be placed at the foot of the royal dais in a position of maximum weakness, with all others seated around her in positions of threat.

Mary entered, supported by Melville and Bourgoing and attended by her surgeon, apothecary and three waiting women. The commissioners dutifully doffed their hats and bowed their heads as she made her painful way to her seat, declaring that she should have been seated on the royal chair under the cloth of state. As she took her seat the Lord Chancellor informed her that Elizabeth 'not without great grief of mind' advertised that 'you have conspired the destruction of her and of England and the subversion of religion'. Mary, still seated, answered with a statement not of her guilt or innocence, but of her position and attitude to the court.

I am an absolute queen, and will do nothing which will prejudice either mine own royal majesty, or other princes of my place and rank or my son. My mind is not yet dejected nor will I sink under my calamity . . . The laws and statutes of England are to me most unknown; I am destitute of counsellors, and who shall be my peers I am utterly ignorant. My papers and notes are taken from me, and no man dareth step forth as my advocate. I am clear of all crimes against the Queen. I have excited no man against her, and I am not to be charged but by mine own word or writing, which cannot be produced against me. Yet can I not deny but I have commended myself and my cause to foreign princes.

Mary then reiterated her personal sovereignty as a crowned queen and Elizabeth's lack of help for her plight. This was simply ignored and the commission drove steadfastly ahead with direct accusations.

Gaudy, the royal sergeant-at-law, vividly robed in blue with a red hood, now described the Babington plot in detail, avowing 'that she knew of it, approved it, assented unto it, promised her assistance, and showed the way and means'. This was crucial and Mary knew it. She could also guess that at least some of her correspondence would have been compromised and would also presume that some evidence against her would have been obtained under torture. However, she had no way of knowing how much detail was in Walsingham's hands and she had been given no notice of the evidence that would be produced at the trial. Mary was certain that the commission would find her guilty and that parliament would sentence her to death, although she may have harboured some fragile hope that the sentence would never be carried out. Therefore, since she now had nothing to lose, Mary had no hesitation in making the most extreme statements.

Opting for the blanket denial she had given to Paulet at Chartley, she denied knowing Babington, Ballard or anyone else. She 'excited no man to commit any offence, and being shut up in prison, she could neither know nor hinder what they attempted'. She did admit that she fervently had wanted to gain her freedom, 'a very natural wish'. Babington's confession was read and Mary simply declared that many men wrote to her and 'it could not thereby be gathered that she was privy to all their wicked counsels'. Then her letters from Babington were read and she denied she had ever written any to him. The response to this was immediate and her incriminating letter of 12 July 1585 was also read.

Now the court could connect Babington's 'six noble gentlemen' who would 'undertake the tragical execution' or the 'dispatch of the usurping competitor' with Mary's request to Babington to know how the 'six gentlemen deliberate to proceed' and when it 'shall be time to set the gentlemen on work', leading to her rescue and the restoration of the Catholic faith. Mary was staggered to find the depth of Walsingham's penetration of her correspondence and realised that if the letter was accepted by the court as having been written by her – and she knew very well that their inclination would be strongly for acceptance – then her guilt was inevitable. She feared that things were being effected now by Walsingham 'who, as she had heard, had practised against her life and her son's', to bring about her death.

Mary had to respond immediately, and her defence was simple. She told the court that while it was true that the letter in question was written in her ciphers, these ciphers had been stolen from her agents in France and the letter was a complete forgery. Mary, reasonably, asked to see the originals of the letters; 'If my enemies possess them, why do they not produce them?' Walsingham could only bite his lip at this. Mary went on to declare that she had not so much as thought of the destruction of the queen, 'And withal she shed plenty of tears.' At this point Walsingham smiled and slowly rose to his feet. He replied that being 'very careful for the safety of the Queen and realm, I have curiously searched out the practices against the same'. Mary said that spies could not be relied upon and burst into more tears. 'I would never make shipwreck of my soul by conspiring the destruction of my dearest sister.'

This was the moment when Walsingham desperately needed the original minute, but lacking it he had to move to the evidence of Nau and Curle. They did not appear in person but their confessions were read out. Given the opportunity to question the pair, Mary might well have been able, by appealing to their loyalty, to gain some retraction of their testimony, but instead she was left with no option but to rise above it: 'The majesty and safety of all princes falleth to the ground if they depend upon the writings and testimony of secretaries . . . If they have written anything which may be hurtful to the Queen [Elizabeth] they have written it altogether without my knowledge . . . sure I am that if they were here present, they would clear me of blame in this cause. And I, if my notes were to hand, could answer particularly to these things.'

On the next day she again protested against her situation and 'saw herself barred from all hope of her liberty' and hoped there might be another trial at which she would be allowed an advocate. She also noticed that the commissioners had all arrived in the chamber in boots and riding clothes, and presumed correctly that this would be the last day of the trial. Mary started by attacking her accusers. 'The manner in which I am treated appears to me very strange. I find myself overwhelmed under the importunity of a crowd of advocates and lawyers, who appear more versed in the formality of petty courts of justice, in little towns, than in the investigation of questions such as the present. I demand that, as this assembly appears to have been summoned for my accusation, another shall be summoned in which I may enter freely and frankly, defending my rights and honour, to satisfy the desire I have of proving my innocence.' Burghley said that her protests would be noted and that the letters held by Walsingham were proof enough. Mary, with some forensic skill, pointed out that 'the circumstances may be proved but never the fact'. Next, Burghley accused her of awarding her inheritance in England to Philip of Spain. Mary said it seemed 'good to some' that the crown should pass to a Catholic. He then told her that Morgan had sent Parry to murder the queen. There was no possibility that Mary could be linked to the intrigues of third parties without any evidence, and Mary leapt on him. 'Ah! You are my adversary.' Burghley responded, 'Yea, I am adversary to Queen Elizabeth's adversaries.'

Mary cut short the slanging match and asked to be heard in a full parliament or that she might speak in person with the queen. She then rose 'with great confidence of countenance' and pardoned the gathering for what they had done. The trial was over. She spoke privately to Walsingham 'which seemed to cause him disquiet' and turned to the now-standing assembly. 'My lords and gentlemen, I place my cause in the hands of God.' The commissioners managed not to say 'amen', and Mary started to leave the chamber. To disguise her need for a rest after only a few steps, she paused by the table of lawyers. 'Gentlemen, you have shown little mercy in the exercise of your charge . . . the more so as I am one who has little knowledge of the laws of quibbling, but may God keep me from having to do with you all again.' The lawyers recognised this as a royal joke and smiled. After she left the room the atmosphere lightened, and with much clearing of noble throats the commissioners mounted their waiting horses and departed from Fotheringhay. Walsingham wrote to Leicester, 'we had proceeded presently to sentence, but we had a secret countermand'. This was the beginning of Elizabeth's procrastination. Mary and her little court were left alone with Paulet and his armed guards in the vast castle of Fotheringhay.

The commissioners reassembled in the Star Chamber at Westminster on 25 October. After Nau and Curle 'had by oath, viva voce, voluntarily without hope of reward, before them avowedly affirmed and confirmed all and every the letters and copies of letters before produced to be most true, sentence was pronounced against the Queen of Scots'. Below a preamble as to dates, it declared that 'the aforesaid Mary pretending title to the crown of this realm of England, [had embraced] divers matters tending to the hurt, death and destruction of the royal person of our sovereign lady the Queen, contrary to the form of the statute in the commission aforesaid specified'. This sentence did 'derogate nothing from James, King of Scots, in title or honour, but that he was in the same place, degree and right as if the same sentence had never been pronounced'. A few days later, parliament made a lengthy list of Mary's misdeeds and declared, 'we cannot find that there is any possible means to provide for your Majesty's safety, but by the just and speedy execution of the said Queen'. Elizabeth's reaction was predictable:

my life hath been dangerously shot at . . . nothing hath more grieved me that one not differing from me in sex, of like rank and degree, of the same stock, and most nearly allied to me in blood, hath fallen into so great a crime. And so far have I been from bearing her any ill will, that upon discovery of certain treasonable practices against me, I wrote unto her secretly, that is she would confess them by a private letter unto myself, they should be wrapped up in silence.

Then, at great length and, it must be said, with polished literary style, Elizabeth promised to 'signify our resolution with all conveniency'. She asked the Lord Chancellor to devise some better remedy that Mary might be spared. The Lord Chancellor and Puckering, the Speaker of Parliament, besought her at length to make a decision and she gave them 'her answer answerless'. Burghley instructed Davison, Elizabeth's private secretary, to urge her to make a decision and order the execution of Mary. Davison's urging had no effect.

Whether Elizabeth delayed making her final decision out of her normal procrastination or out of a deeper reluctance to order the death of a sister sovereign has been long debated to no result, but other factors may have come into play. The execution of Mary would be seen by the Catholic powers in Europe as an attack on them, requiring a response. Rome would see Mary as a Catholic martyr, as would the English Catholics, making Elizabeth the most sought-after target of all Catholic zealots. At Elizabeth's elbow were Burghley and Walsingham, pleading expediency and urgency, although it would not be their throats which would be cut by an assassin's knife. Lastly, Elizabeth had been carefully informed of Mary's physical health and knew that if she could wait long enough, Mary would probably predecease her naturally. For the moment there were more arguments in favour of delay. All Mary could do was await her fate.

CHAPTER NINETEEN

You are but a dead woman

ak

With the departure of the commissioners and the inevitable
verdict expected, Paulet became more lenient towards Mary,
and she relaxed more in his presence. Bourgoing never 'saw her
so joyous nor so much at her ease more constantly in his seven
years of service, speaking only of leisure and recreation, especially
giving her opinion on the history of England, the reading of
which occupied the best part of the day, then spending time with
her court familiarly and joyfully with no appearance of sadness'.

All people suffer from the dread of death, but we are mostly
troubled by the uncertainties of time and circumstance. Mary
now had a certainty that she would die under a law which she
regarded as invalid, and although the method of her death was as
yet undecided, she knew that, given her rank, it would be as
painless and dignified as possible. Mary had witnessed such
executions in the past – the poet Chastelard, for example –
and had seen how quickly the axe did its work, if expertly
handled. She had also seen the butchery of Lord John Gordon's
execution, but, wisely, managed to put it out of her mind.

On 1 November 1586, All Saints' Day, Mary, having prayed all
day, had a long conversation with Sir Amyas, who was astonished at her composure, since 'no living person has ever been
charged with such horrible and odious deeds'. Mary said that she
'had no occasion to feel upset or troubled since she had done
nothing wrong'. She was reconciled to the fact that the commissioners had come with their minds already made up and the trial
had been entirely for show. Mary and Paulet argued over
Elizabeth's claim to be head of the Church as declared by

her father, Henry VIII, and Mary, tired of the now-sterile discussion, said that, in effect, the facts were of no importance since they were whatever Elizabeth wished them to be. Paulet was heartily glad to take his leave from Mary's 'superfluous and idle speeches . . . I have departed from her as otherwise she would never have let me go.'

Two weeks later, on 13 November, Sir Drue Drury came to assist Paulet, and on 19 November, Lord Buckhurst and Robert Beale arrived at Fotheringhay with instructions from Elizabeth to tell Mary that parliament had passed sentence of death on her. They were also instructed to eavesdrop whenever they could and were allowed secret meetings with Mary in case she wanted to 'reveal some secret matter to be communicated unto us'. Elizabeth's conscience was uneasy since she still lacked Mary's open admission of treason. Mary was warned to prepare herself and was told that the Dean of Peterborough would be sent to her. She replied, 'The English have many times slaughtered their kings, no marvel therefore, if they now also show their cruelty upon me, that am issued from the blood of their kings.' She stressed that she was not afraid of death and that she was resolved to meet it with total resolution. She was not guilty of the plots against Elizabeth, but had formed alliances with Christian and Catholic princes 'not for ambition – but for the honour of God and his church and to be delivered from the misery and captivity where I found myself'. Mary was now moving herself out of the temporal sway of politics and preparing herself to die for the honour of God and His Church.

Paulet also found himself in misery, since there seemed to be no end to his hateful duties as gaoler. The obvious end – Mary's death – seemed as far off as ever, and in his letters Paulet finds euphemisms for the act: 'the sacrifice of justice to be duly executed upon this lady, my charge, the root and well-spring of all our calamities'. There was also the terrifying, nagging possibility that Mary might be spared and even outlive Elizabeth. However, Paulet's next action was his most hurtful and petty.

As Buckhurst left Fotheringhay, having delivered his news,

Paulet and Drury met with Mary and told her that she must once again remove her dais and cloth of state, this time permanently. Their reasoning was cold-hearted and sadistic: 'You are but a dead woman, without the honours and dignity of a queen.' As we have seen, these heraldic symbols were of vital importance to Mary. She carried the fleur-de-lis of France, the lion of Scotland and the lions of England, and in this triplet of honours lay encapsulated her past as Queen of Scotland, then of France, then, at her father-in-law's bidding, her claim to the throne of England. In Paulet's view she was the dowager of France and therefore of no consequence in his Anglo-centric mind. She had abdicated from the throne of Scotland and had no right to the throne of England. Condemned to die by the English parliament she was, thus, no more than a piece of unfinished business. Mary remonstrated with Paulet and her servants refused to dismantle either the dais or cloth, but the task was quickly performed by six or seven of Paulet's men. Paulet then sat in her presence, unbidden – a gross insult – and ordered that Mary's billiard table be removed. Mary replied that she had not used the billiard table since it had arrived at Fotheringhay as her mind had been occupied with other things. She then told Paulet that her reading of English history made her compare herself with Richard II as she was stripped of her royal dignities. Paulet did not answer but left her without begging permission to withdraw.

Mary replaced the cloth of state with a crucifix and pictures of the Passion of Christ, thus exchanging secular power for spiritual faith. She also wrote to Elizabeth deploring Paulet's actions and praying that it had not come from her. Mary also told Elizabeth that she was being treated in 'a form degrading to princes and noble women' and she repeated Paulet's insults to her state.

With the pain of rheumatism now adding to her discomforts, Mary wrote four letters on 23 November, one to her ambassador in France, asserting her faith: 'I wished to die and obey the Church, but not to murder anyone in order to possess his rights.' Her second letter was to Pope Sixtus V, hoping to die shriven by a priest. Mary's priest, or almoner, de Préau, was in

Fotheringhay but, in a piece of unnecessary privation, was forbidden to meet with his mistress except on the eve of her death. Mary continued in her letter to ask the Pope to arrange with Henri III that her dowry be used to pay her servants, as well as to pay for prayers for her soul and for the setting up of an annual requiem. Unable to resist intrigue and gossip, Mary warned His Holiness against the Lord de Saint-Jean, since she suspected he was a spy acting for Burghley. The third letter was to Mendoza: 'I have had the heart to receive this unjust sentence of heretics with resignation . . . I have accepted without contra- diction the high honour which they confer upon me, as one most zealous for the Catholic religion, for which I have publicly offered my life.' She continued that her accusers 'told me that, whatever I may say or do, it will not be for the cause of religion that I shall die, but for having endeavoured to murder their queen'. Furthermore she told Mendoza of the removal of her cloth of state and also that 'They are at present working on the hall – erecting the scaffold, I suppose, whereon I am to perform the last act of this tragedy.' Finally she told him to inform Philip II that if her son James were to stay in the Protestant faith then Philip would inherit her claims to the English throne. Mary sent him the diamond which she had received from Norfolk. Lastly, she wrote to the Duc de Guise, whom she had written to in September 'fearing poison or some other secret death'. She repeated the requests she had made to the Pope to pay her servants, clear her debts and to arrange for an annual requiem for her soul.

It might seem that these were simply the business-like letters of someone putting their affairs in order before an expected death, but they help to explain Mary's change of attitude at this time from the much-wronged monarch to the beatific prisoner. Pau- let's removal of her cloth of state and her replacement of it with pictures of the Passion of Christ reinforced her position as innocent victim. Mary Stewart was preparing for her final role, that of a martyr for the Catholic faith.

Four days later, on 27 November, Châteauneuf was sent to Elizabeth to remonstrate against the sentence. On 1 December he was joined by Pomponne de Bellièvre, the personal envoy of Henri III, and they were given an audience at Richmond six days later. They pled for Mary's inviolability as a sovereign princess, invoked the sacred rights of hospitality and pointed out that Elizabeth would gain the enmity of 'Catholic princes' if the execution were carried out. They ended by assuring Elizabeth of the immortal obligation France would feel for Elizabeth's mercy.

Elizabeth largely ignored their arguments, telling them that there were no precedents for the current situation and that nothing they said would make her change her mind, adding 'I pray that God will guard and keep me and give me the power to keep the peace of my people.' She ended by saying that it was impossible to save her own life and preserve that of the said queen.

On 10 December Elizabeth took another tentative step along the road to confirming the death sentence when she told Paulet that parliament had forced her 'against our own natural disposition . . . to yield thereto'. Mary was to stay at Fotheringhay as Paulet's charge but under the overall command of the Sheriff of Nottingham, who would 'without delay do execution upon her', presumably when he received a warrant. Later that month Burghley wrote another memorandum to himself: 'The Queen of Scots is so afflicted as she can live but few years or days and [is] therefore not to be douted [feared] but rather to be pitied over.' But he did nothing to prevent the now-unstoppable juggernaut of justice.

Paulet had made clear that the instructions to remove the cloth of state had come from the Privy Council and not personally from Elizabeth, and on 19 December, after protests and petty obstructions from Paulet, Mary was finally allowed to write to Elizabeth. Mary, who was clearly furious at Paulet's attitude, showed him the unsealed letter, then, mockingly, rubbed it against her face to show the absence of poison, wrapped it in white silk and sealed it with Spanish wax. She then gave it to him for onward transmission.

Mary told her cousin that Jesus Christ had given her the power

417

'to endure the unjust calumnies, accusations and condemnations (of those who have no such jurisdiction over me) with a constant resolution to suffer death, for upholding the obedience and authority of the apostolical Roman Catholic Church'. She then asked to be buried with 'the other queens of France, my predecessors, especially near the late queen, my mother' and hoped that 'a place will not be given to me near the kings your predecessors'. She asked for a public execution so that no rumours of suicide might spread. Mary returned the diamond which Elizabeth had given her on her arrival in Scotland in 1561 and asked permission to send a jewel and a last adieu to her son. She signed the letter 'Your sister and cousin, prisoner wrongfully, Marie Royne.' Previous to the abdication her signature had simply been the bold 'MARIE'.

Giving the feeble excuses of bandaged arms and a lack of direct commands, Paulet delayed sending Mary's letter since he hoped the order for her execution was soon to arrive and would render the letter useless, but 1587 dawned with Elizabeth no nearer to giving the fatal order.

Elizabeth saw the ambassadors again on 6 January and asked them if they saw any other way out of the dilemma since 'she had never shed so many tears . . . as she had done in this unfortunate affair'. They had no solution to offer and both sides knew very well that they were simply performing a diplomatic charade. Mary's dread of assassination was increased when on 7 January a new plot to murder Elizabeth came to light. It involved the confession by a debtor by the name of Thomas Stafford, a 'lewd miscontented person', in a London prison. He intended to poison the queen's shoes or stirrups, by some method which was never revealed. Most people suspected Walsingham of inventing the confessions to break the royal inertia.

Paulet continued his petty privations by removing Melville from Mary's service. He was her mâitre d'hôtel and one of her most long-standing servants. Then, late in January, Elizabeth wrote to Paulet – but not with the hoped-for death warrant. Elizabeth thanked him for his diligence and assured him, 'If I reward not such deserts, let me lack when I have most need of you.' This was puzzling since it seemed to promise a reward for a deed as yet undone, but all became clear on 2 February in a letter from Walsingham and Davison telling Paulet that the Queen was disappointed

> that you have not in all this time . . . found out some way of shortening the life of the Scots Queen, considering the great peril she is hourly subject to so long as the said queen shall live. And therefore she taketh it most unkindly, that men, professing that love towards her that you do, should in a kind of sort, for lack of discharging our duties, cast the burden upon her, knowing as you do her indisposition to shed blood, especially of one of that sex and quality and so near her in blood as that queen is.

Paulet was being asked to murder Mary in secret, and given that Walsingham's letter would have arrived after Elizabeth's, then the English queen could claim ignorance of the whole affair. She could simply say that she was merely congratulating Paulet on his past service and did not intend to provoke him to murder.

Paulet replied immediately: 'I am so unhappy as living to see this unhappy day in which I am required, by direction from my most gracious sovereign, to do an act which God and the law forbiddeth. My goods and my life are at her Majesty's disposition and I am ready to lose them the next morrow should it please her . . . But God forbid I should make so foul a shipwreck of my conscience, or leave so great a blot to my poor posterity, as to shed blood without law or warrant.' Loyal and unimaginative as he was, there was a line Paulet would not cross. Mary told Paulet of her fears of secret death and he was furious that she could have thought him capable of such a deed. 'He did not exercise cruelty like the Turk.'

The rumour mill, its handle vigorously turned by Walsingham, in spite of a severe illness, continued to feed anti-Marian hysteria. 'Information came daily from Ireland and Wales of forces of people in arms, and the report scattered abroad that Fotheringhay Castle was broken, the prisoners gone.' The Constable of

Honiton raised a 'hue and cry' to seek the fugitive Mary in the West Country. Elizabeth realised that she was now cornered. She had 'been backward and unwilling to yield to that which all her realm desired and sued at her hands'. The members of the Privy Council watched her with great care as she met with ambassadors from France and Scotland who pled, unsuccessfully, for Mary's life.

The death warrant had been drawn up, and on the day that these ambassadors left, Lord High Admiral Howard took Davison aside at Greenwich and told him to take the warrant to Elizabeth.

What then took place is, like so much else concerning Mary Stewart, shrouded in legend, but, according to his testimony at his subsequent trial, Davison visited Elizabeth with a bundle of papers for signature. She noted that the weather was mild – this was 1 February – and hoped he was getting enough exercise. He agreed with her about the weather and told her he was quite well. She then asked if the papers he was holding contained the document from Lord High Admiral Howard. He told her that it did and handed them to her. She read the death warrant, called for pen and ink and then signed it where it lay 'upon her mats'. She then asked Davison if he was not sorry to see it done, and he replied that he preferred to see a live queen even at the cost of another. Elizabeth told him to take the warrant to the Lord Chancellor for the Great Seal to be attached and 'to use it as secretly as might be'. He was to tell Walsingham, although Elizabeth felt that the relief might kill him, and to instruct him that the execution was to be performed indoors and not publicly on the castle green. She then gave Davison precise instructions that she should be told no more of the matter until everything was resolved.

Another version of the event, unconfirmed by Davison, was that he gave the bundle of papers to Elizabeth and she signed them all without reading any of them then, turning to Davison, said, 'You know what has occurred?' Davison said he did and left for the Lord Chancellor. This sounds very much like a version of the event after it had passed through the Tudor spin doctors.

The next day, Elizabeth asked Davison if the warrant had been sealed, and, when she was told that it had been, asked him, 'What needeth that haste?' On 5 February, she received the news that Paulet would not undertake a secret assassination. Elizabeth was furious at 'that precise fellow Paulet' but plans for secret assassination were not entirely abandoned and Elizabeth declared, 'I can do without him. I have Wingfield, who will not draw back.' The Privy Council, realising that Elizabeth was wavering again, sent Beale, the Clerk of the Council, to Fotheringhay with the warrant. Beale noted, 'One Wingfield should have been appointed for this deed . . . but . . . by the example of Edward II and Richard II it was not thought convenient or safe to proceed covertly, but openly according to statute.'

To perform the deed, Walsingham sent one Bull with his 'instrument' as executioner. Bull would carry his axe and already knotted 'restraining ropes' should Mary prove violent. He was to be disguised as a servant and paid £10 for his efforts. 'There [was] great care taken to have the matter pass in secrecy' and Walsingham gave precise instructions as to who should attend the execution. Mary's jewels should be seized in case her servants 'embezzle them' and after death she was to be buried 'uppermost' at night in the parish church. George Talbot, Earl of Shrewsbury, as Earl Marshal, would be in overall command, although he tried, unsuccessfully, to resign his earl marshalship in favour of Burghley. He was to be aided by the Earl of Kent, while the legalities would be seen to by Thomas Andrews, Sheriff of Nottingham.

Paulet had been kept fully informed of what was happening in London and was embarrassed on 4 February, when Bourgoing asked for permission to leave the castle in order to gather herbal remedies for Mary's rheumatism. Paulet prevaricated and the next day Mary realised that messengers were arriving at Fotheringhay. One of them was, in fact, Beale. She then told Bourgoing that he need not collect his cures, since she would have no need of them. A controlled sense of calm was descending on Mary Stewart.

By 7 February, the principal characters had arrived at

Fotheringhay, although Shrewsbury was lodged outside the castle, and at about eight or nine o'clock, accompanied by Paulet and Drury, they assembled outside Mary's first-floor apartment to deliver the news. Mary's lady told them that the queen had taken off her mantle and was preparing for bed. Nevertheless they were admitted.

There was an air of embarrassment in the room. The earls were bareheaded but remained standing – a confused mixture of insult and deference. Mary was now wearing her mantle over her nightdress and sat barefoot in an armchair at the foot of her bed with a small table in front of her, flanked by her waiting women with the ever-careful Bourgoing at her shoulder.

Her old gaoler, Shrewsbury, apologised for the necessity of Elizabeth's actions and Beale then read the warrant. Mary listened, then praised God at the news: 'I am of no good and no use to anyone.' She delighted that she was to be freed from her imprisonment and continual affliction. 'All my life has been full of tragedies and I am glad that God is taking me from the hands of my enemies.' For the last time she announced that if only she could have met Elizabeth then their differences could have been settled to everyone's satisfaction. She then put her hand on an English-language Bible and swore that she was innocent of all crimes.

Kent, being 'fiery hot in religion', begged her, since she only had a few hours to live, to think of her conscience and turn to the Church of England. She was once again offered solace from the Dean of Peterborough, Dr Fletcher, but Mary asked for her own chaplain, de Préau. This request, however, was denied. She asked if pleas for her life had been made by other Christian princes and was told there had been, but to no avail. She was not told, nor did she ask, if her son James had been pleading on her behalf. Mary then asked when she would die. 'Tomorrow at eight in the morning,' said a stuttering Shrewsbury. She requested that she be taken for burial either to Reims or to St Denis, only to be told that Elizabeth had expressly forbidden this. Her plea for a guarantee that her dispositions to her servants would be honoured was likewise rejected by the earls, who told her that they had no powers to give such guarantees. She asked after Nau and Curle, and when told that they were both still alive she protested that they had betrayed her and would live, while she, who had been steadfast, would die.

Throughout the interview she had remained calm and almost business-like, much to the astonishment and relief of Shrewsbury and his party. However, by now Mary's servants, including Bourgoing, were all in tears. There being nothing more to say, the officials withdrew.

Mary prayed with her female servants, then, still in a calm, orderly mood, put what money she had left into paper packets, writing names on them. She was brought supper but ate little. She forgave her servants for anything they might have done and then asked their forgiveness for any harshness she may have shown to them. She gave away what was left in her wardrobe – Bourgoing got two rings, two small silver boxes, two lutes, Mary's music-book and her red bed hangings. She then wrote to de Préau asking him what prayers she should say and begging him to give her absolution for her sins.

Mary then made her final testament, appointing the Duc de Guise, the Bishop of Ross and du Ruisseau, her nominal chancellor looking after her affairs in France, to be executors and asking for provision for requiem masses to be said in Reims and at St Denis in the presence of her servants. An annual 'obit' or requiem was to be funded by the sale of property at Fontainebleau. Further, 57,000 francs was to be distributed among her servants and friends after her debts had been settled and after her personal servants had received their arrears. She also made charitable provision for poor children and scholars in Reims.

Mary then wrote a letter to Henri III, her brother-in-law, in her own hand. The large handwriting is firm and clear with no sign of nervousness and the letter covers three pages. Beginning 'Royal brother, having by God's will, for my sins I think, thrown myself into the power of the Queen my cousin, at whose hands I have suffered much for almost twenty years', Mary went on to declare her innocence of any crime and said that she was condemned for the Catholic faith and her 'god-given right to the English crown'. She complained that she was deprived of her chaplain 'although he is in the building', and so could not receive the last sacrament. She commended her servants and her son to him, 'as far as he deserves, for I cannot answer for him' and sent him 'two rare stones, talismans against illness'. She signed the letter 'Wednesday, at two after midnight. Your most loving and true sister, MARIE R'.

Mary then lay fully dressed on her bed and asked Jane Kennedy to read to her from the life of some great sinner. Kennedy read the story of the good thief, but Mary interrupted her: 'In truth he was a great sinner, but not as great as I have been. I wish to take him for my patron for the time that remains to me. May my Saviour, in memory of his Passion, remember me and have mercy on me, as He had of him at the hour of his death.' She asked a lady to bring a bandage to be used to bind around her eyes on the scaffold, selecting a silk handkerchief with gold trimming. Mary then lay on her back on the bed with her arms folded.

At six in the morning, 'The said 8th day of February being come, and time and place appointed for the execution, the said Queen being of stature tall, of body corpulent, round shouldered, her face fat and broad, double chinned and hazel eyed her borrowed hair auburn', Mary dressed carefully in a skirt and bodice of black satin over a russet brown petticoat and an over mantle of black satin embroidered with gold and trimmed with fur. On her head she wore a white crepe headdress and a long lace veil. There were scented beads as a pomander around her neck along with an Agnus Dei, as well as a crucifix and a gold rosary at her waist. Having fully dressed she went into an antechamber and prayed, kneeling with some difficulty at her prie-dieu and surrounded by her ladies. Now everyone could hear the sounds of the construction of the scaffold being completed below them in the Great Hall. Seeing that she was in some physical distress, Bourgoing gave her some bread and wine as the Sheriff of Nottingham knocked on the door for her to accompany him. Bourgoing put him off for a few moments and on the second knock, Mary said, 'Yes, let us go.'

She took her ivory crucifix, promised it to Bourgoing, but, for the moment lacking a priest, she gave it to Hannibal Stuart, acting as her valet de chambre, to carry it in front of her. Then, with an over-harsh regard for security, her servants were forbidden to accompany her any further in case they dipped their handkerchiefs in her blood for relics. Even more absurdly, her guardians were afraid that the female servants might cry out and distress the soldiers. Two of Paulet's soldiers took her by the arms and, with her crucifix in her hand, she came haltingly down the stairs into the hall where she was met by Kent and Shrewsbury. The scaffold was complete, and a huge fire was roaring in the fireplace. The assembled company, thought to number nearly 300, fell silent as Mary entered.

Mary alone was calm, her servants, still separated from her, were weeping to distraction, and the officials – perhaps remembering her remark of the 'theatre of the world' – were nervous to the point of terror that something might go wrong. None of them had any previous experience in what was to occur. Many sovereigns had met violent deaths in both England and Europe, but a judicial execution was totally unprecedented.

Inexplicably, considering the severity shown to her in other respects, Mary was allowed a reunion with Melville at the foot of the stairs. She besought him to serve James as he had served her and he said, 'Madame, it will be the sorrowfullest message that ever I carried when I shall report to him that my Queen and mistress is dead.' She told him that 'today, good Melville, thou seest the end of Mary Stewart's miseries'. In this conversation Mary used the familiar form 'tu'; it was the only time she used it when speaking to a servant. Kent and Shrewsbury, confident that everything would now go according to plan, allowed her five or six servants to accompany her, even, after some masculine prevarication, allowing two women, Jane Kennedy and Elizabeth Curle, to attend her along with Melville, Bourgoing, Gourion, her surgeon and Gervais, her apothecary.

There were so many witnesses to the execution, each with their own unique memory, that the accounts of the subsequent events are varied in many details. Today's police forces will attest that four witnesses to an event will produce four quite different versions; Mary's execution was no exception. According to Robert Wise, who wrote an account for Burghley immediately after the event, Mary climbed the two steps to the twelve-foot-broad scaffold, which was draped in black cloth, as was the block itself – some other reports tell us that the block was only a few inches high. Paulet helped her up the steps and she said to him, 'I thank you, sir. This is the last trouble I shall ever give you.' She then sat on a low stool with Kent and Shrewsbury beside her and listened in silence as Beale read out the death warrant again. Mary was not silent, however, when the Dean of Peterborough launched into a long sermon attempting to convert her to Protestantism. The seventeenth-century historian William Camden called it 'a tedious speech'. Mary interrupted him: 'Good Mr Dean, trouble not yourself any more about this matter, for I was born in this religion [Catholicism], have lived in this religion, and am resolved to die in this religion.' Unperturbed, the dean went on, calling on God to confound Elizabeth's enemies and praying for mercy for all. Mary then prayed aloud in Latin, knelt and prayed in English for the Catholic Church, for James, for Elizabeth and for an end to her troubles. The executioner Bull and his assistant then begged forgiveness, and Mary said, 'I forgive you with all my heart. For I hope this death shall give an end to all my troubles.' As Mary started to remove her outer clothes, one of the executioners took her Agnus Dei since, traditionally, the executioners were allowed the jewellery and clothes of their victim as an extra reward. However, Mary took it back from him saying that she had promised the jewel to one of her servants. Then, as Bull continued and made to remove her sleeves she prevented him: 'I am not used to be undressed by such attendants, or to put off my clothes before so much company.' She took the pins out of her hair herself, while Kennedy and Curle removed her outer clothes down to her underskirt and bodice and gave her fresh sleeves. All these

426

garments were a crimson or russet colour so that not only was Mary now the only person in the hall not wearing black, she was now dressed in the red signifying a Catholic martyr. Mary Stewart had prepared carefully for her apotheosis.

Her women, in spite of promises to the contrary, were now weeping uncontrollably. Dry-eyed, she asked them not to cry and assured them she would pray for them. She made the sign of the cross over her servants and the silk handkerchief was tied around her eyes. Bourgoing, another eye-witness, said that she knelt in front of her stool and recited the penitential psalm '*In te, domine, confido*', then stretched her neck upwards. Perhaps Mary was expecting to be despatched in the French manner with a sword. Bull realised that Mary had not seen the low block and led her to it, where, gropingly, she was laid prone. Other witnesses tell us that she knelt on finishing her prayers. However, now understanding what was to take place, Mary lifted her chin clear of the block and laid her neck down. There was no need for 'restraining ropes', but one of the executioners had now to move her hands clear of the block otherwise they too would have been struck with the axe. Then, in the total silence which filled the hall, Mary, in a loud voice, called out '*In manus tuas, domine, commendam spiritum meum*' 'three or four times' and Bull swung his axe. It was a short-handled woodman's felling axe.

Presumably through nervousness, he mistook his aim and the blade struck Mary on the back of the head. She made no movement and his next blow severed her head from her body except for a piece of sinew, which Bull then sawed through. Finally her head rolled into the straw. 'Thus died Mary, Queen of Scots, in the 45th year of her age, and the 19th of her imprisonment.' It was about ten o'clock in the morning.

According to custom, Bull lifted up her head and declared, 'God save the Queen', while the Dean of Peterborough added, 'So perish all the Queen's enemies' and the Earl of Kent alone said 'amen'. The solemnity of the moment was ruined when Mary's head fell from Bull's grasp, leaving him holding the silk bandage and an auburn wig. The hair of the fallen head was grey and sparse. Bull and his assistant went to pull off Mary's garters and were surprised to find a little dog under her skirts. It had clearly come from her bedchamber and all attempts to remove it failed until it trotted up to lie between her neck and her head, covered in Mary's blood.

Melville led Mary's servants to gather up their mistress's body but they were forced from the hall and locked in their rooms, where, later, the little paper packets of personal gifts were taken from them. Under Paulet's orders the gates of Fotheringhay were locked after Lord Talbot, Shrewsbury's son, had galloped off to take the news to London. The guards removed Mary's body to an adjacent room, used as a presence chamber, where, bizarrely, her body was wrapped in the green cloth taken from her confiscated billiard table. The scaffold and block, along with her clothes, were all publicly burnt and the hall was diligently scrubbed free of blood so that no relics of the dead queen would remain as objects of veneration for her supporters. Even the little dog was washed clean.

An hour later, her severed head was displayed on a black velvet cushion in one of the windows of the hall in sight of the crowds outside in the courtyard. The next day, Mary's corpse was hastily embalmed by 'a country doctor, assisted by the village surgeon' and her internal organs examined by the 'country doctor' who found no abnormalities except for the presence of internal fluid, 'which gives credence to her indisposition being the result of dropsy'. Her organs were then secretly burnt by the sheriff. A wax death mask was taken from her head and her body was wrapped in waxed linen and placed in a double coffin of oak and lead. This huge coffin was left alone in the centre of the great hall. Paulet forbade Mary's servants to pray beside it and had all the locks on the doors of the hall sealed up.

As night fell on 9 February only Mary's servants were still living under strict confinement while Paulet and Drury's guards kept to their own quarters. Mary's little dog refused all food and pined itself to death. The gates of the castle were locked shut and in the centre of the great building the sealed Great Hall was empty except for the double coffin containing the earthly remains of Mary Stewart.

CHAPTER TWENTY

A place near the kings

୬୫

When Lord Talbot reached Greenwich with the expected news, Elizabeth launched into one of the most elaborate, if totally unbelievable, charades of her reign. While church bells were rung and bonfires celebrated Mary's death throughout England, Elizabeth shed 'an abundance of tears' and alternated between hysterical grief and political fury, claiming that her entire Privy Council had betrayed her and that she had only signed the death warrant 'for safety's sake' – whatever that meant – and she immediately had Davison thrown into the Tower. Knowing full well that he was cast in the role of scapegoat, he described his and Elizabeth's actions in detail, realising that he would be found guilty of having betrayed the queen. He was sentenced to imprisonment in the Tower and fined the huge sum of £10,000. The fine was never collected, he continued to be paid his salary as Elizabeth's private secretary, enjoyed a liberal regime in the Tower and was released after a year with a life pension. Burghley was – temporarily – banished from the royal presence, Walsingham remained diplomatically ill, and Hatton, who as Lord Chancellor had affixed the seal to the warrant, expected his arrest by the minute. Beale, who had carried the warrant, was banished to a junior position in York and, unfairly, was perhaps the only one to suffer in the long term. In April Paulet was appointed Chancellor of the Garter and breathed a sigh of relief.

All seaports were closed and traffic with Europe stopped for three weeks, but a garbled version of the events was smuggled out by Châteauneuf. The English ambassadors in Paris were banished from the court and a judicial indictment of Mary's trial as illegal was sent to London. On 12 March 1587 a Requiem Mass was held in Notre Dame, attended by the entire French court in deep mourning, totally ignoring Mary's wishes for either St Dénis or Reims. The funeral oration was given by Renauld de Beaune, Archbishop of Bourges, and was eulogistic to say the least: 'It was not easy to find so many [virtues] centred on one human being, for besides that marvellous beauty which attracted the eyes of all the world, she had a disposition so excellent, an understanding so clear and judgement so sound as could rarely be paralleled by a person of her sex and age . . . she possessed great courage but it was tempered by feminine gentleness and sweetness'. He went on to reminisce on how he had seen her married in the same church. He deplored her execution, horrified 'to see that form which honoured the nuptial bed of a King of France, falling dishonoured on a scaffold . . . It appears as if God had chosen to render her virtues more glorious by her afflictions.' He called on Christian princes everywhere to invade England and avenge the death of the martyr. Antonia Fraser points out that this oration may have been used as the basis of Edmund Burke's eulogy on Marie Antoinette some 200 years later. The point of the oration was not personal grief, however, but rather public show on behalf of the Valois monarchy and this requiem can be taken as the start of the cult of Mary Stewart.

Shortly after the requiem, lives and tributes, some with no regard for truth, flooded on to the market. First to publish was Sartorio Loscho with a wildly romantic tale in which Mary fled Scotland to sail to France but was cruelly diverted to England by contrary winds. Anonymous pamphlets came next the 'Discours de la Mort de Marie, Royne d'Ecosse' was followed by an anonymous life in German. A Latin pamphlet was published in Cologne in which the Dean of Peterborough was a Calvinist minister and his sermon was full of 'diabolical temptations'. The author ended with 'Long Live Mary, a secular martyr in Christ.' Adam Blackwood, probably our first homegrown Mariolater, published his *La mort de la Royne d'Ecosse*, in which the Sheriff of

Nottingham – a bold malapert person – bursts in on Mary while she is in mid prayer, then paces up and down behind her and drags her to the door. The executioners – 'butchers' – attempt to tear her clothes from her, and they drag her corpse unceremoniously away in spite of the anguished screams of the waiting women. Poems of praise also followed in abundance, with Elizabeth cast as Jezebel; there were sonnets, poems with anagrams of Mary's name and funeral odes by Malherbe, Robert Garnier and Cardinal du Perron. Uncomfortable facts were glossed over and events rearranged to fit the accusations. In one pamphlet, Elizabeth was accused of creating the Act of Association solely to entrap Mary in the Babington plot, while the completely innocent Mary was merely seeking her freedom from illicit imprisonment. The smoke of legend was starting to swirl thickly around Mary Stewart.

In Scotland, the execution might have been the cause of immediate and violent reactions, since Elizabeth had murdered their queen and the mother of their 21-year-old king. James's ambassadors had been in London since the previous December, pleading for Mary's life. Indeed, Elizabeth had been reluctant to give them a decision and to let them return to Scotland. Since there was a league of friendship between James and Elizabeth the ambassadors were treading on eggshells and, in any case, the king's view of his mother, carefully formed by Elizabeth and George Buchanan, was ambivalent. He said, 'My honour constrains to insist for her life,' while telling Walsingham, 'Let her be put in the Tower or some other firm manse and kept from intelligence.' There were rumours that 'an unnamed person' had offered to trade Mary's life in turn for James renouncing his claim to the English throne. James begged Elizabeth not to take him for a chameleon, which he seemed to be, and declared, 'How fond and inconstant I were if I should prefer my mother to the title let all men judge.' This statement, like many of James's declarations, could be read in any number of ways. Elizabeth was irritated by his seeming ambivalence and wrote to him, 'The greatest hinder which our negotiations have found is a persuasion that either

431

your majesty deals superficially with the matter or that with time you may be moved to digest it.' Her reply to James's ambassadors was much more direct: 'Tell your king what good I have done him in holding the crown on his head since he was born, and that I mind to keep the league that now stands between us, and if he break, it shall be a double fault.'

In fact there was no co-ordinated reaction in Scotland. The Borderers took Mary's death as a justification to recommence raiding and diplomatic ties were broken for a time by 'the fury of the people'. James himself seemed grief-stricken enough in public, but 'He said that night to some few that were beside him, "Now I am sole King."' Courtiers also reported, 'The king never moved his countenance at the rehearsal of his mother's execution, nor leaves his pastime and is hunting more than before.' There was undoubtedly bitterness in Scotland and James was rebuked for cowardice and foolishness when he merely called for general mourning instead of military intervention; rumours abounded of levies being called up with armed men massing for an invasion of England. But James was very careful of the league of friendship between himself and Elizabeth and he knew very well that all he had to do was wait peacefully and the throne of England would be his. Formally he gave as his excuse for inactivity that he was 'unable to revenge the heinous murder committed against my dearest mother'. In the past he had been too young and 'at all times bygone detained in captivity', then, released from the grip of the rebel nobility, he had lacked money and finally, with regard to 'the divers factions of spiritual and temporal estates, every one regarding himself, and not one me' he could not unify Scotland behind him. He had written to Elizabeth with an ineffectual plea for mercy in which he did not stress Mary's innocence, but merely asked for Elizabeth's forgiveness. At twenty-one years old, he was already growing into his nickname of 'the wisest fool in Christendom'.

A year later Jane Kennedy returned to Scotland and gave James a graphic account of the events she had witnessed in Fotheringhay's Great Hall, which made him 'very sad and pensive'. In May 1588 Elizabeth even proposed that they 'drink a large draught at the river of Lethe' and, at least as a matter of contention between them, the event could be forgotten. Paulet had finally allowed Mary's letters to be delivered and Mendoza corresponded with Philip II as to his claim to the English crown – since it was clear that James would not cloud his own future by embracing Catholicism. In fact, Mary's final will did not contain the clause disinheriting James, and Philip, therefore, had no claim.

Thus in Scotland, England, France and Spain only a charade of outrage was being acted out. Elizabeth claimed she had never intended her cousin's execution and had publicly punished the courtiers she blamed for the deed. In Europe, while the Guise family undoubtedly felt personal loss, a burden was lifted from Catholic consciences as Mary Stewart no longer existed as a wronged Catholic queen to be liberated and avenged. But the body of Mary Stewart still lay, unburied, in the Great Hall of Fotheringhay Castle. Walsingham's instructions for a temporary burial in the parish church had been ignored, but even Elizabeth realised that some more permanent arrangement had to be made, and at the end of July she issued instructions for Mary's burial. Alive, Mary had been a Catholic threat, but dead she was an exiled queen and cousin to Elizabeth and therefore fully entitled to all the pomp of a state funeral. Also, the lavish ceremony might go some way toward easing Elizabeth's conscience.

At ten in the evening on 30 July 1587, Sir William Dethick, Garter King at Arms, set out from Fotheringhay by torchlight with five heralds and an escort of forty horses to accompany the coffin which was now in a royal coach pulled by four horses. The coach was converted into a hearse by being covered in black velvet, 'richly set forth with escutcheons of the arms of Scotland and little pennons' around it. The cortège moved at walking pace and, immediately behind the heralds, walked Melville, Bourgoing and four of Mary's household. The remainder of her household had now been brought from Chartley and were lodged at Fotheringhay. The funeral party reached the bridge

433

over the River Nene outside Peterborough at two in the morning, where it was met by the Bishop of Peterborough, the dean and chapter of the cathedral and the Clarenceaux herald. At the cathedral itself was a reception party of 'choristers and singing men' and inside was a freshly prepared grave in an aisle opposite to the grave of Catherine of Aragon, Henry VIII's first wife. She had died at nearby Kimbolton twenty-one years previously and the cathedral sexton, the 81-year-old Robert Scarlet, could now proudly claim that he had dug the graves of two queens. The huge double coffin, weighing nearly a metric tonne, was lowered into the grave, which was then bricked up.

The following day the participants in what was to be a royal funeral arrived to lodge overnight at the bishop's palace, where the hall had a chair of state with Elizabeth's arms. She was not present but was represented by the Countess of Bedford.

At eight o'clock the next day the countess was escorted by the gentlemen ushers under a canopy of purple velvet and processed in royal state to the Great Hall of the bishop's palace, which now had a wax effigy of Mary, fully dressed. The use of a wax effigy was normal since royal funerals were often held some time after death and the embalming techniques of the day were not totally effective. In Mary's case the corpse had lain undisturbed for five months, the weather was very hot and decomposition was probably far advanced. The funeral procession now formed with heralds, peers, peeresses, knights and ladies in mourning. About 240 people surrounded the effigy as they entered the cathedral, which was draped in black up to six or seven yards in height. Every second pillar was draped with shields, some with Mary's arms, some with François II's or Darnley's, their arms impaled on Scotland's. The choir was also hung with black. Mary's household was allowed to attend, although the Catholic servants withdrew after the procession and waited in the cloister. Melville and Barbara Mowbray, as Protestants, remained. De Préau was allowed to attend 'with a golden crucifix about his neck, which he did wear openly, and being told that the people murmured and disliked it, he said he would do it though he died

434

for it'. There is no record of Paulet attending and he was presumably glad to be totally freed from his duties. The effigy was laid on a catafalque, some twenty feet square and towering above the altar, which was covered in black baize with heraldic arms. On top of the coffin 'was set two escutcheons of the Scottish arms, cut out in paste board, gilded, and an imperial crown gilded and cut out in paste board'. Dean Fletcher had stage-managed the impressive ceremony, but a sermon of astonishing blandness was given by the Bishop of Lincoln. Lord Bedford then laid a coat of mail, a helm, a sword and a shield before the altar, which were afterwards hung above the tomb. The heralds broke their staves into the tomb and the procession returned to the bishop's palace for lunch. 'The servants of the dead queen were in a separate room mingling many tears with their food and drink.' Overall, it was a ceremony lavish enough to have pleased Mary's Valois preferences, and for Elizabeth it meant an end to her relationships with her troublesome cousin. It had cost Elizabeth £321.

There was no inscription over the grave until Adam Blackwood, a servant of Mary, made a pilgrimage to Peterborough and erected an epitaph. The original was in Latin, but, translated it reads:

Mary, Queen of Scots, daughter of a king, widow of the King of France, cousin and next heir to the Queen of England, endowed with royal virtues and a royal mind (the right of Princes being oftentimes in vain implored) by barbarous and tyrannical cruelty, the ornament of our age, and truly Royal light is extinguished. By the same unrighteous judgement both Mary Queen of Scots with natural death, and all surviving kings (now made common persons) are punished with civil death. A strange and unusual kind of monument this is, wherin the living are included with the dead; for with the Sacred ashes of this blessed Mary, know that the Majesty of all Kings and Princes lieth here violated and prostrated. And because regal secrecy doth enough and more admonish kings of their duty – traveller, I say no more.

This was swiftly taken down.

The remaining servants were released two months later. Bourgoing was allowed to return to France and given service at the court of Henri III, presumably when he delivered Mary's last letter. Gourion went to Mendoza and gave him the diamond ring destined for Philip II, who in turn fulfilled Mary's request, and paid her servants' wages. Elizabeth Curle joined Barbara Mowbray in exile and they were buried together in St Andrew's Church in Antwerp. Jane Kennedy returned to Scotland where she married Andrew Melville, and became part of James VI's court. Jane was sent as part of the mission to Denmark in 1589 to fetch the Princess Anne as James's queen and, sadly, got no further than the Firth of Forth; crossing from Burntisland to Edinburgh, her boat capsized and she drowned.

Fotheringhay Castle was abandoned to suffer the fate of all such deserted buildings. Dressed and cut stone is expensive and local farmers and builders used the castle as a convenient and free stone quarry. By the end of the eighteenth century almost nothing remained.

Mary's tomb in Peterborough remained undisturbed until on 14 August 1603, five months after his accession to the throne of England as James VI and I, the new king sent Dethick, Garter King at Arms, back to Peterborough with 'a rich pall of velvet' to be erected over his mother's grave. Sermons in her memory were to be said by the bishop and his omnipresent dean.

Just over ten years later James wrote again to the dean: 'We have ordered that her said body remaining now interred in that our cathedral church of Peterborough shall be removed to Westminster.' With a keen memory and a sharp mind for economy he insisted that the same velvet pall be used during the transfer. James had already overseen the construction of a marble effigy of Elizabeth in an aisle of the funeral chapel of Henry VII in Westminster Abbey. Henry VII had commissioned

436

the chapel for himself and his wife, Elizabeth of York, from the architect Robert Vertue, and it is dominated by the magnificent royal tomb by Torrigiano. Elizabeth Tudor had lain in an unmarked grave until James decided to honour her memory with a white marble effigy. Carved by Maximilian Colt and John de Criz, Elizabeth lies covered with pearls and other jewellery holding the sceptre of power and the orb of omnipotence.

Now James instructed William and Cornelius Cure to make the effigy for his mother Mary, who would lie in the opposite aisle. In contrast to the symbols of royal power held by Elizabeth, Mary Stewart lies with her hands together as if in prayer. Once again she has the widow's peaked headdress and a royal cloak. Although the lion of Scotland is at her feet, it is an effigy more suited to an abbess than a royal queen. The monument is 'of a grander scale as if to indicate the superiority of the mother to the predecessor, of the victim to the vanquisher.'

In September 1612, Mary's body in its great lead coffin was finally transferred from Peterborough and re-interred in Westminster Abbey. All Mary's detailed requests for burial in France among her family were ignored and she was now destined to lie in a Protestant abbey church only a few yards from her cousin Elizabeth. Mary's hope that 'a place will not be given to me near the kings your predecessors' was in vain. However, to be fair, James may never have known that such a wish had been expressed.

Inevitably, Mary's tomb became a focal point for Catholic worshippers and the predictable rumours of miracles began to spread. Some thirteen years later, the Catholic apologist William Dempster, who had never visited the tomb, wrote from Bologna that the place was 'resplendent with miracles'. Ever since her solitary stay in the locked hall at Fotheringhay people had prayed for Mary's intercession as near to her coffin as was possible, but worshippers offering similar prayers to her at Westminster were discouraged.

In 1750, Henry, Cardinal of York – brother to Mary's direct descendant Bonnie Prince Charlie – sought her canonisation from Pope Benedict XIV. Although Benedict was known as the

'Enlightenment' Pope and Mary was found to have shown 'magnanimity and charity' at her death, therefore qualifying as a martyr, Rome found that her case could not be advanced without certain proof of her innocence in Darnley's murder and adultery with Bothwell. Saints Peter, Paul, Augustine and Ignatius Loyola were all sinners forgiven by the Vatican and canonised, and therefore the Holy See's refusal to grant the necessary forgiveness in Mary's case cannot have been entirely on theological grounds. To grant such forgiveness it would have been necessary to accept Mary's guilt; to dispense with its necessity would have been to accept her innocence. Either decision was fraught with political dangers.

In 1887, on the tercentenary of Mary's death, Pope Leo XIII was approached, this time with a well-organised campaign led by no less than Queen Victoria, who was 'enthusiastic in favour of her great ancestress and thankful she had no connection with Queen Elizabeth'. Mary's canonisation was proposed to Rome along with forty other English martyrs. Cardinal Manning, with the recently-restored Catholic Archbishop of St Andrews and Edinburgh, William Smith, and supported by the English Jesuits, led a campaign of speeches and exhibitions, although England's leading Catholic peer, the Duke of Norfolk, opposed the plea. The campaign faltered in 1892 with the deaths of Cardinal Manning and Archbishop Smith, with the result that by 1902, Mary was the sole candidate and the matter came to a halt. According to the Vatican 'her file is still open'. A proposal to mark the 400th anniversary of her death in 1987 with her portrait on a postage stamp was also turned down.

Her burial site in Peterborough was despoiled, as was the tomb of Catherine of Aragon, by Cromwell's men during the English Civil War and today the site is marked by banners presented to the cathedral by the Peterborough Caledonian Society.

Sadly, it cannot be said that Mary had found peace at last in Westminster Abbey. In February 1869 a search was being made among the royal tombs for the unmarked grave of James VI and I. Under the supervision of Giles Gilbert Scott and accompanied by the master mason of the abbey, Arthur Stanley, Dean of Westminster, opened the tomb. Dean Stanley said,

> I was determined to make an entry by removing the stones on the south side of the southern aisle of the Chapel among which one was marked 'way'. This led to an ample flight of stone steps leading obliquely under the Queen of Scots' tomb. A startling, it may almost be said awful, scene presented itself. A vast pile of leaden coffins rose from the floor; some of full stature, the larger number varying from that of the full-grown child to the merest infant, confusedly heaped upon the others.

Along the north wall were two coffins 'much compressed' by the weight of four or five lesser coffins heaped upon them. The second lowest was the coffin of Arabella Stuart, with bones and skull visible through the cracked lead coffin. The lower one was saturated with pitch and was deeply compressed by the weight above but the lead had not given way. This was the huge coffin of Mary, and it was decided not to open it or move it. The other occupants of this royal dumping ground were Henry, Prince of Wales, the son of James VI and I who had died in 1612; two infants of Charles I; Mary, Princess of Orange; Prince Rupert; Anne Hyde, the first wife of James II; Elizabeth of Bohemia; ten children of James II and the tragic eighteen children of Queen Anne, none of whom had achieved adulthood. 'It was impossible to view this wreck and ruin of the Stuart dynasty without a wish if possible to restore something like order and decency amongst the relics of so much departed greatness.' The investigators tidied up the coffins of the children and the various funerary urns but Mary's coffin was left untouched. James's coffin was found in the opposite aisle, nearer to Elizabeth than to his mother.

Mary's tomb in London is magnificent but she lies among people she never knew and who were often her enemies. In Scotland, Mary is remembered by a replica of this tomb in the Museum of Scotland. In France there is nothing.

Mary Stewart, who lived 'at a time when poetry and romance were the prevalent literature of the age' had one of the most eventful lives it is possible to imagine, but it is difficult to find one as passive. Almost every one of the myriad events she experienced was the result of an accident, and the one event she went some way to initiate was the one which finally brought her to the scaffold. Mary Stewart is, therefore, remembered as part of a romantic tragedy – her role in that tragedy being the one of a thrice-widowed queen of great beauty. She was physically graceful, a keen dancer and horsewoman, enthusiastic for outdoor exercise, but intellectually no more than average for her position. When cornered in debate she always referred to her parentage and royal descent. No political or theological lessons had been learned from her Guise uncles, the careful tutelage of Diane de Poitiers in female guile was forgotten and the court diplomacy of Catherine de Medici was ignored. Mary enjoyed gallantry and flirtation but seemed to have had no interest in sex; socially she preferred the company of her close female friends and servants, to whom she was invariably kind, and only encouraged social interaction with male courtiers in the formal ceremonies of dances and pageants.

Her death was made unavoidable by the actions of her supporters – many of whom themselves went either to the block or a less merciful end – and she did nothing to deter these zealots. She allowed the effects of accidents to become overwhelming, until finally she, herself, was overwhelmed in a final accidental tragedy.

Appendix: The Scots Tongue

During the sixteenth century two languages were spoken in Scotland.

To the north and west of Glasgow the principal language was Gaelic, a Celtic language, totally different from English and generally only understood in the Highlands and Western Isles. In Galloway, to the south-west, there were still pockets of Gaelic speakers, although the Gaelic spoken there was closer to the version of the language spoken in Ireland. The rest of the country spoke various versions of Scots, and the argument as to whether these Scots tongues are a language or a dialect rages violently even today, when the debate has become coloured by political nationalism.

In 1074 Malcom Canmore's queen, Margaret – herself Hungarian – complained that the clerics of the Scottish Church spoke nothing but Gaelic, but over the next 200 years the Anglian speech of Northumbria had spread north as far as the Moray Firth, and it is the root of Scots. The Wars of Independence and the physical barrier of the Cheviot Hills meant that from the late fourteenth century on Scots and English developed in different ways. The English court did not abandon French as its language until 1400; in Scotland, the court and the people spoke Scots.

By the sixteenth century Scotland was speaking Middle Scots, which had a rich background of literature and drama all of its own. Here the court, the law and the ordinary people all spoke in the same way and, even as far into modern times as the eighteenth century, the legal profession prided itself on the richness of its Scots vocabulary. The Reformation in Scotland saw a shift

441

towards English – John Knox was heavily criticised for his English accent – and there was no Reformed Bible in Scots.

In *The Complaynt of Scotland*, believed to have been written by Robert Wedderburn in 1549, the author makes a claim for using plain Scots language in place of Latin. When reading these extracts it must be remembered that the spelling was entirely literal and therefore everything should be pronounced precisely as it is spelt. A description of a farmyard awakening gives scope for much onomatopoeia: 'Than the suyne began to quhryne quhen thai herd the asse rair quhilk gart the hennis kekkyl quhen the cockis creu.' The author explains his thinking in using Scots: 'For I thocht it not neccessair til hef fardit and lardit this tracteit with exquisite termis, quhilkis are nocht daily useit, bot rather I hef usit domestic Scottis langage, maist intelligibil for the vulgare pepil.' However, it was not 'intelligibil' for visitors. English ambassadors in Mary's Scotland would have found the speech impenetrable and French would have been used by both sides – much to Mary's relief. Mary's nurses and body servants would use Scots and she would have learnt it from them for use with her courtiers – who, as educated gentlemen would all also speak French.

The official language of government can be found in the minutes of the Privy Council. A case of a disturbance in Leith was raised before the council on 13 April 1572:

Forasmekle as my Lord Regentis Grace and Lordis of Secreit Counsale, considering that not only are the troubles the langar, bot the greittar confusion remains within this toun of Leyth, quhair His Grace, the Counsale and College of Justice remains, becaus of the impunitie gevin to offe-nouris, fautoris and furnissars of the rebellis and disobedient subjectis . . . the former ordinances and proclamationis being neglectit and not put to full execution.

A literary master of Scots was George Buchanan, who wrote *The Chameleon* in 1570. It was an attack on Mary, Darnley and Bothwell, and opens with a description of a strange animal:

Thair is a certane kynd of beist callit chamleon endgerderit in sic contreis as the sone has mair strength in than in this isle of Brettane, the quhilk albeit it be small of corporance noghtheless it is of ane strange nature, the quhilk makis it to be na less celebrat and spoken of than sum Beastis of greittar quantity.

South of the border the Middle English of Chaucer was giving way to the modern English which would flower in the works of Shakespeare at the end of the century. The written English of the sixteenth century is easily understood today, although the richness of local accents would have made spoken English difficult to grasp – as is the case with some strong regional accents today.

The gradual erosion of Scots in favour of English was vigorously encouraged in schools and broadcasting until very recently, and a rich and vivid vocabulary was nearly suppressed. Mercifully the tide was stemmed, and regional speech variations are now encouraged.

Notes on Sources

❦

1   As goodly a child as I have seen

Quotations during the early marriage negotiations are from Sir Ralph Sadler, *State Papers and Letters* (Edinburgh, 1809), or *Hamilton Papers* (ed. Joseph Bain, Edinburgh, 1890–92). Other quotations from ambassadors (throughout the book) are in the various *Calendars of State Papers*, or in *Letters and Papers, Foreign and Domestic, of the Reign of Henry VIII* (Vaduz, 1965). For the condition of Scotland, Robert Lindesay of Pitscottie, *Historie and Cronicles of Scotland* (Scottish Text Society, Edinburgh, 1899), is useful, as is *A Diurnal of Remarkable Occurrents* (Bannatyne Club, Edinburgh, 1833). Knox is quoted from John Knox, *The History of the Reformation in Scotland* (ed. W. Croft Dickinson, Edinburgh, 1949).

2   One of the most perfect creatures

A vital overview of the Rough Wooing is given by Marcus Merriman in the *The Rough Wooings* (East Linton, 2000), while a French view is given by Jean de Beaugué in *Histoire de la Guerre d'Ecosse: pendant les campagnes 1548 et 1549* (Maitland Club, Edinburgh, 1830). Pitscottie and the *Diurnal* give the Scottish background as does John Leslie in *The History of Scotland* (Scottish Text Society, 1888–95). Mary's journey to France is well documented by Jane Stoddart in *The Girlhood of Mary, Queen of Scots* (London, 1908) and Mary's childhood in general is dealt with by Joseph Stevenson, S.J., in *Mary Stuart, the First Eighteen Years of her Life*, (Edinburgh, 1886).

3   We may be very well pleased with her

For a general history in this period I used Frederic J. Baumgartner's *France in the Sixteenth Century* (London, 1995). The same author's *Henry II* (London, 1998) is a worthwhile biography, as are *Diane de Poitiers*, by

445

Ivan Cloulas (Paris, 1997), Henry Sedgewick's *The House of Guise* (London, 1938), and Lenonie Frieda's *Catherine de Medici* (London, 2003). The *Memoires* (London, 1739) of Pierre de Brantôme and his *Oeuvres Complètes* (Paris, 1832), vols 2 and 5, are useful for quotations but are often unreliable, while Baron Alphonse de Ruble is authoritative in his *La Première Jeunesse de Marie Stuart* (Paris, 1891). For Mary's arrival in France, see the recommended Baudouin-Matusek, 'Mary Stewart's Arrival in France' (*Scottish Historical Review*, vol. 69, 1990). Mary's letters are nearly all collected by Alexander Labanoff in *Receuil de Lettres, instructions et mémoires de Marie Stuart* (Paris, 1844–45), and can be identified chronologically. The list of female attributes can be found in *Selections from unpublished manuscripts . . . illustrating the Reign of Queen Mary* (Maitland Club, 1837).

4 The most amiable Princess in Christendom

Mary's Latin 'themes' can be found in *Queen Mary's Book*, by Mrs P. Stewart-Mackenzie Arbuthnot (London, 1907) and her 'donations' of the treaty of Fontainebleau are given in full by Labanoff. Details of her wedding are in *Discours du Grande et Magnifique Triomphe faict au Marriage de François et Marie Stuart* (Roxburghe Club, 1818) and in Douglas Hamer's 'The Marriage of Mary Queen of Scots to the Dauphin', *Library*, vol. 12, 1932.

5 She cannot long continue

Throckmorton's despatches are given in full in the *Calendar of State Papers, Elizabeth* under the relevant dates. Noel Williams's *Henry II, His Court and Times* (London, 1910) provides a thorough background for the reign.

6 She universally inspires great pity

Again Throckmorton's despatches are thorough while the *Histoire de l'Estat de France . . . sous la regne de François II*, by Regnier de la Planche (Paris, 1576) is full of gossip. The coronation of François is covered in *An historical and chronological treatise of the anointing and coronation of the kings of France* by M. Menin (London, 1723). Elizabeth's letters are quoted from the *Calendar of State Papers, Elizabeth* and the Scottish negotiations are in the *Calendar of State Papers, Scotland*.

446

7 We had landed in an obscure country

Mary's arrival in Scotland is covered by Knox and Brantôme and her entry into Edinburgh is given in the *Diurnal of Remarkable Occurrents* and by A. MacDonald in 'Mary Stewart's Entry into Edinburgh – An Ambiguous Triumph' *(Innes Review,* 1991), as well as the same author's 'The Triumph of Protestantism' *(Innes Review,* 1997*)*. The interviews with Knox are one-sidedly quoted from his *History of the Reformation,* and Randolph's despatches are quoted in both the *Calendars of State Papers, Scotland* and *Elizabeth.* A more balanced view of Knox/Mary is given by Jenny Wormald in 'Godly Reformer, Godless Monarch', an essay in *John Knox and the British Reformations,* ed. Roger Mason (Aldershot, 1998).

8 Dynastic entity

Mary's travels were well reported by Randolph and her establishment at Holyrood is described by J.S. Richardson in *The Abbey and Palace of Holyroodhouse* (HMSO, 1978), and also in *Inventaires de la Royne d'Escosse,* ed. Joseph Robertson (Bannatyne Club, Edinburgh, 1863). Details of her library are found in John Durkan's 'The Library of Mary Queen of Scots', an essay in *Mary Stewart, Queen in Three Kingdoms,* ed. Michael Lynch (Oxford, 1988). The interview with de Gouda is detailed in Randolph, who also quotes Mary's enjoyment while on her campaign in the Highlands.

9 The dancing grows hot

Melville's visit to Elizabeth is detailed by him in his *Memoirs of His Own Life* by Sir James Melville of Halhill (Bannatyne Club, Edinburgh, 1827) while the extracts from the official despatches are from the relevant *Calendars.*

10 Yonder long lad

The affairs of the Privy Council are published in the *Register of the Scottish Privy Council of Scotland* (Edinburgh, 1877–98). Randolph and the *Diurnal of Remarkable Occurrents* give full accounts of the events in Edinburgh. Throckmorton's despatches are included with Randolph's in the *Calendar of State Papers, Elizabeth.* Rizzio's murder is dealt with in every history of the period, especially in Antonia Fraser's *Mary, Queen of Scots* (London, 1969).

11 She wished she had never been married

Mary's will is cited by Robertson in his edition of *Inventaires*. Melville in his *Memoirs* supplements Killigrew's ambassadorial reports while du Croc can be found in *Calendar of State Papers, Foreign*. An account of Mary's sickness can be found in *Queen Mary at Jedburgh* by John Small (Edinburgh, 1881). These events are also recounted, unreliably, by Claude Nau in *Memorials of Mary Stewart*, ed. J. Stevenson, S.J. (Edinburgh, 1883). The account of the Craigmillar Bond is in Robert Keith, *History of the Affairs of Church and State in Scotland*, vol. 2 (Spottiswoode Society, Edinburgh, 1844–50) and is quoted by Labanoff. James's baptism is found in the *Diurnal of Remarkable Occurrents* as well as in Melville and du Croc.

12 Some evil turn

Darnley's murder is treated in some detail by Brigadier R.H. Mahon in *The Tragedy of Kirk o' Field* (Cambridge, 1930) and by M.H. Armstrong-Davison in *The Casket Letters* (London, 1965). The aftermath to the murder is given in the *Diurnal of Remarkable Occurrents* as well as in ambassadorial despatches and by John Maxwell, Lord Herries in his *Historical Memoirs*, ed. R. Pitcairn (Abbotsford Club, Edinburgh, 1836).

13 It does not appertain to subjects to reform their prince

Mary's imprisonment on Loch Leven is detailed by Nau, Melville, Keith and the ambassadors. *The Acts of the Parliaments of Scotland*, vols 2, 3 and 4 (Edinburgh, 1814–75) contain the formal results of Moray's dealings. A.M. Scott gives a detailed account of the battle of Langside in *The Battle of Langside* (Glasgow, 1885) and Mary's flight south is found in Herries' *Historical Memoirs* and in *History of the Burgh of Dumfries* by William McDowall (Dumfries, 1867).

14–17

With Mary now a virtual prisoner to the end of her life, her letters as edited by Labanoff become a major source as do the *Calendar of State Papers, Elizabeth* and *Scotland*. The Casket Letters are printed in full in Armstrong-Davison, *The Casket Letters* (London, 1965), and accounts of the examination at York are in *The First Trial of Mary, Queen of Scots* by Gordon Donaldson (London, 1969) and in John Hosack's *Mary Queen of*

Scots and her Accusers (Edinburgh, 1869). Nau gives us useful background, while Edmund Lodge's *Illustrations of British History* (London, 1791) and William Camden's *Annals of the most renowned and victorious Queen Elizabeth*, tr. T. Wallace MacCaffrey (Chicago, 1970) are essential sources. Quotes from Buchanan come from *The Tyrannous Reign of Mary, Queen of Scots: George Buchanan's Account*, ed. W.A. Gatherer (Edinburgh, 1958), 'The Uses of Adversity' is printed in *Queen Mary's Book*, by Mrs P. Stewart-Mackenzie Arbuthnot (London, 1907).

18–19

Mary's letters edited by Labanoff now alternate with *The Letter-books of Amias Poulet*, ed. John Morris, S.J. (London, 1874) and the *Calendar of State Papers, Elizabeth*, combined with the *Hatfield Papers*, vols 1 and 2 (Historic Manuscripts Commission, 1883) give the political background. The Babington plot is detailed in J.H. Pollen, S.J.'s *Queen Mary and the Babington Plot* (Scottish History Society, 1922) while Conyers Read in *Mr Secretary Walsingham and the Policy of Queen Elizabeth*, vol. 1 (Oxford, 1925) gives an overview. Mrs the Hon. Maxwell-Scott's *The Tragedy of Fotheringhay* (London, 1912) is essential as is *Marie Stuart, son Procès et son Exècution, d'après le Journal inédit de Bourgoing*, edited by M.R. Chantelauze (Paris, 1876). Elizabeth's behaviour in signing the death warrant is covered in *Life of William Davison*, N.H. Nicolas (London, 1823). There is an account of Mary's trial in *The trial of Mary, Queen of Scots* by A.F. Steuart (London, 1923).

20   A place near the kings

Accounts of Mary's burial is in *History and Antiquities of Peterborough Cathedral* by John Britton (London, 1828), and in *Collections Relative to the funerals of Mary, Queen of Scots*, by R. Pitcairn (Edinburgh, 1822). *Royal Westminster Abbey* by Bryan Bevan (London, 1976), describes the abbey today while Arthur Penrhyn Stanley's *Historical Monuments of Westminster Abbey* (London, 1868) relates the story of the post-burial investigations. Mary's posthumous reputation is dealt with in some detail by J.E. Phillips in *Images of a Queen* (Berkeley and Los Angeles, 1964).

Bibliography

꽃

The Acts of the Parliaments of Scotland eds. T. Thomson and C. Innes, 12 vols, Edinburgh, 1814–75

Anderson, James *Collections relating to the History of Mary Queen of Scotland,* London, 1727

Arbuthnot, Mrs P. Stewart-Mackenzie *Queen Mary's Book,* London, 1907

Armstrong-Davison, M.H. *The Casket Letters: a solution to the mystery of Mary, Queen of Scots and the murder of Lord Darnley,* London, 1965

Arnold, Janet *Lost from Her Majesty's Back,* Costume Society, London, 1980

Bailey, Aubrey G. *Official Guide to Tutbury,* Gloucester, 1972

Bain, Joseph, ed. *The Hamilton Papers: Letters and Papers illustrating the Political Relations of England and Scotland in the XVIth Century* . . ., 2 vols, Edinburgh, 1890–92

Bannatyne, Richard *Memorials of Transactions in Scotland,* AD MDLXIX– MDLXXIII, ed. Robert Pitcairn, Edinburgh, 1836

Baudouin-Matusek 'Mary Stewart's Arrival in France', *Scottish Historical Review,* vol. 69, 1990

Baumgartner, Frederic J. *France in the Sixteenth Century,* London, 1995

——, *Henry II,* London, 1988

Beaugué, Jean de *Histoire de la Guerre d'Ecosse: pendant les campagnes 1548 et 1549,* ed. J. Bain, Maitland Club, Edinburgh, 1830

Bevan, Bryan *Royal Westminster Abbey,* London, 1976

Bisset, Habakkuk *Habakkuk Bisset's Rolment of Courtis,* ed. Sir Philip J. Hamilton-Grierson, Scottish Text Society, Edinburgh, 1922

Blackwood, Adam *History of Mary Queen of Scots – a Fragment,* ed. A. Macdonald, Maitland Club, Edinburgh, 1834

Bouillé, René de *Histoire des Ducs de Guise,* Paris, 1849–50

Bourgoing, D. *Marie Stuart, son Procès et Exécution, d'après le Journal inédit de Bourgoing,* ed. M.R. Chantelauze, Paris, 1876

Brantôme, P. de Bourdeille, Seigneur de *Memoires,* London, 1739

——, *Oeuvres complètes,* ed. Bouchon, Paris, 1832

Britton, John *History and Antiquities of Peterborough Cathedral*, London, 1828

Bryce, William Moir 'Mary Stewart's Journey to France', *English Historical Review*, vol. 22, 1907

Buchanan, George *The Indictment of Mary Queen of Scots*, ed. R.H. Mahon, Cambridge, 1923

——, *The Tyrannous Reign of Mary Stewart*, tr. and ed. W.A. Gatherer, Edinburgh, 1958

Buchanan, Robert *Scotia Rediviva: a collection of tracts illustrative of the history and antiquities of Scotland*, vol. 1, Edinburgh, 1826

Calderwood, D. *The History of the Kirk of Scotland*, ed. T. Thomson, 8 vols., Wodrow Society, Edinburgh, 1842–49

Calendar of State Papers, Edward VI, Mary and Elizabeth, ed. R. Lenor, 1856

Calendar of State Papers, Foreign, Elizabeth, ed. J. Stevenson, 1863

Calendar of State Papers, Spanish, Elizabeth, ed. M.A.S. Hume, 1892

Calendar of State Papers, Venetian, ed. R. Brown and G.C. Bentinck, 1890

Calendar of State Papers, Scotland, ed. J. Bain 1898

Camden, William *Annals of the most renowned and victorious Queen Elizabeth*, tr. T. Wallace MacCaffrey, Chicago, 1970,

Carpenter, Sarah 'Performing Diplomacies', *Scottish Historical Review*, vol. 82, 2003

Castiglione, Baldassare *The Book of the Courtier*, tr. G. Bull, London, 1967

Challis, C.E. *The Tudor Coinage*, Manchester, 1978

Cherry, Alastair *Princes, Poets and Patrons: the Stuarts and Scotland*, Edinburgh, 1987

Cloulas, Ivan *Diane de Poitiers*, Paris, 1997

D'Orliac, Jehanne *The Moon Mistress, Diane de Poitiers*, London, 1931

Dalyell, J.G. ed. *Fragments of Scottish History*, Edinburgh, 1798

Davies, Norman *Europe, a history*, Oxford, 1996

Discours du Grande et Magnifique Triomphe faict du Mariage de François et Marie Stuart, ed. William Bentham, Roxburghe Club, 1818

A Diurnal of Remarkable Occurrents that have passed within the country of Scotland since the death of King James the Fourth till the year MDLXXV, ed. T. Thomson, Bannatyne Club, Edinburgh, 1833

Donaldson, Gordon *All the Queen's Men: power and politics in Mary Stewart's Scotland*, London, 1983

——, *The First Trial of Mary, Queen of Scots*, London, 1969

——, and Kirk, James *Scotland's History: approaches and reflections*, Edinburgh, 1995

——, and Morpeth, Robert *A Dictionary of Scottish History*, Edinburgh, 1977

Donnachie, Ian, and Hewitt, George *A Companion to Scottish History: from the Reformation to the present*, London, 1989

Dow, James 'Scottish Trade with Sweden, 1512–1580', *Scottish Historical Review*, vol. 48, 1969

Duffy, Eamon *The Voices of Morebath: Reformation and Rebellion in an English Village*, New Haven, 2001

Durkan, John 'The Library of Mary Queen of Scots', in *Mary Stewart, Queen in Three Kingdoms*, ed. Michael Lynch, Oxford, 1988

Edwards, Francis, S.J. *The Dangerous Queen*, London, 1964

Fleming, David Hay *Mary Queen of Scots: from her birth to her flight into England*, London, 1897

Forbes, P. *A Full view of the Public Transactions in the Reign of Queen Elizabeth*, London, 1740

Frieda, Leonie *Catherine de Medici*, London, 2003

Fraser, Antonia *Mary, Queen of Scots*, London, 1969

Goodall, Walter *An examination of the letters said to be written by Mary, Queen of Scots, to James Earl of Bothwell*, Edinburgh, 1754

Goodare, Julian *The Government of Scotland 1560–1625*, Oxford, 2004

——, *State and Society in Early Modern Scotland*, Oxford, 1999

Gore-Browne, Robert *Lord Bothwell*, London, 1937

Graham, Roderick *John Knox – Democrat*, London, 2001

Guy, John *My Heart is my Own: The Life of Mary Queen of Scots*, London, 2004

Hamer, Douglas 'The Marriage of Mary Queen of Scots to the Dauphin; a Scottish printed fragment', *Library*, vol. 12, 1932

Hamilton Papers, ed. J. Bain, 2 vols, Edinburgh, 1890

Harrison, G.B. *Letters of Queen Elizabeth I*, New York, 1968

Heape, R.G. *Buxton under the Dukes of Devonshire*, London, 1948

Henderson, T.F. *Mary Queen of Scots: Her Envoroment and Tragedy*, 2 vols, London, 1905

Hepburn, James *Les Affaires du Conte de Boduel*, pr. H. Cockburn and T. Maitland, Bannatyne Club, Edinburgh, 1829

Herries, John Maxwell, Lord *Historical Memoirs of the Reign of Mary, Queen of Scots, and a Portion of the Reign of King James the Sixth*, ed. R. Pitcairn, Abbotsford Club, Edinburgh, 1836

Hicks, Leo *An Elizabethan Problem: some aspects of the careers of two exile-adventurers*, London, 1964

Higgenbotham, Frank *Codes and Ciphers*, London, 1973

Historic Manuscripts Commission, Hatfield Papers, vol. 1, 1883

The Historie and Cronicles of Scotland . . . by Robert Lindesay of Pitscottie, vols 1 and 2, ed. A.J.G. Mackay, Scottish Text Society, 3 vols, Edinburgh, 1899–1911

The History of Scotland . . . by the most reverend and worthy Jhone Leslie, vol. 2, ed. E.G. Cody, 2 vols, Scottish Text Society, Edinburgh, 1888–1895

Hosack, John *Mary Queen of Scots and her Accusers*, Edinburgh, 1869

Houston, R.A., and Knox, W.W.J. *The New Penguin History of Scotland: from the earliest times to the present day*, London, 2002

Hume, David *History of England: from the invasion of Julius Caesar to the Revolution in 1688*, vols 3 and 4, Indianapolis, IN, 1983

Imrie, John *Scottish Royal Palaces: the architecture of the royal residences during the late Medieval and early Renaissance periods*, East Linton, 1999

——, and Dunbar, *Accounts of the Masters of Works: for building and repairing royal palaces and castles, Vol. 2: 1616–1649*, Edinburgh, 1982

Inventaires de la Royne d'Escosse, Douairière de France: catalogues of the jewels, dresses, furniture, books and paintings of Mary, Queen of Scots 1556–1569, ed. Joseph Robertson, Bannatyne Club, 1863

Jackson, G. *Bolton Castle*, Clapham, 1946

Jebb, S. *De Vita et Rebus Gestis Serenissima Principis Marie Scotorum Reginae*, London, 1725

Keith, Robert *History of the Affairs of Church and State in Scotland from the Beginning of the Reformation to the Retreat of Queen Mary into England anno 1568*, Edinburgh, 1734; eds. J.P. Lawson and C.J. Lyon, 3 vols, Spottiswoode Society, Edinburgh, 1844–50

Knox, John *The History of the Reformation*, ed. W. Croft Dickinson, London, 1949

Lang, A. 'The household of Mary Queen of Scots in 1573', *Scottish Historical Review*, vol. 2, 1905

Leader, J.D. *Mary, Queen of Scots in Captivity*, London, 1880

Lettenhove, Kervyn, Baron de, *Marie Stuart: l'oeuvre puritaine, le process, le supplice, 1585–1587*, Paris, 1889

Letters and Papers, Foreign and Domestic, of the Reign of Henry VIII, Kraus reprint, Vaduz, 1965

Lisle, Leanda de *After Elizabeth: how James King of Scots won the crown of England in 1603*, London, 2005

Lockie, D. McN. 'The Political Career of the Bishop of Ross', *University of Birmingham Historical Journal*, vol. 4, 1953–54

Lodge, Edmund *Illustrations of British History, Biography and Manners*, London, 1791

Lynch, Michael *Scotland: a new history*, London, 1991

——, ed. *Mary Stewart, Queen in Three Kingdoms*, Oxford, 1988

——, 'Queen Mary's Triumph: the baptismal celebrations at Stirling in December 1566', *Scottish Historical Review*, vol. 69, 1990

MacDonald, A. 'Mary Stewart's Entry into Edinburgh – An Ambiguous Triumph', *Innes Review*, Autumn, 1991

——, 'The Triumph of Protestantism; the Burgh Council of Edinburgh and the entry of Mary Queen of Scots, 2 September 1561', *Innes Review*, Spring, 1997

Mahon, R.H. *Mary Queen of Scots, A Study of the Lennox Narrative*, Cambridge, 1924
——, *The Tragedy of Kirk o' Field*, Cambridge, 1930
Mapstone, Sally 'Scotland's Stories', in *Scotland, a history*, ed. J. Wormald, Oxford, 2005
Marshall, Rosalind K. *Mary of Guise*, London, 1977
Mary, Queen of Scots, *Receuil de Lettres, instructions et mémoires de Marie Stuart, Reine d'Ecosse* ed. Alexandre Labanoff, 7 vols, Paris, 1844–45; English trans. William Turnbull, 7 vols, London, 1844–45
Mason, Roger *John Knox and the British Reformations*, Aldershot, 1998
Maxwell-Scott, M.M., Mrs the Hon. *The Tragedy of Fotheringay*, London, 1912
McDowall, William *History of the Burgh of Dumfries*, Dumfries, 1867
McKean, Charles *The Scottish Château*, Stroud, 2001
Melville, Sir James of Halhill *Memoirs of His Own Life, 1549–93*, ed. T. Thomson, Bannatyne Club, Edinburgh, 1827
Memorials of Transactions in Scotland 1569–72 by Richard Bannatyne, ed. R. Pitcairn, Bannatyne Club, Edinburgh, 1836
Menin, M. An *Historical and chronological treatise of the anointing and coronation of the kings of France*, London, 1723
Merriman, Marcus *The Rough Wooings: Mary Queen of Scots, 1542–1551*, East Linton, 2000
Mezeray, E. *Histoire de France*, Paris, 1643
Michel, Francisque *Les Ecossais en France*, vols 1 and 2, London, 1862
Mignet, F.A. *The History of Mary, Queen of Scots*, London, 1851
Murdin, William *Collection of State Papers relating to Affairs in the reign of Queen Elizabeth*, London, 1759
Nau, Claude *Memorials of Mary Stuart, or the History of Mary Stewart from the Murder of Riccio until her Flight into England*, ed. J. Stevenson, S.J., Edinburgh, 1883
Neale, J.E. *Queen Elizabeth I*, London, 1960
Nicolas, N.H. *Life of William Davison*, London, 1823
Paris, Louis *Négotiations, Lettres, et Pièces Diverse relative au Règne de François II*, tirées du portefeuille de Sébastien de l'Aubespine par Luois Paris, 1841
Parkinson, David '"A Lamentable Storie", Mary Queen of Scots and the Inescapable Querelle des Femmes', in *A Palace in the Wild*, ed. L.A.J.R. Houwen, Leuven, 2000
Phillips, J.E. *Images of a Queen: Mary Stuart in Sixteenth Century Literature*, Berkeley and Los Angeles, 1964
Pitcairn, R. *Collections Relative to the funerals of Mary, Queen of Scots*, Edinburgh, 1822
——, *Criminal Trials in Scotland*, Edinburgh, 1833

Platt, Colin *Carlisle Castle*, English Heritage, 1982

Pollen, J.H., ed. *Papal Negotiations in the reign of Mary Queen of Scots, during her Reign in Scotland, 1561–67, Edited from the Original Documents in the Vatican Library and Elsewhere*, Scottish History Society, Edinburgh, 1901

———, ed. *Queen Mary and the Babington Plot*, Scottish History Society, 1922

Poulet, Sir Amias *The Letter-books of Sir Amias Poulet, Keeper of Mary Queen of Scots* ed. John Morris, S.J., London, 1874

Rait, R.S. and Cameron A.I. *King James's Secret*, London, 1927

Read, Conyers *Mr Secretary Walsingham and the Policy of Queen Elizabeth*, vol. 1, 3 vols, Oxford, 1925

Register of the Privy Council of Scotland eds. J. Burton *et al*, HMSO, 1st series, 14 vols., Edinburgh, 1877–98

Regnier de la Planche, Louis *Histoire de l'Estat de France, tant de la république que de la religion, sous le règne de François II*, Paris, 1576

Richardson, J.S. *The Abbey and Palace of Holyroodhouse*, HMSO, 1978

Ruble, Baron Alphonse de *La Première Jeunesse de Marie Stuart*, Paris, 1891

Sadler, Sir Ralph *The State Papers and Letters of Sir Ralph Sadler, Knight-Banneret*, ed. Arthur Clifford, 2 vols, Edinburgh, 1809

Scott, A.M. *The Battle of Langside*, Glasgow, 1885

Sedgewick, Henry D. *The House of Guise*, London, 1938

Selections from unpublished manuscripts . . . illustrating the Reign of Queen Mary of Scotland, MDXLIII–MDLXVIII, ed. J. Stevenson, Maitland Club, Edinburgh, 1837

Scottish Correspondence of Marie of Lorraine... to 15th May 1560, ed. Annie I. Cameron, Scottish History Society, Edinburgh, 1927

Small, John *Queen Mary at Jedburgh*, Edinburgh, 1881

Smith, Gergory G. *Specimens of Middle Scots*, Edinburgh, 1902

Stanley, Arthur Penrhyn *Historical Memorials of Westminster Abbey*, London, 1868

Starkey, David *Elizabeth*, London, 2000

Steuart, A. Francis, *The Trial of Mary, Queen of Scots*, London, 1923

Stevenson, Joseph, S.J. *Mary Stuart, the First Eighteen Years of her Life*, Edinburgh, 1886

Stoddart, Jane T. *The Girlhood of Mary, Queen of Scots*, London, 1908

Strickland, Agnes *Letters of Mary Queen of Scots*, London 1842

———, *The Life of Mary Queen of Scots*, London, 1873

———, *Lives of the Queens of Scotland and Englisg princessesconnected with the Regal Succession of Great Britain*, vol. 7, Edinburgh and London, 1858

Stuart, John *A Lost Chapter in the History of Mary Queen of Scots Recovered*, Edinburgh, 1845

Teulet, A. *Papiers d'état, pièces et documents inédits ou peu connus relatifs à l'histoire de l'Écosse au XVIe siècle*, Paris, 1851

Tytler, Patrick Fraser *History of Scotland*, Edinburgh, 1845

Williams, H. Noel *Henry II: His Court and Times*, London, 1910

Willson, D.H. *King James VI and I*, London, 1963

Wormald, Jenny *Court, Kirk and Community: Scotland, 1470–1625*, Edinburgh, 1991

——, *Mary Queen of Scots: a study in failure*, London, 1988

——, ed. *Scotland: a history*, Oxford, 2005

——, 'Godly Reformer, Godless Monarch', in *John Knox and the British Reformations*, ed. Roger Mason, Aldershot, 1998

Index

꽃

NOTE: Throughout the index Mary is referred to as MQS. Where a relationship for a person is given it denotes that person's relationship to MQS unless stated otherwise. Places beginning with 'St' are indexed as spelt.

459

Babington, Anthony 352, 392–97 *passim*, 401,
    408
Bacon, Sir Nicholas 322
Bailly, Charles 351–53, 355
Balfour, Henry 13
Balfour, James 229, 236, 238, 243, 246, 247,
    257, 258, 261, 269, 271, 287, 325
Balfour, Robert 236
Ballard, John 391–92, 393, 396, 408
Band of Congregation 125
Barker, Edward 404
Barlow, Robert 330
Barnard Castle 339
Bartly, George 336
Bassett, William 364
Bastard of Angôuleme 54
Bayard, Pierre du Terrail, Chevalier de 166
Beale, Robert 379, 414, 421, 422, 426, 429
Beaton Mary 217
Beaton, Andrew 370
Beaton, David, Cardinal 12–13, 17, 20, 24–25,
    32
Beaton, James, Archbishop 201, 368, 369, 372,
    378, 389, 396
Beaton, Janet 224
Beaton, John 285, 346, 347, 370
Beaton, Mary 39, 171, 189, 216, 224
Beaugué, Jean de 37, 38
Beaune, Renauld de, Archbishop of
    Bourges 430
Bedford, Countess of 434
Bedford, Earl of 181, 185, 203, 230, 231, 232,
    234, 250, 435
Bellenden, Patrick 205
Bellièvre, Pomponne de 417
Benedict XIV (Pope) 437–38
Berry, Marguerite, Duchesse de 81, 85, 88
Bess of Hardwicke *see* Shrewsbury, Elizabeth,
    Countess of
Bible 94, 95, 132, 150, 442
billiards 415
birth customs 7
Black Death 94
Black Turnpike 262–63
Blackadder, Captain William 241–42, 251, 268
Blackwood, Adam 430, 435
Blois, Palace of 51, 101, 141
Bochetel, Jacques 63
Bocosel, Pierre de, Sieur de Chastelard 166,
    167–69

Bog, Sandy 333
Boleyn, Anne 26, 81
Bolton Castle 305, 306–07
Bond of Association 380
Bond of Congregation 125
Book of Articles, The 319, 323
Book of Common Prayer 307, 308
Book of Discipline 127–28
Book of Hours 373, 400
Border raiding 4–5, 12, 26, 190, 223, 432
Borromeo, Carlo, Cardinal 146
Borthwick Castle 257
Bothwell, Adam, Bishop of Orkney 253
Bothwell, James Hepburn, Earl of 119, 145–46,
    152–53, 197, 210, 221, 231
  ascendancy 219, 222, 223–24, 247, 249–50,
    251–52, 254
  brief life overview 223–24
  Carberry Hill and defeat 259–62, 267, 319
  Chase-about Raid 198
  and Confederate Lords 257–58, 282
  Darnley murder and plot 228, 229, 235, 236,
    238, 240–249 *passim*, 257, 268, 270, 281,
    283, 325
  and Elliots 223
  female relationships of 255
  flight and death 261–62, 369
  insanity 262, 369
  and Lady Jean Gordon 198, 242, 252
  MQS and 188, 246, 248, 251, 252, 253, 269,
    270, 283
  post-Carberry judgements/concerns 312,
    314
  Privy Council 137, 212, 226, 257–58
  Rizzio plot 207
Bothwell, Patrick, Earl of 21–22, 23, 32, 223
Bouillé, René de 93
Boulogne 31, 55
Bourbon, Antoine de *see* Antoine de Bourbon,
    King of Navarre
Bourbon, Antoinette de *see* Antoinette de
    Bourbon
Bourdeille *see* Brantôme, Pierre de Bourdeille,
    Seigneur de
Bourgeois, Loys 62
Bourgoing, Dominique 398, 399, 406, 413,
    421, 422, 423, 424, 425, 433, 436
Bowes, Sir George 306, 307
bowls 189, 365
Boyd, Lord 196, 203, 271, 311, 337

470

471

473

474